MW00353623

PADDLING EDNA

Mona,
Jump off YOUR bank!

LaNae Abnet

PADDLING
EDNA

*How a Backyard Creek Provided One
Couple Access to the Sea by Kayak*

LaNae Abnet
(Appearances by John Abnet)

Palmetto Publishing Group
Charleston, SC

Paddling Edna
Copyright © 2018 by LaNae Abnet
All rights reserved

No portion of this book may be reproduced, stored in a retrieval system, or transmitted in any form by any means–electronic, mechanical, photocopy, recording, or other–except for brief quotations in printed reviews, without prior permission of the author.

Second Edition

Printed in the United States

ISBN-13: 978-1-64111-202-4
ISBN-10: 1-64111-202-6

In Memory

Many river angels shared themselves with us during our trip. Some gave food, lodging, coffee, gifts, conversation, and friendship. Unfortunately, some of our heroes passed away since the completion of our trip. *Paddling Edna* is dedicated to their memories.

- Dawn Wanner
- Toby
- Jeff Gosnell
- John (Mad Dog) Fewkes

Coffee houses

I like coffee. A lot. In fact, as I wrote this book, I felt most productive when drinking a cup or two (or three) of joe while enjoying the atmosphere of a coffee house. I know I could have put a pot of coffee on at home, but it's just not the same. There is something creative about sitting at a café table, listening to Pandora through my earbuds, and inhaling the aroma of coffee. Focused on my computer, I'm not distracted by the laundry that needs moved from the washing machine to the dryer. And eating a lunch I don't need to prepare on dishes that I don't need to wash is a luxury. A big thank you to the following coffee houses for allowing me to occupy a table for hours and reinforcing my coffee snobbery.

4 Soils Coffee Café Bakery	Franklin	KY
Alpine Rose	Berne	IN
Angel's Bakery	Decatur	IN
Bailiwicks Coffee Company	Tiffin	OH
Billy Goat Coffee Café	Mt. Juliet	TN
Grounds and Grains	Bluffton	IN
Hazelnut Coffee Company	Celina	OH
Hugh's Bakery and Coffee	Bluffton	IN
Java Bean Café	Decatur	IN
Mocha Lounge	Ft. Wayne	IN
Modoc's Market	Wabash	IN
Sabaidee Coffee House	Tiffin	OH
Shaka Shack	Monroe	IN
Spencer's Coffee	Bowling Green	KY
The Edge Coffee House & Roasting Company	Crete	IL
Yazoo Pass	Clarksdale	MS

The Story Behind the Chapter Titles

As you read this book, you may ask, "What's up with the chapter titles?"

Well, actually, there is very little meaning behind them. Considering the book follows the daily journal of our trip, there didn't seem much point in chapter titles. So, I decided to simply use odd quotes and one-liners (and random odd sayings by John) that I heard and apply them randomly to the chapters. In fact, if I know you personally, you may recognize something YOU have said!

Enjoy!

LaNae

Read This First

Dear Reader,

I know you have dreams. Some you have expressed—others you have kept to yourself, thought about accomplishing but decided them too far-fetched. If you express your dreams, you either have to make a move to accomplish them or admit failure. If you don't voice your dreams, they don't seem real. You watch others realizing "your" dreams; you read about their adventures—living vicariously through them. You can almost see, hear, and taste the experience.

However, you are never quite brave enough to jump off the bank. *What will others think? How much will this adventure cost? What will I have to give up? How much time will I have to sacrifice? Are there dangers?* These are a few questions that keep you on the bank—the safe bank. You think that even though you may never live the adventures yourself, at least you can read about them.

I have been where you are. I wanted to stay safely on the bank. At the same time, I didn't want someone else to live "my" dreams while I lived vicariously through them. I used to lament as I watched a travel show, "How can I have a job like that? How can I travel and write about it?" I discovered the answer—JUST DO IT!

As I thought more about how to live out my own dreams, I realized the travels that interested me were unusual to the ordinary person. I consider myself ordinary—I climb out of bed, brush my teeth, exercise, eat breakfast, read my devotions, complete my household chores, eat lunch, work in my garden, take a shower, prepare and eat dinner, watch *Dark Shadows*

(OK that's not ordinary), and then climb back into bed. Maybe some would describe me as boring.

Thank goodness, I have John to help me discover ways to jump off the bank. We both want to live the unusual and then share. John always expresses, "If you don't experience adventures for yourself, you don't have anything to share with others." I want my kids and grandkids to hear about the exciting places I have traveled and voyages I have completed. I don't want to remain a typical grandparent. I want my grandchildren to desire to do the unexpected and know they too can accomplish the extra-ordinary.

As you read about how we jumped off the banks, I hope you will live vicariously through our journey, but soon that will not be enough. May our story encourage you to jump off your bank and into a world of excitement. My purpose is to show you ordinary people can accomplish the extraordinary. You are never too ordinary for an adventure. Don't settle...

May you live out-doors, out-loud, out-rageous, out-dreams. Just LIVE OUT!!!!!

LaNae

The Inspiration

Why? you ask would anyone want to live out of a small boat for four months—no mattress, no plumbing (running water, shower, toilet), no microwave, no air conditioning, no electricity, no comfy sofa, no TV, no radio, no... All comforts of home left behind. *Why?* is a very valid question. We sometimes asked ourselves the same thing.

Then we remember *why?*... Life is too short to sit on the banks watching the water go by, wondering... wondering where the water flows, wondering what we could see at the water's edge, wondering whom we could meet, wondering.... Sitting is safe while we never answer these questions and stay in a state of wondering, sitting in silence, so.... We decided to LIVEout-loud.

Then we remember *why?*... Life is too short to exist inside four walls. We work there, eat there, sleep there, groom there, socialize there, and attend church there, everything there.... We wanted to change where we lived our lives, even if only for four months. The opposite of inside is outside, so.... We decided to LIVEout-side.

Then we remember *why?*... Life is too short to be predictable. We live by a schedule dictated by a society that at some point determined life consists of working 40 (plus) hours for someone else, taking care of all our STUFF, and sleeping eight hours (does anyone really accomplish this?). Shouldn't there be more to our life? We wanted to break society's schedule and create our own, knowing that most of society will think we are crazy, so... We decided to LIVEout-rageous.

Why? you ask did we decide to take this particular trip to LIVEout-loud, -side, -rageous.

Hmmm. A few possible additional answers...

Romans 12:2

"Do not conform to the pattern of this world, but be transformed by the renewing of your mind. Then you will be able to test and approve what God's will is- his good, pleasing and perfect will." A stretch? You decide.

Ms. Janet Mooreland

While at the Quiet Water Symposium (a frequent spring pilgrimage to Michigan State University) we met Ms. Janet Mooreland and immediately saw how her Love Your Big Muddy adventure mirrored a potential trip for us. Soon after returning home from the symposium, we selected a date and launched the planning.

Follow along as we LIVEout-loud, -side, -rageous.

The Beginning

The best books in literature begin with a catchy line, quoted for years to come and becoming an answer on *Jeopardy*. Since I am a kayaker and not a novelist, I am borrowing one of my favorite lines in literature from Lewis Carol's *Alice's Adventures in Wonderland:* "Begin at the beginning and go on till you come to the end: then stop." So that is my plan, start at the beginning of our trip and continue until I come to the end: then I will stop.

The beginning. This is the daily journal of our kayak adventure, which interestingly, begins with a day of walking. Yes, walking—not to the river, but along the river since the Wabash River is not navigable for the first 18 miles.

04-01-2015

The Walk

Weather conditions:

High: 70

Low: 32

Skies: clear

Wind: S 4-12 mph, gusts to 16 mph

Today's mileage: 18 miles

Total: 18 miles

Where we traveled: Wabash River source to Fort Recovery, Ohio

In preparation for our adventure, a couple of weeks ago we took a road trip to talk with John Will, the owner of the field that contains the Wabash River headwaters, which is nothing more than a drainage tile with water flowing from it. We asked if we could park our truck by his barn and cross the short distance through his field to the creek-like body of water. He gave us the permission we sought.

"Oh you're not the first ones to come and see where the Wabash starts," John (not my John) declared as he rubbed his chin. John was an unassuming figure. His camouflage ball cap and jeans were typical for this part of the country. If a livestock farm can have a lobby in the barn, then that's where we stood and talked. Oh, I guess it could pass for a man-cave as well, including the obligatory refrigerator, sofa, and TV. The eaves of the low ceiling encircled the room with an array of mostly purple 4-H award banners, proudly displaying successes of this family farm. John seemed indifferent to our intent, and I wondered if others had expressed such grandiose ideas in the past without bringing them to fruition.

Today, almost exactly one year after we had discussed the possibility of taking this trip, we began our journey. The original itinerary indicated hiking on Friday, April 3, 2015, but because of a rainy and cold forecast, we decided to be "comfortable" and journey in the sun forecasted for today, the first day of April. This morning John and I drove our Volvo and Nissan Xterra to Fort Recovery, Ohio. We first dropped off the car at Ambassador Park—the end of our trek for today. We then drove the truck to farmer Will's barn, parked, and prepared to tramp to the source of the Wabash. What was once a dream was becoming reality.

Before crossing the field to the drainage tile, we pondered wearing our coats. The temperature this morning started out brisk, in the 30s and ended close to 70 degrees. John ditched his heavier coat, leaving it in the truck while I chose to enjoy the warmth of mine a bit longer. I knew I could eventually stuff my discarded jacket into John's backpack, filled with our snacks, lunches, water, GPS, and other essentials for the day. John always brings a backpack when we hike. Like a boy scout, he wants to be prepared for anything—sort-of like a woman and her purse. (But don't ever make that comparison to him.)

Wearing our chosen outerwear, we strode to the beginning of the Wabash River and our journey. Approaching the less-than famous drainage tile, I stared at a meager Wabash River. I had read and heard the source was only an overflow, but I couldn't visualize it. I guess I expected it to look different from other creeks. It was, after all, the origin of a major river, flowing across the state of Indiana to the Ohio River. Shouldn't there be a sign or something distinguishing it from any other drainage tiles in the field? Before me stood a submerged tile, emerging through a short cement wall built as the initial bank of the river. Perpendicular on each side of this bank two other cement fortifications formed a "U," creating a small pool of water. Sod and tall dead grass, from the previous fall, covered the sides. I strutted to the starting point of the Wabash River and stood above the drainage tile on the cement shore. Positioning myself in the grass, I looked at my reflection in the water below. I existed at and in the source of the river. I opened my arms wide to embrace the beginning of a new way of life, Life on the River.

Obligatory pictures taken to record the commencement of the trip, we began traversing the first mile of our almost 1600-mile, four-month kayak journey to the Gulf of Mexico. Our plan was to walk today what we thought would be 12 miles along the river from the headwaters of the Wabash to Fort Recovery, Ohio, where we will launch our kayaks this Saturday, April 4, and begin the in-water portion of the trip. We chose a Saturday to begin the paddling portion of the excursion because several of our family and friends indicated they want to be present at the launching of our adventure. And since most people work other days…

Leaving the drainage tile, we strolled along the waterway with the sun in our eyes towards a nearby woods. Anticipation of our journey's start caused my step and spirits to be unusually light. Entering the woods John picked up various sticks, checking their length and sturdiness. Thinking he had lost his mind, I asked, "What are you doing?"

"I'm gathering the perfect walking sticks because everyone needs a walking stick," he answered. He handed me the stick he had decided was ideal for me. I didn't understand why he needed a stick to walk along the river—not up a mountain—but accepted his gift anyway. I hate to admit this, but the stick did provide stability as we trudged the uneven ground of the fields.

Sticks in hand we continued until we reached mile three. Thinking we had completed a fourth of our 12-mile trek, we stopped to eat our first home-made granola bars of the trip. During the last month, I prepared and packaged 224 of these for the trip. Stopping at regular intervals during our hike was part of the nutrition plan for the day. Anyone who knows me realizes I would have an organized agenda determining when I am going to eat throughout the day—already planning the next snack/meal before I have finished my last bite of my present snack/meal. *Is this an indication I am obsessed with food or just structured? We all need routine nutrition, right?*

Between our nutrition/rest breaks, our jaunt along the creek-river took us behind many farmhouses. Dogs barked, alerting their owners someone was intruding on their space. However, even with the announcement of our presence we didn't encounter any humans. John and I discussed the absence of people. Was everyone at work? Then again, how often, as we pass homes while driving or walking, do we encounter anyone outside? Have we become an "inside" society, only venturing outside to climb into our vehicles or retrieve the mail? What are we doing "inside" that is so important? Are we avoiding interaction or merely too busy? Will interacting interfere with our precious schedule? Are we losing the art of socialization? Hmm…

As planned, upon reaching the halfway mark of six miles, we stopped to consume a nutritious lunch of peanut butter wraps, pretzels, and oranges while sitting on the bank by a bridge. My feet were hot and uncomfortable. During the last few miles before lunch my left foot whispered with each step, "I hurt. You are walking too much. My heel is uncomfortable. Please stop."

I was eager to remove my shoes and identify why my foot was complaining. I untied my shoes as I sat down, promptly removing my hiking shoes. The air's coolness brought the temperature of my feet down at least five degrees. The next step towards relief was discarding my socks, revealing some blisters. Ouch! No wonder my feet were complaining!

John examined my blistered feet compassionately, "Oh, Babe. I can't believe you have blisters. I think you need new shoes." He reached into the backpack. "In the meantime, I have something that might help." He pulled out a roll of duct tape. John's brother Paul had suggested we bring duct tape along for such a scenario—duct tape can fix anything, right?!

Duct tape, a strong cloth-based tape originally used during World War II to seal ammunition cases, can be found in a toolbox, craft room, car, junk drawer, submarines, NASA spaceships, and, in our case, backpacks. Those who are creative have fashioned sandals, ties, purses, space suit costumes, and more. Repairing such things as shoes, boats, motorcycles, and cars is easy with this silver tape. I once witnessed a duct-tape-attached driver's side-view mirror of a Cadillac on Interstate 90 in Chicago. Before today, though, I hadn't even considered using it to relieve the pain of blisters.

As my feet cooled and we ate, bitter smoke wafted into my nostrils— not the sweet smell of a campground fire. I scrunched my nose. My ears detected cackling and popping. I scanned the area for visual confirmation. Thick gray smoke rolled in the sky. A fire not posing a threat to any nearby buildings or us blazed across the bridge in a small wooded section next to the river. What do you do when you encounter a fire in the middle of no- where? Was the fire accidental or intentional? Opting to believe the fire was part of a plan, we did nothing and proceeded with our day. Is this reaction a result of being an "inside" society? Avoiding interaction with other peo- ple? Assuming someone else has everything under control? Is this the same reasoning we use when we notice someone sitting in a stranded car along the road? Of course, the driver has used a cell phone to call someone. Of course, someone is on the way. They don't need *us*. Making it evident that even when we are "outside," we can still be "inside."

After making the decision to ignore the fire, John gathered our empty lunch containers and stashed them in the bag. "We better keep moving. Let's put the tape on your feet. I hope this helps." John ripped pieces of tape from the roll, tenderly placing them on my fluid-filled bumps. With a wince, I pulled on my socks and shoes, and we traveled onward to mile nine for another snack. (Planning!) Thinking we had only three more miles to go, we limped (I limped) along.

The scenery as we covered the un-navigable portion of the Wabash River varied from farmland to beautiful woods, from flat land to rolling hills. I wonder what the landscape (or should I say riverscape) of the rest of the river will look like. Except for the portion of the Wabash I have previously paddled (Linn Grove, Indiana, to Markle, Indiana), I have viewed the Wabash River only from bridges. I am anxious to experience a different view.

As we enjoyed the view, creativity is the word I would use to describe our entertainment—singing, praying, and telling the alphabet story. Let me explain how to create an alphabet story, just in case you are in need of an innovative way to pass time at some point. The alphabet story consists of words beginning with each letter in the alphabet. One person comes up with a word starting with "A," the next person adds a word beginning with "B," and so on, until you create an entire story. Here's an example…. A Bird Carried Dead Elephants Far… I wonder how we will entertain ourselves for four months. Surely, more than the alphabet story will keep us entertained. How many times can you tell an alphabet story in four months? This could be interesting! However, any trip with John is interesting.

During an intermission in our entertainment, John referred to the GPS and noted we had reached mile nine and should eat our snack to provide our nourishment for three more miles. Three more miles should not have been a problem, but my blisters were speaking more loudly, "Hey, you! The duct tape isn't working. You NEED to stop and take these shoes off your feet."

I tried to be brave and not say anything since we were so close to being done. I kept telling myself I could continue three more miles—*it's only three more miles.* By now the sun beat down on us and the temperature had reached the predicted 70-degree high (I had long ago stored my coat in John's backpack), so we sat on the ground under a tree, enjoying our last snack. Even with the snack, my stomach growled as I looked forward to eating at home.

Soon after our snack, we reached an area along the banks of the Wabash that is not accessible, not even by foot, and progressed parallel to the river on the edge of road. On foot along the highway brought us to Eldora Speedway. Recognizing the racetrack, John's brow furrowed, "We have gone nine miles and should have only three more miles to go, but I

KNOW Eldora Speedway is farther from Fort Recovery than three miles. I am guessing it is more like nine miles."

I cried! My feet had gone from whispering to screaming, "I CAN'T go another step. You MUST take this shoe off. WHY are you still walking? Please STOP! Are you seriously STILL walking!" *There is no way I can walk another nine miles! What am I going to do?* This was only the beginning of the trip, and I felt like a liability. Not only did I want to strip off my shoes, but I also wished I'd worn shorts. I needed to sit down and rest in the shade. I perused my surroundings—a flat black top road with nothing but barren fields on each side—no shade. I gazed farther in the distance and noticed a small town around the corner. There must be some shade there. We walked (I limped) into town, finding shade under an awning in front of a store. I sat down on the sidewalk, slipped out of my shoes, and sighed.

Sitting on the sidewalk in front of the store, I thought about the upcoming trip. I felt like I was already a hindrance to John. Many times over the last year, I had worried about a scenario such as this—a time when I would slow down the progress of the trip. *Will John become annoyed with me if I can't keep up or pull my weight? Will I be honest with John? Or will I push myself too far, causing injury? Is today an indication I don't have the stamina for a trip of this magnitude?* I was embarrassed. I didn't' want to admit any of these feelings to John, afraid he may think he needed to fix the situation by cancelling the trip. Hopefully, after two days of rest, I will have a different outlook on the situation. At that point I simply wanted to return to the car.

After resting and contemplating my situation, I picked up my walking stick, my much-needed friend, and concentrated on taking one step and then another and then another. With each step, I experimented with various positions of foot placement, hoping to find the magical combination to provide relief. My step and my spirits were no longer light, and the songs and alphabet story no longer entertained me. Prayers were all that remained from earlier in the day. *Surely, paddling will be easier than this.*

Our breaks became more frequent as we proceeded. Taking advantage of each stop, I removed my shoes. Since we had eaten our last snack during our mile-nine break, we were "snackless." My stomach groaned. I started scheming about what I was going to eat as soon as I entered the door of our house. Planning helped take my mind off my feet and stomach, at least for a little while. Absorbed in my discomfort, I sulked. *This is more than I signed up for. Will this ever end?* I craved to set my eyes on our car in the distance. I kept telling myself, "This too shall pass and become part of our story. Tomorrow at this time, this will be a memory." Finally, we reached our goal—Ambassador Park in Fort Recovery. The grey Volvo beckoned me to claim my prize.

Shuffling the last few feet to the car, I anticipated the moment I would slump in the seat allowing the Volvo to transport me home to shower, eat, and relax on the couch—my rewards for a tough day. However, today is the last day for four months these luxuries will be my end-of-the-day payment. After a long day paddling, my compensation will be putting up a tent, making dinner, and journaling. No shower, comfy couch, or bed. Oh well, this is the trip!

04-04-2017

The Launch

Weather conditions:

High: 50

Low: 30

Skies: clear

Wind: W 13-20 mph, gusts to 24 mph

Today's mileage: 15 miles

Total: 27 miles

Where we traveled: Fort Recovery, Ohio, to near the Ohio/Indiana line

What do you eat on your last morning before beginning a four-month journey? Half a hotdog, of course. What else? The lone hot dog was the last food sitting on the shelf in our fridge, so we cut the hot dog in half and ate it. After eating our "nutritious" breakfast, we began the task of closing the house for our extended absence.

Of course, I had my "to do" list, hoping I wouldn't forget anything major.

- Unplug all electronics (except fridge and freezer)—check.
- Take batteries out of all gadgets—check.
- Disconnect water softener—check.
- Turn off water heater—check.
- Empty fridge (eat last hot dog)—check.

- Turn heat to air conditioning and set temperature at 80—check.
- Turn off all lights—check.

In preparation of this unusual experience, I had written and completed another, lengthier, "to do" list over the past year. Some items I had recently checked off were...

- Dog baby sitters (relocate?)—arrange; buy food; (relocate?)
- Dog heartworm—arrange; buy heartworm
- Stop mail—speak with mail carrier—place mail into totes in entryway (Post office will hold mail for a maximum of 30 days.)
- Lawn care—prep mower; train; arrange; purchase diesel
- Bill payment—pre-pay as many as possible; arrange for payment method while on river
- Food cache delivery—pack in shipping boxes; store; arrange
- Food prep—prepare; pack 720 meals and snacks
- Holden's (grandson) birthday (6-11) gift—purchase, wrap, deliver
- New grandbaby (due end of June) afghan—finish, wrap, deliver
- Internet—cancel
- Dentist appointment—change
- Birthday checks—write checks, cards, send
- Homecoming bag—pack "normal" clothes, extra make-up, pampering items, etc.
- Plant babysitters—arrange; deliver

Preparing to be gone for an extended period requires more time than we realized, causing us to leave later than intended. *Could we possibly be late to leave on OUR four-month trip?* Since this is OUR trip, we couldn't literally "miss the boat." However, a few people wanted to see us off, so we scheduled our departure for 9:00 a.m. We didn't want to keep them waiting. We also didn't want to deal with the awkward feelings triggered by packing our kayaks while everyone watched. We discussed if we should allow them to help. Would they feel we were taking too long? Did they have schedules for the rest of their day? We began to feel rushed but soon realized we would be without a time schedule for the next four months. Meeting this last time commitment was significant—we were leaving one way of life and entering another.

Even though I cried when I heard the house door click as John closed it, I felt like skipping. We were leaving the known and entering the unknown. We were leaving our comfort zone and entering a different way of life. A million thoughts filled my mind: *Do we have everything we need? Will we be safe? Will our family be safe while we are gone? What if something goes wrong? Will we have enough money? Whom will we meet? What sights will we see? What adventures will we live? How will we change?* I tried quieting the thoughts. I prayed for peace and softly sang the chorus of "God Will Take Care of You."

God will take care of you
Through everyday o'er all the way
He will take care of you
God will take care of you

This wasn't the first time over the past year I had sung or thought those words. When I was nervous and scared about the pending expedition and all the unknowns, the words to this chorus comforted me and provided peace.

Strolling to the truck, I stared at the kayaks—our means of transportation for the next four months—loaded on the truck. In the back of the truck lay everything we needed to survive during that time (minus the weekly boxes we will pick up at stops along the way). At least we thought it was everything we would need. How could we be sure? We hadn't taken a trip of this magnitude before. We had completed kayak trips in the past few years; but the longest we had lived on the river was a few days, not four months. Over the last year, John did his best to research, purchase, and pack our gear. *Did he remember to include all of my necessities? My sleeping bag liner? Does he understand how concerned I am about being cold? My flip-flops? My...? How can he know what I need?* It was at this point I realized I hadn't been sufficiently active in creating the gear list. So focused researching and preparing our food, I hadn't taken the time to research needs. I had placed my trust in John. Now I was beginning to worry little too late.

John opened the passenger door for me, as he always does. I climbed into the truck, buckled my seatbelt, and tried to relax as John started the engine and backed out of the driveway. Pulling onto the road resembled the beginning of any normal vacation, but this trip was different—we wouldn't be returning for several months. I tried to grasp the immensity of what lay ahead. *Do I really want to leave?* My stomach churned. "God Will Take Care of You."

As we drove to Fort Recovery, Ohio, my stomach growled. Half a hotdog was not enough sustenance and nutrition to begin a full day of paddling. We decided to find somewhere in Fort Recovery to grab some breakfast before launching. Deciding to eat breakfast created a dilemma. Should we remove our kayaks from the top of the truck and pack them with our gear first, or eat first? Again, we discussed the uncomfortableness of packing our kayaks with an audience. But we were hungry. Our stomachs won—we decided to eat one last un-dehydrated meal at the Northend Bar and Grill in Ft. Recovery.

We parked our kayak-topped truck, moseyed across the street, and entered the Northend Bar. The interior of the restaurant was as I expected of a small town bar. On the right of the long, narrow room, a bar with stools provided seating for many patrons. A space of about four feet separated the bar from a row of tables with four wooden chairs each. Red and white tiles covered the floor while outdated paneling decorated the walls. Beyond the

13

bar, a window opened to the kitchen. Next to the window, a gray plastic cart housed a dishpan for dirty dishes, napkins, and other essentials. The papers on the bulletin board above the cart advertised goods and services for sale.

We sat at a table and examined the menus. When eating out for breakfast, I usually order oatmeal. For years I have eaten oatmeal every morning at home and have carried that routine over into my restaurant breakfasting. However, this morning was different. I knew I would need more energy today than I do during a normal day of activity at home. I ordered biscuits and gravy topped with scrambled eggs and two pieces of dry wheat toast. I didn't want to get hungry. John ordered his usual—two eggs over easy, bacon, hash browns, and dry toast. We both try to remember to request dry toast because we don't enjoy butter dripping off our food. *I wonder if later in our trip, dripping butter will become a luxury after eating dehydrated, unbuttered food.*

We were finishing our coffee when a gentleman came in the door, glanced around, and approached our table, apparently eager to talk with us. With furrowed brow, I studied him as he approached our table—I didn't know this man. *Why is he seeking us out?* He, Ralph, introduced himself, explaining he had read the article in Portland, Indiana's, *Commercial Review* about two crazy people paddling to the Gulf of Mexico and was intrigued. He said he recognized us from our picture and couldn't miss the yellow truck equipped with two yellow kayaks atop parked on the street. *I guess the residents of Fort Recovery don't observe a yellow kayak-topped truck every day.* Ralph talked with us for a few minutes, wished us luck, and moved to a stool at the bar to order, eat his breakfast, and read the newspaper. I wondered if he will follow us on our website or even remember meeting us this evening when he sits down in his recliner to watch *Wheel of Fortune* on T.V.

This interaction with Ralph makes me ponder about how many people will spot us in the next few months as we paddle down the river. John and I are private people—we hate to draw attention to ourselves. Actually, there are times I recognize someone in the grocery store and quickly push my cart down another aisle. *Is that wrong? Will I feel more comfortable around strangers on the trip than I do around people with whom I am familiar? Am I afraid of the preconceived notions of those who already know me? Since I probably won't encounter the strangers I meet on the trip again, will that diminish my lack of comfort in that department? Interesting thoughts.* I don't want to wish my life away, but I am anxious to see who I am in August. If a trip like this doesn't change me, there is something wrong.

After paying for our breakfast, we drove to Ambassador Park. The time was only 8:30 a.m., so we were surprised when people started arriving within minutes. Many were eager to help pack, but John had created a map indicating where everything belonged. The goodwill of others simply would not fit into the routine needed to stay organized.

John has approached this trip much like a business and has applied many of his philosophies in the planning. John is structured in many areas of his life—especially work. His organizational skills have given him success in his career in quality assurance. In the business world, he creates processes that decrease the probability of problems occurring and receives a paycheck to do so. Therefore, creating a gear location map is not out of the ordinary for this man. In fact, for the past three weeks, instead of our car parked in one side of our garage, our kayaks rested in the midst of all our dry-bags and other essentials as John packed and unpacked the kayaks several times to be sure everything fit. Every item had a place. Or so I thought!

Today, as John packed, I brought him my pillow and asked, "Where does my pillow go?"

"It's not on the map. You can't take it." He didn't even glance up.

I stared at him. Then, I laughed. I was sure John was kidding, as he often does. He had to be. My compact camp pillow, when compressed, fits into a small 4" x 6" stuff sack. *Why won't that fit? How can I sleep for four months without a pillow?* I wanted to make sure he wasn't serious, so I asked, "You're kidding, right? Seriously, where does it belong?"

"I'm serious. Your pillow didn't make the list—there isn't any room. You can use a jacket or a dry bag for a pillow," he stated sternly.

I stared at John's kayak, realizing his guitar strapped to the back of his kayak had made the list. Now I was confused. How did his guitar make the inventory and not my pillow? Yes, it is a small "backpacker" guitar, but the guitar is still much larger than my compact, made-to-travel pillow!

Were we fighting? ("Pillow fight"?) John and I rarely fight, and when we do, we fight quietly. Seldom does either of us raise our voices. I believe we get along better than most couples do. This fact was evident from the re-action of many people when John and I told them we planned to spend the next few months together, just the two of us. Almost every one exclaimed, "I could never spend that much time with my spouse. We would kill each other!" Unlike those couples John and I have found in the eleven years we have been married (the second marriage for each of us) that the more time we spend together, the better we get along. *Will this be true after four months of being together day after day after day after day after...*

Once John announced my pillow might not be traveling with us, I tried not to express my reaction to what I interpreted as thoughtlessness—un-successfully. He noticed my grimace and tried to appease me, "Leave it over there. I'll see if there is any room after I load everything else."

So there was hope! Packing continued. I watched my pillow's position, hoping it would eventually disappear into one of our kayaks' four small holds. Soon the spot where my pillow had been sitting was empty. I ex-pressed my gratitude. "John, thanks for packing my pillow."

"I didn't pack your pillow," he said, perplexed.

Hmmm... *Did someone put my pillow back in the truck?* I searched the truck. It was empty. Bud Heare, who was watching as John packed, mo-tioned me over to a hold John had finished packing. There was my pillow, safely stuffed into a small empty corner of my rear hold. *My hero!*

While John packed, my oldest son Travis, his wife, Katie, and their two-year-old daughter Emerlynn arrived. Between the two of us, John and I have four children (three mine—Travis, Tiffany, Trent; one his—Kasie), four children in-laws (Katie, Zach, Jillian, Chris), and five and seven-ninths grandchildren (Haleigh, Emerlynn, Jensen, Holden, Hazel—Calvin is due in June). Travis, Katie, and Emerlynn were the only ones available to see us off.

Emerlynn, dressed in her pink and purple plaid winter coat and monkey hat, ran to me with outstretched arms calling, "Ma-mah." I scooped her up and gave her a big hug and kiss. *I will miss this little girl.* As I held her, I noticed a plate of marvelous goodness in Travis's hands. He brought a no-bake bar containing Cheerios, chocolate, pretzels, peanut butter, and caramel sauce creation for us and other bystanders to indulge. Unfortunately, these bars do not have a name, and Travis didn't write down the recipe, so no one will ever enjoy their yumminess again. I wasn't surprised since Travis likes experimenting with food but often fails to record his creations. I savored every bite of my last sinful treat! John, the I-really-don't-care-for-sweets man, even ate one. Although my meal planning for the trip includes dessert every day after dinner, after four months I am sure I will crave fresh homemade treats.

Enjoying my treat, I considered the view in front of me. In addition to Travis and Katie, many family and friends had come to say good-bye and wish us well. Twenty total. Wow! Tears fell onto my cheeks as I realized the support demonstrated by these special people. As I mentioned before, John and I are private people, so sharing this moment with others overwhelmed me. In addition to those we knew, there were three other gentlemen, whom we did not know from the Ft. Recovery area (Bob, Oscar, and Dean), who left their warm homes on a sunny, chilly, spring, Saturday morning to watch the launch. Group picture time!

The group of well-wishers included our pastor, Jeff Horsman. We feel this trip has a purpose, even if we aren't sure what that purpose is yet, and realize the importance of covering the journey in prayer, so we asked Pastor Jeff to pray before we carried our kayaks to the water, beginning our four-month journey. The entire group gathered around as he prayed for our safety in addition to peace for our family and us. I began crying as I realized the time to leave everyone was drawing near. *Why am I crying again?*

After the prayer, many hugs, and a few more tears (four months is a long time to be away), the time arrived to transport our kayaks down the steep bank to the water. Most of the Wabash River's banks are nearly vertical, and the banks in Ft. Recovery are not an exception. In addition, with all our gear, our kayaks weigh in at around 150 pounds each. The steep, high banks and gear-laden vessels were not a good combination. This is when having twenty people in attendance comes in handy. Dan Abnet (John's brother) and Bud Heare (my hero) helped us slide the kayaks gingerly down the bank and into the cold spring water. They carried and launched John's kayak first. More tears brimmed in my eyes as I watched him paddle away from me. *Why am I crying again?*

It was my turn. The long, dead grass crunched as I took my first step. *Concentrate. Don't fall.* I caught myself. The grass was sharp under my hand. Someone offered advice. *Who is talking to me? What are they saying?* The onlooker's buzz at the top of the hill was undiscernible. *Why are they here?* My feet were like heavy weights on the end of my legs. I couldn't concentrate enough to take another step. I sat down and slid the rest of the way to *Pray. How do I climb into my kayak?* I think Dan and Bud helped me. I don't remember. It's all a blur.

My kayak felt foreign and uncomfortable. The seat was hard and the small cockpit claustrophobic. *How many hours will I have to sit in this position before I will be able to unfold and walk?* Since every day over the next few months I will be sitting in my kayak for many hours each day, will my kayak ever feel as comfortable as home? At the same time, floating on the river felt familiar, like home, providing a sense of freedom and calm. I inhaled and exhaled slowly, allowing myself to shed the stress I had felt moments before. This was really happening!

The official "set sail" time was 10:00 a.m.—an hour later than planned. I guess one hour doesn't make much difference on a four-month journey. Time is relative, right?

Catching up with John, I beheld him through tear-filled eyes and exclaimed, "We're doing it!"

A year of planning was coming to fruition. Over the past year, as we were planning our four-month trip, I don't think I believed we would really be paddling in the Wabash River, to the Ohio River, to the Mississippi River, and finally to the Gulf of Mexico. I didn't have any memories on which to base my feelings and experience in order to conceive what lay ahead. When previously planning a weeklong vacation, I knew what to expect and how to prepare because I had taken many trips of that length to similar places. This excursion is much longer and unlike anything we have attempted before. I had created my usual "to do" list, but knowing what to include was difficult. *Did I remember everything? Will something I forgot to put on my list cause us difficulty later?* I didn't know anyone personally who had completed a similar journey in order to ask them for advice. *What will be required of me to finish the trip successfully? Will I grow tired of sitting in my kayak day after day after day? Will John and I get on each other's nerves?* All these thoughts flew through my mind at once. Then, overwhelming pride soon replaced them as I considered what we had accomplished over the past year. Today, as I sat in my kayak, the preparation time seemed like a blink of an eye. The many hours spent researching, purchasing, planning, discussing, packing, dehydrating, vacuum packing, recording, etc. were worth every moment. Even if we don't complete the trip, we have accomplished more than most. We moved from dreaming to planning to executing. Most are stuck in the dreaming stage. We're DOING it!

The first few miles were curvy and included some unexpected near Class I rapids. John referred to them as fun—I prefer the word *scary!* These fun (scary) rapids caused me some difficulties. I hadn't paddled in six months, so my kayaking techniques were mediocre and not sufficient for maneuvering through water bubbling over rocks. I was actually sideways and backwards (yes, backwards) a few times. *How can I be this bad?* I did a lot of praying accompanied by a few tears, "keep me upright and safe, keep me upright and safe." Oddly enough, I began thanking God for the rapids. Here is my logic… Water flowing over rocks creates rapids. If the water level is too low to flow over the rocks, rapids don't exist. If there isn't enough water to flow over the rocks and create rapids, there isn't enough water for our kayaks to float over the rocks. The result of unfloating kayaks is clambering out of the kayaks and pulling them down the river. Walking instead of paddling really isn't a better option. Bring on the rapids!

When we kayak in rivers, John usually paddles a little ahead of me, especially when we go around a curve or hear rushing water, so he can assess certain situations and provide direction. "Follow me." "Go left." "Paddle hard." Once today, as we approached a deadfall, a pile of trees and brush washed into the river, John climbed out of his kayak to check out the state of the river. I hung out in my kayak until he came back to report his evaluation. "No problem," he assured, "we can make it through."

We were not as fortunate as we approached the Ohio town of Wabash. This time, John reported there was a problem—a fallen, impassable tree, known, sadistically, as a strainer. We couldn't stay in our kayaks and still go through, under, or around it. We both climbed out of our kayaks this time. John attached a rope to my kayak pulled it under the tree to the other side. Once beyond the strainer, he placed my kayak between a rock and the shore. He then helped me down a 60-degree, muddy bank to my craft, placed me in, and sent me on my way. Confident I was safely paddling downstream, he performed the same routine with his kayak. However, he didn't have anyone to help him down the steep, muddy bank to his vessel. I was worried. I found a place downstream and waited and waited and waited. I strained my neck to see a sign of his arrival. I strained my ears to hear the signal we use when paddling to relay safety—"I love you." *We are only on the Wabash. I don't know if I can handle all these emotions and fear. This is only the first day. Can I do this?* It felt like years before I finally caught a glimmer of his white paddles rotating in the air. Then, I cried with relief when I heard "I love you." He joined me, and we continued on our way together.

As I paddle on the river for the next few months, I am going to relish my view as I pass slowly through nature. Previously, as I passed swiftly over a bridge, my view of nature was brief, and sometimes easily missed. Actually, there were times I couldn't see the river from the bridge. Now, from the river, I am watching the squirrels run along the bank, jump over fallen trees, and accompany me on part of my journey. Birds fly overhead, creating a shadow on the water, as they break the silence with their calls. Trees barren of leaves provide a view of nests built for the use of nurturing baby birds. This slower pace will enable me to become one with nature as opposed to a brief passer-by. Hmmm… Becoming one with nature. Have I officially left the "inside" society?

Approaching a slightly sloping grassy area we deemed suitable for lunch, I caught sight of a pile of trees and brush. Then, a beaver glanced at me from in front of the pile before scurrying into the brush. Unfortunately, I didn't have a chance to gain John's attention in order to share the view with him. I don't remember ever catching a glimpse of a beaver from my road view.

After paddling a total of fifteen miles, which was much easier than hiking eighteen, our next challenge was to find a place to pull off the water and set up camp for the night. Bill Knapke had offered his property farther downstream as a stop for the night, but with the fallen tree adventure, we didn't have the time or energy to travel any farther. Since the banks close to the origin of the Wabash River are not sandy and flat, finding a place to exit our kayaks and camp becomes a difficult task. We finally found a-less-than perfect place—an out-cropping of discarded, broken-up pieces of cement on a ten-foot high bank with a 45-degree incline. A flat, weedy area sat at the top of the hill. Transferring our gear from our kayaks by the water to the crest of the 45-degree incline was a challenge. John removed the gear needed for the night from the kayaks and threw them to me at the top of the hill. No pressure, considering, if I missed an article, it would roll down the hill into the water. What a way to begin the trip! Fortunately, my catching prowess was up to speed.

Having overcome the challenge of the steep bank, we had to contend with the wind. This campsite came furnished with what seemed like 70 mph wind. Trying to hold onto and put up an ultra-light tent was not easy. Not to mention, this was only the second time we had erected this particular tent. I'm sure we would have entertained anyone watching as we tried to hold, reach, and chase during our attempt to raise our "home" for the night!

Tent securely in place, John and I proceeded to carry out our individual tasks. John put up a makeshift clothesline—a stick—to dry his gloves and socks while I created a comfy place to sleep in our "home." Satisfied with his clothesline, John prepared our first dehydrated meal of the trip while crouched behind a rock in order to avoid the incessant winds. Since we were so tired and cold after a long day of paddling, we found eating the rations of our first supper, noodles and sloppy joe, difficult but ate as much as we could. Dinner complete, John did the dishes (his job when we camp), using only a few ounces of water. I'm amazed how little water John needs to do dishes when camping. At home, he uses so much water that, occasionally, he needs to drain some from the sink before the task of washing dishes is complete. I guess he is adjusting his actions in response to the limited quantity of safe water available.

Once we secured the food prep essentials in their proper place in the front hatch of John's kayak, the hour was 8:00 p.m., time for me to establish a going-to-bed routine. Go pee, brush teeth, and wash face before entering the tent. Once in the tent, take out contacts, apply moisturizer, and quickly change from outdoor clothes into long underwear, a down vest, wool socks, and a head covering. We had "just settled down for a long winter's nap," when a farmer nearby started his target practice for the evening, lasting for over an hour. Since no one alerted the farmer of our arrival and need for rest, the echo of the gunshots delayed the long winter's nap.

Lying here with my head resting comfortably on my pillow and listening to gunshots pop in the distance and the wind roar, I realize the end to our first day was not what I imagined. I had imagined pulling our kayaks onto a somewhat flat bank and easily setting up our tent on the grass under a tree. I forgot we wouldn't have a fire to cook on or warm our weary bones by while replaying the day's activities. I had based my expectations on previous camping trips. I didn't anticipate a steep, rocky hill or the wind. I didn't know I would be this cold. How many other expectations of the trip will be incorrect?

At the end of day one on the river, I am exhausted and cold! The weather forecast for tonight is brisk and breezy—in the 30s. *I left my warm bed on purpose?*

04-05-2017

Easter on the River

Weather conditions:

High: 53

Low: 26

Skies: sunny

Wind: WSW 13-26 mph, gusts to 35 mph

Today's mileage: 16 miles

Total: 43 miles

Where we traveled: Near the Ohio/Indiana line to Ceylon, Indiana

Guess where I found my pillow this morning. Under John's head! Apparently, MY pillow was more comfortable than HIS makeshift pillow of wadded up clothing stuffed in a dry bag. And he had suggested I leave my pillow at home and use a jacket or a dry bag for a pillow. I guess I was the one who was right!

Last night was so cold. Even with my long underwear, down vest, wool socks, hat, gloves, sleeping bag, sleeping bag liner, and wool blanket, I couldn't stop shivering. My feet felt like I had walked barefoot in the snow for a mile. Between trying to stay warm and thawing my feet, I didn't sleep much. First, I tried pulling my head deeper into my sleeping bag, warming my face a little; but the rest of me still shook. Then, I scooted closer to John. Unfortunately, our sleep pads soon separated, leaving me scrunched in the gap between them. The only material protecting me from the hard, cold ground was the tent floor and a wool blanket. I climbed back on my sleep pad. When I began losing the feeling in my feet, I pulled off my socks and placed my bare feet on my bare leg—skin on skin.

John taught me the skin-on-skin trick several years ago when we were hiking through the woods in the snow. I was wearing a cheap pair of boots, and my feet were becoming numb from the cold. When I told John I couldn't feel my toes, he told me to sit on a stump. What he did next surprised me. He removed my boot and sock. Yes, he totally exposed my foot to the elements. I knew better than to ask any questions as I watched him lift his coat and shirt and place my naked foot on the skin of his stomach. John held my foot on his stomach as we talked and watched snowflakes float to the ground around us. I'm not sure when the temperature of my feet changed from frozen to normal, but I do know John was my hero that day.

Unfortunately, the skin-on-skin trick didn't work last night.

This morning after I left the tent's protection, the cold wind blew through my Columbia shell, down vest, wetsuit, and Under Armour. The thought of taking off my gloves to cook a warm breakfast wasn't appealing, so I opted instead to prepare peanut butter wraps and oranges my friend Dawn Wanner brought from Florida—what a treat! Fresh fruit! *When will I enjoy fresh fruit again?*

After fighting the wind as we took down the tent, we placed all the stuff we had used last night in a pile. John then climbed down the hill to the kayaks while I stayed by our dry bags and other gear. Consulting his gear map, John indicated which item he was ready to pack, and I threw it precisely to him. This game of pitch and catch caused me stress. One poor pitch or catch would result in a piece of our gear rolling into the river. After catching an article, he placed it where the map indicated.

Waiting to throw the next dry bag, I studied the names John had painted on our kayaks while they sat in our garage the last few weeks—*Work* and *Pray*. St. Augustine's often recited quote "Work as if everything depended on you and pray as if everything depended on God" is the inspiration for the our kayaks' names. The choice that *Pray* was mine and *Work* was John's came when I arbitrarily stated, "I'll do the praying while John does all the work." Not sure he sees it the same way.

In the middle of loading the kayaks, John stopped in his tracks. "What am I stuck on? I hope it's not something man-made." He stood motionless—he didn't want to damage his wet suit.

Climbing down, I assessed the situation. "It's a wire. Hold still."

I carefully removed the neoprene of John's wetsuit from the offending wire sticking out of a random chunk of concrete. John was ticked, not because he might have damaged his wet suit, but because the snag was the result of a man-made hazard rather than nature. Nothing infuriates John more than man-made hazards causing a problem. John forgives nature because nature is not the result of someone else's laziness or carelessness. In other words, he would not have been as upset if a stick had been the culprit. Thankfully, upon closer inspection, his wet suit was fine, but he did push down the wire so it would not cause more damage to himself or anyone else. Obstacle disarmed, we checked for other hazards and deemed the area safe.

We finally, and painstakingly, moved *Work* and *Pray* off the steep, rocky hill and into the water about 10:40 a.m.

Keep us upright and safe.

Today was a monumental day to us. We traveled under the bridge west of New Corydon, Indiana, a bridge we have crossed over by car many times. This bridge represents more than a means of traveling from one side of the river to the other side; it is part of the inspiration for this craziness. Many times before this trip was even a thought, as we drove over the bridge and glanced at the water, John would say, "You know we could put our kayaks in here and go anywhere in the world." Little did he know how prophetic his statement would be.

After we decided to put our kayaks in the water and set a date to start our trip, his statement changed to, "Can you believe we are going to go under this bridge to the Gulf?"

Today we paddled under the bridge and viewed the underside of it. We regarded it from a different view—the river view. WOW! Few people have seen the underside (river view) of the New Corydon Bridge and other bridges on the Wabash. Perhaps they have traveled by kayak, canoe, or jon boat (a flat-bottomed aluminum fishing boat); or fished from the bank under the bridge. However, while they have viewed the undersides of SOME of the bridges, they have not had the privilege to catch a glimpse of the underside of ALL of the bridges on the Wabash River. We will experience the river view of every bridge on this historic river. Ordinary John and LaNae Abnet doing the extraordinary.

Passing under the bridge this morning, I thought about last year when we went from "we could go anywhere from here" to "we are going." As a result, I began considering the river through different eyes. What was once something to admire for a brief moment as I traveled became an object of anticipation and trepidation. While excited about the experience that lay ahead of us, I envisioned the dangers we would encounter. With new eyes as we had crossed over the New Corydon Bridge, I spotted a tree partially obstructing the river. From the bridge, the tree appeared dangerous.

Almost every time we drove over the river, I fretted, "Boy we will have to be careful when we reach this point." John snickered, sometimes aloud and sometimes to himself.

Today as I cautiously approached the dreaded tree that's been the source of John's taunts, I paddled under the bridge, hugging the left bank, wanting to avoid the tree obstacle on the right. Hmmmmm… The closer I came to the tree, the more I realized it was no big deal. It appeared different from the river view than it did from the bridge view. I barely noticed the hindrance as I paddled by.

Of course, as soon as I caught up with John, he relished in the fact that the tree was benign. He chortled, "Wasn't that tree dangerous?" I hate it when he is right.

A different view—a different perspective.

I have come to appreciate different views. I think I first started recognizing them as I inspected my surroundings while waiting for my order to arrive at a restaurant one evening. I took inventory of the picture behind John's head. I then turned around and scoped out the artwork John was enjoying on the wall over my shoulder. I shared my thoughts with John, "You realize that even though we are both here, if we were asked to describe our evening, our memories would be different. My memory would be of Van Gogh's *The Starry Night* and yours would be that colorful abstract painting." Same experience—different memories.

Soon after paddling by the harmless tree, we came upon two Amish boys fishing. John was little ahead of me and passed them first. I could hear him talking to them but couldn't make out their conversation. Apparently, the boys thought of another question after John had paddled farther downstream. As I came upon them, they were trying to gain John's attention one last time. "Hey!" they yelled after him.

Focused on John, they didn't hear me approaching and jumped when I greeted them, "Hi." Then the following unexpected dialogue occurred.

Amish boy: Where are you going?
Me: Gulf of Mexico.
Amish boy: I heard about you.
Me: We're them.
Me: See ya. (What else do you say to someone you don't know and probably will never see again?)

For some reason, John thought the conversation was one of the funniest things he had heard in a long time. I thought the interchange was just odd. Since Amish live such a simple life-style without electricity and with limited access to information, how had they heard about us? Hmmm…

There are many dangers, toils, and snares on the river. Since this portion of the Wabash is narrow and winding, encountering some adversities today did not surprise us. Even so, we stayed upright and safe the entire day. Although we were safe, I did experience an unfortunate encounter. The weather conditions were sunny, a little cool, with an occasional gust of wind. Unfortunately, a gust of wind caused a sad situation. I had just passed a debris pile when a gust of wind easily whisked my hat from my head. Frantic, I immediately shouted, "I lost my hat!"

This wasn't any hat; it was my special hat. It had traveled with me on a previous kayak trip to Hudson Bay and provided protection from the sun through many years of gardening. I cried. The tears flowed easily because I tend to become emotionally attached to objects that represent special times in my life. *Why? Am I afraid that without items as reminders I will forget? To what pieces of this adventure will I become emotionally attached? Maybe our kayaks?* I've heard of others selling their crafts upon completion of similar trips. Why? Maybe they spent so much time in their boats they didn't want to look at them any longer. Did they need money to pay bills after being unemployed while on their excursion? Maybe they didn't have room to store them. Had they realized after their expedition, their boats wouldn't add value to their life—they would be in the way, collecting dust? How much emotional stuff could I eliminate because it doesn't add any value to my life? I read a hint once that suggested taking a picture of an object you are keeping because of the memories and then discarding the article. Something to contemplate.

Enough about my emotional attachments—back to today's hat drama… John immediately paddled back to the place of loss. "I see it, and I think I can get it." I was thrilled —my hero!

My hopes were high until John shouted, "Oh, no! Don't go in there!" Pause. "It's gone. The current sucked it under the pile of debris. Sorry, babe."

Now the practical impact of losing my hat set in. *What will I do without a hat to keep the sun from beating down on my face, especially in the South?* I couldn't simply drive to the store to replace it.

John, knowing my thoughts, took off his olive green, brimmed hat and offered, "Here. You can have my hat." What a sweetheart!

"I'm not taking your hat. You need one too. We'll figure something out." I still accepted his hat—for now.

We continued paddling to Ceylon, Indiana: our destination for the night. After passing under another bridge we have driven over many times, we assessed our options of landing and moving *Work* and *Pray* off the river. Since the banks were not steep like last night's, we thought clambering to land would not be a problem. Wrong. The banks consisted of muck and mire, making every step an adventure. If we didn't slide, the mud held our boots firmly in place, making pulling our foot up difficult. We used our Epic carbon fiber paddles in a way not recommended by the manufacturer—as a mountain climbing stick. *Whatever works, right?*

With *Work* and *Pray* finally out of the water, the next goals were to put the wheels on the kayaks; then transport them through a small creek, up the hill (everything is up hill from the river) to the road, over a bridge, and to our camping spot. We put the wheels on *Pray* first and transported it through the small creek.

Let's take a moment to discuss the process of putting on the wheels. The wheels attach to a collapsible framework. Once taken apart, the entire assembly fits into and is stored in our rear holds. Mine in mine and John's in his (makes sense, huh). When we are ready to use the wheels, we remove the framework and sometimes muddy wheels from our hold (Hmmm, mud makes a mess in *Work* and *Pray*... we may need to address this in the future), unfold the frame, and slide the wheels onto the axles. Next, we retrieve the latch pins and straps from the stuff sack and push the pins through the axle holes to secure the wheels. Then, with me on one side of the kayak holding the wheel construction and John on the opposite side, John lifts the stern, and I slide the unit into place below the cockpit. With the kayak balanced on the wheels, we secure the assembly to the kayak with the straps. Voilà! Instantly transforming our water vehicles into amphibious crafts.

Muck and mire can cause more problems than the obvious sliding and potential loss of a boot. (Can you have muck without mire?) After pulling *Pray* through the small creek, I was trekking back to help John retrieve *Work*. I moved carefully through muck and mire, watching my feet so I wouldn't fall, when my forward motion stopped abruptly, and I was in severe pain. While watching my feet and being diligently careful, I failed to notice the massive tree branch overhead and ran into it—hard! I heard the thunk deep in my head. My vision was fuzzy. (I understand where the phrase "I saw stars" comes from.) Since John was the only one there, I didn't need to scan the area to see if anyone witnessed my clumsiness. However, I did immediately check for blood—none. Phew! No trip to the ER for stitches.

John, hearing the thunk, turned around to determine the origin of the noise. Surprised to see me stumbling around dazed, he then noticed the tree branch and knew what had happened and wondered how I could accidentally run into an obstruction that large. He was soon at my side. If he hadn't been so worried about me, I know he would have allowed his laughter to escape his head. Later in the day, however, he didn't use as much self-control during the retelling of the story.

I sat down for a while and, as a bump began to form, knew I needed ice. *Where am I going to find ice?* Then I remembered Irene Heare, my pillow hero's wife, planned to bring us dinner later and sent her a text…

Me: Can you bring me an icepack?

Irene: Sure. Why?

Me: I hit my head on a tree.

Irene: In the boat?

Me: No, while I was walking.

No response from Irene. I'm sure I heard her laughing. I was so embarrassed. This was only day number two, and I had hit my head on a tree while on land. Injuries should have cool stories attached.

Sure I would live, we began the task of pulling *Work* and *Pray* up the hill, over the bridge, and to the place we planned to place our tent. Except for some brief trial runs at home, this was the first time we had used our wheels to transport *Work* and *Pray*. Even with the wheels, I found pulling my kayak difficult. An aching head didn't help any. What seemed like a short distance became longer with each step. I even had to stop several times to rest.

After pulling the kayaks today, I am NOT looking forward to hiking around the town of Markle, Indiana, in a few days. This town will present us with our first man-made impediments. Apparently, years ago, the Army Corp of Engineers constructed a levee along the town. On one side of the levee, a dam allowed a small amount of water to pass down the original channel, affording access for swimming and fishing to the locals. The river proper, on the other hand, was redirected to the other side of the levee and under the bridge at Highway 3. We knew these roadblocks existed and had driven over to scout the area earlier in the year. From our investigation we believe the only safe passage is to put the wheels on *Work* and *Pray* at the take out point upstream from Markle and then portage about two miles into town. We will then hike about half a mile south on the highway and a mile down a dirt road to the Division of Natural Resources access point. A long, mostly uphill hike, but doable. At least that is what John keeps telling me.

Back to today... Safely across the bridge, we pulled *Work* and *Pray* onto a flat, grassy area, which was more appealing than our camping spot last night. Erecting the tent was also much easier without the gale-force wind— no acrobatics needed!

As I was homemaking in our tent, Bud and Irene arrived with Easter dinner. I didn't realize how much they were going to spoil us. I thought they were simply bringing us a meal. Boy, I was wrong!

Before I emerged from the tent, Irene brought me some Easter candy. *Who doesn't like chocolate on Easter (or any other day)?* I was finishing my before-dinner chocolate treat when I heard Irene approach the tent again. I expected her to announce dinner. Instead, she surprised me with a hot washcloth—like an airline attendant! (Oh yeah, I forgot—the first gift Irene presented me was an icepack.)

Finished "making the bed," I emerged from the tent to see Bud, with his normal two pair of glasses—clear lenses on his face and sunglasses on the top of his slightly bald head, Irene, dressed warmly in her black wool mid-thigh pea coat, and John sitting on chairs at a table. Real dinner plates (not a pan and lid) placed neatly on the table awaited the Easter meal. Bud, Irene, and John smirked as I sat down sporting an ice pack sticking out from under my purple wear-around-the-campsite ball cap. I was embarrassed and would have removed the ice pack if it hadn't felt so good.

As we enjoyed the cheese and cracker appetizers in the center of the table, John thought he should provide us with some before dinner entertainment by telling Bud and Irene his version of my hitting my head on the tree… no sympathy here. He proceeded to describe the tree branch as an entire 18-inch diameter Sycamore tree that had fallen across the path. He then mentioned his wonder at how I could of have failed to spot the tree. "LaNae actually had to duck under to avoid planting her face into it." Hmmm, that's not quite how I remembered the incident, but then considering my recent head trauma, I was glad I could remember my name. Oh well, only 3 months and 28 days left. What more could possibly go wrong?!

Once we finished our appetizers and Bud and Irene finally stopped laughing, we moved on to our next course—salad. *I am enjoying this pampering. Maybe we should take a trip more often.*

After our second course, Irene instructed us to pick up our real plates and carry them to the back of the van. My stomach growled as the aroma of the main entrée of our Easter dinner—ribs, baked potatoes, and green beans—wafted through the air. What Easter dinner (or any dinner) is complete without dessert? Irene served us strawberries on shortbread covered with a creamy sauce. *I need this recipe.*

As I relished my final bites of dessert, Irene whispered, "Would you like to ride with me to my mom's? I want to take her some of the leftovers. You could also use her restroom."

Hmmm… all I heard was restroom! The idea of sitting on a toilet sounded EXTREMELY appealing. The thought of riding in a heated van was an added bonus.

Over the last couple of days, every time I have felt the urge to relieve myself, I have had to retrieve the red "poop bag" from the front of *Work* or the tent's rain fly strap. The "poop bag" contains a collapsible shovel, toilet paper, plastic bags, tampons, and hand sanitizer.

Going poop isn't as easy as…
- walking into the bathroom
- shutting and locking the door
- pulling down my pants
- sitting down on the toilet
- pooping
- wiping
- pulling up my pants
- flushing the toilet
- washing my hands

No. While in the wilderness, going poop requires many more steps …
- retrieving the red poop bag
- locating a discreet place far from camp
- finding a sturdy stick
- removing toilet paper; shovel; plastic, re-sealable bag from red bag
- placing toilet paper within reach

- removing the shovel from the sheath
- digging a hole—this is taking some practice to achieve the correct depth and width
- removing coat
- pulling my wetsuit down to my knees
- squatting in the proper position to insure my clothing doesn't gets wet
- aiming for the hole
- pooping
- reaching for toilet paper and hoping it hasn't moved
- tearing off an adequate length of toilet paper
- wiping
- placing toilet paper in proper re-sealable, plastic bag
- using stick to cover hole—the shovel touches only dirt
- re-clothing
- placing shovel back into sheath
- returning shovel, toilet paper, and plastic bag to red poop bag
- removing hand sanitizer
- sanitizing hands

I hope I don't have diarrhea in the next four months. I don't think I can move that fast.

So, when Irene asked if I wanted to ride along and use her mother's restroom, I responded with an enthusiastic, "Of course!"

A few minutes into the ride I lamented, "I lost my hat." I almost cried.

She sympathized, "Oh, no. You really need a hat. I might have one at home. I think Bud's planning to bring you coffee in the morning. I could send it with him."

"Does it have a string? That's a necessity!"

"I don't think so. But I'm sure we could make it work."

"Thanks."

I hate depending on other people: I like being independent. If I were at home, I would put *hat* on my grocery list and buy one the next time I went shopping at Walmart. However, I don't have a grocery list and won't be going to Walmart any time soon. I am supposed to be self-sufficient—everything I need for the next four months is in *Pray*. I have a feeling allowing others to "do" for me will be merely one of the many lessons I will learn on this trip.

On the rest of the ride to Irene's mom's apartment, we carried out the obligatory small talk about kids, the weather, etc.

I am going to miss Irene. We have spent many hours philosophizing over a cup or two or three of coffee. I call her my boring, coffee-drinking friend. She's anything but boring. We labeled ourselves as boring one evening while sitting in a restaurant on Broadway in New York City. We realized we were "too boring to know" when we couldn't identify the famous people being photographed in front of a publicity backdrop across the street. I am going to miss girl-talk. I will be spending four months with John. I love him dearly, but he doesn't understand the mind of a woman. He focuses on facts not emotions. I sometimes need someone who will think with his or her heart. Will I become frustrated when I can't express myself to someone who will hear and understand? I hadn't considered this as we planned our trip. I thought we were so prepared, but as I focused on physical needs, I forgot about emotional needs.

Irene and I discussed the amount of time I will spend with John, talking to only him. I expressed my concern. "I wonder if we will run out of things to discuss."

To be honest, I wonder if in John's lifetime he will ever run out of subjects to talk about since he always seems to have something interesting and random bouncing around in his head and out of his mouth. Unfortunately, sometimes thoughts bounce out of his mouth before he can stop them, creating some interesting, and perhaps embarrassing, moments for both of us. I realized this soon after we started dating when he complimented me by saying, "Your skin is soft... Like lard."

However, for the next four months, we are going to spend almost every waking moment together—that's a lot of discussion time. His thoughts may actually quit bouncing.

Irene had a solution. "I could text you discussion topics."

"Sounds like fun." I am already looking forward to her discussion topic texts. Her topics will be anything but normal (or boring)—perfect for John and me.

Arriving at Irene's mom's apartment, I immediately found my way to the bathroom. As I had thought, I enjoyed the toilet seat in a room with a door and heat. Sitting, not squatting, and having privacy have already become a luxury—and this is only day two of our trip. *Will peeing in the woods ever feel natural?*

After I took care of my bodily functions, we returned to Bud and John.

Bud commented, "We better get going."

"Thanks for dinner." John, smirking, had to add, "And the ice pack." Everyone chuckled, except me.

Still smiling, Irene added, "Just a minute."

Irene stepped to the back of the van, retrieved a Styrofoam cooler, and placed it by my feet. I opened the lid and stared at the boiled eggs, fruit, yogurt, and an extra ice pack.

Irene explained, "I thought you might like these for breakfast. Bud will pick up the cooler in the morning when he brings your coffee."

I hugged her. "Thank you so much for everything!"

After prayers, more hugs, and thanks to Bud for stuffing my pillow into *Pray*, they left. Sigh… and a few more tears. *When will I quit crying?*

Tonight, we are staying seven miles from home, but we might as well be 200 miles away. Instead of a double bed, we will sleep in a tent wide enough for two sleeping bags and only a couple of inches longer than John is. Instead of a mattress, we will lie on thin sleep pads. Instead of a down comforter, we will cover up with summer-weight sleeping bags. (Our winter North Face sleeping bags were too large to bring.) Instead of a furnace, our breath will heat the "bedroom." We are so close, but so far.

Would asking Bud and Irene to drive us to our home for the night be cheating? Probably. There isn't anything to eat there anyway—not even a half of a hot dog.

04-06-2017

Not My Store

Weather conditions:

High: 62

Low: 37

Skies: overcast with occasional light rain

Wind: S 6-17 mph, gusts to 21 mph

Today's mileage: 9 miles

Total: 52 miles

Where we traveled: Ceylon, Indiana, to Linn Grove, Indiana

John stole my pillow again last night—the pillow he didn't think there was enough room for. The one I thought should be included on our journey. Hmmm… So we are sharing a small pillow, which wasn't even on the list. Technically, the pillow isn't even here! We may need to change the name of our web site from "Separate Boats" to "Separate Tents."

Shivering instead of sleeping, I attempted all of my try-to-stay-warm tricks with the same unsuccessful results as the night before. I know I will welcome a little chilliness later in the trip, but, right now, I am shaking from dusk to dawn. This morning, snuggled in my sleeping bag but still cold, I imagined the warm bed we will be enjoying at the home of our friends Mark and Myra Moore in Linn Grove, Indiana, tonight. (And probably a full-size pillow of my own.)

• • •

This morning for breakfast, we enjoyed the hard-boiled eggs and fruit Irene left us last night. *I just realized today is the day after Easter. I'm sure many people ate hard-boiled eggs for breakfast this morning—I guess we're not so special.* Soon after we finished eating at 7:15 a.m., Bud pulled up in his white work truck. He climbed out of his truck and handed us each a white convenience store to-go cup of coffee. We are so spoiled!

Bud also brought a beige, brimmed, Panama Jack hat for me to borrow that Irene purchased in the Florida Keys. Although thankful for the gesture, I was hesitant to accept the assistance. "I don't want to use Irene's souvenir hat. What if I ruin or lose it? I would feel awful."

"Believe me; she's not attached to it. She bought it to protect her scalp from the sun."

"OK. Are you sure?"

"Yes. Please, take it."

Sadly, the design of Irene's hat didn't include a chinstrap, which, as I have learned, is essential during bursts of wind. Confession time—my original hat had the necessary strap; however, I was negligent and didn't have the strap under my chin. In my vanity, I thought the strap looked "hickish," and since the wind was mild, I had tucked it behind my head. Unfortunately, even during a mild breeze, gusts can appear out of nowhere. (Thus the term gusts.) The rest is history… Since everything we brought we need, losing my hat was more than an inconvenience, it was unnecessary. *Will this trip teach me the frivolity of vanity?*

Back to Irene's hat—Bud, being resourceful and knowing the necessity of a strap, brought shoestrings to serve as makeshift straps. To make the hat useable, we will somehow need to punch holes through the fabric of the brim. I didn't want to ruin her hat; there had to be another alternative. I accepted the hat and shoestrings from Bud, hoping I wouldn't have to use them. Until we decide if we want to punch holes in Irene's hat, John is letting me borrow his hat, even though without a head covering, the sun will beat down on his face. I think he believes my skin needs more protection than his does. I am a woman after all. John being without a hat right now is OK; but once we are farther south and summer approaches, we will both need a hat.

After presenting me with the hat, Bud announced, "Well, I better get going."

"Are you sure you can't stay a little while and drink some coffee with us?" Even though I wasn't at home, didn't have a chair to offer, and hadn't provided the coffee, I still wanted to offer hospitality. To be honest, I wasn't ready to say goodbye.

Bud glanced at his watch. "I guess I have a little time." He sat on the tailgate of his truck and drank a cup of coffee with us before taking the leftover eggs and fruit and traveling on to work. I was disappointed we couldn't keep the leftovers with us, but we didn't have any extra room. We did make room, however, for the leftover Easter candy—priorities.

Watching Bud drive away, I cried. John put his arm around me and held me tightly as I sniffled, "I hate to see him leave. We won't see Irene or him for several months. I didn't realize how much I am going to miss certain people." Leaving our life is proving to be more difficult than I had expected. During preparation for the trip, the anticipation of what was to come and the unknown veiled the fact we were leaving people we knew and loved. Eventually, the only person with me will be John. Will he be enough?

Once Bud left, we prepared to launch, which included tearing down the tent, packing our gear, and pulling *Work* and *Pray* back across the bridge. We didn't, however, go through the little creek next to the injurious tree but found, instead, a place a little less muddy with easier access for launching our kayaks.

All launching prep accomplished, we left Ceylon about 10:00 a.m., heading for Mark and Myra's for some more pampering. I will be sad when we leave this area and no one will continue to spoil us. On the other hand, think of all the new people we will meet—waiting for those divine appointments.

Keep us upright and safe.

Today, we noticed a pileated woodpecker and several owls. We've en-countered these birds before but in different settings. Watching them from the river appeared different than on land. I wondered why? Is interacting with them more natural in their environment, an environment humans haven't intruded upon? How often do animals on the river encounter a human? Not often, I assume, since they ignore us.

A few miles after we left Ceylon, we passed under another familiar bridge—US Highway 27. Although we have driven on this bridge several times over the course of many years, our experience today was as if we were seeing this area for the first time. Approaching the bridge, I wasn't sure which road we were going to be floating under since, from the river, even familiar banks and bridges seem foreign. They are the same but different— like the animals.

Today's drizzly, eight-mile paddle was uneventful. Arriving at our des-tination, we faced the same dilemma we encounter every time we prepare to leave the river—where to pull out. Linn Grove previously had a boat ramp, but it had washed out several years ago (I don't remember it being there) and had not been replaced because this portion of the river is rarely suitable (too low) for water transportation. Since Mark and Myra live on the river, we decided to scope their conveniently located back yard. In prior years, we had launched another pair of kayaks, which were smaller and not loaded with gear, by their house, but requirements for launching are dif-ferent from landing. After assessing the situation, we decided pulling our long, heavy kayaks out at this "convenient" location was not convenient. So we paddled upstream to another option we had spied earlier. (Don't be impressed by our paddling upstream, the current isn't very strong on this part of the Wabash.)

As we were turning around, we spotted Chase Moore taking some pic-tures of us from the bridge. Our friend Dawn Wanner had asked Chase to snap some pictures to help her have a record of our journey. I had texted her during the day to update her of our progress. When we thought we were close to Linn Grove (on the river knowing exactly where you are is sometimes difficult), she called Chase, who then drove to the bridge to wait on us. We were thankful for some pictures that included the both of us.

After talking with Chase, we reached a place suitable to pullout and did so. We put the wheels on *Work* and *Pray* (wheels—a great invention) and began pulling them through the yard of Alan Neuenschwander's, with whom we chatted awhile. Then we pulled our kayaks through Linn Grove—population of 60 (maybe). You get the idea—traveling across town wasn't difficult and didn't take long.

We arrived at the Moore's earlier than expected. Since they are responsible members of society, they were at work—unlike us. Hungry, we decided eating would be the perfect way to pass time while we waited. Sitting at their picnic table, we prepared and ate one of our dehydrated (only boil water) meals—spaghetti with mud pie for dessert. Unfortunately, I added too much water to the mud pie, and we had to drink our treat. However, the thin pudding did make delicious chocolate milk; we may be drinking "pudding" for breakfast in the future. (Haven't some great foods been invented by mistake? Like the invention of Reese's Peanut Butter Cups—"You got your chocolate on my peanut butter." "No, you got your peanut butter on my chocolate.") The spaghetti and pudding made a satisfying snack. Most people would consider this a meal; but when burning off extra calories kayaking each day, meals sometimes become snacks.

Sitting at the picnic table, we reflected over the past couple of days. John commented, "You know, this was only our third day on the river, but it seems like we have been gone weeks."

I agreed, "Yeah. You know what's weird is we've traveled 52 miles, but are only 11 miles from home."

John asked, "What is one thing that has surprised you?"

"I'm surprised my muscles aren't sore. It's not as if we could have trained for this. While I am tired after a day of paddling, my muscles don't hurt." John and I are active and work out regularly, but did no training specific for this trip. "Do yours hurt?"

"No, actually, they don't."

Now it was my turn to ask, "What has surprised you?"

"I'm surprised we have had such high winds to deal with." He paused a moment before adding, "I still can't believe we are doing this."

After our discussion, we went into the house to clean ourselves and our clothes before Mark and Myra arrived home. I'm sure they appreciated our fresher fragrance. But then again, this is only our third day on the river—how dirty can our clothes or we be? I enjoyed a hot shower and wondered what will be the longest stretch between showers later in the trip—when we don't have friends living by the river to exploit. Clean may become relative.

Refreshed and warmer, I put on my going into town clothes. Replacing my shampoo, conditioner, deodorant, and face moisturizing in my toiletries bag, I caught sight of my make-up. I had almost forgot to put it on. Vanity!

When Mark and Myra arrived home, Mark informed us we should "park" *Work* and *Pray* in the garage while their vehicle would spend the night outside. This is the second time our water vehicles have taken a road vehicle's parking spot in a garage.

Mark and Myra (fit and in their early fifties and late forties) became friends with John several years ago when John coached their daughters in club soccer. Mark perceived John needed help and became one of John's biggest assets, and a friendship was a resulting benefit. Although we live only eleven miles from the Moore's, we haven't taken time to get together for quite a while. Life (kid's activities, household upkeep, work, etc.) seems to fill our calendar, leaving few available dates for socializing. We have good intentions to "give me a call," but soon months become years before making a call. I wonder how much time we will allow to pass before we reconnect again; will we need to take another kayak trip? We took advantage of tonight to catch up. Somewhere during our conversation, Mark blurted,

"Oh, by the way, I contacted the *Berne Tri-Weekly* (the local newspaper). They may call."

Not long after Mark's announcement, his phone rang. The voice at the other end was a reporter from the *Berne Tri-Weekly*. He said he would arrive at Mark's within the half hour, putting dinner on hold. I was glad we had eaten our dehydrated "snack" earlier because the interview was lengthy. This was our second interview. Our first was about a week before the beginning of our trip for *The Commercial Review* of Portland, Indiana. Again, we are private people, so the media coverage is out of our comfort zone. If we had our way, we would have told only our kids, close relatives, and friends about our trip, so they wouldn't worry when we disappeared for a few months. We definitely wouldn't have announced our trip to the public, but we are willing to leave the privacy of our own little world in order to promote our chosen charity, The Fortress (a home for unwed mothers in Uganda).

After the interview, Mark and John grilled some of the best steaks I have ever tasted. Last summer when we told Mark about our trip, he declared enthusiastically, "You have to stay at our house when you come through Linn Grove. We'll share a steak and a beer." He fulfilled his promise. Inside, Myra and I created a pasta dish and salad. Once all courses were prepared, we enjoyed steak with sautéed mushrooms, salad, California blend, pasta dish, and bread, accompanied by beer and wine. Our final course was a delicious strawberry dessert. I was sooooo full!

Then we retreated to the family room and talked until I couldn't keep my eyes open any longer. "I need to go to bed."

Myra said, "I'll bring you some jammies to sleep in and comfy clothes for tomorrow morning."

"Thank you so much!" How thoughtful. My trip jammies are long johns—too warm for a heated bedroom. In addition, we are carrying only three sets of clothing—one for going into town, one dirty, and one clean. When we were packing, there wasn't room for my pillow so there definitely wasn't' room for comfy lounging clothes. Earlier this evening, I had wished I had some comfy clothes to relax in and had already thought (worried) about what I was going to wear to bed. How did she know? With limited room, packing for every scenario was impossible.

"Good night. Thank you so much for everything!" We withdrew to our warm bedroom for the night. We have slept in our tent only two nights, but with the temperatures so cold, I am looking forward to having warm feet and not shivering all night.

We have been so blessed with friendship. The Moores opened their home to us, invited us to use anything, and served us a wonderful meal. In addition, don't forget the shower, washing machine and dryer, jammies, comfy clothes, a warm comfortable bed, and my OWN pillow!

04-07-2017

"Hey, Roger! Watch this Jump Shot"

Weather conditions:

High: 53

Low: 40

Skies: overcast with occasional light rain

Wind: ENE 14-25 mph, gusts to 30 mph

Today's mileage: 15 miles

Total: 67 miles

Where we traveled: Linn Grove, Indiana, to Bluffton, Indiana

A warm bed and full-size pillow I didn't have to share. I slept GREAT! How long before I experience these luxuries that I previously viewed as necessities again?

Actually, despite my complaining, I love camping. Most people perceive our adventure as a four-month kayaking trip with camping almost every night as part of it. I describe it as a four-month camping trip with kayaking from campsite to campsite as a part of it. The description of the trip is a matter of perspective. However, no matter how much I love camping, I'm not fond of cold feet or shivering all night. I will be a happier camper when the temperature is above 50 degrees.

This morning, Mark and Myra had to leave for their paying jobs before we left for our non-paying, kayaking job. (It is, after all, work!) As they left we offered our thank yous and exchanged good-byes. They wished us good luck with the rest of the trip. Hopefully, the next time we meet them, they will be offering us congratulations. *I still can't believe we are doing this!*

Before Myra left, she explained our breakfast options—none of which required boiling water to rehydrate our food. We chose the egg sandwich on wheat bread option. (Roughing it, I know.) Clean clothes and toiletry dry bags packed into our kayaks, we backed *Work* and *Pray* out of Mark and Myra's garage, rolled them back through Linn Grove, across Alan Neuenschwander's yard, and down to the river. We removed our wheels and placed them into the back hold of each kayak, exactly where John has them listed on his map.

Everything stowed in its proper place, John placed *Pray* into the water. (He always puts mine into the water first, and then I stay near while he launches his.) Holding on to *Pray*, John turned to me and instructed, "Grab your paddle."

I scanned the area, "I don't see our paddles. " *Had the proverbial "up a creek without a paddle" literally manifested itself at this moment?*

I recognized the realization on John's face. "Oh no. I forgot to grab the paddles. Stay here." He turned around, hiked across Alan Neuenschwander's yard, through Linn Grove, back to Mark and Myra's garage, and retrieved the important gear. Even after John traipsed through Linn Grove three times, we paddled our first stroke of the day around 9:00 a.m.

Keep us upright and safe.

Sometimes as I lie shivering all night because the temperature is in the thirties, I wonder why we started this trip on April 1 and not on a later, warmer date. Today, I remembered why we chose this starting date—we didn't want to climb out of *Work* and *Pray,* dragging them as we waded through the water. Unless there has been a lot of rain or snowmelt, a common occurrence in March and April, the first parts of the Wabash River are usually shallow.

We have previously experienced the shallowness first hand. The stretch of the Wabash we kayaked today between Linn Grove and Bluffton is familiar territory to us and brings back memories. I remember one time in particular. We launched our kayaks at Mark and Myra's house in late summer even though the water level appeared low. We had set aside a day to paddle from Linn Grove to Bluffton, followed by eating at Pizza King. (Eating a Royal Feast pizza is how we reward ourselves after a twelve-mile paddle. *Doesn't everyone?*) Realizing we were spending more time out of our kayaks pulling them than in our kayaks paddling them, we clambered out one last time, pulled them back from whence we came, loaded them back on the truck, and drove home. Yes, we drove home, not to Pizza King. I thought we should still eat at Pizza King, but John thought otherwise. I was devastated. *What, no Royal Feast? Now, I have to cook.* Thus, the reason we left April 1, despite the less-than-desirable temperatures, was to avoid pulling *Work* and *Pray*, which we have avoided. So far.

The river conditions today were similar to what we have experienced the last couple of days, including trees to paddle around and some minor rapids. We thought we were going to experience an uneventful day, until we heard a scraping sound on the bottom of our kayaks. We peered over the side of our boats. Gravel. I quickly raised my rudder, which is important when encountering shallow water and approaching land to avoid damage to the rudder. Hearing and seeing the limestone river bottom means the water depth is probably inches, not feet of water. Kayaking in inches of water can be difficult if not impossible. I wondered, "Can we make it? We think we can, we think we can…" *Oh yea, that story is about a train not a boat.*

I heard the grating sounds of stones scarring the bottom of my brand new polyethylene (really hard plastic) kayak. I slowed down. Slower… Slower… Slower… I almost stopped. I used my paddle to push myself. The push helped for a couple of "strokes." I looked up. John was climbing out of his kayak. *Poor guy, he has to pull his kayak.* Then I stopped too. I joined John as I scrambled out of *Pray* and started pulling it. Then I remembered why we left on April 1 and are enduring cold nights. I HATE pulling my kayak.

Afloat again, we continued to Bluffton, also known as Parlor City and a familiar place to us. We have traveled to the Parlor City by river many times to shop (frequently at Lowes), and I drive there by road every three weeks for a hair appointment. However, since our travel time has been four days and not the usual 30 minutes, today felt as though we were journeying to a foreign land. Approaching Bluffton, everything seemed new and exciting. Then I heard a familiar voice.

"John! LaNae!" River Road (creative name) runs next to the river, so I glanced over my left shoulder to identify the origin of the voice. Someone in the passenger seat of a passing car was waving frantically at us through his or her rolled-down window. I didn't recognize the car nor arm. Then the head belonging to the arm appeared out the window. It was Connie Moore. Sixty-something Connie with straight chin-length dirty blond hair and a smile that makes me forget I have a care in the world, is a friend from church who makes me feel like her long-lost soul mate every time I bump into her. She repeated, "John! LaNae!"

"Hi, Connie!" I shouted over the bubbling water of some small rapids we were approaching.

The car drove a little farther down the road and stopped.

Connie and her husband, Billy, stood next to the guardrail, waiting on us to catch up to them. Connie explained their presence there, "We are on our way to the chiropractor. We had just commented, 'Wouldn't it be crazy if we saw John and LaNae,' and there you were!"

Billy had retired a few years ago from a local factory where he and John first met in the mid-eighties. Many years before John met him, Billy had served in Vietnam as a Marine. That is who Billy is—a marine—loyal, regimented. He wears his marine jacket and hat with pride. I've heard him say more than once, "Once a marine, always a marine."

Ever since we told Billy about our trip, he has been one of our biggest fans. He has stated many times, "I am so proud of you guys." Billy is one of the reasons we have to complete this trip. He makes us feel pleasantly accountable.

"It's so good to see you guys," John said.

We couldn't talk long because we were still floating downstream and trying to maneuver around the small rapids. Rapids scare me enough when I am paying attention, let alone while distracted. How embarrassed I would have been if I had flipped while someone we know was watching us. These chance meetings with people we know are unexpected blessings.

As quickly as we said hi, we blurted, "Bye. Thanks for stopping," and continued safely on our way.

Soon after our chance encounter with our friends, we pulled up on shore. As soon as we landed, before anything else, I went over the river and through the bridge, not to Grandma's house, but to Hardee's restaurant to use the restroom. I'm not sure if John was out of *Work* yet.

After checking out Hardee's restroom, I returned back over the bridge and down the hill to where John was waiting. We put the wheels on *Work* and *Pray* and pulled them up the hill (everything is uphill from the river), past a parking lot, down the hill, to a grassy area on the banks of the Wabash located behind the Kehoe Park's pavilion. Last week John had called the parks department to gain permission to camp. Little did he know his call would create a domino effect of activity and encounters.

During last week's phone call, the parks department employee instructed John to call them when we arrived in Bluffton. John and the employee agreed that after our call someone from the parks department would in turn alert the police of our presence. Today John made the we-are-here phone call.

John's phone call caused the first domino to fall. We had set up the tent and were securing all our gear in preparation for the incoming rain when Dave from the *Bluffton News Banner* strolled up. A parks department employee had contacted him, and he thought us newsworthy. At the completion of the video and audiotaped interview, he added, "The article may be an on-line video or in print tomorrow." Domino number one down.

Interview complete, we enjoyed a quaint, and late (3:00 p.m.), lunch in the tent. Each morning after breakfast, I prepare our lunches of peanut butter wraps, granola bars, and fruit roll-ups. I then place our lunches into a small mesh bag located conveniently in our cockpits.

After lunch we gathered the items we needed for a jaunt to Hardee's. Before this excursion visiting Hardee's didn't require many preparations. The only planning might have included checking my hair and makeup, grabbing the keys, and driving. However, going anywhere on this trip has a purpose (no frivolous activities) and requires organization. Preparing for our trek over the bridge to Hardee's included packing our iPads (to use the free Wi-Fi and to charge the batteries), the Sherpa (Our battery pack we use to charge our phone and iPads. We can charge the Sherpa using either electricity or our solar panel. Cool, huh?), our phone (to charge and be in touch with the world), and courier dromedary (a water bag made with a Cordura nylon shell). We have five dromedaries—two in each of our muddy cockpits. Of those two, one has a tube and a bite valve, providing us with hands-free hydration. The fifth dromedary is generally empty and housed in John's front hatch. This empty bladder, the courier, is clean and carried into businesses to obtain and transfer water to our filthy dromedaries. Necessary items gathered (I will admit, I did apply a little makeup, but my hair was already pulled up in a ponytail—nothing to fix.), we hiked across the bridge to our destination.

Sydney, a cute energetic young woman, greeted us as we approached the counter, "Welcome to Hardee's. How can I help you?"

John said, "Good afternoon, Sydney. We would like to order two black coffees."

"Sure."

As she was filling the disposable cups with the hot, dark liquid, John continued, "Sydney, we are kayaking to the Gulf of Mexico." Showing her the dromedary, he asked, "Is there someplace we can top off with water?"

Coffees in hand, Sydney stopped mid-step and stared at us skeptically, "Where?"

"The Gulf of Mexico."

"No way!"

"Honestly. We are."

She considered us a little longer and decided she didn't have any reason not to believe us. Handing us our coffee, she pointed, "You can use the water tap on the soda machine over there."

"Thank you. How much do we owe you?"

"No charge."

"Thank you so much, Sydney." We (especially John) find accepting help from others difficult, as we try to be self-sufficient. However, John has agreed on this trip we should say "yes" to offers of help unless the gift or help offered won't fit in our kayaks or impedes our progress or success.

I have tried to say yes as often as I can ever since my grandpa gave me some wise advice. I don't remember how old I was or the situation, but I do remember one particular visit. As I was sitting on the couch in front of the window in the sunny living room of my grandparent's small country home, Grandpa advised, "If someone wants to give you something, you should accept it. If you don't, you deprive them of their blessing." Ever since he offered that advice, I have tried to say yes even though my pride makes acceptance difficult. I tell myself that receiving help doesn't mean I am deficient in any way. I am merely participating in being human with the rest of society.

Coffee accepted and water container filled, we searched for the perfect place to charge our devices and take care of some Internet business. Posting pictures and journaling were at the top of my list. We found a quiet booth in the corner equipped with an electrical outlet. For us, working in a warm building with a restroom was as luxurious as relaxing by a fireplace in a lodge while drinking a mug of hot cocoa. Ready to work, I slid into the booth, plugged in my battery-powered objects, turned on by iPad, and connected to the Wi-Fi. I attempted moving some pictures to our website (www.separateboats.com) but was soon frustrated when the pictures disappeared into cyberspace, causing the arrow on the website to continue spinning. How could such a simple task become so stressful? I love technology—when it works. However, when it doesn't work, it is such a time-waster. I know I'm not the first one to complain, but being able to express my frustration has lowered my stress level from an eight to a six.

Having spent over an hour on the photos and not able to check "post pictures" off my to-do list, I moved on to journaling. I had scarcely began journaling when the iPhone rang. John and I both studied the phone as if we had never seen nor heard a phone ring before. I don't think we had heard a phone ring (Mark's was on silent last night) since we left home three days ago. (Really, only three days. If feels like three weeks.)

Hearing the phone made me realize how much I have enjoyed silence. Silence. Hmm... What is the definition of *silence*? The absence of any sound or noise. Is silence what we have been experiencing? Not really. We have heard the birds, wind, water, raccoons, etc. Nature. So there has been sound. Has there been noise? What is the definition of *noise*? A sound that is loud or unpleasant. No noise. Nature is definitely a sound and not a noise. I would define the ringing of a phone as a noise. Therefore, I guess what I have been enjoying is "half silence"—the absence of noise.

I waited to see if John would answer the phone—he did. "Hello, this is John." He is always so professional. I am proud of his business-like approach to life, especially during this trip. I think his approach has caused people to take us more seriously, realizing we aren't some fly-by-nights who decided last weekend to throw our kayaks in the river and paddle as far as we could. This is a serious venture.

Tilting his head to the side, John's brow furrowed and his eyes narrowed as he digested the caller's identity. The voice on the other end articulated, "Hello, this is Marge Ellis, the mayor's wife. We would like to host you in our home for dinner tonight." John later conveyed that he originally thought he was listening to a recording and almost hung up. Boy, am I glad he didn't.

Since John had recently made the decision to become a "yes man" in regard to accepting kindness, he responded without hesitation, "Yes, we would love to have dinner with you and your husband."

"Good. I will pick you up at your tent at 5:30." We had a dinner date with the mayor and his wife. *How did she know we were here?* This series of events seemed surreal for a multitude of reasons. One, we live 22 miles from Bluffton. Two, we have paddled from Linn Grove to Bluffton and from Bluffton to Markle several times. Three, we haven't done anything yet! So I wondered why the mayor and his wife would feel compelled to invite us to dinner at their house. I didn't have a clue, but I wasn't going to complain.

We quickly finished using the free Wi-Fi and gathered our stuff. We double-checked to be sure we had everything. "Back away," John instructed as we stepped away from our temporary office. This is a practice he began using as a soccer coach to help ensure his team members didn't leave anything before boarding the school bus and returning home from an away game. I remember watching his team, as I sat in the bleachers across the soccer field, turn around in unison after a match, and inspect the bench before leaving the area. Even without hearing him, I knew what he had directed. On this trip forgetting even one thing would be detrimental since we need everything we brought with us.

Before leaving close proximity to a restroom, we used it one last time and then rushed back to our tent to prepare for our dinner date.

I felt like skipping as John and I, holding hands, approached the tent— we were going to dine with the mayor. "Meet you in the tent," we said in unison as we released hands and each entered opposite sides of the tent. I didn't pay any attention to John's entrance until I heard the rustle of the paper bag. He held up a small paper sack (or is it called a bag?) and announced, "Look what someone left us in our vestibule." (Our rainfly creates an area outside each entrance, which we have given the name vestibule. Having a vestibule makes us feel important. Small pleasures.) Handwritten on the side was "Welcome to Bluffton." I wish we had been there to greet our visitors and accept our gift in person. *How do all these people know we are here? Did another domino fall?*

"What's inside?" Anxious as a kid on Christmas morning, I watched John pull the articles out one at a time. An orange (yum, fresh fruit), a bottle of water (always welcome), lemonade packet (water enhancement), homemade energy balls (made specifically for us?), granola bar (healthy), and a Little Debbie coffee cake (who doesn't like a Little Debbie treat). *Who left this for us and why? Why all the fuss? We haven't done anything yet!* Since we were going to dinner at the mayor's house, we stuffed everything back in the bags for tomorrow.

Getting ready didn't require much time. What did we have to do? We didn't need to change our clothes—we were already wearing our going-to-town clothes. I had already applied my make-up, and my ponytail was still tidy. Ready, we each crawled out our side of the tent and stood holding hands scanning the area for Mrs. Mayor. We wondered how we would recognize her but soon realized not many people visit this area of town on a cold, early April evening.

Soon a shorthaired blonde woman with glasses meandered up to the tent. She introduced herself, "Hi, I'm Marge." We shook hands and progressed to the parking lot. Her welcoming manner helped put me at ease as I compared my going-into-town clothes of kakis, blue t-shirt, and cleanest paddling shirt with her black pants, jacket, teal blouse, and flowered silky scarf. Approaching the car, John checked his pockets for his keys and wallet, neither of which he has on this trip. Habits. Since John is much taller than I am, he opened the back door of the vehicle for me before climbing into the front passenger seat, and relayed, "Boy, it's weird not to be in the driver's seat."

"We have to ask you how you knew we were here," John asked.

"Remember when you called the parks department last week? Well, my husband, Ted, was in the room when the call came in and told me about it when he got home that evening. As soon as I heard your story, I decided I wanted to meet you. We do many out-of-doors activities, and our children are adventurous. Today, I was at The Creative Arts Council and noticed you setting up your tent from across the river. I called you as soon as I got home." The last domino had fallen.

Marge drove us to her home. She explained her husband was still may-oring (Is *mayoring* a word? It is now.) and would be joining us shortly.

As we entered the Ellis's comfortable home through the back kitchen door, the aroma of soup simmering in the slow cooker on the counter greet-ed us. The Ellis home matched Marge—homey and comfortable. Marge offered us a glass of wine, which we willingly accepted. Wine is difficult to dehydrate. (Well, maybe even impossible.) My pillow didn't make the list even though it is small and light. Wine definitely wasn't included because of its weight. Also, what would we do with an open container? Would we be obligated to drink it all? Is there a law against drinking and paddling? John and I enjoyed our wine while Marge stood at the sink, washing grapes.

We were enjoying our wine and conversation when Mayor Ellis, wear-ing his mayoring attire, a suit and tie, entered through the kitchen door. He had distinguished slightly gray hair and an infectious smile. After intro-ductions and greetings, Marge checked the soup. "It isn't quite ready. Let's take our wine to the living room."

Time passed quickly as we shared stories about our families and our adventures—past, current, and future. I soon understood why Mayor Ellis has served in his position for four terms—he and his wife are caring, down-to-earth people who are not afraid of stepping out of their comfort zone. We learned the Ellis family does not limit their time to Bluffton, spending much of their free time out-of-doors. Being like-minded people, they em-braced our trip instead of questioning our sanity as others have.

While we were talking, the aroma of the simmering soup continued taunting my empty stomach. I hoped no one would hear my rumbling stomach as it complained. Luckily, when Marge checked the soup again, she declared, "It's ready." Yes! My stomach would soon quiet down.

We carried the soup, bread, wine, and grapes to the dining room, which was more elegant, with a chandelier and draperies, than the other two rooms we had been in. Frequent offering of hospitality was evident in the presence of a cloth covered dining room table in addition to an extra table sitting perpendicular to the main table.

I sat down. Marge began serving the soup while the Mayor stood behind her loosening his tie. My stomach growled once more as I admired the meal displayed on the table before me. Everyone seated and the blessing said, we inhaled (at least I did) the delicious meal. I was so hungry; I think liver and onions would have been delicious. (Well, maybe not.) We have been on the river four days and have eaten only one dehydrated meal (and one meal as a snack). At this rate, we won't have to worry about running out of food. After the main course, Marge served my favorite course—dessert. *It is my opinion that we should always eat dessert first, avoiding the possibility of being too full after the main course.* Apple pie with coffee. Marge and Mayor Ellis were spoiling us.

Before leaving, we snapped the obligatory selfie with our new friends. (Selfies are what friends do, right?) Picture captured and approved, Marge returned us to our home for the next few months—the tent.

Another day complete. Did we leave Linn Grove, Indiana, (and a warm bed) only this morning? Wasn't that a week ago? Did we leave Fort Recovery, Ohio, only three days ago? Wasn't that a month ago? In the last few days we have reconnected with some old (not in age) friends and made some new friends. *This is the trip*—meeting wonderful people and making new friends!

04-08-2015

What's the Point

Weather conditions:

High: 70

Low: 38

Skies: severe thunderstorm in the morning followed by overcast skies

Wind: E 10-32 mph, gusts to 38 mph

Today's mileage: 13 miles

Total mileage: 80 miles

Where we traveled: Bluffton, Indiana, to Markle, Indiana

Routine. Essential for any excursion.

Without routine, I think we would be concentrating more on our fears and the length and breadth of the excursion we have undertaken. With routine, our focus is on the moment and not on what could happen over the next four months. Even though John hasn't voiced his fears of potential dangers or of being overwhelmed with what will be required to live on the river, he must feel what I am feeling. How can he not be concerned about overturning or getting hurt? How can he not be worried about having everything we need? I guess he did say once he felt responsible to bring me home safely to our kids. That is a lot of pressure. If we spend our time focusing on routine, we are too busy to be worried or frightened. The trip is manageable one task at a time. Contemplating the trip's enormity is daunting.

While we are focusing on our tasks, I am concerned we are missing some of nature's beauty around us. Although I have observed some of the sights as we float down the river, I want to notice ALL the spring flowers, the birds, the banks, the smells, and the changes. I hope that as we become comfortable in our wilderness life, the river becomes our home and not something to overcome, giving us permission to examine our environment and note its contrast to society life.

Even though we are only four days into our trip, we are already developing routines. We spend the first few minutes of our day responding to e-mails and texts, checking our blog, reading our devotions, checking the radar, and verifying the weather forecast. The radar this morning was very colorful, containing a lot of yellow and red—not safe colors when planning to be in a kayak on a river. The hourly forecast indicated the storms would arrive this morning and would be out of the area soon after noon. (Isn't technology great?) With this information in mind, John determined our goals for the day.

Goals for this morning were to tear down our tent and stow our gear in the kayaks before the forecasted thunderstorm arrived in Bluffton. Then for breakfast eat the treats from our gift bags left yesterday by a random angel. Next head to Hardee's to use their Wi-Fi and wait for the storms to pass, return to *Work* and *Pray*, eat our peanut butter wrap lunch, and then paddle to Markle.

Tent down and store gear—check.

Breakfast enjoyed—check.

On our way to Hardee's—almost check.

As we walked by a parking lot on our way to Hardee's, a car pulled in and parked close to us. We didn't think anything of the car; it's a parking lot after all. Two ladies emerged from the vehicle. We recognized the driver as Marge, Bluffton's First Lady. What a surprise to run into her this morning. She introduced us to her passenger and friend, Liz Ortiz Mock. Marge had told Liz about this couple (us) kayaking to the Gulf of Mexico. Liz thought she should meet us, so Marge and Liz drove to our camping spot, hoping to catch us before we left town. Lucky for them, the forecasted storm had delayed our departure.

Soon after the introductions, another vehicle parked a few spots away from Marge's car. No big deal; it's a parking lot after all. A fifty-something man climbed out of his vehicle and strolled look towards us. Obviously, he knew someone in our group. I assumed he recognized Marge, Liz, or John because I couldn't identify him. I broke rule number one of avoiding someone in society—I made eye contact. He continued on his path towards me. *Oh no, I am the one he knows.* I tried to pull the recognition information from a small area in the back of my brain. No clue. I hoped during our conversation I would be able to piece together bits of information and avoid embarrassment. *Please, don't ask me if I recognize you.* Of course, his first words to me were, "You don't know who I am, do you?" *Why is it when someone asks you if you know who he or she is, you usually don't?*

After I apologized for my lack of memory, he put me out of my misery, "Rod Gerber." Oh yeah, we graduated from high school together many years ago. Rod has changed a lot since then—he has grown up. He once was a boy with short, dark brown hair covering his forehead with bangs that touched his rectangular, gold, wire rim glasses. The man before me was a mature, taller version of that boy with a little less, and graying, hair that barely reached his forehead. He still wore rectangular, wire rim glasses, but they were now silver instead of gold.

"I've been following your trip on your blog. Last night I read that you were staying in Bluffton. I was on my way home from work this morning and thought I would take a chance and see if you were still here." The forecasted storm, which caused a delay in our departure, was forcing us to be social.

I chatted with Rod while John talked with Marge and Liz. During John's discussion with the ladies, he was brave enough to ask if they would drive us to Walmart so we could buy a new hat to replace the one I lost on day two. They agreed to do so. Since the loss of my head covering, I have been wearing the hat I stole, I mean borrowed, from John—leaving him hatless. I said good-bye to Rod and climbed into the back seat of Marge's vehicle, and away we went—Walmart bound.

Wanting to be at Hardee's before the storm hit, we decided to divide and conquer when we reached Walmart —John to sporting goods, Marge and Liz to women's apparel, and me to gardening—all of us on a quest to find my hat replacement. We live 22 miles from Bluffton; I have shopped at this Walmart many times and am familiar with its layout. But since traveling here this time took days and not minutes, when I entered the doors, I felt I was entering this particular store for the first time. I found myself reading the signs to direct me to the proper department. I finally located the lawn and garden sign and scampered towards it.

Where are the hats? Down this aisle? No—seeds. This one? No—fertilizer. This aisle? Yes! I scanned the small selection and decided not many people wear hats while gardening, at least not in April. I always wear a hat when gardening or mowing the lawn for a couple of reasons. One—to protect the color in my hair. Two—to protect my skin from sunburn and sunspots. Vanity.

Inventorying the miserable collection of hats, I tried to recall the requirements for a hat: a brim for shade, a string for security, and flexibility for stuffing it into my deck bag. *This one has a nice brim and is flexible.* I tried it on. *I like it.* No string. *How about this one?* No string. *Don't they make hats with strings anymore?* Discouraged, I set off to find out if the others had been more successful. I found Marge and Liz exiting the women's apparel area. Empty handed. Together we moved to the sporting goods department in search of John.

As we reached sporting goods, John turned the corner with a smile on his face and a camo hat in his hand, the only hat in the entire store with a string. For a brief moment, I had a vision of me in the camo hat paddling down the river. *I certainly hope he doesn't intend for me to wear that.* I kept the concern in my head since he was so proud of his find. He eased my mind when he disclosed, "Why don't you keep my hat? I'll wear this one." I'm glad I kept my thoughts in my head. I hadn't given him enough credit. He DID realize I am a girl (and vain) and the new hat was a little too masculine for me. I miss my hat!

Hat in hand, I stood in the checkout line. Rumbling, sounding like an avalanche, echoed through the building. I said, "Listen to that thunder." (Why does thunder sound more ominous in a store?) Our decision to tear down first thing this morning was, indeed, a wise one.

Approaching the doors, I surveyed the view—the darkness in the sky resembled 8:00 in the evening not 10:00 in the morning. The automatic doors opened. The thunder's roar and rain's hammering increased in intensity. The forceful rain struck the ground and bounced. This was not a peaceful spring shower. More affirmation that our tear-down-early-and-wait-out-the-storm decision was the correct plan of action this morning. We scurried (well maybe ran) to the vehicle, and Marge drove us to Hardee's, where we parted ways. We darted into Hardee's and worked toward checking the next goal off our list.

Wait out storm at Hardee's while enjoying coffee and free Wi-Fi—check.

Sitting in the booth at Hardee's, I pondered the camo hat lying on the table. Thankful I didn't have to wear it. I mourned the loss of my hat. Life would have been simpler if I hadn't been so vain and had put the string under my chin. Oh well, this is the trip—another part of our story.

Once the deluge of rain became a drizzle and the thunder grumbled in the distance, John checked the radar. "The storm is past us. Let's get going." We packed up, backed away from the booth, returned to our belongings, and ate lunch. Included in our lunch today were homemade fruit roll-ups. We are enjoying these fruity pleasures.

Eat lunch—check.

Launch *Work* and *Pray* into the water at 12:30 p.m.—check.

Keep us upright and safe.

I love the moment when I finally insert my paddle blade into the river, take my first slice of the water, and glide away from the previous night's shore downstream to another location. Leaving the banks, I wonder what new sights I will discover along the way from my river view.

Each day I am amazed by, and in awe of, my river view. Only a privileged few have seen what I witness every day. The Wabash winds more than I realized. Anticipation fills my core as I near a bend in the river, wondering what new sights await me as I round the corner. *Will I observe a deer that has wandered down a wildlife path to the water's edge, drinking from the flowing river? Will I set eyes on of an eagle soaring? Will I catch a glimpse of an eaglet poking its head above the edge of its nest, waiting for its parent to return with lunch? Will a squirrel race us from the banks?* Anticipation.

Today we traveled to Markle, where the river is re-routed, creating a three-foot drop as the re-routed river joins the original river. Paddling over a three-foot drop with all the possessions we need for the next four months didn't sound safe or appealing. Over the last year, John investigated our options and found there is a boat ramp above the re-routing. Since boat ramps are more difficult to recognize from the river than from the road, last April we paddled from Bluffton to Markle to make sure we would recognize the take out.

Last year while paddling this section, I spotted shadows floating across the water's surface. I probed the skies for the origin. Then I perceived the birds—several large birds—soaring over us. I slowed down to get a better view. I tried recalling what large birds I had previously noticed flocking in a group—turkey vultures. Since John is familiar with many varieties of birds, I thought I would try impressing him with my recognition. I asked, "Are those turkey vultures?"

"I don't think so." He studied them a little longer. "I think they are great blue herons." Hovering herons seemed unusual because great blue herons tend to be skittish and usually fly away. Then again how much time have I spent on the river to be an expert?

Soon after identifying the birds, I counted approximately thirty spindly nests high above us in the tops of some sycamore trees. At first I thought they were squirrels' nests. But as I grew closer, I realized the nests were blue heron nests, some with chicks' heads peeking above the top of their home. Large birds sitting in trees on frail looking twig bowls seemed contrary to reason. I also didn't expect to come across blue herons in groups. Think about this… great blue herons nest in a rookery but do not usually live in a community. Geese do not always nest in groups but live and travel as a gaggle. Opposites in nature. I deemed the nesting area a great blue heron maternity ward.

This year as we came near what we thought was the same area, we scoured the trees with eagerness for the rookery. Our confidence level was low that we would locate the maternity ward because locations on the river are difficult to identity; the river is a living body of water as it and its banks constantly change. But like last year, we first become aware of the birds soaring above followed by the nests in the trees. Great blue herons apparently use the same nests year after year as the eagles do. Recognizing the maternity ward again today made me feel even more connected to the river—this is OUR river. Our view from the river, rather than the road, is proving to be educational. A different view—different knowledge.

Along with the unexpected maternity ward, we encountered some expected wildlife—raccoons, squirrels, and muskrats. Still waiting to see eagles.

Today was a relatively calm fifteen-mile paddle with no portages. Approaching the fifteen-mile mark, I was concerned we would not recognize the boat launch. Last year our yellow Nissan Xterra waited for us there, making recognition much easier. *With a year of changes, will we paddle by? If we miss the boat ramp, then what?* The possibility of not recognizing the area because this year's river is not the same as last year's river reminded me of the words of the philosopher Heraclitus, "No man ever steps into the same river twice, for it is not the same river and he is not the same man." (I need to contemplate the "not the same man" portion of this statement later.) Soon I detected something that appeared familiar. *Is that it?* No, false alarm.

I was ready to be done. Pulling the paddle through the water became more and more of a chore; the water became thicker and thicker. I tried coasting as much as I could and still keep up with John. *Isn't he tired?* He wasn't slowing down at all. This had been a long day. Was it only this morning we had combed Walmart for a new hat, run through a storm, and spent time at Hardee's? *We have to be close; we just have to be.*

With relief in his voice, John proclaimed, "There it is!" I wondered if his relieved tone was a result of worrying about missing the boat ramp or tiredness or both. We ended our day of paddling around 3:50 p.m.

Routine. Essential for any excursion.

The first goal after pulling *Work* and *Pray* out of the water is selecting a camping spot. Criteria for the perfect spot—flat, free of a lot of debris and low branches, and far enough from the water to ensure no tent floatage (Is *floatage* a word?) in the event of rising water since the Wabash River rises and falls quickly, sometimes in a matter of hours. After tripping over a couple of branches and trying to avoid thorns, John chose the almost perfect spot. With gusto, John attempted to make the spot more perfect by using his machete to murder some offensive roots and limbs. (Interesting, the machete made the list instead of my pillow.) All hazards were removed. Or so we thought.

"Wait, what is that?" John asked pointing to the seemingly featureless ground. "Slobs!" John reached down and began pulling yards of buried and twisted barbed wire. More man-made hazards (MMH), the perfect tool for ripping a hole in our expensive MSR(Mountain Safety Research) tent, tearing our paddling boots, or tripping us—you get the picture. Once we had relocated as much of the vile offender as we could, we assembled the tent.

While I was making our sloppy joe, rice, and veggie supper, which was prepared and served on our foil emergency blanket "table," the crunch of tires on the stone driveway alerted us of another human in the area. We didn't pay any attention to the vehicle since others had driven down the path from the road to the river, turned around, and returned to the road without stopping or climbing out of their vehicle. I find this ritual odd since the boat ramp is several miles from town. I think if I went to all the trouble to climb in my vehicle and drive to the river, I would stay and relax awhile.

Since this wasn't the first vehicle to drive to the river, hearing the tires quit crunching, the engine cease its humming, the door click open and closed, and footsteps squish in the dead leaves on the moist ground surprised us. A DNR (Department of Natural Resources) officer, dressed in his typical green uniform sporting his DNR equipment of guns, walkie-talkies and handcuffs, sauntered from his truck to our self- appointed camping site. DNR officers are employed by the state government to protect Indiana's natural resources. In addition, they enforce state law. I was afraid he was going to tell us we couldn't camp there and ask us to leave. *Where will we go? We can't go back to Bluffton. We don't know anyone in Markle. I'm so tired.*

He asked us where we had come from and where we were headed. After John provided him a brief overview of our trip, he asked, "What do you have for protection?"

We wondered what the officer's motive was. John told me later he had thought about responding "condoms" but decided on a more proper response. John answered truthfully, "Bear spray." John had chosen bear spray to protect us against bears, other wildlife, and any threatening humans. John's reply satisfied the officer.

With another glance at our kayaks, he caught sight of our PFDs (personal flotation devices) and gave his approval. Then he returned to his truck. I relaxed as I heard the crunch of the tires on the gravel fade and disappear in the distance. Whew!

Another visit came after dinner from John's brother Delno and his wife, Becky, and dog, Cocoa. Previously in the evening, Becky had texted us, asking if there was anything they could bring us. John started to type "nothing" when I remembered our packing-of-muddy-wheels dilemma— Walmart bags! I told him to ask her to bring four Walmart bags. She didn't even question the odd request. How often does she receive a request for four Walmart bags?

Upon their arrival, Delno was the first to open his car door. Delno is John's oldest brother. He and John are the bookends of the four Abnet boys and are opposites in looks. While John has a full head of dark black hair, Del's hair is gray, forming a ring around the back of his head. Blonde-haired Becky, who is much shorter than Del, climbed out of the passenger side and opened the rear door. Cocoa, a cockapoo with tight black curly hair, jumped from his perch in the back seat. He wagged his stubby tail (entire body?) as he put his nose to the ground, investigating all the new scents of nature. Coming from a city, he doesn't experience riverbank smells on an ordinary walk down the street.

After we discussed our day, Becky opened the trunk and produced our treats. We had joked that anyone who came to visit us on our trip had to bring us some non-dehydrated food. Becky brought us lemon meringue pie, coffee, ham, and buns. And four Walmart bags.

Since we have only two of everything, John and I sat on our small collapsible stools while Becky and Del sat on the edge of their trunk. Becky served the pie on white Chinet plates with purple paisley design (what a luxury) and a real fork. I didn't realize how much better food tastes when eaten with a real fork. And of course, we enjoyed a cup of coffee with the pie. (You can't eat pie without coffee. It's like eating cookies without milk, or celery without peanut butter. Some things must be consumed in pairs.) Although lemon meringue pie is one of my favorite pies, and I love to bake, I have never made one. This special dessert was a delight!

Having already eaten our supper, we decided to save the ham and buns for tomorrow.

As Delno and Becky packed up and prepared to leave us for the evening, Delno mentioned, "We hope to visit you at least one more time next month before we go to Spain for a month. Then we will see you the end of July when we pick you up at the end of your trip." Wow—the completion of our trip seemed so far away. It is only April. We have a long way to go.

As part of our routine, we reached our goals for today. Our goal for tomorrow is to portage six miles around Markle. I am NOT looking forward to pulling *Pray* that far! I hope the six-mile portage won't be anything like our twelve (eighteen)-mile hike the first day of our trip. I still don't have new shoes.

04-09-2015

You Can't Push a Boat with a Rope

Weather conditions:

High: 74

Low: 45

Skies: severe thunderstorm in the morning followed by partly cloudy skies in the afternoon

Wind: SE 13-25 mph, gusts to 32 mph

Today's mileage: portage 2 river miles

Total mileage: 82 miles

Where we traveled: Above Markle, Indiana, to Rock Creek just below Markle, Indiana

Living in the wilderness has provided the gift of living with the animals. Day and night. The number of creatures that choose not to sleep at night amazes me. And since they are wide-awake, they feel the need to make sure the rest of creation is awake with them. Last night the nocturnal animals in the area caused the evening to be a noisy one. The interruption to our sleep began with a coon dog howling in the distance, causing every dog within a five-mile radius to respond. I had barely fallen back asleep, when the dog decided to move closer to our tent and howl. I jumped and hit John! "What's that?"

John mumbled through his still sleeping lips, "The same hound that's been howling all night."

I am certain the proximity of an animal to the tent affects the fierce-sounding capacity of the creature. I didn't realize the relationship between the two until all that separated me from the wildlife was a thin layer of nylon. Not long after the dogs serenaded us, the coyotes began singing. Luckily, they didn't come as close as the coon dog did. A coyote next to my tent would have caused more than a jumping reaction from me. Once I was sure the coyote was going to stay in his area of the world, I fell asleep in mine.

Upon waking this morning, we started our day with our regular routine, which includes checking the radar. This morning checking the radar affected our decisions again. More yellow and red. John suggested, "I think we should pack up before we eat breakfast. I'd rather eat in the rain than pack in the rain".

We completed our packing in less time than yesterday. "How did we get done so fast?" I asked.

John informed me, "We didn't have to take off the wheels." Oh, yeah. Since the plan was to pull our kayaks around Markle, we could leave them on.

"I think I felt a raindrop on my face," I reported. I felt another drop, "Yep, I'm sure it is a raindrop." We were packing the last of our dry bags into *Work* and *Pray* when the rain arrived, so preparing a dehydrated breakfast was not an option. (This is the trip!)

"This is the trip!" In the midst of our preparation prior to starting this journey, that statement became a trip mantra. During one of our planning sessions, John opened a discussion with, "We need to talk about something."

I hate it when he starts a conversation with those words and answered hesitantly, "Whaat?"

"I want you to be prepared for what can happen while we're out there. Gear will fail us, the weather won't cooperate, we will dump, food parcels won't be available for pick up, we will get sick, we might be injured, etc. In society things can indeed go 'wrong.' A drunk driver can run into us. Businesses can cheat us. Man-made things can fail us before they're intended. Yes, things in society can indeed go 'wrong.' But on the river, in the wilderness, bad things aren't 'wrong,' they're just part of the trip. In fact, they're not even bad; they're just not what we had hoped for. If a tree falls and crushes a kayak, the tent, or even one of us, nothing went 'wrong.' It's just the earth turning on its axis. The earth is and the earth will. We're just along for the ride. So, I want to make sure that when things don't go as planned or hoped, we have our minds prepared to react and not stress. Whatever happens or doesn't happen, this is the trip."

So the fact that the rain was falling and we couldn't eat a warm breakfast didn't come as a surprise. It was part of the trip. Today marked the fifth morning of our trip, and we still have not eaten dehydrated food for breakfast. I am looking forward to eating breakfast casserole, one of our favorite trials at home. Today instead of dehydrated food, our best option was to eat the ham sandwiches Delno and Becky brought us last night. Soft buns instead of tortillas, yum!

Breakfast eaten, we started rolling *Work* and *Pray* to begin our long portage. Not only did the kayaks begin rolling, but also the thunder, preceded by the lightning flashes. John glanced at the radar once again to determine how long the thunder would roll, the lightning flash, and the rain fall. He showed me the colorful phone screen, "Look, it is freight training." He pointed to a clearing on higher ground farther from the river. "Let's pull *Work* and *Pray* up there. We'll have to wait until tomorrow to portage." (This is the trip! This is our story!)

Not wanting *Work* and *Pray* to float away without us in the event the river rose quickly, we rolled them to the place John had indicated. Instead of standing unprotected in the open, we took cover by crouching under some trees. We didn't say much as we squatted there watching the rain and lightning. What is there to talk about while hunkering next to a tree in a storm contemplating your position in life?

I considered our decision to leave the dry, comfortable shelter of our home and withstand uncomfortable times such as these. Squatting any length of time and becoming wet are uncomfortable. Am I a product of our 75 °, sunny, dry, slight breeze, and temperature-controlled society? I become uncomfortable if the temperature varies 5 ° from the ideal. Or it rains. Or it is too windy. Or... From where did this idealistic society emerge? I think that as an indoor society we transfer our idea of what perfect conditions are from the controlled indoor environment to the uncontrollable nature. If conditions aren't ideal outside, we pack up our belongings and go back inside. I gazed at John; tears filled my eyes as I realized how fortunate I was to be experiencing these uncomfortable moments with him. "God, help me to be aware of my blessings in the midst of unplanned, and sometimes unpleasant, circumstances during this trip and in life. Broaden my comfort zone literally and figuratively." I wonder how many crouching-under-trees experiences we will endure during our trip.

As I pondered my life, the lightning became less frequent, followed by a quieting of the thunder. Finally, the steady rain became a sprinkle. John thought we should take advantage of this break in the storm and instructed, "Hurry, let's set up the tent." We raced (well, walked quickly) to the location of *Work* and *Pray* and removed the tent from the rear hatch of John's kayak.

As we were attaching the tent to the poles, the wind increased, indicating another storm cell would soon arrive. *Hurry... Oh no, I felt a raindrop on my face again.* Tent erected, awaiting the protection of the rain fly, the raindrops began falling more intensely. The water falling from the sky found its way in to the tent through the exposed screen. *Hurry...* Finally, the rain fly was in place, preventing any more rain from entering. A glance into the tent revealed some unwanted puddles shimmering on the nylon floor. Then we remembered two of the most usable, but inexpensive, line items on our gear list—a sponge and towel. In the midst of the continuing rain and approaching thunder and lightning, we soaked up the puddles with the sponge and dried the tent's floor with the towel.

As I mopped the floor, John unpacked the fundamentals needed to exist in our tent for the duration of the storm—food, bedding, iPads, maps, dry clothing, and our clothesline. How can a clothesline be of any use in the rain, you ask. We put it up in the tent to dry our wet clothes and towels. Our small tent provided everything we needed—shelter, food, warmth, comfort, entertainment, and a drying station. Who needs a large house?

Tent-duration essentials thrown in, we entered the tent and made ourselves comfortable (well, as comfortable as you can in 29 square feet). Clothes drying and the rain falling, John put on his dry long johns and napped, using MY pillow! Boom, crash, whoosh, rustle. *How can John sleep through the sounds created by the thunder, wind, and tent?* I watched John sleeping peacefully on my pillow, oblivious to all that was going on outside our tent world. He was so relaxed. Then I realized being stuck in a tent during the storm was resulting in forced relaxation. I journaled, pondering our current situation. *How often do I allow myself to experience forced relaxation at home? Did I even know there was such a thing as forced relaxation? Can I create forced relaxation without being trapped in a tent? Do I even remember how to relax?*

I took a break from my journaling and closed my eyes as I thought back to a time when I knew how to relax. I was ten years old. I gathered my favorite book and blanket my mom made from scrap material she brought home from her job at Berco, a local producer of overalls. I sashayed barefoot through the grass, feeling its cool blades tickle my feet, to my favorite tree, a boxelder, which over the years provided many summer hours of shade and a cool breeze. (As I imagined this scene, I could almost feel the breeze in my face and hear the leaves rustle.) I unfolded the blanket and spread it out perfectly, no bumps or wrinkles (my princess and the pea syndrome). Then I lay down, opened my book, and allowed myself to slip into another place and time created on the pages bound together in the book I held in my hands. As a kid I knew how to relax. Free time existed. When was the last time I read a book while I lay on a blanket under a tree? When did the stresses and busyness of life decrease my ability to relax? Without my usual stresses and busyness of my society life, I plan to take advantage of these moments when there isn't anything else to do but relax. Forced relaxation—I like it.

Almost without realizing the change, the tent appeared brighter. Here comes the sun! (That should be a song.) Even though I was enjoying my forced relaxation, I was ready to leave our quaint little dwelling and venture into the wet out-of-doors. Emerging from the tent's seclusion to view the results of the storm created anticipation. What happened beyond the tent's walls while we were safe and secure inside? Without windows the tent hid everything outside from our view. I unzipped the door and put on my boots. As I unfolded I surveyed my surroundings. Branches and leaves littered the ground. Mud and puddles replaced dry ground. The sun and moisture created warm, humid air.

I unpacked a Grand Trunk compact stool from the back hold of *Work*. I unfolded it, placed it on the stones, and continued journaling. I relish my time journaling because, as I capture the moments of our trips and my life, my writing grants me the opportunity to reflect. These reflections and memories provide a record of special times in my life. Many of these times were trips John and I have taken together. Since we have been married, we have embarked upon a variety of adventures, ranging from Italy to the Arctic Ocean. For each trip, I created a journal capturing our moments and my reflections. Many times I reread my words, and my thoughts amaze me—did I think and write that?

I continued writing and reflecting until John woke up and joined me outside. Since the sun had replaced the clouds in the sky, John retrieved our solar panel and Sherpa from *Pray's* rear hold and set up a charging station on top of her bow. Even though we had recently charged the Sherpa with electricity in Bluffton yesterday, we needed to take advantage of every ray of sun. The sun has become a necessity for a different aspect of survival. I used to view the sun as nature's way of providing the necessities for growing my garden and comfort for enjoying outdoor activities. Now I have expanded my view of the sun's purpose to include the need to collect the rays as an alternate to something manmade—electricity. How quickly we adapt our activities to meet the needs before us.

Detecting the flashing of the I-am-charging lights on the Sherpa, John grabbed his stool from *Work's* stern, sat down, and considered what to do with his time. He uttered, "I think I will shave." (Who doesn't shave outside after a thunderstorm?) He gathered his shaving basics, razor and shaving cream, and had started lathering his face with shaving cream when he realized he was missing a crucial element—a mirror. Picture this…. John standing outside wearing his long johns tucked in his black, knee-high paddling boots, lather on his face, looking a little bewildered about his predicament. Imagine his astonishment when he heard tires crunch on the stone path. Embarrassed to be caught in such a state, John ducked behind the tent. The driver of the vehicle honked the horn, causing John to duck his 6' 1" frame a little farther behind our small, two-man, 4-foot tent. The quizzical look on his face said so much, "Seriously!?"

The driver and passenger came into view, and I realized our intruders were Tom and Candy Moore, friends of ours from Fort Wayne, Indiana. Tom and Candy have infectious smiles, laugh easily and often, and look too young to be retired but are. They enjoy life and cause others in their presence to enjoy it as well. I smile thinking about them.

John decided he could safely come out of hiding when I blurted, "It's Tom and Candy."

Tom parked their gold minivan next to our stools. John moved to the vehicle and checked out the reflective surfaces. I could almost hear his mind working, *Hmm… Which surface would provide the best reflection for shaving—the outside mirror or the darkly smoked back windows?* He chose the darkly smoked back windows and began shaving. Having overcome the embarrassment of his state of undress, John carried on a conversation with the Moores while he shaved. As John finished wiping the shaving cream remnants from his cheek, Tom lowered the window. Candy smiled, motioned to the back seat, and announced, "By the way, I'd like you to meet our son-in-law Matt and grandson Jakob."

I wish I had a picture capturing the wide-eyed look on John's face. "Nice... to... meet... you," John greeted them slowly while secretly glad Tom and Candy's daughter wasn't also present.

After the four visitors climbed out of the minivan, we explained our trip to the younger guys and relayed some of the events of the past five days. (Wow, a lot has happened in five days.) As the group prepared to leave, Matt confessed, "Yeah, when we pulled up I couldn't figure out why Tom and Candy were bringing us down here to see some homeless people."

If the definition of *homeless* is having no home or permanent place of residence, then living out of a tent in a different location each night could indeed be considered homeless. If Tom and Candy hadn't confirmed we were safe people, how would Matt have treated us? With pity? With judgment? Would he have ignored us? For the next few months I will not look, smell, dress, or live like the rest of civilized society. Will others assume we are homeless? How will they receive us? If I were in their shoes, how would I receive us?

As I mused about how I would receive us if we were homeless, I remembered an event a couple of years ago when John and I visited Seattle between Christmas and New Year's Eve. Since I grew up and still live in a rural community, I have not encountered many homeless people. While in Seattle, instead of taking public transportation, we walked everywhere. Exploring the city we came across many homeless sleeping under heavy blankets, sitting on the sidewalk and leaning against the buildings, some asking for money. John often says, "We are all one crisis from being homeless."

One evening a brown-haired woman in her forties approached us as we were waiting outside a restaurant for an available table inside. She peered at us with desperation in her eyes and pled, "I'm not a typical homeless woman. Honest. Could you give me some money for...?"

I don't remember why she said she needed the money. I do remember, however, the conflicting thoughts in my head. *She didn't look homeless. Was she lying? What if she was telling the truth? Should we give her money? Should we invite her to eat with us? Could I ever be her? Was I judging?*

She walked away...

After Tom, Candy, Matt, and Jakob left, we decided to enjoy the beautiful weather and sit outside on our small campstools. Everything we have is small (even my pillow). These stools are perfect—they fold up and fit into their own little pouch. (Hmm... My pillow fits into its own little pouch.) Sitting on our stools, I journaled and John played his guitar. John hadn't even finished one song when a white commercial truck pulled in and drove to the river. (Luckily after the Moores left, John had decided to change into clothes more appropriate for receiving visitors.) Considering we are on a trip in the wilderness, the number of people we were encountering in this spot surprised us—DNR officer, relatives, friends, and now a random person. Where is the peace and quiet of the wilderness? John, learning to be more social, joined our latest visitor by the river while I continued journaling.

After what seemed like a lengthy conversation, John returned with his new acquaintance, a man in his mid-thirties with sandy hair, mustache, and goatee. John introduced him to me, "This is Jeff Miller. He is going to transport us around Markle so we don't have to hike tomorrow." Remember, tomorrow we were going to pull *Work* and *Pray* on the highway, through Markle, over the bridge, down a hill on a stone road to a spot down the river in order to miss a waterfall created by a small dam? Jeff was our hero! Jeff just happened to have built a hitch extension rack for the back of his truck in order to haul his canoe.

Hearing our plans to drag our kayaks around Markle, he offered, "Heck, I'll run home and grab my boy and truck. We'll get you around Markle easier than that." He drove his company truck home to bring back his truck, the rack, and his son, Drew. While Jeff was gone, we tore down the tent the second time today.

Jeff returned in his dark blue Chevy Z71 truck with his son. Approximately ten-year old Drew helped his dad and John load *Work*. The bracket Jeff built for his canoe worked perfectly to carry our kayaks. John and Jeff climbed into the truck and drove off.

Strangers left alone together, Drew and I awkwardly studied each other. While John and Jeff were gone, we discussed every topic I could think of—family, school, friends, hobbies, etc. When I ran out of topics, Drew, not afraid to make his Nikes muddy, built a dam of sticks and stones in a puddle. We both began feeling the discomfort strangers experience when the length of time spent together exceeds the duration of safe topics and non-conversation activities. *How much longer can they be gone?* I started worrying, and my imagination began creating scenarios to explain the delay. They seemed to have been gone longer than the time needed to drive eight miles and unload a kayak. However, if I had been sharing a cup of coffee with Irene, would the length of time they were gone have felt as long?

Finally we heard the welcome crunch of the tires rolling over stones. The rack was empty, and Jeff was the only one in the cab of the truck. Jeff explained his long absence. The bridge we had planned to cross on our portage tomorrow, the one he had driven over this morning, was now closed. He and John had to take an eight-mile detour. Think about this, tomorrow we would have hiked six miles to the bridge, only to find it closed. Then we would have trekked that same six miles back to where we started and then another eight miles to our destination. The portage would have taken two full days to complete! I don't think it was a coincidence it just happened to rain, causing us to wait until tomorrow to portage. I don't think it was a coincidence Jeff just happened to drive to the river. I don't think it was a coincidence Jeff just happened to have the perfect vehicle and hitch extension. I don't think it was a coincidence... God just happens to be good.

Jeff and Drew loaded *Pray* and transported us to John. John and I set up camp the second time in one day (not in the rain this time) and ate sloppy joes, macaroni and cheese, and rice pudding! So yummy!

At the end of an eventful day, we are in bed listening to the hum of I-69 in the background. I hope dogs or coyotes howling in the middle of the night won't join the hum. Tomorrow we will travel to Huntington Reservoir and the boat ramp, where, with any luck, the bathrooms will provide running water so we can do laundry and somewhat bathe. Ahhh! The little things in life!

04-10-2017

I Can't Nest Here

Weather conditions:

High: 69

Low: 42

Skies: mostly cloudy

Wind: W 24-38 mph, gusts to 50 mph

Today's mileage: 6 miles

Total mileage: 88 miles

Where we traveled: Rock Creek just below Markle, Indiana, Huntington Reservoir—Huntington, Indiana

A storm came through during the night with strong winds, bringing much colder temperatures. John slept through the entire storm while I listened to the tent moan as the wind howled and thrashed against it. I shivered.

This morning when John announced we should leave our tent and face the strong winds and cold temperatures, I crawled a little deeper into my sleeping bag. I thought staying in the tent protected from the elements sounded much more appealing than paddling down the river unprotected in a plastic tube. John didn't agree. Having convinced myself to leave the warmth of the tent, I realized it was too cold and windy to prepare the dehydrated breakfast casserole we have been eagerly anticipating. My mouth watered as I thought about the egg, bread, and mushroom entrée. I could almost feel the heat of the food warming my insides. Instead, we ate cold peanut butter on a cold tortilla—again!

Since returning to the tent for the remainder of the day wasn't part of the trip and we needed to travel to Huntington Reservoir to meet up with our friends Terry and Dawn Wanner, we packed up the tent, stowing it in *Work's* back hatch. We then walked the short distance to our launching spot and realized the conditions were far from ideal. The already swollen river had risen overnight, and the current had increased, causing whitewater conditions. The turbulent waters alone would have been enough to cause me to want to retrieve the tent, set it back up, crawl into it, and curl up like a baby. However, even more daunting was the large log jutting out of the water barely off shore and downstream from where we would slide *Work* and *Pray* into the frigid waters. The waters boiling around the log revealed the unforgiving power of the current. Trying to hold back my tears, I relayed my fears to John, "The current is going to push me right into the log."

"I'll give you a big push. Dig hard with your paddles, and you'll shoot clear of the log on the upstream side." He was trying to convince me everything would be fine—I wasn't convinced.

"Oh, and, by the way, if you do hit the log and tip over, hold onto your kayak and kick to shore on the outside of the next bend. Whatever you do, don't let go of the kayak! I'll be right there."

Wow, how comforting. Apparently, he too realized there was some danger. And who was going to push HIM past the log? *Be brave. I can do this.* I put on my life jacket and spray skirt, which covers the cockpit and is essential in rough waters—when there is a strong possibility waves will wash over and swamp the kayak. Although I knew the answer, I asked, "Can't we wait until tomorrow when the water is calmer?"

John tried comforting me as he kissed me, "Sorry, babe."

After a prayer, John placed *Pray* into the water. *I'm not brave. I don't want to do this.* I laid my paddle across the back of the kayak and perpendicular to the shore. Placing my hands on the paddle, I lowered myself into *Pray*, positioning my bottom on the seat. After hooking my drinking tube to my spray skirt, I secured my spray skirt around my cockpit cowling and zipped it up. Trying to hold the tears back, I lied, "OK, I'm ready."

Keep us upright and safe.

John pushed me off. *Paddle hard. Keep me upright and safe. Keep me upright and safe. Focus downstream. Paddle hard. I can do this!* I glanced to my left. Sure enough, I had passed the log safely and the foaming waters swirling around it. I was still alive!

Now that I was safe, I began worrying about John. I experienced the same feeling I had a couple of days ago when I waited for John to portage *Work* around the fallen tree, scale down the steep muddy bank, climb into his kayak, and launch without any assistance. *Can he push himself off with enough force to miss the log? Keep John upright and safe. Keep John upright and safe.* The current carried me farther and farther from him. I couldn't turn around and watch for him; I needed to watch where I was going. All I could do was listen for our signal—"I love you." I kept listening. The wind roared in my ears and the waves slammed against my kayak. *Did I hear a voice?* I listened more closely. *Or was it my imagination?* I pulled back the hood that covered my ears. *He should be getting close soon. I wonder how far I have gone. This is awful!* Finally sure I heard his dear voice behind me saying "I love you," I sighed! *Thank you, God!* Once he had joined me, we continued on our way to Huntington Reservoir.

The incessant 40-50 mile per hour headwinds diminished the progress we should have been making since there was a strong downstream current. We encountered whitecaps and had to continue paddling if we didn't want to lose our momentum and go backwards. *Keep paddling.* In the midst of the tiring paddle, however, we saw some cool wildlife: an eagle guarding its nest, a small herd of deer running along the shoreline, and swallows diving at and playing with us. The chaos of the river was juxtaposed against the *c'est la vie* attitude of the creatures around us.

Seeing the swallows reminded me of home. Arriving around Memorial Day each year, these beautiful birds with their shimmering blue-black bodies build nests in our barn. During the summer, we sit on our porch while they entertain us with their acrobatic flying and swooping as they catch insects mid-air. Mowing the yard becomes a game. The mower causes a flying smorgasbord for our feathered friends. Feasting on the displaced insects, they come within inches of my head, giving the impression they are playing with me. I miss my friends when they move on to their new home at the end of August. (I just now realized the swallows are here before Memorial Day this year.)

Upon entering Huntington Reservoir, I was surprised by the lack of water—it was merely a river, not a lake. It didn't look anything like I remembered. John and I have paddled and water-skied in the reservoir many times. *It is flooding upstream, so where is all the water?* Oh, yeah! The Army Corps of Engineers opens the dam to release water over the winter. *Now I understand John's previous conversation with someone from the corps.* Discussing the releasing of water from the dam, he had asked, "Will we be able to get to the boat ramp?" I thought that was an unusual question. *Why wouldn't we be able to reach the boat ramp?* In all the times we had been there, we hadn't had any trouble finding or reaching the boat ramp.

However, today I felt I was paddling in a different place altogether. New sights replaced familiar landmarks. As I paddled, drift (short for driftwood) lay on the shore where there once was water. Herons appeared displaced as they strutted on the land where they previously waded in water. I felt as if I were passing through a ghost town—everything seemed abandoned and barren.

I thought I hit something as I placed my paddle in the water. *Is the blade of my paddle hitting a rock?* I performed another stroke, meeting the same resistance. *I think I am hitting the bottom of the river.* When the dam wasn't open, the banks defined the man-made lake and sufficient water allowed us to paddle anywhere within the confines of the shores. Now, where there once was a reservoir, a river without distinct borders remained. Without banks to provide direction, we had "lost" the river and found ourselves in shallow water. I was concerned we may have to clamber out of *Work* and *Pray* and pull them. I found it odd that while the rest of the Wabash was flooding, I would be worried about having enough water in which to paddle.

Eventually spotting the boat ramp. John pulled up parallel to the shore and prepared to climb out of *Work*. Unfortunately, as he pulled off his skirt, a wave washed over his kayak, filling it with water. I tried not to laugh as each consecutive wave poured more water into his cockpit causing an expression of "really!?" on his face. I wished at that point I that had the iPhone (John usually has it around his neck) so I could record his misfortune. Once the waves settled down, he emerged from *Work*, pulled her on shore, removed the bilge pump from its storage place on top of his kayak, and pumped the water from his cockpit.

The bilge pump is stored on top rather than in a hold so it is readily available. In the unfortunate event of capsizing, once the craft is upright, one of us would use the pump to rid the kayak of unwanted water. Too much water in the kayak would cause it to be unsteady and heavy during the trip to dry land. I didn't realize the pump would be necessary on shore too.

Work emptied of water, the process of putting on the wheels took place in order to roll the kayaks up a steep, sandy hill. Proving to be one of the best investments we made, along with the sponges and towels, the Wheeleez wheels have revealed we couldn't have made the trip without them.

After pulling *Work* and *Pray* to the top of the hill (everything is uphill from the river), my goal was to check out the restroom. From previous visits I knew there were restrooms here, but I was concerned they may not be open since Memorial Day is a month and a half away. Happiness—they were open AND had hot water! Laundry and bath!

Now the task of finding a place to camp. We knew there was a campground on the property, but neither of us had camped there and did not know where it was located in reference to the boat ramp. John appointed himself as campground searcher; I stayed with our kayaks and all our earthly possessions. I watched John leave and then gathered our lunch of peanut butter wraps, granola bars, fruit roll-ups, fruit and nut packs, and the last oranges Dawn Wanner had sent with us before the trip. I had all the food presented neatly on a concrete picnic table when John returned with news of no campground spotting. We decided to first eat lunch and then pick out a site to camp in the boat ramp area.

Picking a place to camp caused a difference of opinion between John and me. Thinking of late night bathroom treks, I thought we should set up residency for the night on a mowed spot conveniently located next to the restroom. John suggested we camp farther from the washroom in an un-mowed area. When I inquired why he thought his spot was superior to mine, he replied, "It's not as likely that we'll be asked to leave if we're away from the mainstream of activity." Okay—you win.

Setting up the tent required some acrobatics again today, similar to our first night's antics. There were times we thought the bundle of nylon would blow away. The wind maneuvering under the tent and lifting it off the ground reminded me of playing with a parachute in gym class as an elementary school student. You know, when the entire class surrounded a parachute. At the teacher's instruction, everyone picked up their portion, raised and lowered the nylon object together, catching air beneath and creating an igloo-shaped hideout. After the raising of the parachute, all students simultaneously, on command, ducked under it. I remember being amazed the dome didn't collapse, trapping us all inside. Despite the wind's effort to transport the tent to another location, we successfully erected our nylon home without it blowing away or trapping us.

We were attaching the rain fly to the tent when Rebecca, a reporter from *The Huntington County TAB*, came to interview us. Today's interview was our fourth, which is amazing because we haven't contacted a single newspaper, and as of yet, have not accomplished anything significant. I wonder how many of these newspapers will run a follow-up story if we are successful? We may be more interesting during our journey than after.

Interview complete, I began organizing our home. When preparing our bed for the night, I unfold and spread out a wool blanket, which provides warmth and padding, followed by our Klymit sleep pads. These inflatable thin sleep pads are a unique design with open slits for ventilation. In addition, instead of the customary symmetrical rectangle, the foot area is narrower than the top. I guess that makes sense, since my feet take up less room than my shoulders. I then zip our sleeping bags together for warmth and place them on the pads. Inside the sleeping bag on my side of the bed is a Sea to Summit Reactor Extreme red sleeping bag liner, which is supposed to (supposed to) increase my sleeping bags performance up to 15 degrees. Each night, I wiggle into the liner for an additional layer of warmth. John doesn't have a liner on his side—he is too macho for one. So far, I haven't had to share it with him—like my pillow. I then place another wool blanket over all, creating one final protective layer from the cold. Unfortunately, even with the wool blankets and sleeping bag liner, our lightweight Lafuma sleeping bags with a 45 degree rating haven't kept me warm on these thirty-something degree nights. (Oh, and don't forget my pillow on my side of the bed—unless John steals it.)

Bedroom preps almost complete, Terry and Dawn arrived (why do our visitors arrive when I am making the bed?) with four Nelson's chicken dinners, salad, wine, and our Week #2 package. Terry, in his late fifties, with gray hair, mustache, and goatee, wore an insulated sweatshirt to protect him from the incessant wind. Auburn-haired Dawn sported a sweatshirt under a lightweight brown hip-length jacket.

Dawn and I have known each other over thirty years, but first became friends through a women's Bible study at church twenty-two years ago. Our separate names soon changed from "Dawn" and "LaNae" to "Dawn and

LaNae." Through the years we have spent hours together drinking coffee, co-leading bible studies, and making cards using rubber stamps. Actually, when we first started making cards, we bought stamps together so we could have more by splitting the cost. Having been youth sponsors together, we attended a youth summer conference (CDYC) together at Calvin College in Grand Rapids, Michigan. During that youth conference, I decided to room with Dawn to protect myself from her practical jokes. She was well known for placing pepper in pillowslips and plastic wrap on toilet seats.

At church every Sunday night, since our husbands didn't come, we sat in a pew towards the front on the right side of the sanctuary. She sang alto; I sang soprano. We often laugh at our differences: she is outspoken, I listen and watch; Dawn has beautiful handwriting, and she brags that she is the only one who can read my writing; Dawn answers my questions while I ask more than my share. Even with our differences, we are surprised at how much we are alike; we both are organized, live with a list, love to camp, are the oldest of our siblings, and have a bunion. (Well, she still has her bunion; I had mine removed.) I remember when we discovered our bunion connection. Lying on the floor of my camper with our feet propped up on the sofa, we chuckled as we noticed we both had a bunion on the big toe side of our right feet.

We planned the first and many ladies' retreats for the women in our church. Unfortunately, our connection at church changed sixteen years ago after my divorce. Since that time, I have missed our church connection, but we have continued planning retreats by combining the women of my new church with hers. We don't make cards together any longer because we think we are too busy. However, we still find time to share our lives over a cup of coffee once in a while. Some things are too important to give up.

Doctors diagnosed Dawn with stage four melanoma a little over a year ago. We have added another chapter to our relationship—attending doctor's appointments and treatments. Even though the situation isn't ideal, the time we are "forced" to spend together is treasured.

When I first told Dawn about our trip, she asked, "Are you going through a mid-life crisis?" As time passed, she realized John and I really were going to follow through with our plan and found ways to support us, such as giving us oranges, coming to visit us, providing us a meal, and bringing our first resupply box.

Today after Terry and Dawn arrived and we exchanged hugs, we discussed two locations as options for a place to eat in order to escape the cold and wind—hiding behind the restroom or in their heated vehicle. Zipping our coats up farther and pulling our hood strings tighter, we chose to hide behind the restroom.

John and I assembled our stools without a back, and the Wanners unfolded their red floral padded chairs—with backs. (Visitors have to BYOC.) Opening the Styrofoam container of a Nelson's chicken dinner engages all the senses: the sound (and anticipation) of the Styrofoam crackling as it opens; the smell of the barbecue; the sight of the chicken, roll, and cookie; the feel of the slightly greasy chicken; the taste of the smoky, barbecued, tender, juicy meat. Even the wind couldn't diminish this pleasure. Don't forget the perfect companion to the chicken dinner— wine out of real wine glasses.

After dinner Dawn and I took advantage of the running water and great breeze (I guess a more accurate word would be wind. At what point does a breeze become a wind?) by washing a "load of laundry" in the bathroom sink. I washed the dirty clothes and wrung them out the best I could before handing each article to Dawn, who wrung them out even more. Then down the hill to our campsite to hang the clothes on the line. This is the first time during the trip I have hung laundry on the clothesline. During this process I realized I should have been more involved in some of the packing—I would have brought a few more clothespins. The inadequate number of clothespins required us to be creative by hanging the excess clothing on branches, which ordinarily would have worked well, but today the wind was intent on blowing the clothes off the makeshift clothesline.

With the laundry chore completed, we had one more task to accomplish—dehydrated food sorting. Each of our food boxes contains seven breakfasts, seven lunches, seven snacks, and seven dinners (including dessert)—the exact amount that will fit in *Work* and *Pray* and provide us with a week of nutrition. This amount of food wouldn't normally be a problem except we haven't eaten a dehydrated breakfast yet and have had four dinners provided. If you do the math, we have too much food for *Work* and *Pray*. Dawn volunteered to store some at her house. Sorting complete, Terry and Dawn headed back to their warm home. I was a little jealous.

After the Wanners left, John and I carted the things we carry to the tent every night, the stuff we want to protect or have handy: our hiking boots, toiletry bags, water bottles, clothing bags, stools, any un-dry laundry, and John's guitar. John set the stools up in his foyer. He places anything we don't want wet or dirty on the stools or in the attached pouch underneath the stools—his guitar, our shoes, and wet clothes. He props his toiletry bag, water bottle, and clothing dry bags next to the stools. In my foyer my bags and water bottle are stored on the ground. In addition to using every inch of our kayaks, we utilize every inch of the tent, including the foyers.

Everything organized, we climbed into the tent. I pulled on my long johns, down vest, wool socks, and hat, edging myself deep into my red sleeping bag liner inside our combined sleeping bags next to John; not an inch of me exposed in preparation for another cold night. When will I quit shivering?

04-11-2015

Well, the Tick Is Up

Weather conditions:

High: 60

Low: 32

Skies: clear

Wind: WSW 5-10 mph

Today's mileage: portaged 6 river miles—paddled 17 miles

Total mileage: 111 miles

Where we traveled: Huntington Reservoir—Huntington, Indiana, to between Lagro and Wabash, Indiana

Today was a day of milestones: traveled a week on the river, paddled 100 miles, overcame last man-made impediment, performed last mechanical portage, reached the most northern part of the Wabash River (and our trip), and began making our way south. All that in one day—wow!

Emerging from the tent this morning after another brisk night, we gazed at a layer of white, glistening crystals that frosted the grass, our kayaks, and tent like icing. (Thus the name frost?) With the warming of the sun, the frost-covered objects became water-soaked gear.

Luckily, the wind died down overnight, making our first dehydrated breakfast finally possible. I can't believe we have been on the river a week and this is the first time I have boiled water in one of our two pans over our MSR propane stove to prepare breakfast. We enjoyed the breakfast casserole that has caused our mouths to water. This breakfast entrée—bread, eggs, cheese, and mushroom combo—was one of our favorites during our try-this-at-home era. The steaming food warmed our bellies and souls on such a cold morning.

I'm amazed how delicious the dehydrated meals taste because the food stored in the vacuum-sealed plastic bags resembles compacted dried twigs. A sound of relief escapes the plastic bag as our utility knife punctures a hole in it, allowing air to enter the bag and give the food breathing room. The bags. Although we re-use some of the bags for lunches, the preserver of our food creates a lot of trash. We stuff the empty bags into every nook and cranny of *Work* and *Pray*, awaiting disposal. We find ourselves inspecting every boat ramp area for trashcans before we even climb out of our kayaks.

Warm breakfast consumed, we welcomed John's second oldest brother, Paul, with his carpeted trailer to help us past the Huntington Dam, our last man-made impediment. Climbing out of his truck, Paul pulled on his beanie before zipping up his insulated hooded sweatshirt. "Man, it's chilly out here." I made note of the fact that he didn't have his hat on or his coat zipped before exiting his vehicle. Hmmm… the truck cab must be warm. All I could think about was crawling into the heated truck and escaping the frigid air.

So why was Paul here, you ask? Last fall, we had scouted out a manual portage route around the dam. We decided we would hike up a grassy hill on the dam's east side, over a bridge, across the road, and downhill on a stone road to a rocky spillway on the west side of the dam. A lot of work—but manageable.

However, due to the recent rains, the Army Corps of Engineers is releasing massive amounts of water from the dam, causing the launching of *Work* and *Pray* so close to the spillway on the other side to be unsafe. We needed to find a safe place to put our kayaks in several miles downstream—too far for a manual portage. John texted Paul. Paul, learning of our dilemma, offered to bring his trailer and transport us downstream.

Before placing the kayaks on the trailer, we removed and placed all the dry bags and the gear attached to the outside of the kayaks inside the truck. As John and Paul loaded *Work* and *Pray* on the trailer, I noticed a small blue, collapsible, nylon cooler sitting on the picnic table. *Hmm... Could there be something hiding inside for us?* Ready to leave, and the cooler untouched on the table, I asked, "Is this your cooler, Paul?"

"Oh yeah," Paul said. "I brought you some treats."

I unzipped the container of goodies—donuts, orange juice, and two giant-sized Snickers bars. Even though we had recently eaten breakfast, my stomach growled with delight at the sight of such unhealthy goodness. Climbing into the truck, I handed John his donut and bit into the first donut I had eaten in a long time. The initial bite was delectable, but the second brought a smile to my face as I licked creamy vanilla pudding from the corners of my mouth. This was probably the best donut I had ever eaten. The orange juice chaser that followed helped override my guilt of eating a cream-filled ball of fried dough. We decided to save the Snickers bars to satisfy our hunger later.

We hadn't planned on this scenario and hadn't investigated available launching locations. So John used Google Maps on our iPhone to identify roads near the river, providing verbal directions to Paul until we found a place within walking access to the shoreline. Parking the truck along the road, we first carried all our gear down a steep, narrow path from the trailer because *Work* has 105 pounds of gear; while *Pray* has 75 pounds. (Small bites, one piece of gear at a time.)

Having carried and deposited the gear in a pile, John and Paul carried the kayaks down the hill. Even without our possessions, *Work* and *Pray* are still heavy—63 pounds and 60 pounds respectively. I was glad Paul was there because carrying the kayaks is not only tiring but also painful: the strap handles hurt my hand.

Returning with *Work*, John removed his coat and shirt, unzipped his wet suit, pulled his arms out, took off his long-john shirt, and put everything back on minus the long-john shirt he had just removed. He commented, "Boy, that feels better."

Jealously, I grumbled, "I'm hot too."

I think he forgot I am a girl and more modest than he is. He quipped, "Then, take off YOUR long-john shirt."

I glanced around. There was a public park across the river, a busy road next to us, and Paul was standing nearby.

Scanning under the bridge, he countered matter-of-factly, "There's a perfect spot."

I disagreed, "It's muddy, and the people across the river might see me. And what about Paul?"

John replied tautly through his teeth, "First, I don't see anyone across the river. Paul and I will be going back up the hill soon. And, you've walked in mud before."

Stubbornly, I huffed, "Forget it. I'll just leave it on."

He turned and stalked up the hill. I felt like crying. I didn't like being a girl. I couldn't go pee just anywhere. I couldn't stand up to pee. I couldn't take my shirt off in public, especially since I don't wear a bra under my wetsuit. I didn't like living out in the open. I couldn't always find a place to hide. I resented that John didn't understand or care.

I was still pouting when John returned. He asked, "Well?"

"I don't want to go under the bridge."

Still annoyed, he snapped, "I'll hold up my coat to hide you."

Moping, I muttered, "I don't want to delay us."

Ignoring my whining, John took off his coat and shielded me with it. I removed my long-john shirt.

The I'm-too-warm saga resolved, we used John's kayak map to place all our stuff in its pre-determined locations.

I wonder when we will no longer need the gear map or if we will even realize when we're no longer referring to it. The normals in our lives morph to new normals without our realization. One day, we examine our life and recognize things have changed—something new has been added and the old has slipped away. We ask ourselves, "Where did that come from?" or "When did that disappear?" We usually don't have answers because the change doesn't happen all at once or even overnight—it is gradual.

As we were packing, I grabbed the solar panel, which we use to charge our Sherpa power source, and asked, "John, it's sunny out. Should we place the solar panel on *Pray* to charge it?"

"Good call, Babe." John proceeded to attach the Goal Zero Nomad solar panel to the top of *Pray* with small carabiners arranged on my deck for that purpose. John then slid the power source into my cockpit up under the front deck and into a "basket" he had constructed from nylon webbing, out of the way and safe from most spray. It reminded me of my after-market 8-track player mounted under the glove compartment in my early '70s hatchback poopy brown Ford Pinto, which did not EXPLODE. (Those of you who lived through the '70s know what I'm talking about.)

Everything in its place, including the solar panel, the time to launch had finally come. Peering down at *Pray* in the water, I wondered how I was going to slide from the bank into my kayak without tipping. Then I made the mistake of surveying the other side of the river. I began coveting. The opposite bank slanted gradually into the river. The bank on our side, however, gave the impression that someone had used a machete to whack off a portion and then removed it, leaving a two-foot vertical drop to the surface of the water. The proverbial grass was greener on the other side, but we decided to stay where we were. The thought of carrying all the gear and kayaks back to the truck seemed like too much work. Not to mention, we would also have to identify the coveted slanting bank from the road, presenting its own difficulties because the road view and river view are different.

"Let's go, babe."

Lying on their stomachs on the once-glistening-frost-covered-now-soggy grass, John and Paul held *Pray* while I lowered myself into my water vessel.

Keep us upright and safe.

Unlike other difficult launches, this time Paul could aid John, giving me peace as I hung out and waited for him to join me.

Enjoying our river view today, we encountered some sites we wouldn't have seen from our land view at home—three eagles and nests. We are finding eagles are not unusual on the river. However, the next thing we saw was unique.

We heard voices (not in our heads—real voices). Since we have rarely encountered anyone outside while we have traveled down the river, hearing voices was unusual. (More evidence we are an inside society.) Hearing the voices caused us to scour the banks, looking for the source. We located it—a couple of men on the bank constructing a small building—maybe a utility shed.

They jumped when John broke in, "Good morning. What'cha buildin'?"

They claimed they were building a food shack so "folks, like you, travelin' down the river can stop and enjoy a sandwich and a beer." For some reason I didn't believe them. This conversation reminded me of the odd river-to-bank conversation held with the Amish children on day two—somewhat short and segmented. Although, how meaningful and complete can any conversation be during the brief moments that pass as someone floats by?

Today's beautiful weather brought many fishermen out to test their luck on the banks, catching crappie and catfish. As we passed by, the conversation with these river users was more normal. "Hi, how ya doin'?" "Whatcha' catchin'?"

With the sun overhead, we maneuvered (landing is always a maneuver) off the river next to the beautiful and historic Hanging Rock. Hanging Rock is a large example of how the banks are changing. They are still steep but not as muddy and becoming striations of rock, making departure from the river different from before but still a task. Hanging Rock is a national natural landmark with parking, a deck with benches, and a path to the top of the hanging rock. Many people come to climb the path to the lookout point at the top of the hill and gawk over the edge at the river. However, while they observe the beauty of the river, they miss the river view of the striations, representing 420 million years of geologic history. Personally, I love my river view.

In addition to its archeological significance, there is the legend that two Native American braves fought there over a maiden. Watching her true love fall to his death, she threw herself off the cliff as well. Because of this legend, Hanging Rock is the focus of many poems and songs.

Once we had landed, climbed out of *Work* and *Pray*, trekked up the hill, disposed of our trash, and read the obligatory information plaques about the site and rock striations and legend, we ate our lunch in a shaded seating area on the deck. Even though we had sat in our kayaks for several hours, relaxing on a seat with a back where our legs could hang down was a welcome change of position.

Having finished our relaxing and educational break, we trekked down the hill, climbed into *Work* and *Pray*, and launched. After an uneventful afternoon on the river, John began searching for a place to stop for the evening.

John has certain criteria for a campsite, one of which affects the ease of approaching the bank despite the current—the presence of an eddy. An eddy provides a respite from the current, allowing for an easier approach and landfall.

This afternoon, John located one of these gems, which formed a small lagoon parallel to the river between the towns of Lagro and Wabash. (The town's name really is Lagro—not Largo.) Even though the location of our home tonight is far from any roads that would connect us to civilization, from here we can still hear the train, which has become a near constant companion on our journey. When we hear the train whistle, we often look at each other and say, "Home."

After landing, we hunted for the ideal spot to place our tent. We found a flat place somewhat debris-free. However, the path leading from our kayaks to the tent was not debris-free, containing many tripping and clothing-snagging offenders. Having methodically removed the major impeding obstacles, I started carrying dry bags from *Work* and *Pray* to our camping spot.

Carrying my first load, I noticed John was still moving sticks. Confused, I asked, "What are you doing?"

Boy Scout John proudly proclaimed, "I am making a 'road' for us to walk safely on." He continued to build a shoulder out of sticks to guide our way. I love that man!

When setting up camp, one of John's first chores is locating two trees or large bushes, close together, to stretch our clothesline for drying laundry that hasn't dried from the day before, along with wet clothes from the day of kayaking. Yesterday, we did laundry at Huntington, and a few clothing pieces weren't dry, some of which were John's cotton underwear. John has decided bringing cotton underwear was a bad idea for a trip like this—they take forever to dry. We avoided bringing other items made of cotton but didn't consider the material of John's underwear. When you have only three pair of underwear, you do need them to be fast drying. John, frustrated with the slow-drying cotton underwear, is threatening to burn them and go commando. Yikes!

Having everything in its place and settling into our home for the night, we hit a technology glitch. (The more you have, the more things that can go wrong.) John was charging the phone with the solar panel, but when he checked on the status, he discovered the phone wasn't charging—the amount of charge of the battery had actually decreased. Upon further investigation he decided the phone cord had failed. John called Travis, my son, asking him to retrieve a cord at our house, transfer it to Rat and Sam Boyce, who would deliver it to us at Wabash, Indiana, tomorrow. John hung up and turned off the phone to save battery life.

Later, when he turned the phone back on to check for a response, a picture from Travis awaited our viewing with the text, "Before I leave, this is what you want right?" Travis had apparently traveled to our house as soon as he hung up and sent a picture of the cord he found—an iPad, not iPhone, cord. Now what?

John called Travis again, explaining the error. Evidently, we didn't have another iPhone charging cord. John thanked Travis, "Thanks. We'll figure something out."

Powering off the phone, we contemplated our dilemma. Maybe we could find a cord in Wabash. The problem is we are not familiar with Wabash; therefore, we do not know which stores are close (within walking distance) to the river. John turned on the phone to check the Internet for the location of possible carriers of phone cords and quickly turned it off and put it back in his pocket.

Confused, I asked, "What's wrong?"

"I don't want to waste the battery in case we have an emergency later." This was hard for John. His immediate reaction to any unknown is to pick up the phone and Google it. He can't stand to live in the world that exists between not knowing and knowing for more than a few minutes (maybe seconds). One time, when we were sitting in a coffee house in Japan enjoying a romantic cup of coffee and sharing a dessert, I ate almost the entire dessert alone while he investigated—get this—JAPANESE TOILETS.

Later this evening, John turned on the phone long enough to read another text from Travis stating he drove his own phone cord to Rat and Sam. What a great son!

Even as we are trying to live a simple life, technology has us in its grasp! Over the past year, as we planned our gear list, we determined certain technology as needs and not wants. Considering many people made similar trips ten or more years ago without modern technology, why do we now consider these pieces of technology needs? Our daily life in civilization continues to influence our definition of *need* and *want* here in the wilderness. I wonder if our experiences on this trip will alter our definitions when we return to civilization. What will our definition of *need* be in August?

Fix for the phone cord arranged, we ate a delicious dinner of chili, corn-bread croutons, and apple pie. Yum! I love that we have dessert every night after dinner—my favorite part of a meal. Many times, I eat my main course just so I can have dessert. To be honest, sometimes I am tempted to eat my dessert first. When I grow up, I think I will eat dessert first—life is short.

Settling in for a relaxing evening after the cord drama, me journaling and John playing his guitar, we heard a nasty ruckus of raccoons fighting about 100 yards away. Then, about ten noisy geese flew over; a couple landed and continued yelling at us. While we were admiring the lagoon, a beaver swam towards us. River sounds and sights of nature!

These river sounds and sights of nature are different from our land sounds and sights of nature. While relaxing for the evening on the porch swing of our country home, we experience land sounds and sights of nature. We may watch robins steal portions of my moss planters for their nests or hear a house wren yell at us because we are too close to her birdhouse located on our porch pillar. Sounds and sights of nature, whether from river or land, cause me to sigh and smile as my body relaxes. Emerging from my inside world to the outside world never disappoints.

Relaxing to the river sounds and sights of nature, we discussed which pieces of clothing and other articles we should send back home when the weather becomes warmer to free up some space in *Work* and *Pray*, making John's daily job of packing easier. While I am still shivering myself to sleep, I have a hard time planning for warmer temperatures. During the conversation, John mentioned he wanted to keep his down vest. Confused, I asked him, "Why?"

He smirked, "It will make a great PILLOW." Maybe, then, he'll quit stealing mine.

What an action-packed, milestone-surpassing day! It seems like a week since I climbed out of our frost-covered tent this morning, but in actuality, it has been only a few hours. The first week of our trip is over! So much has happened in that week as I have traveled farther and farther from home—100 miles—and the ones I love. Reaching the northern-most part of our trip seems weird because I thought we had been heading mainly west towards the Indiana-Illinois border—not north. We reached each of these milestones without thinking about them—we hadn't defined them as goals—they simply happened. Would they have meant more if we had pinpointed them ahead of time? Maybe we are too busy focusing on the end goal and missing the joy of accomplishing some of the less impressive milestones along the way. What is our next milestone? I think I'll sleep on that one.

04-12-2015

And God Just Shook His Head and Moved on to Something Else

Weather conditions:
High: 68
Low: 41
Skies: clear
Wind: SSE 8-15 mph, gusts to 20 mph

Today's mileage: 4 miles
Total mileage: 115 miles
Where we traveled: Between Lagro and Wabash, Indiana, to Wabash, Indiana (campsite set aside for those using the Wabash River Corridor)

After another cold night and morning, the unique sound of Pileated Woodpeckers hammering close by serenaded us as we ate our dehydrated breakfast of eggs, sausage, and hash browns. I had forgotten what loud, large birds they are.

My first sighting of a Pileated Woodpecker happened one fall a few years ago while John and I were strolling through a youth camp on Birch Lake in Michigan. The caretaker had locked the buildings for the season. The sun was shining, the air crisp and clean, and the leaves on the trees were changing from their summer green to autumn yellow and orange. The leaves that had lost their battle of holding tightly to the branches crunched under the weight of our walking shoes. Shuffling in silence, we imagined the voices of excited children running to the dining hall. The empty flag-pole is surely the center of flag-raising and lowering ceremonies each summer day. We peeked in the windows of the nurse's station. How many children does the nurse nurture each week? Do the campers count down the days each summer until they finally pick out a bunk? I know I did for several weeks before church camp each July.

First, we heard the monkey-sounding call. Since we were sure monkeys don't typically inhabit Michigan, we listened more closely. A large shadow moving across the browning grass, speckled with colorful leaves soon followed the call. We gazed up to locate the creator of the floating black shadow. Shielding our eyes from the sun, we spotted a large black bird with white under its wings. When the bird landed, we detected its red crown and long beak. Then we heard the noise—a hollow, hammering sound—classifying the bird as a woodpecker. Studying a bird book later, we identified the bird as a Pileated Woodpecker. The range indicated this species could also be found in Indiana although we have never seen nor heard one. Now, if I hear a monkey in our woods, I won't be surprised.

From the time we wake up each morning on the river, we spend three hours preparing to push off. Three hours seems like a long time since I don't need to decide what to wear, put on my make-up, or do my hair. So what takes so long? Here's how our morning progresses…

- The alarm interrupts our sleep.
- John turns off the alarm. (I groan, "No way.")
- We read devotions.
- I check Facebook, e-mail, and our web site statistics.
- John checks the radar and weather.
- John peruses the charts, noting any points of emphasis.
- John fetches our wet suits from the kayaks.

- John pulls up and zips his wetsuit.
- I go pee and wash my face (not at the same time).
- I put in my contact lenses.
- I pull and tug my wetsuit while contorting my body into unflattering positions in an attempt to put on my glue-like layer of clothing in the confines of a small, barely, two-man tent.
- John starts making breakfast.
- Once I am ready, I finish preparing breakfast and make our lunches.
- John begins packing *Work* and *Pray*.
- We eat breakfast.
- I brush my teeth.
- John goes pee and brushes his teeth (at the same time).
- John does the dishes. (Good for me!)
- I roll up the bedding.
- John continues packing the kayaks.
- We tear down the tent.
- John finishes packing our gear in the kayaks.
- We police the area. John promotes backing away from our site, ensuring we leave nothing behind.
- If we have pulled the kayaks from the river the day before, we roll them to the launching area.
- We apply sunscreen and Carmex Chap Stick. (I love how Carmex tingles on my lips.)
- We put on our hats, kayaking gloves, yellow (easily seen) life jackets, and, if needed, spray skirts.
- We physically view and touch all lashings and hatches on our own kayak, ensuring all is secure.
- We physically view and touch all lashings and hatches on the other person's kayak, ensuring all is secure.
- We pray and give each other a kiss.
- *Keep us upright and safe.*

- I climb into my kayak.
- John shoves *Pray* in the water.
- I launch.
- John launches.
- FREEDOM!

Performing today's morning rituals without a glitch, we left our peaceful, well somewhat peaceful, campsite.

Although the antics and noises of the wildlife as they performed their routines entertained us last night, nature still provided a sense of peace. I love that nature continues its routine around us despite our presence. What a privilege to live in the midst of nature first-hand, day after day. I hope the sights and sounds of nature never become wallpaper—like so many aspects of life. What parts of life at home have become wallpaper without my realizing the transition? What activities used to create excitement and wonder but now occur without notice? An interesting question I can't answer because the transition from exciting to normal has happened without my realizing.

This morning, after leaving our wildlife neighbors, we experienced a non-eventful paddle to Wabash, Indiana. Non-eventful is good—we were upright and safe. Approaching Wabash, we caught sight of an "overnight camping" sign. Awesome! This was an unexpected treat since Jerry Hay, author of *Wabash River Guidebook*, hadn't mentioned a camping option in Wabash.

Early in our yearlong investigations for this trip, John discovered the *Wabash River Guidebook* by Jerry Hay. This valuable source of information includes towns and amenities located close to the river. In addition, he provides other helpful landmarks, indicating our location and possible campsites.

Today, as we came closer to the unexpected sign, confusion replaced our excitement. The steep and high bank caused landing and exiting our kayaks at that location a less-than-perfect scenario. John stressed there wasn't any way we could stop there. As we passed, I set eyes on a picnic table and fire ring. I was so sad! I surveyed the area and could almost picture our tent and *Work* and *Pray* nestled under the tree. (If it were a bowl of moose track ice cream, I would have been salivating.) Was this a joke? Why would anyone place an "overnight camping" sign by the river and not provide an access point? I was a little bitter.

John reassured, "The Jerry Hay chart shows a boat ramp about a quarter of a mile downstream. We can pull out there."

"Okay," I mumbled, trying not to express my deep disappointment with the campsite tease.

Exactly as Jerry had noted, there was a boat ramp. We pulled up to it around 11:45 a.m. Before I landed and stepped out of *Pray*, some blue, green, and orange objects sticking above the green grass caught my eye. How odd?

We emerged from our kayaks, made sure they were secure, and checked out the colorful items in the grass. We found two gallons of water with blue caps and two bottles of orange juice with green lids. An attached note indicated the identity of the givers—our friends Chad and Tera Myers, who were in town for their daughter's softball tournament. Having corresponded with them over the last couple of days, we knew they would be in the area today. Earlier today, they had asked us, in a text, if we needed anything. We gave our usual answer—water. However, since the timing of our arrival in Wabash conflicted with a scheduled game, we assumed we wouldn't cross paths and were surprised they made the effort to ensure we received their gifts.

We guzzled the orange juice in three gulps. (Well, maybe more, but it seemed like three.) That was the best orange juice I have ever tasted! Things I used to take for granted are now treats. Will I still view them as treats even after I return to normal, or should I say society, life? Will I notice the back on a chair when I plop down on the couch? Will I appreciate the opportunity to enjoy a shower (maybe even two) daily? I hope so.

• • •

What will my life look like when I return to my society life? This question keeps appearing at the forefront of my thoughts and as a recurring conversation in my mind. When did I start to distinguish a difference between my society life and wilderness life? I don't know when the switch started or if I will experience a complete evolution, but I do know I am beginning to appreciate my life in the wilderness and almost resent parts that resemble my old life at home. It's interesting that some of the things of my society life that I used to view as necessities now seem meaningless and frivolous. For example, I have a closet and drawers full of clothes, many I haven't worn in years. For the last week, I have been clothed each day in one of my three sets of clothes, which fit into a medium-sized dry bag. I don't need to hold on to all my clothes at home "just in case I might want to wear them sometime" or "just in case I lose weight." I know I am not the first person who has complained about an excess of clothes. However, living with only three sets of clothes proves I **can** live with less. Once I return to society, I hope I remember that I **can** live without. Or should I say what I **can** live with? It's a matter of perspective. If I say I am living without all this or that, I feel deprived. If I say I can survive with only this or that, I feel I have accomplished something. Maybe the biggest difference between a society and wilderness life isn't what I have or don't have, but a matter of perspective. I will need to ponder this a little more. For now, I am content living with three sets of clothes.

Once we guzzled our orange juice, we placed our kayaks on the dollies, gathered our water, and pulled *Work* and *Pray* to the top of the hill (everything is uphill from the river). At the top of the hill, we were happy to find a restroom, a trashcan, a bench, and a paved walking path. I felt like I was in heaven—all these luxuries in one place. After eating our lunch on the bench, we deposited our trash in the proper receptacle and cleaned up in the restroom. (In other words, I put on clean clothes, redid my hair, and put on some makeup.)

Immediate needs met, John left in search of a new phone cord. While John trekked around Wabash, I sat on the bench journaling.

I jumped when I heard someone yell, "LaNae."

I stared at a couple walking towards me holding hands. As they approached, I recognized the couple—our friends Rat and Sam Boyce. Rat and Sam are not their real names; they are Donald and Marilyn. I haven't a clue where their nicknames came from, but I have grown so accustomed to their nicknames that on the rare occasion someone calls them Don or Marilyn, I am confused. I remember when I first met them; I assumed Rat was a nickname but thought Sam was short for Samantha or something similar. I was surprised to learn much later their real names.

After exchanging greetings and hugs, Rat pulled Travis' phone cord out of the pocket of his leather jacket. Our heroes!

The three of us sat on the bench watching people traveling down the path, taking advantage of the beautiful, crisp spring day. As the sun beat down on us, Sam unzipped her yellow sweatshirt, and Rat pulled his brown camo baseball cap down farther over his sunglasses. Several people stopped to talk to us—I think the kayaks behind the bench lured them in.

When John returned, he gave us a blow-by-blow of his experience. First, he hiked to Speedway, where their employee, Ashley, allowed him to try the cord before leaving the store. Hmmm…the aftermarket cord had molded plastic around the plug, which would have fit the iPhone fine, but it would not fit through the opening of our Lifeproof case. Strike 1.

John then trudged to Phillips 66. "We ain't got no phone cords." Strike 2.

Then, John walked the three-mile round trip to a Dollar General, where they also had a cord with the large molding around the plug, which, of course, would not fit through our Lifeproof case. Strike 3.

However, John decided to purchase the Dollar General cord, assuming he could whittle the plastic housing down until it would fit—or because he simply felt compelled to buy something after walking so far.

After telling his tale, John handed me the phone so I could verify whether Travis' cord would work. I plugged the cord into the phone and then into the Sherpa. The familiar "ding" sounded as I engaged the plug. I smiled. We will be able to use our phone for more than an emergency again. I didn't realize how dependent on technology I had become on our wilderness trip until I was without. "Don't it always seem to go, that you don't know what you've got 'til it's gone?" (Hey, that should be a song. Those born before 1980 know it is a song.)

Even though the cord John purchased wouldn't work, John's trip across Wabash wasn't a total waste: he found the campsite we had passed on the river. The paved path next to the bench led directly to the coveted camping area. We would have a fire and picnic table tonight after all! I felt guilty for being bitter earlier.

As Rat and Sam were leaving, we received a text from Terry and Dawn Wanner, who had driven to Wabash to visit the Harley Davidson dealer, wondering where they could find us. We gave them directions to the area where we would be staying. (We don't socialize this much at home. Honest.)

Grabbing *Work*'s strap, John started down the path. "Let's do this. The campsite isn't very far."

Yay! Even though we had paddled only four miles, I was tired and ready to relax for the day. And we still had to set up our tent. I have a hard time relaxing until I complete my chores, and I wanted to have my home in order before the Wanners arrived. The longer we plodded, the more I questioned John's definition of *isn't very far*. Resembling a little kid, I asked, "How much farther? Aren't we there yet?"

Not only had we surpassed my definition of *isn't very far,* but we were also going up and down steep hills. Pulling the kayaks up and down several hills was tiring. Going downhill was almost as difficult as going uphill, because, depending on the grade of the hill, *Pray* sometimes rolled faster than I moved. I remember, before we left, someone stated, "Boy will you have buff arms." To which I replied, "I know, right. But I'm afraid my legs will become wimpy." Let me make this clear—I was wrong! My legs will be anything but wimpy by the end of our trip. Finally reaching the campsite, I plopped down at the picnic table and rested my weary (un-wimpy) legs!

Our physical condition after paddling for a week surprises me. Although my muscles are tired at the end of the day, they don't really ache. I honestly thought they would feel sore like they do the day after an intense workout. I think the reason they don't is I use my core to pull the paddle through the water, not my arms. One thing John and I have noticed on the inside of our left thumbs right where the "v" forms with our hands is a small bump, known as a paddler's callous. It doesn't hurt; it's simply there. This bump isn't present on my right hand. Again, I think this is a result of the way I paddle. I can't explain exactly what I do; I just do it. Our backs become stiff during the day, so we take a break from paddling and float while we lean back over the rear of our kayaks to stretch. Once the banks are more accessible, we will go ashore and walk more often. Overall, I feel pretty good physically—until I lie in bed shivering all night. Luckily, there is an end in sight to this temperature discomfort.

Approaching our home for the night, we noticed a sign only observable from land. We read the sign…

Campsite Rules

This campsite is for the exclusive use of those exploring the Wabash River Corridor on foot, bicycle, or water vessel. Please observe the following rules.

Camping in this area is restricted to this site only.

Maximum capacity: 8 persons.

Maximum stay: 24 hours.

All campfires must be confined to the fire ring. Please extinguish your fire before leaving.

Help us preserve the Wabash River Corridor. Please burn only downed trees.

Please place all trash in the trash containers.
Those not abiding by these rules will be asked to
leave.
Thank you for your cooperation.
Wabash Park Department
Wabash River Defenders

The campsite beyond the sign was as inviting from land as it appeared from the river, with its tree, picnic table, trashcan, fire pit, and firewood. The table, can, and pit were without the dings and dirt of older, frequently used campsites. How many others have taken advantage of this spot provided by Wabash Park Department and Wabash River Defenders? I wondered who presented their ideas to one or both of these groups and made these luxurious accommodations happen. I wanted to thank them personally. If there were more places like this along the river, would more people use the river and experience nature as we have?

Deciding we could abide by the site's rules, we prepared our camp. While we were organizing our home for the night, Terry and Dawn arrived. (Didn't this happen a couple of days ago?) Hungry, we decided the Wanners would provide burgers from the nearby Speedway, which were surprisingly good, while the Abnets would supply a dehydrated apple pie dessert. To me, sitting and eating at a picnic table was plush. Small things in life. What was a luxury to the Abnets was roughing it to the Wanners who eat at a dining table every evening. Again, it's all a matter of perspective.

Since we had Travis's correct cord, we gave the Dollar General cord to the Wanners for delivery to Travis, assuming it would work with his case.

After Terry and Dawn left, we were enjoying the campfire, discussing the day's events and the potential thunderstorms in tomorrow's forecast, when a middle-aged man bounded down the hill and boldly sat on the bench of the picnic table. "We need to talk," our visitor announced as he pushed back his red baseball cap and unzipped his sweatshirt, revealing a lime green t-shirt. I avoided making eye contact. *Did we do something wrong?* The sign clearly stated this campsite was for those traveling on the river—our kayaks were a good sign we were doing that.

Crossing his arms, he continued, "I'm Mike Beauchamp." He began asking questions about our trip and relaying information about the Wabash River most people wouldn't know. Finally, everything became much clearer, "I've taken your trip. Not from the headwaters—but from here."

Actually, he had completed three similar trips with each of his three children as high school graduation gifts. For their adventures, instead of paddle crafts, they had used a flat-bottom, motorized boat. Our view of Mike changed from a strange interruption to a provider of information. Realizing what he had accomplished, we started asking the questions.

"What did you eat?"

"Where did you stay?"

"Do the tow boats make a large wake?"

We soon ran out of questions because, even though we had an expert who could give us all the information we needed concerning the trip ahead of us, we didn't have the basic information to perform a successful interrogation. We were like first graders who can't ask about multiplication tables because they don't know they exist.

In addition to answering our limited questions, Mike offered some advice about the Mississippi River, such as rooster tails. They spout unexpectantly in the tows' wake as a result of the churning water unseen under the surface. This phenomenon was new to us.

John asked one final question, "How did you know we were here?"

"You know the runner who stopped to talk to you earlier?"

John answered, "Adam Stakeman?"

"Yes. He ran into my wife. (Fortunately, she wasn't hurt.) He knew I would be interested in talking with you, so he told her you were here. She, of course, rushed home to tell me. And here I am." This is a perfect example of the domino effect as a result of, what we have termed as, "just happened to be" moments we are observing on this trip.

Through the conversation that followed, we discovered Mike is the founder of the Wabash River Defenders. The River Defenders' main objective is to clean up the river, and they have hosted several "Clean Out the Banks" events. He told us to watch for white "Wabash River Water Trail" signs, which have a blue map of Indiana in the center, alerting us to locations of boat ramps.

Mike is also active in establishing small campsites, like the one we are staying at, along the river for water travelers. Seriously? We actually met one of the people responsible for these luxurious accommodations and had a chance to say thank you.

Tonight as I sit at a ritzy campsite, reflecting on my day, I realize the sounds of society (of which I am a participant) have replaced the sounds of nature that I witnessed last night and this morning (as a bystander). How I long to return to the place where I find peace in the midst of noise like the monkey-like calls and the hammering of a Pileated Woodpecker.

04-13-2015

At the Appropriate Time, Ten Minutes Prior, You Will Receive a Call

Weather conditions:
High: 60
Low: 51
Skies: light drizzle with an occasional rain shower
Wind: WSW 14-22 mph, gusts to 30 mph

Today's mileage: 23 miles
Total: 138 miles
Where we traveled: Wabash, Indiana, to Peru, Indiana

Baa! Yes, I hear a sheep bleating as I write tonight. No, we didn't find a herd of sheep on the banks of the Wabash. Let's start at the beginning of our day and progress to the bleating of sheep.

Today started out with an oatmeal breakfast and the ordinary three-hour prep before I executed my first stroke in the water. I wonder if, as we become more efficient with our routine, we will eventually launch earlier in the morning. Even if we don't—*this is the trip*—we don't have a schedule after all. After eating and cleaning up breakfast, packing up, and rolling

Work and *Pray* up and down hills for what seemed like six miles (no wimpy legs here), we launched our kayaks and prepared for a 20-mile paddle to Peru with a forecast of rain later in the day.

Keep us upright and safe.

Aware of the forecast of rain, I opted not to wear my sunglasses. Later, since no rain had fallen yet and the sky had lightened some, I thought I should put on my sunglasses. I wear sunglasses because I am vain. (Not because I look like a movie star in them, but because I am trying to avoid wrinkles from squinting.) I opened my deck bag, rummaged through its contents (much like a purse), and located my sunglasses at the bottom (much like a purse). Literally, within two minutes after putting them on, the lenses were speckled with raindrops. *Oh well, it is only sprinkling.* Unfortunately, the sprinkles turned into major raindrops. My vision was then impaired because not only were the skies not sunny enough for sunglasses, but my lenses were also covered with water, causing images to be blurred and distorted. Not a good combination! Glasses removed, case retrieved, lenses cleaned, and then all replaced in my deck bag. You know your day of paddling has been relatively eventless when an error in sunglass options makes the journal entry.

So, what else do I do on uneventful days—other than put on and take off my sunglasses? I work on my kayaking techniques by paying attention to how I hold the paddle, place the paddle in the water, and pull the paddle; noting what part of my body I am using during my stroke. The ideal stroke is to use your torso more than your arms. You know, twist at the waist to allow your core to do most of the work. The "off" (top) hand should push the paddle forward until the blade reaches far up towards the bow, as the "on" (lower) hand pulls its blade back against and through the water. For long-distance paddling, keep the paddle as low (parallel to the horizon) as possible. I also try not to grip the paddle too hard…easier on the hands.

Regardless, if you paddle frequently, you won't be able to avoid the paddler's callous (I mentioned this yesterday) at the inside base of your thumbs near the webbing. Badge of honor.

In order to stay focused on my paddling technique, I talk to myself, sometimes in my head and sometimes out loud. "Twist, push, reach, pull… Twist, push, reach, pull … loosen your grip… Twist, push, reach, pull… Twist, push, reach, pull". I also remind myself to tighten my ab muscles with each pull. I'm hoping to tone my core as a side benefit to surviving the trip.

The most eventful parts of today were the sightings of six eagles and one nest. One of the six welcomed us as it stood sentry at the confluence of the Mississinewa and Wabash Rivers. I had goosebumps as I admired the beautiful, majestic bird welcoming those traveling on the Mississinewa to the Wabash—a promise to watch over them. With the addition of the waters from the Mississinewa, the river's size has increased—it's definitely not a creek any longer. The river's landscape is also beginning to change— lower banks, sand bars, and larger islands. A welcome change!

Giving directions on the river is different from giving directions on land. On land, street and road names provide descript location identifiers. Even now, in Indiana, finding someone's house is much easier than when I was growing up. When I was a young child, country addresses were assigned based on the mail route, such as rural route 1. With the implementation of the new 911 system, addresses were changed to provide emergency vehicles a simpler method of locating a residence or business. Try finding someone on rural route 1. The new system uses the numbered country roads, based on miles, as its foundation. Houses were numbered similarly. For example, a home with the address 8322 S 600 E indicates the house is 0.322 miles south of 800 South on road 600 East. A division road gives a reference for north and south roads, as well as east and west: 800 South is eight miles south of the division road.

Unfortunately, giving directions on the river isn't as easy. There aren't ANY signs. So, when we asked Amber Kuhn, our hostess for the next couple of nights, where she lived, she wasn't sure what to say. "Beside the big tree on your left" won't work—there are millions of big trees on our left. "Just past the bend" still doesn't work, especially if the person providing the directions hasn't traveled on the river and isn't familiar with all the bends. The same problem happens with "Soon after the island"—which island? And, by the way, how far is "soon"? Correcting a missed landmark on the river is not as easy as turning around and backtracking as one does with a car on the road. On the river, an overshoot requires an upstream paddle. Paddling against the current requires more energy to overcome the pressure of the river as it flows in its natural direction. I am usually too tired to work against the water.

During our conversation with Amber last night, she confirmed she would put a pink ribbon on the tree. We knew Amber's tree was about 20 river miles from the town of Wabash. Having traveled what we thought was approximately that distance, based on *Wabash River Guide Book*, we started combing the left bank descending (LBD) for a pink ribbon around a tree.

After searching for, but not locating, the ribbon for about twenty minutes, we became concerned we may have missed it. We didn't want to paddle upstream. Approaching a large island that appeared to be a notable landmark, I sent Amber a text. (Isn't technology wonderful?)

Me: Are you before or after the island?
Amber: After island.
Me: We are just passing the island now.
Amber: Oh, you are so close.

We looked for the pink ribbon on a tree "soon after the island." (By the way, deer hunters also use pink neon ribbons to mark the way to their stands.)

John peered ahead. "I think I see a ribbon. You hang tight while I confirm it is the right ribbon and check out the landing situation."

I back paddled as I "hung tight." Back paddling is like going upstream—backward—and is tiring. While I paddled backward upstream ('hanging tight'), I continued my text dialogue with Amber.

Amber: I work(ed) night shift. Just woke up n brewing vanilla coffee. Would you all like some?
Me: Yep
Amber: OK I'll be down when it's done. Y'all should be here by now or shortly.

Coffee! Flavored coffee! Amber had no idea how happy she made me. One: Coffee is a luxury we have chosen to do without on this trip. Two: I like flavored coffee while John doesn't. Since I also like unflavored coffee, and being the nice person I am, I generally brew the boring (I mean unflavored) variety at home. Anticipation. *Come on, John, hurry up and confirm the pink ribbon!*

Finally, John returned. "I think this is the place. But there is no way on God's green earth we can get our kayaks off the river there." Last night, Amber clarified there was a place to land on her property. I'm sure pulling a short boat with no gear up the bank was doable, but not our long, heavy kayaks.

I fretted, "What are we going to do?" I had been looking forward to staying at Amber's for a couple of days. Maybe enjoy a little pampering. Where would we stay if we had to keep going? And, would a cup of flavored coffee be waiting for me there?

"We passed a private makeshift boat ramp upstream. Let's turn around and try that."

Remember, turning around on a river means navigating upstream. I was tired after traveling 20 miles and back paddling for several minutes. I cried—I didn't want to paddle upstream. I also didn't want to keep paddling downstream. I wanted to be done.

John doesn't do well with my tears. He usually responds in one of three ways. If he feels uncomfortable with the situation, he tries to diminish it by saying something (usually silly) to make light of the circumstance. This only makes me feel worse because I feel foolish for being upset. Or, he tries to fix the problem. This doesn't always work because, although he is wonderful and my hero, he can't fix everything. Or, he becomes angry because he doesn't know what else to do. Today, he tried to fix the situation by reminding me we would be done soon. I had to remind myself, *This is the trip.*

We turned around and paddled upstream about half a mile in order to access the easier exit point. Since we were traveling upstream, we had to paddle past the ramp, turn around, and approach from upstream. We performed the required pass-turn-around-and-approach routine in order to land our kayaks.

Once *Pray* was resting on land, I regarded a large chain across the path to the road. Another obstacle in what I thought was going to be an easy landing. *This is the trip.*

We dragged *Work* and *Pray* ashore and put on the wheels. Thirty-something Amber, dressed for her day off in a rust-colored hoodie and glasses, arrived as we were trying to maneuver our kayaks under the chain. We set them down, ducked under the linked barricade, and walked to the road. Obligatory welcome hugs exchanged, Amber, her ponytail bouncing, strolled around to the passenger side of her gray Kia Sportage and opened the door. The aroma of vanilla coffee floated out of the SUV. My mouth watered! There is something soothing about the smell of coffee.

Then I spotted it on the floor—an entire pot of coffee. She picked up a mug, preparing to pour me a cup. I reluctantly turned it down, knowing if I took the mug, I would enter another world and forget I had a kayak waiting on the other side of the chain. The act of holding a cup of java in my hand as the aroma of the dark liquid rises and enters my nose causes the stress in my body to lower ten notches before I revel in the first sip. I told myself to practice self-control. "Thanks, but I better wait until we bring the kayaks up here."

Amber held up the chain as John pulled and I pushed *Work* and *Pray* under it. Once the kayaks were resting by the vehicle, I accepted—without guilt—the cup of joe. Amber poured us each a mug of coffee. I closed my eyes as I relished my first sip. *When was my last cup of coffee? Five days ago? At Markle? With lemon meringue pie? I remember. Yum.* Even though the enjoyment was only five days ago, it seems like five weeks. So much has happened since we relished the taste of pie and coffee!

Although John and I proudly call ourselves coffee snobs, resisting convenience store brew, we gave up coffee early in the trip. When packing our sixteen supply boxes in preparation for the trip, I included a zip-lock bag containing enough coffee and tea to drink each morning with breakfast. With a three-hour prep to launch, we soon realized taking time to for coffee wasn't practical. In addition, the inaccessible banks present another obstacle—they are unavailable for peeing (coffee is a diuretic after all).

After savoring our cups of coffee and talking about our trip, we assessed the portage situation.

I saw a house across the road. "Is that your house?"

"No honey, our house is about a mile and a half away—up the hill in that woods over there." She pointed to a woods on the other side of a large field. I couldn't even see her house. "Then our driveway is almost half a mile."

Hmm... I considered the woods in the distance, wondering how we were going to transport *Work* and *Pray* from here to there. I thought yesterday's and this morning's hikes were long. They seemed like a brief stroll compared to the miles ahead. Jokingly, I blurted, "Too bad we can't pull the kayaks behind your vehicle."

John got a gleam in his eye. (Oh, no.) I could almost hear the gears clanking in his brain. Examining the rear of the vehicle, he asked, "Do you have anything in the back? If not, we could open the back hatch. LaNae and I could sit there and hold our kayaks by their carrying handles while you drive slowly."

Amber opened the back hatch, "Nothing here. I think we can do this."

John proposed, "Let's do it. What's the worst that can happen?"

Let's see...*What's the worst that can happen?* ... I drop *Pray* and it rolls down the road and crashes into a tree? How would we explain that scenario to the insurance company?

Even worse, how would we explain the reason we cut our trip short. I can hear the conversation now...

"Why didn't you make it past Peru?"

"My kayak ran into a tree."

"Oh, you poor thing. Did you get hurt?"

"I wasn't in my kayak."

"Didn't you tie your kayak off when you were on shore?"

"Umm... My kayak was on land."

"Well, then how....."

Imagine the embarrassment.

Despite my misgivings, John and I hopped in the back of the vehicle. With our feet dangling, we grabbed the carrying handles on the fronts of *Work* and *Pray*, and away Amber drove at a pleasant four mile per hour. Even though Amber was creeping, I was nervous. I was concerned about falling out, dropping *Pray*, or bumping the kayaks into each other. Then we reached the hills. Going up and going down were both a challenge. Going downhill, I found keeping *Pray* from running into the rear bumper strenuous. Going uphill, its weight almost pulled me out—I held onto *Pray* with my right hand while I white-knuckled the back of the rear seat with my left. Part way up the largest hill, I gave up. I couldn't hold on to the seat any longer. I had Amber stop the vehicle. I then jumped out, sat *Pray* on the road, and walked; John sat in the back of the SUV, alone, holding on to *Work*.

He and Amber pulled it to the top of the hill and then returned to perform the same procedure with mine. What an interesting way to portage. Where there's a will, there's a way!

Amber turned into her driveway at the top of the hill, and I returned to my position in the back beside John. Both kayaks once again in tow, I surveyed our surroundings from the back cargo area where I could see what we had only this minute passed. Were we still in Indiana? To my left, cattle grazed on rolling pastures more akin to Kentucky than the featureless portions of Indiana with which I am familiar.

We reached her house and stopped. Before I could put *Pray* down, a large tan dog approached us. His entire body wagged as his tail moved from side to side with joy. He tried several times to jump in the vehicle with us. With each jump, he failed to find any free space to place his white paws and fell back to the driveway. Giving up, he stood by Amber's car, asking us to please exit our spots and give him some attention.

Amber introduced us, "This is Toby."

Lowering our kayaks, we crawled off the back of the vehicle. John playfully petted the dog's head, "Hi, Toby. You're a good dog. I miss my dogs, Olive and Lilly."

We have two beagles at home, who are opposites. Olive is timid and takes a while to warm up to you. Once she does, she can't snuggle close enough, often pushing herself up against you in order to initiate more petting. Lilly, on the other hand, doesn't know she is a dog. She usually could care less if you pay attention to her unless you feed her a piece of cheese or something she likes. While Olive will eat anything, Lilly sniffs the food offered before deciding if it fits her culinary tastes. More often than not, while she delays, Olive jumps in and steals the food from under Lilly's nose. Lilly also climbs trees. Yeah, she's weird.

In addition to Toby, chickens running freely around the yard cackled (cluck, cluck), another dog panted (ah uh ah uh), and Bailey the sheep bleated (baa, baa). In the distance, hound dogs bayed (aaarrrrrrOOOOOO) in their kennel, making their presence known. Even with the auditory sensual overload of the farm, a peace washed over me. Since tomorrow is our day of rest, this is home for the next couple of days, and I couldn't be more thankful.

We placed our tent in Amber's yard beside her rustic log cabin with its exposed, genuine chinking while tall and thin Croydon, Amber's dark-haired 12-year-old son, did the same with his tent so he could "camp" beside us. As we set up our tent, Bailey sniffed our kayaks and supplies. At first, he simply appeared curious. Then he started nuzzling the straps that held my boots on top of *Pray*. Recalling stories of sheep and goats eating everything in sight, I asked, "He won't eat my straps, will he?"

"Absolutely," Croydon offered. Amber proceeded to escort Bailey to a safer environment inside the fenced corral. We proceeded to organize our nylon bedroom.

Bedroom complete, I asked Amber if I could take a shower and wash some laundry. Of course, she said yes. I'm not sure if she agreed because she wanted to be hospitable or because we… um… how shall I say it… um… stank (for lack of a better word). After all, our last shower was a week ago.

Entering the bathroom, I turned on the heater. OOOHHHH!! Warm air. I turned on the water. OOOHHHH!! Warm water. The sound of the water splashing at the bottom of the tub brought a smile to my face. *This is going to feel so good.* I pulled my shampoo, conditioner, razor, and shaving cream from my green toiletries dry bag. *This is going to feel so good.* I lifted a full-size, plush (not small, quick dry) towel from the shelf. Pulling the shower curtain to the side, I stepped into the tub and stood under the warm water, watching the grime of the river flow down the drain. I used my fingernails as I shampooed my hair. On the river, I wear my hair in a ponytail, so it didn't look unkempt and dirty, but man did my scalp itch. Warm air, warm water, full-size towel, clean scalp (and a little make-up). Small luxuries.

As the new and improved LaNae exited the bathroom and entered the kitchen, Amber, glancing up from the kitchen table, explained, "When I was deciding what to have for supper, I tried to think what you couldn't get on the river. Pizza!"

Later, when she returned with two large pizzas, I had to exercise self-control once again. I wanted to snatch the boxes from her, retreat to another room, and consume both pizzas by myself. I couldn't remember the last time I had pizza. I know we have been on the river almost two weeks, but it feels like we have been away from civilized eating establishments for two months. She placed the cardboard boxes on the table and took drink orders—water or Pepsi. Even though I rarely drink pop, I chose Pepsi. Everyone knows pizza can't be washed down with water.

As Amber fulfilled our beverage preferences, I lifted the box lids. The sight and smell of grease, pepperoni, sausage, and melted cheese caused my stomach to make feed-me noises. More self-control. I had to wait until everyone sat down and a prayer said. At the appropriate time, I chose a sausage piece. Removing the triangle from the box, I watched its pointed end sag down from the weight of the toppings and cheese, leaving a grease-soaked spot on the cardboard where it had rested. My mouth watered as I lifted the slice to my mouth and took a bite. Just as the orange juice yesterday was the best orange juice I had ever tasted, this was the best pizza. At first, I tried to be polite and eat slowly, but my self-control lasted only a couple of bites. I don't know how many pieces I had, but I was a good girl and didn't eat the last piece.

With my hunger satisfied, I sat back and studied my surroundings. Parts of Amber's log home were original with the chinking visible. The large eat-in kitchen, laundry room, and bathroom were a later addition. The atmosphere was relaxing and inviting (and there was a coffee maker on the counter). I am going to enjoy spending tomorrow here.

Dinner complete, Amber announced, "Croydon, it's time to feed the cows. I will make the bottle for the calf. You feed the other cows."

They stood up and gathered the items needed to complete their chores. We followed behind. John and I live on a three-acre "farm" but do not have any livestock (except for our dogs), so watching Croydon and Amber do their farming chores interested me. On the other hand, John grew up on a farm, so he could relate somewhat with their daily routine. We watched as Amber bottle-fed a calf whose mother had abandoned it.

At the same time, Croydon fed the rest of the cows bales of hay from the skid loader he had driven from the barn. Because of the recent rains, the heavy cows create thick craters and slimy mud as their hooves push the solid ground below the surface, bringing the sticky substance to the top. Croydon's vehicle began to slip and slide on the unique, bumpy mud. The engine whined as it tried to provide enough power to keep the tracks from spinning in the slime. I kept waiting for him to stop moving at any time, which he eventually did. For a while, he could only spin in his tracks as he futilely switched from forward to reverse. Croydon then used the hydraulic bucket to leverage himself into a position where he could gain enough traction to keep moving. He took pleasure in every minute of his conquest—as most 12-year-old boys (and grown men) would.

Chores finished, we returned to the house and relaxed on comfy chairs—with backs—while catching up with Amber until my eyelids would not stay open. Strolling outside, we climbed into our familiar tent. Home.

That brings me to the bleating sheep. I am sitting here in the tent (Croydon is sleeping in his tent beside us) writing while I listen to Bailey baaing in the background, asking to be untied. The sounds of nature have been replaced by the sounds of the farm. Home.

04-14-2015

I Suppose THAT Is out of the Question

Weather conditions:

High: 64

Low: 43

Skies: mostly cloudy

Wind: NE 5-13 mph

Today's mileage: 0 miles—day of rest

Total mileage: 138 miles

Where we are: Peru, Indiana

What do Tuesday and Sunday have in common? They are both days of rest—at least for us. We started the day taking the term "day of rest" literally by not setting an alarm and sleeping until we woke up. After another chilly night, we slowly emerged from the tent and sauntered to Amber's log home. What a great place to live!

Entering the kitchen, I called, "Helloooo..." No answer. The kitchen and rest of the house were quiet and void of activity. Croydon was at school; we assumed that since Amber's vehicle was in the drive, she was performing the daily morning farm chores. Even though no one was in the house, we decided to make ourselves at home. I chose (pulled from the bag of food in *Pray's* front hatch) a dehydrated breakfast. Hmmm...I just realized that since I have all the food in *Pray*, she and I are essential to John's survival. Maybe he should have considered this before he attempted not to bring my pillow.

I leisurely started preparing breakfast on a stove I didn't have to light, using water from a faucet. While waiting for the water to boil, I thought visiting the bathroom would be safe. Wrong! I returned to a strange scene in the kitchen. Weird image number one—John standing by the stove. *Why is John standing by the stove? John rarely stands by the stove, and boiling water doesn't need stirring.* Weird image number two—a metal bowl upside down on the burner. *Why is the bowl upside down on the stove? From where did John retrieve a bowl?* Weird image number three—a frazzled John met me with a blank stare. *How can boiling water frazzle John? I wasn't gone that long.*

I gave him the what-happened-here look.

John proceeded to explain like a kid without bangs caught holding a pair of scissors and a hank of hair, "There was a fire. I don't know what happened."

I started my interrogation. "Uh…. How did a boiling pot of water start on fire?"

"The fire was in the drip pan—grease, I think. The first thing I spotted was the bowl on the counter. I used it to cover the fire. Everything is under control." So we thought.

John lifted the bowl off the burner. Flames shot up! Apparently, he needed something larger in order to cover more of the burner. I remembered glimpsing a pan lid in the cabinet earlier as I was searching for a pan to boil water. I retrieved said lid and used it to smother the fire.

All dangers of fire gone, we enjoyed our delicious couscous with fruit breakfast eaten with a regular spoon instead of a collapsible plastic spork, out of a regular bowl instead of a lid or pan. Before this trip, I had never had couscous for breakfast. I found a recipe for hot breakfast couscous on the Internet during my investigation of dehydrated food ideas. The only dehydrated portion of the meal is the fruit. The prep directions are easy: Add

½-cup boiling water to couscous; set 5 minutes; add fruit and nuts. I wonder how many of our trip recipes I will continue making when we return home. Or, will I be so tired of them I never want to eat these meals again?

Unfortunately, I was not able to scrub all traces of the fire from the bottom of the blackened lid. I guess Amber should be glad the house is still standing!

I jumped at the creak of the door opening. It was Amber. I'm not sure why I was surprised, it is her house. Shutting the door, she asked, "Do you want some coffee?"

"Absolutely!"

Amber put on a pot of French vanilla coffee. Between John (Yes, John drank flavored coffee.), Amber, and me, we finished the pot in less than an hour.

We spent the balance of our "day of rest" taking care of details like catching up on my journaling, determining our Week # 3 package pick-up, practicing with the VHF radio, etc. We don't have much time to accomplish administrative duties while we are on the river because we are busy tearing down camp, loading the kayaks, paddling the kayaks, setting up camp, being interviewed by reporters, and socializing with new and old friends. We commandeered Amber's kitchen table with two iPads, an iPhone, charts, a VHF radio, and several charging cords. *After all, she did tell us to make ourselves at home.*

While John played (I mean practiced) with the VHF radio, I took advantage of an indoor clean space with running water to clean our muddy wetsuits. Before placing the suits into the water, I asked Amber if she noticed any difference between John's suit and mine. And if she did, was there a problem? Immediately, she noticed the lack of a zipper on my suit. Yes, my wetsuit does NOT have a zipper. It closes at my top left shoulder with a snap and extra sticky Velcro. (I shouldn't be bitter—at least, unlike my pillow, my wetsuit made the packing list.) Before the trip, John did a lot of research on all of our gear. Unfortunately, he didn't notice the lack of a zipper on my women's wet suit. This design oversight causes much consternation when the need to eliminate MY fluid (and solid) waste arises.

Imagine this scenario… I have been in *Pray* for four hours, drinking plenty of liquids to prevent dehydration, causing my bladder to be quite full. When we finally stop, John climbs out of *Work*, unzips his coat and wetsuit, and relieves himself without any effort. In the meantime, I do the I-have- to-pee dance while trying not to wet my pants (it may be a wetsuit, but I don't want it to be wet in that way). Dancing, I remove my coat and shirt, placing them safely on a non-muddy surface. Without the protection of my coat and shirt, the cold wind easily penetrates my bare arms, chilling me to the bone. Now I am shivering, in addition to dancing. The next step before I can pee is to pull down my wetsuit by unsnapping and releasing the extra strong Velcro. Once the strap is free, I pull the wetsuit, which clings to my body like a second skin, down to my knees. (I don't wear any underwear—one less piece of clothing to pull down during this time of urgency.) Now, I am naked down to my knees and COLD. (You don't need to visualize this.) However, don't forget to visualize my I-have- to-pee dance during this procedure. Then, I have to squat with my feet spread apart far enough to avoid splashing or sprinkling on my boots. John gets to stand. Sometimes, I HATE being a girl. After taking care of business, I reverse the order of all the previous steps (eliminating solid waste requires even more steps). By now, John is back in *Work* and ready to go. Don't forget, John was warm this entire time—while I am STILL shivering. Nonetheless, both our wetsuits were filthy from coming in contact with Wabash River mud both in and out of our kayaks.

For lunch, we shared one of our homemade river lunches with Amber—a peanut butter wrap, Parmesan cheese chunk, fruit roll-up, and granola bar. We served all menu items on white dinner plates. Let me tell you, the meal resembled an elegant dinner at a 4-star restaurant more than a bagged meal from *Pray's* hold. Amber was impressed!

"This doesn't seem right," John muttered. He was working with the Marine band radio in preparation for the eventual ship traffic we will encounter on the Ohio and Mississippi Rivers. "I don't expect to pick up any signal around here, but I do expect static when I turn down the squelch." A quick call to the customer service line at Standard Horizon confirmed there was an additional level of squelch reduction John hadn't noticed. Once he tried their suggestion, he received the all-is-well static he expected to hear. Check. Radio ready to go.

Next on John's gear-care list was finding the slow leaks that have developed in our Klymit sleep pads. We really like these pads, and at less than a pound each, they add very little size or weight to our stash of gear. However, half way through the night we have woken up to find the extra protection they provide from the hard, COLD ground gone. John hauled the pads into the house and inflated them. Then he tried scrunching them down small enough to fit in the kitchen sink. A little investigation under the slowly running water determined that while there were no punctures, there were slow leaks from each of the auxiliary pump valves. The pads inflate quickly and easily with a few puffs into the primary valve. However, in the event we desire a tighter fill, we can use a small hand pump bulb to add additional air via the auxiliary valves. From the website, John determined how to carefully open and clean the valves. Even after cleaning the valves, one of the pads still had a slow leak at the valve. Hmmm...

A call to Klymit met with an enthusiastic and helpful customer service associate who offered two options. One—she could send replacement pads in a style of our choosing. Two—she could send us valve caps that would completely seal the auxiliary valve. Even though both options would be at no cost to us, John decided option two would likely fix the problem and be easier. The Klymit associate assured John she would be glad to send the valves to some place along our route, so John provided the address of the post office in Logansport, Indiana, where we will be stopping to collect our next food drop. Since I am in charge of making the bed each night, I may take the liberty of placing the leaky pad on John's side of the tent. (Pillow—need I say more?)

Tasks completed, we sat at the cleared table relaxing while we anticipated the arrival of our good friend and mother of Amber, Phyllis Hull, from Fort Wayne, Indiana. Phyllis and I have been friends for over thirty years. Over the years, we have birthed our youngest sons, cruised together, lived through divorces, married the loves of our lives, struggled through blended families, traveled by kayak and canoe in the Canadian wilderness, and created more memories than I will ever be able to remember.

Tires rolling over the stones, a motor silencing, and a car door opening and closing announced her arrival. I rushed outside to say hi to my dear friend. Tall and thin Phyllis approached me. Even though I was wearing going-in-to-town clothes and had put on a little make-up earlier, I felt a little underdressed as I compared my attire to Phyllis's gray pants, navy jacket, and red purse. We exchanged our usual it's-so-good-to-see-you hug. Since this would be our last chance to spend time together for three and a half months, she drove the hour and fifteen minutes required to reach Amber's. I was touched she would leave her busy schedule and travel to see me!

Soon after Phyllis arrived, my stomach began growling; indicating the time for dinner was approaching. Amber suggested driving to Peru, purchasing roasted chicken, and bringing it back to the house. After some discussion, we decided eating in a restaurant was more enticing. (I have going-in-to-town clothes and makeup on, you know.)

Amber suggested, "How about Chinese?"

Anything not requiring boiling water sounded wonderful to me. "Sure."

We piled into Phyllis's silver minivan and were on our way to Peru to enjoy egg rolls and egg foo young. Pulling into the Chinese restaurant parking lot, we questioned the absence of vehicles. Upon closer inspection, we realized the building's interior was dark. Conclusion—this establishment was closed.

Phyllis asked Amber, "Now where?"

Amber gave us the options, "Mexican or Harvey Hinklemeyer's."

Given the opportunity to eat at a restaurant named Harvey Hinklemeyer's, what other choice is there? Who doesn't want to say they had dinner at Harvey Hinklemeyer's? We made the decision—we would eat at the restaurant with the fun name. Pulling out of the empty Chinese restaurant parking lot and onto the street, Phyllis drove the short distance to the restaurant of choice and parked in Harvey's full parking lot. The building wasn't fancy. Yellow, vertical siding covered the top three-fourths while stones adorned the bottom fourth. Humorous sayings hanging on the interior walls provided us with entertainment while we waited for our meals. The diverse menu included Italian and Mexican cuisine, pizza, and sandwiches. Not only were the entrées delicious, but also the dessert was fabulous. Yes, I had dessert—undehydrated. Actually, it wasn't cooked at all: I had lemon custard ice cream! (Have I mentioned I love ice cream?) If you ever visit Peru, Indiana, look up Harvey Hinklemeyer's. You won't be disappointed. Then you too can say you had dinner at Harvey Hinklemeyer's. (Harvey Hinklemeyer is just fun to say.)

Back in the vehicle, Phyllis asked if we needed to stop anywhere. During our planning, John had estimated how many propane fuel canisters we would need, but now he has decided we might be consuming them faster than anticipated. John asked if there was a Kmart or other business that might carry them. Kmart located, Phyllis pulled to a stop in the parking lot. John and I hurried into the store, combed the recreation department—no luck—returned to the vehicle, climbed in, and buckled our seatbelts all within five minutes. Since the fuel isn't an urgent need yet, we will try again in Logansport tomorrow.

Not long after returning to Amber's log house, Phyllis climbed back into her vehicle and returned to Fort Wayne. Just think, we will have passed through spring and part of summer before we connect in person again. One and a half seasons seems like a long time. However, in reality, with our busy schedules, more time than we like passes between our moments together—sometimes four months or more. Why, then, did watching her van become smaller and smaller, finally disappearing over the hill as she drove down the driveway feel so final? Maybe because we won't have the *option* of seeing each other, making the interval apart more dramatic.

Since John and I will return to the river again tomorrow, we chose to go to bed soon after Phyllis departed. Amber asked if I stayed warm last night. I replied, "Honestly, no." She disappeared for a moment and returned with a couple of blankets. As she handed them to me, I anticipated a warm night ahead, the first since April 4.

Right now, I am snuggled under Amber's blankets journaling and wondering if she would miss two blankets. Oh well, there probably isn't room for them in the kayaks anyway since John didn't think there was enough room for my small pillow.

Curled up under the blankets, all is right with the world after a "day of rest."

"Baa," says Bailey, the sheep.

04-15-2015

The Cheese Will Get Grated

Weather conditions:

High: 68

Low: 44

Skies: clear

Wind: ENE 10-25 mph, gusts to 32 mph

Today's mileage: 12 miles

Total mileage: 150 miles

Where we traveled: Peru, Indiana, to Logansport, Indiana

Boring breakfast prep today—no fire. (Sometimes boring is good.) The standard hum of the microwave (the microwave—a safer option than the stove?) filled the air as it zapped our water for our quinoa breakfast.

Kayaks packed, we said good-bye to Amber's animals: dogs—Toby (the sentry), Shelby (the hostess), Bonnie and Clyde (loud); cat—Lucky (slacker); sheep—Bailey (mad and wanted us to leave so Amber would untie him); cows and chickens—unnamed.

Toby wagged his tail as he chased *Pray* and *Work* while we sat in the back of Amber's van, holding onto the kayaks. On our way to the boat ramp, we executed a repeat performance of the towing portage from a couple of days ago. We launched our kayaks into a river that was much lower than it was a day and a half ago. The water levels on the Wabash can rise or lower drastically in a matter of hours. I still don't understand how a body of water that extends for miles can change so quickly.

Keep us upright and safe.

Paddling today, we noticed more banks consisted of rocks and limestone. We hope the addition of these hard minerals means less mud. Rock Island displays this transformation with its different colors of striations—visible from the river but not the road. The gray, brown, and tan levels of the layers demonstrate many years of development of the earth with green moss covering the lowest ridge. The latest phase of earth holds trees while their roots poke out from lower striations of dirt. Many of these trees will eventually be in the river as the dirt erodes from the top level across the layers below and into the river.

Other changes we have observed along the river represent not years of change but a yearly change. In the midst of the barren tree trunks and branches, green patches dot the view as leaves appear on early-budding trees. While the trees are preparing for spring, we still have not noticed any wild flowers brave enough to make an appearance in the fluctuating spring weather. I am becoming more comfortable with our routine and my paddling skills, providing me the opportunity to notice the changes both of terrain and of season. Watching as my river view changes creates anticipation. What transformations will I encounter each day?

Today we encountered our first boat, a blue kayak, which a gentleman was paddling to shore. I felt like a lonely dog roaming in the woods when it spots another dog on the path. I wanted to wag my tail, display the play stance, and bark, "Let's play." The other vessel was not long like *Work* and *Pray*; it was a shorter, recreational kayak. I assumed our potential playmate had gone out for a brief paddle as exercise. We watched as he pulled his kayak on shore and dragged it effortlessly to its place of storage. John was jealous of the light-weightedness (I don't think that is a word, but it works) of the man's water vessel. Because of the weight and length of *Work* and *Pray*, we struggle to move them anywhere when they are not in the water or on their wheels.

Even though we are experiencing less mud on the banks, today's search for an appealing place to exit our kayaks and eat lunch was not successful. We parked next to the mud shore, holding ourselves secure with one paddle blade stuck in the river bottom while we ate lunch in *Work* and *Pray*. Enjoying my peanut butter wrap, I spotted cement support pillars in the water downstream, remnants of an old bridge, the only sign there once was a connection between the opposite banks of the river. I began pondering. (Surprise, I know. But what else can you do when you are trapped in a kayak hour after hour after hour?) I thought about the road the bridge used to support. Why was the road no longer needed? What communities did the bridge connect? Who traveled on the lone direct path linking the populations? Today, a woman drinking coffee while sitting on her front porch could wave at a woman working in her garden on the other side of the river, but without the bridge to join the opposite banks, traveling to share a cup of coffee could be, at the very least, inconvenient. Why would homes no longer need a bridge to connect them? Who decided easy access was no longer necessary? Did heated discussions concerning the bridge's removal occur during several meetings? How does a bridge become, as John often quotes the Japanese, "kankeinai" (irrelevant)? So many questions, and no answers, evolving from seven cement pillars existing in the river.

Soon after passing under the non-existent bridge, I heard a gurgling noise. I've learned to equate noise with danger.

With a little panic in my voice, I asked John, "Is that bubbling water? I haven't heard that since the beginning of the trip. Seriously! Don't tell me there are rapids ahead. The river has been rising. The water must be too deep here for rapids." I know some people, John included, consider rapids fun. Maybe if I wasn't so worried about dumping and either losing or drenching everything I own, I might be able to enjoy the challenge.

Speaking of dumping. This has to be my biggest fear so far. When people question us about the fears of the trip, some have asked if I am afraid of shady people. No. Everyone we have encountered so far has been either someone we know or someone who has gone out of his or her way to help us. I can't imagine this view of people changing. Maybe I am naïve. Also, John makes sure we carry out necessary precautions—we have our bear spray. Speaking of bear spray. Others have asked if we are afraid of bears. Not yet. Ask me when we are on the Mississippi River. Snakes. I HATE snakes, but we use snake precautions by making a lot of noise when we climb out of the kayaks. We step on and then over rocks and logs for a better view. Most of the dangers people ask about are situations we can avoid by being smart and cautious. While I can be careful by preventing *Pray* from contacting dangers I can see while traveling down the river, there are unseen dangers barely below the surface—weird currents, downed trees, large boulders. Any one of these dangers could potentially cause me to land in the water before I know the enemies exist. Also, the repercussions of dumping are huge— possibly the end of our trip! John continues to emphasize, "If you tip, whatever you do, DON'T LET GO OF YOUR KAYAK." Although I know he is worried about me, I think he is more concerned about *Pray* and our food floating away from us down the river. At least for now, my biggest fear is dumping.

As we rounded the bend, the water was indeed low enough to bubble over the rocks (hence the gurgle), creating small rapids. We did learn later that even when the river levels are up, the water is often low in and around the Logansport area. I have a hard time wrapping my mind around this. How can the water level all of the sudden become so much lower? Where does all the water go? Whether the rapids being there made sense or not, they existed; and I didn't like the situation. Following the same protocol we established the first day of the trip, John paddled ahead to investigate while I held back, which is not always easy because the water seems to flow faster near rapids. John decided his plan of action and shouted, "Follow me." At that point, I watched his every move so I could determine if I wanted to follow him or explore my own route. Taking my own route would have meant he had encountered an undesirable result while executing his plan. In this case, I liked his course, so I followed.

Approaching Logansport via the river, we relished a view those entering Logansport from the road cannot see: the steeple of a white church peeking over the railroad bridge. To me, the steeple represents a place of peace and rest. I let out a contented sigh as I used my iPhone to snap a photo, probably one of our favorite pictures so far. I know I have stated this before, but one of my favorite aspects of traveling by kayak is appreciating the trip from a different point of view (my river view) than we would have traveling by car. Neither view is better; each view is unique and beautiful! However, only a few have witnessed the view I am living with every day. I never tire of my river view.

Landing at Logansport was both difficult and easy. We maneuvered through some difficult and scary (I mean fun) rapids prior to reaching a flat limestone ledge jutting from the bank. The Logansport waterfront provides easy access to the river for those on land with an elaborate concrete block lookout above and unique steps of different heights at the river's edge. These steps provide a place to fish or sit and enjoy the river. After landing on the hard and not muddy surface, we heard voices coming from the upper look out.

The standard conversation took place. "Where ya goin'?"

We glanced up. The heads of three college-age girls jutted above the lookout.

John answered, "Gulf of Mexico."

"No way!" They weren't easily convinced that our destination was the Gulf. I wonder what answer most people expect to hear.

Two other ladies taking a stroll during their lunch also yelled the same opening questions regarding our travel itinerary. However, they believed us more readily than the girls did. (I wonder why. Age?) They took pictures of us, which they later posted on our Facebook page. We appreciated the shared pictures because since there are "just the two of us" (Shouldn't that be a song? Oh yeah, it is…Thank you, Bill Withers.), pictures of John and me together are rare.

Work and *Pray* secured, John hiked to the post office to pick up our Week # 3 package and replacement parts from Klymit. This was the first food box we have picked up at a post office because the Wanners personally delivered our Week # 2 package to us at Huntington Reservoir, and our Week # 1 package left with us from Ft. Recovery. Luckily, the post office was only six blocks from the river. John had to show his ID to prove he was who he said he was and then carried our goodies back to the kayaks.

While John trekked through Logansport, I sat on a park bench enjoying the sun, writing in my journal, and watching people. When I observe people, I wonder about their lives. (John usually judges.) I make assumptions from the clothing they are wearing and the speed they are walking. A business attire and quick speed could indicate they may be late for a meeting. The same attire and slower pace leads me to believe they are enjoying the sun during their break. Power walking while wearing shorts, t-shirt, and athletic shoes could be a sign of someone trying to lose weight but not enamored with running. If they are sporting exercise garb and running, they may be training for a 5k. Most people greeted me with a, "Hi," as they passed by. I wondered what observation (judgment) they made of me as I sat on the bench dressed in my multi-colored wet suit with black knee reinforcements (which resemble knee patches), yellow coat, boots, sunglasses, and purple and gray baseball cap. What would I assume if I were to notice me sitting on the bench? Hmmm…

In the midst of my people watching, a guy probably in his late twenties, wearing a blue t-shirt and jeans, sat down beside me. I felt a little uncomfortable at his proximity to me for a few reasons. One, he sat too closely. Two, I couldn't judge his sincerity because his sunglasses hid his eyes. Three, his story about his girlfriend, work, and kids didn't sound logical.

(As a friend of ours says, "It didn't pass the smell test.") Four, he asked for a hug before he left. I declined. I made sure I mentioned John's impending return but didn't reveal that we hoped to camp nearby. I know I stressed earlier that I am not scared of sketchy people. I still stand by that statement. I didn't feel scared as he sat next to me, simply uncomfortable. We were in public and John would be back soon. I still believe dumping my kayak is the scariest. Again, maybe I am naïve and too trusting.

Not only did John pick up our food, but he also found a restroom. (Perfect civilization stops include water, trashcan, and a restroom.) He found one on the corner of Melbourne and 5th at Amelio's bar. John provided directions, and I left my place on the bench and headed to the bar. Entering the building, I waited for my eyes to adjust to the dark room before searching for a "Women's" sign. I located one on the back wall of the rear dining room and hustled towards it. Approaching the door, I read the hand written sign. "Closed" *Oh, no.* I remembered a door next to the bar with a "Men's" sign. At this point, I didn't care whose restroom I used. Thinking I should be polite, I asked the bartender if I could use the men's restroom. He affirmed, "No problem."

Upon exiting the restroom, I noticed a couple in the booth across the room. A partially eaten plate of fish and chips sitting in front of the woman and the gentleman signing the credit card receipt indicated they must have been sitting there when I entered a few minutes before. Apparently, focused on the location of the bathroom, I failed to notice their presence. Although they were dressed casually in jeans, the dismissive attitude of the woman led me to believe they were finishing a business lunch. My judgment was confirmed when the woman received a phone call, picked up her laptop, stepped to the vacant back room of the restaurant, and sat at a table. She was still there when I left.

The sixty-something gentleman ran his hands through his graying hair as he asked if I was a horse rider. I'm sure my outfit of boots and pants with knee patches gave him that impression. (I have thought people might think we are homeless, but a horse rider never entered my mind. I wish more people would ask questions, so I would have a better idea how others perceive us.) I told him the real reason for my attire. He asked the usual questions and then proceeded to tell me about himself, giving me a business card. I'm learning people are interested in our story for about a minute and then are ready to move on to a more interesting topic—themselves. Which is fine. I'd rather hear about them—I know my story.

Amelio's bar became our restroom stop and water fill-station for the day, thanks to "Nick the bartender." Nick reminded John of another "Nick the bartender" in *It's a Wonderful Life*. He quoted the movie all night. (*It's an Interesting Life* with John.)

Returning to the kayaks, I found John starring at the open box of food lying on the limestone beside *Pray*. "Where are we going to put all this food?" John asked.

The box of packaged, dehydrated, vacuum-packed food brought back memories. Had only a few weeks passed since I stood in my study with my blonde-haired, thirteen-year-old granddaughter, Haleigh, filling the numbered containers with essentials of survival? I remember stressing over the possibility of not having enough food. I am realizing I didn't need to worry. Even after sending some food home with Dawn Wanner at Huntington last week, the addition of today's package proved to be a problem since so many people have been kind enough to feed us "real" food.

I provided a solution to our dilemma, "Give me a couple of bags. I think I can stuff a couple in my front hatch." He tossed me a couple of "breakfasts," which I stuffed next to my hiking shoes. We proceeded to cram all the food in every available nook and cranny. (Where does that term come from?) A few bags even found their way next to my pillow. (See, there was room for food AND my pillow.)

As we packed our food in *Work* and *Pray,* clinking limestone and jingling keys alerted us to a sandy-haired man's arrival. The man put his phone in the pocket of his jeans and shook John's hand, "Hi, I'm Rich Brewer, the parks commissioner."

Apparently, while I was using the restroom, John called the parks department to receive permission to camp somewhere by the river. The parks department employee indicated someone would come to the river to help us.

"I'm John Abnet and this is my wife, LaNae."

Noting my reflection in his sunglasses (Did you ever notice how distorted sunglass reflections are?), I greeted Rich, "Glad to meet you." His handshake was firm and confident.

We discussed our trip a few minutes before Rich asked, "Is there anywhere I can take you or anything you need?"

John immediately thought of our propane needs, "Is there a Walmart close? I'd like to see if they have any fuel canisters."

Little did we know when we met Rich he was going to put out a wonderful welcome mat. He drove John to Walmart to buy a fuel canister. Unfortunately, they didn't have any. Since Rich had been so willing to drive John to Walmart, he felt obligated to buy something, so he bought another essential, toothpaste. Shopping trip complete, Rich provided John with a tour of Logansport. Logansport (Population 19,000—saaaaa-lute!) supports nineteen parks and houses one of three hand-carved Dentzel carousels. A special building houses the carousel. The sign on the railing surrounding the carousel indicates its significance.

LOGANSPORT CAROUSEL

HAS BEEN DESIGNATED A

NATIONAL

HISTORIC LANDMARK

THIS SITE POSSESSES NATIONAL SIGNIFICANCE

IN COMMEMORATING THE HISTORY OF THE UNTIED

STATES OF AMERICA

1987

NATIONAL PARK SERVICE

UNITED STATES DEPARTMENT OF THE INTERIOR

After John returned, he stayed with *Work* and *Pray* while Rich provided me with a similar tour. Instead of driving me to Walmart, he treated me to a sundae at an ice cream shop. (Have I mentioned my love for ice cream?)

Rich gave us permission to camp in the corner of the Little Turtle Park, a beautiful riverside park with a paved walking trail. Lumbering on the path to our campsite, we passed through an area with bricks bearing dedications to various important people. I read the bricks as I pulled my kayak.

IN MEMORY OF TONI JEFOSKI 1922-2013.
WE HAVE MET THE ENEMY AND HE IS US.
I MISS MY 700 LB WIFE.

What?! I put *Pray* down, unzipped my coat, and removed the iPhone from its waterproof holder. I can safely say I have never photographed a dedication brick, but I HAD to snap a picture of this one.

A large stone monument with a three-dimensional inlay of the Wabash River and its watershed bordered one side of the brick walkway. Admiring the work of art, I was speechless as I ran my hand along the depiction of the river I am becoming one with. The replica reminded me how much of Indiana the 503-mile long Wabash touches as it crosses the entire width of the state before turning south at mile 241 and eventually running along the Indiana-Illinois border its last 187 miles. My river.

Finding our spot in the corner of the park, we set up our home for the night. As I was arranging our bedding, the tent began spinning. "John, I don't feel well."

Concerned, John asked, "What's wrong?"

"I don't know. I just feel odd."

"I'll finish up out here. You lie down."

I didn't argue. I was surprised how quickly I fell asleep because I hate taking naps: I don't want to miss anything while I am asleep. I woke up to an unfamiliar male voice outside the tent.

The unfamiliar voice asked, "How long do you expect the trip to last?"

John answered, "Four months."

"How do you plan to get home?"

"My brother and his wife are driving our truck to pick us up."

I soon realized the unfamiliar voice was interviewing John. After the reporter left, John filled me in on what I had slept through. "The reporter was Mitchel Kirk from the *Pharos Tribune*. Rich called him. A photographer is coming tomorrow to shoot a picture or two."

Since I felt better after my nap, I ate a little of the leftovers John had saved for me.

After dinner, we received a phone call from another reporter, Emma Rausch, who reports for *The Wabash County Paper*. She had learned today that we had stayed in Wabash a couple of days ago but still wanted to do an interview. Therefore, she drove 37 minutes to interview us. *Are we that big of a deal? We haven't done anything yet.*

Emma's red hair bounced as she bobbed up to our campsite. From her casual dress of jeans and purple Adidas shoes, we could tell she wasn't the typical reporter. (Actually, we weren't sure she was a reporter until she introduced herself to us.). She unzipped her olive green jacket as she sat on one of our two Grand Trunk collapsible stools. Her smile was contagious as she pulled something other than a camera from her brown camera bag, "I brought you something just like my grandma would have." She handed me a bag of sliced apples and a container of caramel. Even though I hadn't felt well an hour before, my mouth watered. She instantly became our favorite reporter.

Emma asked us if she could do anything for us. Since John's trip to Walmart earlier wasn't successful, we asked if she could drive me to Rural

King in search of the propane canister. (John felt he should stay with *Work* and *Pray*.)

My trip with Emma was as unfruitful as John's was to Walmart. However, unlike John, I didn't feel obligated to buy toothpaste. Even though the trip to Rural King was not successful in the sense of purchasing a propane canister, it was successful—I made a new friend.

At the completion of a social day, we climbed into the tent, ready for a peaceful night's sleep. Wrong! This little corner of Little Turtle Park is the loudest campsite yet. Two train tracks, each about 50 yards away, intersect merely a block from the park. However, after first hearing a train in Bluffton and traveling close to the tracks ever since, sounds of the train have become familiar and comforting. In between the horns blasting and tracks rumbling, another comforting sound pacifies our ears, not the baaing of Bailey the sheep, but the soothing sound of the river splashing outside our door. Home!

04-16-2015

Did You WANT a Bag

Weather conditions:

High: 60

Low: 44

Skies: light rain in the morning with overcast skies in the afternoon

Wind: SSE 9-15 mph, gusts to 20 mph

Today's mileage: 15 miles

Total mileage: 165 miles

Where we traveled: Logansport, Indiana, to French Post Park Lockport, Indiana

"I have to pee! I wish we were still in the wilderness." I can't believe I uttered those words. If someone had asked me before the trip which I would prefer, civilization or wilderness, I would have declared "civilization" because I assumed restroom options would be more accessible there. Again, a preconceived notion is often incorrect. Actuality is only accurate after obtaining experience. (That sounds impressive, maybe even quotable.) In the wilderness, I can pee anywhere, anytime. In civilization, peeing anywhere, anytime is frowned upon. Designated peeing stations were created to prevent this social faux pas. Yesterday, Amilio's was my designated peeing station. Sadly, this morning when I woke up, Amilio's was not yet open. (It's a bar after all.) Translated into how this affects me? My designated peeing station was closed. Yikes! John left in search of another available restroom.

Upon his return, John asked, "Hey, where did these come from?"

"Where did what come from?" I unzipped the tent and poked my head out. John held an apple, a container of caramel, and a canister of fuel. "Are you sure they weren't sitting there when you left? I didn't hear anyone."

"I bet Emma snuck up and placed them on my kayak while I was gone." She secured her position as our favorite reporter.

John grinned and pointed to his cheek, "You can kiss me right here."

I scrambled out of the tent. I know when John asks for a kiss on his cheek he is wanting recognition for something he did that he thinks is hero-worthy. "Did you find a restroom for me?' He nodded, giving me a shy expression of feigned modesty. I stood on my tiptoes and kissed his cheek. Then, to boost his ego more I cooed, "My hero."

"It's at a car dealership a few blocks away. It's easy to find." He pointed. "Walk down the street and past the old train station. Then, cross at the light. Walk through the parking lot to the car dealership. You'll see a big door. You can't miss it. Once you're in the building, you'll see Tom and Dan sitting at their desks. Walk to the end of the showroom. The restroom is on your left." *Seriously! He thinks that is supposed to be easy to find?! He lost me at "Walk through the parking lot."*

I followed John's direction to a tee. (What does "to a tee" mean? Where does that saying come from?) Everything was exactly as he said, except Tom and Dan were NOT at their desks. Regardless, I enjoyed a warm restroom. I took my time peeing, tugging and pulling on my un-zipped wet suit, washing my face, fixing my ponytail, and brushing my teeth. I didn't want to leave the warmth of the building. I contemplated putting on some make-up while I had access to a mirror but decided against the extra vanity since we were leaving civilization. Having completed my car dealership "to do" list, I strolled back to the campsite.

Approaching our corner of Little Turtle Park, I noticed John talking to a red-haired, Irish-looking gentleman with a camera around his neck. When I reached the campsite, John introduced me to our visitor, "Babe, this is Kyle Keener from the *Pharos*. He's here to photograph us for Tuesday's paper."

I reached out to shake the photographer's hand. He had a light complexion with many freckles. "Nice to meet you, Kyle."

Any doubts of his nationality were squelched when he returned the niceties expected when shaking the hand of a new acquaintance. "Nice to meet you, LaNae," he greeted with an Irish brogue that could only come from The Emerald Isle. Talking with Kyle, we learned he has quite the resume. He worked as a photographer for *Detroit Free Press* and a Philadelphia paper. Even more impressive was his coverage of Mandela's release and the genocide in Rwanda. I wonder how he ended up in Small Town, Indiana. Kyle surprised John and me when he told us he was planning an entire photo shoot, not the picture or two we were expecting. He shot us performing all our morning tasks from different angles: eating breakfast, tearing down camp, packing *Work* and *Pray*, rolling them to the river, and maneuvering them down a steep rocky slope. A yellow plastic scraping left behind on a sharp rock from the bottom of *Work* is a reminder of how difficult transporting the kayaks across the large jagged rocks is. Don't worry; our heavy roto-mold polyethylene choice of kayak material can withstand a little scraping. This is one reason we decided not to go with the lighter, composite boats. If we had chosen that material, the injury may have required a Band-Aid. Once the kayaks were resting by the river, Kyle continued taking pictures of us removing wheels, re-packing *Work* and *Pray*, launching, and paddling downstream.

Keep us upright and safe.

And the photo shoot continued. Periodically we caught glimpses of Kyle or his car on the banks as he followed us downstream adding action shots to the photo gallery he plans to post on-line in the next few days.

For the first few miles on the river, we encountered many shallows (rapids) again today. This is stressful to me—John enjoys the challenge. I expected the rapids prior to Markle but not this far downstream. Before yesterday, I can't remember the last time I heard John say, "Follow me." Interesting, how something can disappear from your life without you even realizing it's gone. Fortunately, about half a mile after leaving Logansport, the North Eel River pours into the Wabash, causing the river levels to increase and the rapids to disappear. A disappearance I was aware of and thankful for.

The water levels aren't the only things changing: the foliage is becoming lusher, the soil sandier. In addition, the river flows around more islands. John's distinction between an island and a sandbar is an island contains a tree. After John told me his definition, I asked, "If an island has only one tree on it and the tree dies, does the island become a sand bar?" He didn't have an answer. (John without an answer?—Amazing!) Although through research, I discovered islands exist in the Mississippi, I didn't realize there are islands in the Wabash. Another example of the education my river view is providing!

Our wildlife spotting from our river view today consisted of our first Cormorant of this trip and a pair of Pileated Woodpeckers. John and I reminisced about another Cormorant encounter we had experienced on our way home from the Arctic Ocean near Inuvik, Northwest Territories, a few years ago. We had decided to spend a few days at a campground on a small lake in Nebraska. Kayaking in the lake one day, we observed a tree with dozens of black birds, wings outstretched in a drying position—a perfect picture for a Halloween poster. Before we could investigate, they flew away. (Question: What's more eerie than an assembly of black birds in a tree? Answer: An assembly of those same black winged creatures flying over your head.) We were, however, able to snap pictures for identification. With the modern technology of a digital camera, we didn't have to wait several weeks to have the pictures developed. Pulling up the pictures on our camera when we returned to our tent, we searched in a bird book and identified the birds as Cormorants. Now, every time I recognize a Cormorant, I fondly remember the campground in Nebraska and our Arctic Ocean trip. Several years from now, what will spark fond memories of this trip?

• • •

We spend most of our days in silence. A comfortable silence that comes with familiarity. We've all experienced the opposite, uncomfortable kind. You know, when you sit beside an acquaintance and the silence becomes loud. When the only way to quiet the silence is to say something. When the something you finally say is forced and usually makes no sense at all, and then you want to grab your words and stuff them back in your mouth. When you ask something like, "What uh, shoe size do you wear?" After which you turn red and say to yourself, *I can't believe those words just came out of my mouth. You dummy*!

John broke one of our comfortable silences when he asked, "Hey, did your sleep pad hold its air last night?"

I tried to remember. "I think it did. I don't think I woke up on the ground."

This started a deeper conversation. It seems we either paddle in silence or engage in deep conversation. (Or sing, or John does an impersonation—or I wish he were silent.) I commented, "I was aware of when the pad didn't work but not when it did. We take so many details for granted."

John paddled in silence, a sign of serious thought. I've learned to equate a pause in the conversation with an indication he is thinking. No pause means he is bloviating. (Cool word, huh?) He concurred, "I agree. I think we can apply this logic to many areas of our lives, not just things."

I jumped in, "Yeah. We are aware of absences more than presences. We take a person for granted until they are gone. Then it is too late."

John thought a moment longer, "Kinda like a chair. You don't pay any attention to it until you go to sit on it, and it's not there."

"But then again, sometimes things disappear from your life before you even realize they aren't there. Like the rapids or the wind. They are there, and then they aren't, but you can't pinpoint when they disappeared."

And the conversation continued until we couldn't remember how it started.

• • •

John, our chief camp spot locator, found a campground tonight along the river; a historical French fur trading post, French Post Park. Landing and exiting *Work* and *Pray* at the boat ramp, we started our investigation of the premises by lumbering up the hill. (Have I mentioned everything is uphill from the river?) A pavilion, port-a-pot, and teepee awaited us at the top. *Why wouldn't a French fur trading post have a Teepee?* Guess which of the three I visited immediately.

After emptying my bladder in the Teepee (kidding!), I joined John in the green-roofed pavilion, which was open on three sides. Outlets on the white posts and lights in the ceiling made me smile. "Maybe we can charge our IT devices," I suggested. John tried the lights—nothing. A water pump outside the pavilion caused a hesitant smile. "What are the odds the water is on?" John pulled the handle—nothing. At least the port-a-pot was open.

Excitement about the potential IT charging and water filling dashed to the ground, we trudged towards a wooded area on the other side of the stone parking lot. "Do I see fire rings? Is that a camping area?" I could almost feel the fire warming my feet.

We spotted a gate. "Surely, the gate isn't locked?" I questioned. Then I caught sight of the chains and padlock. Sarcasm oozed as I quipped, "Of course, it's locked. Why wouldn't it be?" The elation I felt when we first arrived slid one step at a time to discouragement.

Glancing above the gate, we detected a sign nailed to a tree. "Call ...... for camping." John called the number and spoke with the caretaker. He said he would drive over.

A few minutes later, a white van with "Buttice & Sons Produce" painted in green on the side pulled in the driveway. The driver's door opened; a man in his late fifties wearing jeans and a gray t-shirt jumped out. While the driver's gray hair was thinning, his beard of the same color was thick. He held a pink spiral-bound receipt book in his left hand as he offered his right hand to John, "Hi. I'm Al Buttice,"

Shaking his hand, John replied, "I'm John Abnet and this is my wife, LaNae."

Al took care of business right away. "The fee is $10."

John slid his waterproof money pouch off his left arm, removed a ten-dollar bill, and handed it to Al. Although this is the first time we have paid for a place to lay our heads this trip, a ten-spot is a small price to pay for a place to sit and pee.

Al filled out our receipt, explaining, "My wife usually takes care of this, but she wasn't home. Let's see… What was your name again? I think this is right." He continued talking as he filled out the rest of the receipt. "You're lucky you didn't come last week. I had the port-a-pot delivered yesterday. I will turn on the water and electricity for you." He tore off the white original receipt from atop the pink copy and handed it to us. "See that fire wood over there? You're welcome to it." The thought of a campfire brought the smile back to my face.

Talking with Al, we came to realize what a small world we live in. Al lives near here on Indiana SR 218, which runs one and a half miles from our home. He also buys seeds for his produce business at ER, a seed store outside Monroe, Indiana, where I buy seeds. In addition, he transports antique trucks to the Tractor and Engine Show in Portland, Indiana, only 30 minutes southwest of our house. Since we have traveled on the river two weeks and paddled 165 miles, I sometimes forget we are still in Indiana and only about two hours from home by car.

Al left us to set up our campsite and eat one of our favorite dinners: southwestern lasagna and strawberry shortcake. After dinner, we called Cyndy Evers, our Food Cache Coordinator, to arrange delivery of our Week #4 package to Covington, Indiana. Before sending our parcel, we asked her to remove some food. Each box contains a week's worth of food—all *Work* and *Pray* have space for. Since many people have offered us meals, we have stuffed dehydrated food packages everywhere—even by my pillow. We won't arrive in Covington for six more days, but that will not provide us enough time to consume enough food to create adequate space in our storage hatches for our next cache. However, we assume since we are traveling farther from our friends and family each day, not as many people will be feeding us, and Cyndy will no longer need to remove food from the parcels. So many details to manage.

We used the electricity in the pavilion; and since the campground was vacant, we left John's iPad and the Sherpa plugged in all night. Our Sherpa works great to power our iPads and phone as long as the sun shines enough to charge the solar charging-panel. Before the trip, we thought the Sherpa would allow us to be self-sufficient. Now we're beginning to wonder.

Oh, I just remembered. We encountered our first powered watercraft today. A fishing boat launched at the French Post Park boat ramp. I thought we would have happened upon more watercraft by now. Maybe April is too early in the season.

Now as I write, I hear the crackle, smell the smoke, and feel the heat of the fire—what a treat! The only luxury missing is a stick with a marshmallow roasting over the hot coals. I love roasted marshmallows. The perfect marshmallow has a crunchy, golden exterior and a white, warm, gooey center. Having roasted the outer layer to perfection, I pull it off and eat it. Then, I roast the gooey center until it is crisp. I pull the new crispy outer layer off and eat it. I continue the process until there isn't enough gooey center left to roast. Sometimes this process can take up to five minutes. John catches his marshmallow on fire, waits till the fire is out and his marshmallow is totally charred, and then eats it. He is so impatient.

Believe me, even without the marshmallow, the fire warms my body on this chilly night. Soon I will move my toasty body to the tent, slip into my sleeping bag, and cool down quickly. When will I sleep without shivering?

P.S. Tomorrow morning my designated peeing station won't be closed.

04-17-2015

Whoever's Snoring, Mute Up

Weather conditions:

High: 75

Low: 46

Skies: fog in the morning becoming clear

Wind: W 2-9 mph, gusts to 12 mph

Today's mileage: 20 miles

Total mileage: 185 miles

Where we traveled: French Post Park Lockport, Indiana, to Americus, Indiana

"The Wabash River in the area of French Post Park is under a two-hour FOG DELAY!" I loved hearing the words *fog delay* when I was in school. However, hearing Mom yell, "There's a two-hour fog delay" up the stairs didn't create as much excitement if I was already up and ready. What a waste! I couldn't go back to bed to gain some extra sleep. That would mess up my hair—heaven forbid!

Today, we awoke to the sound of drip, drip, drip on the tent. "Is that rain? Was rain in the forecast?" I unzipped my side of the tent and peeked out from under the rain fly. The dripping wasn't a result of rain. Instead, the ground-hugging clouds created pea-soup-like fog. The leaking sky had soaked the tent, our boats, and all gear attached to the outside of *Work* and

Pray. Unlike school days, we didn't even consider going back to bed since preparing to launch requires three hours.

We performed our regular morning routine; eating a taco macaroni and cheese dinner for breakfast (okay, that isn't regular), packing up all our belongings, and rolling *Work* and *Pray* to the ramp. Standing by the river this morning provided an interesting view. "Where is the other side of the river? And where's the bridge? I could have sworn we paddled under a bridge a few yards upstream yesterday." The brown trees silhouetted against the white-grey fog-generated background created eerie, false surroundings. The green patched earth with sprigs of weeds appeared to end at the bank's edge, where our current world ceased to exist. Conditions such as these would warrant a school closing but not a river closing, only an indefinite delay. While waiting for the fog to lift, we sat on a bench facing a river we could not see, delighting in our last Snickers bar. I guess if you can't sleep during a fog delay, eating a Snickers bar is the next best thing. Satisfying!

Once the other bank and the bridge were visible, John lifted the fog delay, and we launched *Work* and *Pray*.

Keep us upright and safe.

Nature sightings today included two Bald Eagles close to their nests and two heron rookeries—small and large. From our river view, we are becoming more familiar with the eagles' and herons' nesting habits. We have learned that as soon as we spot a Bald Eagle's nest, we should watch for eagles; they are usually close. Conversely, if we glimpse an eagle, we search for a nest. Likewise, when we recognize several wiry nests in the crooks of sycamore trees as heron rookeries (maternity wards), we scan the treetops and banks for herons.

During a calm, straight section in the river, I stopped paddling, allowing *Pray* to drift while I adored nature's beauty. Three trees in danger of losing their grip from their eroding perch formed a 45-degree angle with the waterway. The banks' mirrored images grew closer and closer together, joining in the distance. In between the merging banks, the reflection of the sparse, fluffy clouds created a second sky in the water, which I slowly and easily broke through. These are images not enjoyed on a brief drive-over while crossing the river via a bridge. I am blessed to experience my river view.

John and I emphasize communication as an important aspect of safety when traveling with two or more people. (I have a hunch John communicates even when he is alone.) Kayaking is not the only non-motorized form of trips John and I have taken with each other. We have traveled by pedaling bicycles together. Our day trips have been as short as ten miles and as long as seventy-five. During even the shortest trips, we have certain danger signals to alert others riding behind us of the hazards ahead. Since we have also encountered risks on the river, we, likewise, have developed some danger-alert signals. "Danger right." "Danger left." "Follow me." "Hold back." "Come ahead." Today, since we have begun encountering motorized boats on the river, we discussed the need for additional calls, "Boat up," or "Boat back." I wonder how many other dangers we will encounter, requiring additions to our alert signals.

Communication strategies aren't only important when relaying dangers, they are also necessary when sharing the location of something. Out of necessity, we created the "time-degree system." Oh, it's not like we invented it. Navigators long before us have communicated similarly. We simply adjusted it to meet our needs. For example, if one of us sees an eagle flying directly ahead of us (12 o'clock) and its approximately 30 degrees above the horizon, he or she would yell out "eagle, twelve o'clock thirty." Now, hopefully, the recipient of the information can quickly locate it. Likewise, if someone detects a deer directly to his or her right (3 o'clock) standing along the water's edge, he or she would simply yell out "deer, three o'clock zero." Simple!

. . .

The days can become long when the river is calm. John and I can find only so much to talk about so we have been creative in finding ways to pass the time. One way is to sing. Too bad our repertoire is so limited. We know the first one or two lines of quite a few songs but knowing an entire song is rare. One song we do know in its entirety is "Do Wah Diddy" as sung by Manfred Mann. John sings the main portion while I sing the "Do wah diddy diddy dum diddy do's" and echoes of the chorus. The song has become a welcome friend and a permanent part of the trip, singing it at least once every day. After the trip, I don't think I will be able to hear the song without smiling and tearing up at the same time. I love the memories John and I are creating together. Memories we will never share with anyone else. Memories that define us as a couple—John and LaNae memories.

Today was a long, hot twenty-mile paddle. Hot is a relative term compared to what we expect to experience on the lower Mississippi. We decided to ditch our coats when we got too warm under our layers of long johns, shirt, coat, and life jacket. To perform this stripping, we headed towards the bank. The steep and muddy potential landing spot made emerging from *Work* and *Pray* implausible. A place to pull to the side of the river chosen, we shoved our paddles vertically into the sandy mud to keep us from drifting away from the shore. Being out of the boats to divest ourselves of our coats would have been an easier task. Just in case you ever need to remove your coat while floating offshore in a kayak, here are the steps…

1. Unzip life jacket and remove it. (Remember, one arm is wrapped around the paddle this entire time.)
2. Place life jacket securely on lap.
3. Remove coat. This step is much more difficult than the removal of the life jacket since the sleeves are long and maneuvering in a

kayak with its limited space is challenging. (Did I mention one arm is wrapped around the paddle this entire time?) Another consideration while removing the coat is attempting to keep any part of it from making contact with the water.

4. Stow coat securely between legs. The resulting bulk creates an uncomfortable situation.
5. Move life jacket from lap to body, carefully slipping arms into holes. (Remember to maintain hold on the paddle.)
6. Zip life jacket.
7. Enjoy coolness that is worth the effort.

As I mentioned, we traveled twenty miles today. Twenty miles! We have paddled over twenty miles only one other time on this trip—twenty-three from Wabash, Indiana, to Peru, Indiana. However, the thought of setting up camp, fixing a meal, or doing anything else today seemed like huge tasks— more than any other day. Maybe due to a temperature of seventy degrees?

Most days John doesn't have a camping spot picked out when we launch in the morning. Today, however, thanks to *Wabash River Guidebook* by Jerry Hay, John was aware of Wolfe's Leisure Time Campground in Americus, Indiana. Our arrival was well timed since the campground opened yesterday for the year. God is preparing a way—port-a-pot yesterday and a campground today.

We selected our campsite behind a "No Camping in this Area" sign. Hiking up the hill (Have I mentioned everything is uphill from the river?) to the campground office, my wet suit felt like it was made of four-inch thick rubber. I was uncomfortable. I was hot and had to pee. Although anxious to find a restroom, I was NOT looking forward to peeling the rubber off my body and then, once my bladder was empty, trying to pull it back up over my hot, sweaty frame.

After I finally unpeeled, peed, and pulled, we hunted for and located the registration office. A plastic sheet hung from the ceiling on one end of the room, separating a construction area from the rest of the room. Thirty-something Candy bounced in from the kitchen. Her long curly hair partially covered the howling wolf symbol of the campground on the left breast of her white sweatshirt. We explained we were traveling by kayak and would like to camp in the "No Camping" area by the river. She asked the expected question, "Where are you traveling to?"

John answered, "Gulf of Mexico."

She responded with the usual, "Really?" then added, "Will you be stopping in New Orleans?"

"Yes, we will."

She beamed, "I love New Orleans!"

"We have never been to New Orleans."

"You will love it!" She proceeded to give us tourist tips. Since I didn't have anything to write the tips on and didn't have a clue how long we would be there or where in New Orleans we would be, I pretty much forgot most of what she said.

Revisiting the camping subject, John peered at the campground map on the wall, pointed to the site we had picked out, and asked Candy, "Can we camp in this spot?"

"Sure."

After we registered and paid the nightly site-rental fee, she gave her campground-information speech. "The restrooms and showers are on the far side of the building with a guest laundry in the middle. Also, this evening, come to the recreation room for free hot chocolate and homemade cookies to celebrate the beginning of this year's camping season." Usually, I would have focused on the cookies and hot chocolate, but my ears quit listening at the mention of a shower and laundry. A shower AND laundry? Are you kidding? I was in heaven. After a long, hot, exhausting paddle, I could almost feel the perspiration sliding from my body and disappearing down the drain.

Deciding we were hungrier than we were dirty (Candy may have had a different opinion), we ate dinner back at the campsite before taking a shower and doing laundry. Tonight's feast consisted of lazy lasagna with dehydrated garlic bread croutons made from homemade bread, finished off with pineapple upside down cake.

During my investigation of dehydration, I found two ways to dehydrate food. One is to make the meal and dehydrate the finished product. This method is a great way to use leftovers and provides the opportunity to taste the entrée before the trip. The other method is to dehydrate all the ingredients separately and combine them before vacuum sealing. The disadvantage of dehydrating and then combining the meal is our first opportunity to taste it is on the trip. If we dislike the entrée, we still have to eat it again later when another bag of it appears in another food box. Tonight's dehydrated leftover meal is one of John's favorite meals.

Speaking of meals, I have realized I didn't calculate the calories provided by each meal. Oh, don't get me wrong, the planning was meticulous in regards to the contents, serving size, preservation, and preparation of the required 720 meals. But what about caloric intake vs expenditure? Would our meals suffice?

Hunger satisfied, we strolled to the white building at the top to the hill to give some attention to our dirty bodies and clothes.

Showered! What a great feeling—clean and fresh. I don't think we realize how offensive we smell—gamey has become the norm—until after we shower. Smelly bodies cleansed, we washed our smelly clothes.

While our laundry is drying, John is savoring a fresh homemade cookie and I am journaling on a bench outside the laundry room. Notice, I am not eating a cookie—I already had a dessert. What self-control!

We will sleep well and refreshed tonight—and smell better too! I wonder if we will have a fog delay again tomorrow.

04-18-2015

I Don't Need No Fancy Lawn Chair

Weather conditions:

High: 77

Low: 47

Skies: clear

Wind: E 3-15 mph, gusts to 19 mph

Today's mileage: 15 miles

Total mileage: 200 miles Yahoo! (only 1391 more to go)

Where we traveled: Americus, Indiana, to Lafayette, Indiana

I love living without a schedule! I could get used to this! We relaxed this morning, putting off our paddling until 10:45. Really? 10:45? I felt guilty. Almost. No really. Other mornings we have traveled ten miles down the river by 10:45. However, we didn't rush this morning because we knew our paddle today was a short one, only 12 miles to Lafayette, Indiana. After 20 and 23 mile paddle-days, 12 miles is a breeze. It's all relative.

We ate dinner for breakfast again today—black bean stew. The serving sizes on "The Backpack Gourmet" website are generous: sometimes eating the entire portion is difficult. I know John is almost full when he picks up his lid (his plate) and starts pacing around while continuing to eat. I remember the first time he did this; thinking he had lost his mind, I asked, "Umm... What are you doing?"

He answered matter-of-factly, "I'm making more room." I don't know if changing position really helps; but when he does this, he is able to finish everything on his lid. He doesn't want to waste any calories; he will need those later.

Stuffed, we completed our morning chores, preparing to leave. Departing from each campsite is bittersweet as we leave the comfort of home every morning and travel to another home, which then becomes comfortable. As a result, we spend the majority of our day in transition. Pulling *Pray* from our previous night's residence, I glanced over my shoulder. The only indication we had lived in this place was the matted grass where our tent had stood—our footprint. Our camping philosophy is to leave only our footprint behind. We purposefully vacate a campsite the same as, or better than, we found it by picking up and discarding at least one piece of someone else's trash. Again this morning, we pulled away from our home and proceeded to the boat ramp on our way to our next home.

Before launching *Work* and *Pray*, we discussed charging the Sherpa since we will be in civilization the next couple of days and should have access to electricity. Deciding there are never any certainties and preparing for the worst-case scenario, John attached the Sherpa solar panel to the top of *Pray* to catch some rays and charge the Sherpa, which he secured in my cockpit 8-track tape deck style. (Some of you are old enough to remember the not-so-smooth transition from track to track in the middle of a song.)

Keep us upright and safe.

Twelve miles. Lafayette, here we come!

Since we have set tomorrow, Sunday, as a day of rest, I was looking forward to arriving in Lafayette, a college town with the potential for a coffeehouse. I love the smell of coffee and the relaxed atmosphere of cafés. We could spend, and have spent, hours in such establishments reading, using the Internet, and, of course, drinking coffee. In fact, a couple of years ago, John and I flew to Seattle for a week with the sole purpose of relaxing and reading in as many coffeehouses as possible. One rule—privately owned shops only, no chain stores. Reading *Wicked* at the time, I asked a barista in each shop to sign the inside cover, creating a record of every java shop we frequented.

Being in civilization on a Sunday also presented the possibility of attending church. Hoping we could find someone to drive us to church, John had sent out a Tweet requesting a ride and had received several offers. Although we have not attended church since before our trip, while on the river, I have sensed God's presence in a special way. In nature, I experience God in a manner not clouded by outside interruptions. Even though I can see evidence of my Creator everywhere on the river, from the antics of the animals to the changing of the seasons, I miss the music and atmosphere found in a church.

In addition to offers for rides to church, we had another exciting offer—lunch. Don't get me wrong, our dehydrated food gratifies our hunger and tastes satisfactory, but it doesn't compare to freshly prepared food. Especially if I don't have to cook or do dishes.

As we were singing the last note of our daily rendition of "Do Wah Diddy," we noticed the sun glimmering off a silver aluminum canoe, carrying two boys and a man paddling upstream, coming towards us. (I was concerned they heard us sing—we're not very good.) Until today, we haven't had to share the river or maneuver around other boats. Therefore, we weren't only surprised to encounter another craft, but we were also surprised to see them paddling upstream and coming right at us.

Becoming more nervous the closer they came to us, I asked John, "Are they going to hit us? Which way should I paddle?" I'm not sure why I asked, I knew John's answer. Repeatedly, he has stated that one of the rules of the road (water) for watercraft is to steer right.

John answered, "Paddle right." (I knew it!) We paddled right—so did they. We paddled left—so did they. Apparently, they didn't know the rules.

The thirty-something man in the canoe yelled, "John!" What a surprise! *Did we hear him correctly? Who knows we are here? We don't know anyone in the area.*

After closing a few more yards, we could distinguish the occupants of the canoe, *Happyhooker II*. John exclaimed, "Hey, Kit!" His response convinced me he knew the guy. "How are you? What a surprise!" OK, so he DID know them. However, I still didn't know their identities.

"LaNae, this is Kit Minnich, the son of Dan Minnich." John worked with Kit's dad several years ago. Kit then introduced us to his sons, Kayden and Kolton, who were probably both under 10.

This meeting was not as unplanned as we first thought. Kit had contacted us earlier in our trip through our website stating if we needed anything while in Lafayette, he would love to help us out. Through additional correspondence, we learned he would be out-of-town at his dad's home when we traveled in the area. Imagine our surprise to bump into him on the river.

"From your website, we calculated when you would pass through this area. We knew we would have a little time to put in and paddle with you for a while before traveling to Dad's." ("Dad's" just happens to be about ten miles from our house.) They paddled with us as we talked, the boys periodically snapping pictures, until we came to the spot where they had put in and their car awaited them. Exchanging good-byes, we floated passed their slowing canoe, continuing on our way.

The day progressed uneventfully until a fish swam to the surface next to John, studied him, blew bubbles, and then swam back down. John shared his version of the series of events that followed the fish's disappearance...

"The fish swam back to his school and bragged, 'You'll never guess what I did.' The other fish swam closer so they wouldn't miss a word. 'I swam to the surface.'

Mortified, the other fish declared, 'Say it isn't so! What did you see?'

'Oh, it was no big deal. I saw a man in a yellow kayak and swam right up next to him.'

The other fish thought he was so brave since they would have swum away as soon as they saw a yellow object floating in the river. The fish continued, 'When I swam next to the kayak, I made eye contact with the human and then I...' He paused in order to add emphasis to what he was about to tell them. He liked being the center of attention and knew the others were impressed. He continued, 'I bubbled him.' The other fish gasped..."

If John finished his story, I didn't hear him. I laughed so hard. My life with John for four months!

I was still giggling at John's "fishy encounter" when we approached our first option for camping—a boat ramp close to the road with little grass. *Work* and *Pray* secured on the bank next to the boat ramp, we surveyed the area. John investigated the back of a brick building. (In other words, he took a leak.) The building appeared to be a city building—maybe part of the water treatment system. I am jealous of John's ability to "investigate" just about anywhere. Again, the wilderness is more convenient than civilization. Noting all the commercial and residential *busyness*, John declared, "Let's keep going."

Back in *Work* and *Pray*, we paddled and approached our second option—a beach with a small boat ramp. Unfortunately, the beach was close to the downtown area with a lot of activity. I don't know what we were thinking. Why would the city allow camping in the midst of a downtown area? Sadly, John declared again, "Let's keep going."

We kept paddling. Each stroke moved us farther from civilization and all chances of enjoying a coffeehouse, attending church, or sharing a non-dehydrated meal. I was disappointed but kept reminding myself, *This is the trip.*

We approached our third option—a beautiful, sandy island. Yes, even though we are still in Indiana, sand is replacing mud on the banks. John uttered some welcome words, "We're staying here." Home for two days! The island gave the impression of perfection—a beach to easily exit the river, shade trees to hang a clothesline and provide shade from the late afternoon sun, and higher ground to protect us from the rising water level of the river.

But I was sad. Unfortunately, staying on an island, even if it is beautiful, prevents access to the road and a relaxing afternoon enjoying a cup of joe, attending church, or eating a freshly made lunch.

Soon after placing my feet on land, I started sweating. How can the air temperature change so much once we are on shore? I know it doesn't really change, but the air feels either warmer or cooler than on the water. Today, the air became warmer. Much warmer. My wet suit and blue and yellow plaid button-up shirt added two too many layers so I peeled them off. My neon yellow-green short-sleeved shirt allowed the soft breeze to cool my exposed arms. To cover my bottom half, I put on my black Under Armour pants and a black skort. I replaced my (or should I say John's) heavy, green wide-brimmed hat with my cute purple, girlie baseball cap. Even if no one was around, feeling girlie lifted my spirits.

While setting up camp, we realized the island wasn't as quiet as we first thought. Airport traffic, a factory, and a train interrupted the peaceful bliss we "observed" from the river. Although the train replaced the bliss with noise, the train's clickety-clack on the tracks and "waank" of the horn generated feelings of home because we have continued traveling close to trains since Bluffton, Indiana.

And now—we have neighbors. Yes, neighbors. We first noticed a van parked on the bank. No big deal. Then, the van's inhabitants climbed over the fallen-tree-bridge, setting up camp at the other end of the island. Fortunately, when sitting at our campsite, we can't see them and wouldn't know they existed if we hadn't witnessed them arriving. The best kind of neighbors, right?

Since we are staying here a couple of days and have neighbors, we realized the necessity of establishing a pee corner for privacy. Two downed trees forming a "V" protected us from the view of people on three sides. Another downed tree perpendicular to the other two provided a shield on the fourth side. A pee corner—I almost feel civilized.

After a black bean stroganoff dinner and one of John's favorite desserts, chocolate pudding with homemade granola, known as mud pie, we are now relaxing. I am looking forward to a day of rest tomorrow—no packing up and setting up! Kayaking is the easy part of the trip.

Sitting on my stool with no back, I am enjoying my view of the sunset's pink and blue hues reflecting on the water. Geese periodically visit and peck around on the sandy beach, keeping us company and drowning out the hum of the downstream factory with their honk and squawk song. This is good.

I'm using this time to reflect on my day. Today, I spotted many signs of spring—daffodils, tulips, and other wild flowers. In addition, the trees are beginning to show promises of leaves to come. I don't have a favorite season: to me, every season is a special time. I love the newness of spring, the long days of summer, the colors of fall, and the relaxation of winter. As we travel on this journey, I am eager to observe the transformation in nature. Our adventure began in what seemed like winter (a couple of inches of snow fell a few days before we left), will pass through spring, and complete the trip in summer. I am going to sit back and watch the transformation not only in nature but also in me. This is indeed good.

04-19-2015

It's Just Ed

Weather conditions:

High: 60

Low: 51

Skies: clear early turning to rain with periods of heavy rain

Wind: ENE 12-20 mph, gusts to 25 mph

Today's mileage: 0 miles—day of rest

Total mileage: 200 miles Yahoo! (only 1391 more to go)

Where we stayed: Lafayette, Indiana

Today was an N.A.S.—No Alarm Sunday! I love No Alarm Sundays. Actually, I love No Alarm Any Days.

Part of our daily routine is checking the radar—even before we unzip the tent, crawl out the small opening, and leave the coziness of our home. Today's observation showed rain would arrive within the hour, continuing most the day. Needing to make a plan to use each rain free minute wisely, John instructed, "OK. You get breakfast ready. I'll put a tarp over the tent to provide one more layer of protection and double check the security of *Work* and *Pray*." One, two, three, go….

I prepared the granola.

- Measure one cup water.
- Pour measured water into bag of dehydrated milk.

- Shake bag.
- Pour granola into cups.
- Pour milk over granola.

"Breakfast is ready when you are."

Eating out of our cups, we scarfed down our granola while sitting on a log. What a great way to live—simply. Eating out of a bowl at a table is overrated. After breakfast, John returned to his task of preparing our campsite for the impending rain. I cleaned our breakfast dishes and performed other daily routines, such as washing my face, brushing my teeth, and using the designated pee corner one last time before tent confinement.

Dishes, face, and teeth clean, and tent and kayaks secure, we reconvened to decide how much longer we could enjoy standing in an upright position. Sitting is barely an option in our 39-inch tall (in the center) tent. Six foot one John's head brushes the ceiling when he sits on his "bed." Lying down in the seven-foot long area doesn't provide comfort either since gear rests at the foot of his sleeping bag. He always sleeps on his side with his knees bent. Needless to say, we were avoiding the tent as long as we could.

John examined the radar and sky and exclaimed, "We better get in the tent NOW!" We climbed into the tent, zipping up the zipper as we heard the first pitter patter on the tarp. Excellent timing! Now to take advantage of a literal day of rest.

Settled in for the day, John asked, "What do you want to do?"

"I haven't journaled since our last rainy day outside of Markle ten days ago. I have to catch up!" I kept notes each day but needed to put them into a logical, readable version so I could post them in our daily journal on our website.

John tried to think of a way he could also be productive but unable (unwilling?!) to do so declared, "I think I will take a nap!"

That is exactly what happened. John napped. I journaled.

We have been lucky we haven't had a rainout since our stormy day spent in Markle. Today resembled that day (sleeping and journaling) except for two details. First, something was missing from our tent today, a clothesline. Since we didn't put our tent up in the rain, we didn't have wet clothes and towels to dry. Another difference was the rain's duration. In Markle, we escaped the tent mid-afternoon. (Remember, John's being-caught-shaving-in-his-long-underwear incident that day.) Today, the rain continued and continued and continued and continued some more. The time is now 8:00 p.m., and the rain is still falling. Rainy days like today force us to relax. As I decided in Markle, I'm a forced relaxation fan.

Here's a recap of our day…

Earlier today, during a lighter time in the rain (Notice, I didn't say the rain stopped.), John put on his rain suit and slipped outside to retrieve some snacks from *Pray* and verify the water levels. Climbing back into the tent, he tried not to transfer the wetness from his rain gear to the tent's interior. "Ugly day. However, going outside in the rain was worth it. I saw a Blue Herron fly over the river. It's amazing how silently they glide." I hope we never lose our sense of wonder. Hey, that should be a song. (Actually, it is, thanks to Lee Ann Womack—"I Hope You Dance.")

Since we prefer to be in our kayaks when they are floating, John continued to check the water levels throughout the day to see if he needed to move *Work* and *Pray* to higher ground. Luckily, he didn't have to relocate them. During one of John's check-on-the-kayaks absences, I encountered a candy dilemma. Let me explain how I came face-to-face with THE dilemma. At the beginning of the day, we still possessed four Easter candy treats from Irene Heare. (Amazing any remained after 14 days. Right?) Now, there are none. Here's the recap of how the candy total went from four to none…. We each ate one soon after entering the tent this morning. Then there were two—a Baby Ruth in a pink wrapper with a bunny on it and a blue-wrapped Snickers with the picture of an Easter egg. While completing my journaling marathon, I ate the Snickers, which, if you do the math, left one. Then, John put on his rain suit to make his rounds and left his (the last) candy alone in my presence. Hmm… *Should I collect the last candy as rent for the use of my pillow?* I considered holding it hostage for a ransom. I even captured a picture of the Baby Ruth bar lying on his sleep pad but soon decided John didn't have anything to offer as a reward. *I could pretend I ate it and then produce it once he showed his disappointment, or I could eat it and face the consequences.* What would you have done? John is lucky he returned before I could make a decision.

Rain gear removed, John noticed the candy on his sleep pad and decided to eat it. Watching John tear the top off the wrapper, I realized what a good person I was and shared this with John, "I was tempted to eat the last Snickers but was nice and left it for you."

He kept my gaze as he continued unwrapping the milk chocolate covered peanuts, nougat, and caramel. My mouth watered as he offered me a bite. I reached for the bite-size candy bar. *He's nicer than I thought.* My fingers brushed it. In one swift move, John popped it into his mouth, smiling as he slowly chewed the final chocolate treat. I think he even made a yummy sound. *Bastard. (I never say that!)*

Sometime during the day, I needed to pee. I have no idea when since time becomes unmeasurable when stuck in a tent all day. Unfortunately, the rain didn't care if nature called. I started to do the I-have-to-pee wiggle and began paying attention to the plip - plip - plop - plip - plip - plip - plip – plop on the tarp, which didn't help the situation. The pitter-patter continued at a steady pace. Soon my wiggle progressed to placing my hand in the I-don't-think-I can-hold- it position. Not caring about the rain, I grabbed my rain suit, stuffed my hand into the armholes, unzipped the tent, and braved the rain-soaked environment. I unclipped the red poop bag from the tent rope and squished through the mud to my established pee corner. I performed the steps required when peeing in the wilderness. You know, dig a hole, place toilet paper in a convenient place, pull down pants and underwear, squat, etc. You get the picture. However, peeing outside in the rain requires some resourcefulness to keep the toilet paper dry. You know what happens to a toilet paper roll once it's wet—it becomes a hard white clump, no longer good for anything except to throw at an intruder. I decided leaving the toilet paper barely inside the mouth of the poop bag wise. When the time came to use the T.P., I snatched it from the bag, tore off the amount needed, and stuffed it back where it belonged. This plan apparently worked, since the toilet paper is still an un-wind-able roll and not a clump. I don't think I will take pulling down my pants, sitting on a toilet, pulling dry toilet paper off a roll attached to a wall, and flushing for granted after this trip. Having successfully saved the toilet paper roll from the rain monster, I returned to the tent, wet but relieved. John barely noticed my absence.

I finally grew tired of journaling and needed a break. I scolded myself for falling so far behind. I should have heeded my own motto, "It's easier to keep up than to catch up." *I need to take a break. What should I do? I know, play two-handed euchre.* I turned my head to ask John if he wanted to play. But when I observed a peaceful John resting comfortably on MY pillow, I knew he wouldn't be playing euchre any time soon. *I guess I will play solitaire.* The sequence of writing, playing solitaire, writing, reading, and writing continued throughout the day. (Boy, I was glad we charged the Sherpa yesterday. I used it several times to charge my iPad.) Relaxing was refreshing, but I was lonely. I missed John's random comments and stories. *How can he sleep this much?*

Since John lay in silence, I decided to text Irene. Before we launched, she mentioned sending us conversation starters. I thought if I could wake John up, maybe we could talk.

Me: How are you? Still waiting on those daily conversation topics… John and I ran out of things to discuss yesterday at 8:47 a.m.

Irene: If you could live anywhere in the world, where would you live and why?

Me: That sounds interesting.

Irene: Here's another one… Trying on swimsuits at the store… Do or don't?

Me: Thanks. I miss you.

Topics in hand, I couldn't wait to start discussing them. I tapped John on the shoulder, "Johnny, I'm lonely. Aren't you done sleeping?"

He rolled over and opened one eye, "I guess."

I needed to convince him to stay awake, "Irene sent us some discussion topics."

He closed his eye.

"Please wake up. I miss you."

He slowly opened both eyes, "OK. I give. What did Irene say?"

"First question."

"Wait. There's more than one topic?"

"Yeah. There are two. Please…"

"Ok."

"Here's the first one… If you could live anywhere in the world, where would you live and why?"

"Myanmar."

"Myanmar, why Myanmar?"

"Because I get to add, '…formerly known as Burma,' when people ask me where I'm from."

"You're weird."

"That wasn't so bad was it?" I asked. Before he could answer, I read the second question, "Trying on swimsuits at the store… Do or don't…"

He tilted his head to one side and furrowed his brow. "I don't know what that means."

"She's asking if you try on swim suits with your underwear on or off."

"Ok, so I don't really wear a 'swimsuit.' If I were to buy one, I'd probably grab a medium. Definitely no trying on. Definitely no commando happening."

Wow, not the lengthy, time-killing conversation I had hoped for. *Oh well.*

Tent-bound (except for the occasional checking the kayaks and peeing) and unable to use our stove to heat water, we ate cold meals of peanut butter roll-ups for lunch and dinner. In addition to our roll-ups at lunch, we enjoyed cheese and homemade granola bars. For dinner, we added salt and vinegar potato chips I made from potatoes grown in my garden last summer to our menu of peanut butter roll-ups. I am proud of the way we are eating; most of our food is homemade, and a considerable amount came from my garden. Eating this way has saved us a lot of money, not to mention the fact we can pronounce every ingredient we are placing in our bodies. Well worth the time and effort involved in preparing our food before the trip.

We have now reached the end of our day of rest. Although some would call our day boring, we deemed our day set aside to relax successful—we relaxed. I caught up on my journaling, read, and played SOLITAIRE. What else could I play while John slept on MY pillow?

04-20-2015

If It Ain't a Rock, It's a Pillow

Weather conditions:

High: 57

Low: 42

Skies: 20% chance light rain

Wind: WSW 30 mph with gusts 40-50 mph

Today's mileage: 13 miles

Total mileage: 213 miles

Where we traveled: Lafayette, Indiana, to Fulton Islands at the mouth of Flint Creek

The wind!

Sometime during the night, wind replaced yesterday's rain, drying our tent, tarp, and outside gear. However, the wind became quite an unpleasant presence as the day progressed.

Let's start at the beginning of the day. After examining the charts and performing the usual do-before-leaving-the-tent chores, John unzipped the tent, climbed out, and disappeared. As usual, I had no idea what he was up to and knew not to ask. (John disappearing is always a little scary.) I stayed in the tent preparing for the day until I heard John say, "You're gonna be happy!" (I was still a little scared.)

My curiosity got the best of me. Peeking out of the tent, I saw a tarp stretched at an angle from the ground to two trees, creating a windbreak. The emergency foil blanket lay on the ground prepared for breakfast. Although using the foil blanket as a table is our norm, John's preparation of the windbreak and table as a surprise made the scene resemble a picnic rather than a regular occurrence. I fell in love with him all over again and with tears in my eyes approved, "My hero."

We enjoyed a beef and bean burrito dinner for breakfast. Tomorrow, instead of dinner for breakfast, maybe we'll eat breakfast for breakfast. That's a novel idea!

As we packed up, what the wind had previously dried soon became wet again when the skies started leaking. "I think I will use my cockpit skirt today," I mentioned as raindrops pelted my face and whitecaps claimed the river.

Keep us upright and safe.

The wind! The forecast today called for 30 mph winds with 40-50 mph gusts, causing waves large enough to break on *Pray's* bow and splash in my face. With each breaking wave, I congratulated myself on my foresight to cover my cockpit with its skirt today. Soon, pebbles of rain—a wind and rain combination—struck my face. The combination of cold, rain, and wind penetrated my bones. *I left my warm, dry, wind-free home on purpose?*

About four miles downstream from last night's campsite, we received a respite from the elements of nature when we stopped at Fort Ouiatenon. *Work* and *Pray* secure on the kayak-friendly boat ramp, we hiked to the top of the hill. (I'm sure I haven't mentioned everything is up hill from the river.) *Wow! Did I enter heaven?* The beautiful park in front of me included all the ingredients of a great place to camp with restrooms, water, electricity, picnic tables, and trashcans. (All the comforts of home—right?) And trees. Lots and lots of trees to block the howling winds.

All of this waited for us a mere four miles downstream from where we camped last night. I lamented to John, "If only we had gone four more miles Saturday. We would have enjoyed all this, been able to go to church, and feasted on brisket barbeque for lunch."

"Reflect don't regret," John reminded me.

"Reflect don't regret" is a statement we recently adopted on this trip and have decided to apply to our lives. Many times, we make a decision we later wish we could change. We become aware of information we did not know when making the choice. However, we can't change our decision. We can reflect, deciding that next time we will go about our decision-making process differently, but regretting the choice won't change anything or bring about any benefit. Regretting causes us to develop a negative attitude and perhaps start complaining.

"Reflect don't regret" is another example of the power of perception. This trip is teaching me so much about life. For example, I have learned the power of perception. How I choose to view circumstances changes my attitude about the situation, my mood, my demeanor, and the manner I interact with John. I choose. This choice affects the atmosphere. I decide if the atmosphere will be positive or negative. I choose. I decide. Reflecting has allowed us to avoid fights. During regret, we often place blame on something or someone. During a blame session, becoming defensive is easy. When one person is in defense mode, the other assumes an attack stance. I choose. I decide. I reflect.

Before exploring, we took advantage of the abundant luxuries. We used the restrooms, filled our dromedaries, plugged in our electronics, enjoyed eating a snack on the picnic tables, and disposed of our trash.

Chores completed, we relaxed and investigated the park. *Were we tourists?* A sign provided the significance of the area.

POST OUIATENON SITE
French and Indian Trade
was significant in this area
prior to 1700.
To protect it, Post Ouiatenon was established:
One mile West

The mulch squished under our feet as we lumbered on the well-maintained path to various buildings and displays, each with a sign describing a different aspect of life at the fort. Because of my love for baking, the large cement bread-baking oven with its own chimney caught my attention. Reading about the process of heating it to the correct temperature made me appreciate my gas oven at home. All I do is push a button to program the desired temperature and then wait for the oven to do the work. Although I appreciate my modern conveniences, I would love to go back in time and live for maybe a week as one of these women to experience their way of life. Even though their way of life was hard, it seemed simple. Hard, but simple. Hmm… I could use those two words to describe my life right now on the river. Hard, but simple. My river life is even simpler than those who used the bread-baking oven years ago—I don't even possess a bread-baking oven. Henry David Thoreau wrote in *Walden* concerning modern conveniences "Our inventions are wont to be pretty toys, which distract our attention from serious things." Without the distraction of the oven convenience, my goal is to use this time to pay attention to more serious things.

A Native American living village stands in a corner of the post. Right now, only shells of the actual wigwam dwellings exist, awaiting their canvas covering. In addition to the wigwams, various "living areas" are on display making up the rest of the village. Right now, however, the area resembles a ghost town.

Other buildings closed for the season are the blacksmith shop and fort. A sign on the fort indicates the museum will open May 30. What a great place to bring kids!

After our history lesson, we returned to the river and the weather. In the midst of the wind and rain, several swallows swooped down, barely missing our heads. Animals "playing" with humans make me smile.

In addition to the swallows' antics, what resembled a live *Mutual of Omaha's Wild Kingdom* episode entertained us. This episode focuses on a domestic battle between two Bald Eagles. Picture this. (Don't forget to add the peaceful music with an air of suspense playing in the background.) At first glance, two graceful birds appear to be gliding peacefully through the air, oblivious to one another. Upon closer inspection, one eagle can be seen carrying a fish while being pursued by the other. Unfortunately (at least for one eagle), the fish-carrying eagle loses its grip on its next meal, dropping the prize. The pursuer deftly snatches it out of mid-air in one graceful swoop.

Now, switch channels from PBS to Comedy Central. Picture the same video clip. Instead of background music, dialogue accompanies the same clip. The Comedy Central episode might sound a little like this...

..."Hey Brad, that's my carp...now bring it back."

"No way, Kevin. You snooze, you lose."

"&%%$#@. You didn't even know it was there until I pointed it out to you. Now, give it back, or I'll pluck your tail."

"Ow!... Now look what you made me do."

"Did ya see that?! Grabbed it with one talon. Thanks for passing it to me."

Back to this business at hand—kayaking. Paddle, paddle, paddle...interrupted by our "Do Wah Diddy" song and several other random partial tunes. "Do Wah Diddy" may be the only song we knew all the words to, making it the only one we sang in its entirety, unless we (John) made up words to go with a tune whose lyrics escaped us.

During our concert's intermission, I tried taking my mind off the incessant wind by paying attention to my river view. Almost all the trees possess budding leaves. Changes in the seasons happen gradually yet quickly. Only five days ago, I made note that only a few trees had leaves. At home, because of my perceived busyness, I don't usually make time to notice the changes in the seasons as they happen, but since I searched for the change today, I observed it. I am thankful this slower pace is prompting me to take time to observe. I hope I remember at home this fall to watch for the signs of the seasons.

Another change I don't think I would have noticed if Jerry Hay hadn't written about it in his book is the widening of the river. He points out that the Wabash River is up to 150 yards wide in some areas. This change is even more gradual than the changes in the seasons. The wider river influences my safety because the width allows me to paddle farther from the banks. The banks represent danger because unseen downed trees could be looming below the surface. Deeper water also puts space between dangerous submerged rocks and me. If I collide with a downed tree or rock, I could end up in the water. Remember, my greatest fear is dumping.

Paddling *Pray*, singing partial songs, fighting the wind, and observing changes in nature were the activities for the rest of the day until the time arrived to find a place to camp. Finding camp is not as easy as in the movies. In the movies, the muscular tan man and his beautiful maiden discover a sandy beach as soon as they decide to stop for the day. In our real life today, we tried THREE different spots before finding a suitable spot to camp for the night.

Of course, the SHE in the movies has every lock of hair in place and perfectly applied makeup, even though she hasn't glanced in a mirror for days and has paddled six hours in the wind and rain. Not to mention, her legs are smooth as silk without any stubbles. Of course, MY hair is sticking out all over and I am not wearing any makeup. I am most thankful I haven't encountered a mirror for days. I clumsily climb out of my kayak after paddling six hours in the wind and rain. Not to mention, the stubble on my legs is sharp enough to draw blood should I cross my bare legs or put them next to some unsuspecting human. I think I last showered and shaved a week ago. Yes, I did pack a razor AND shaving cream. There are some society conventions I hesitate to let go of.

One requirement for today's campsite was to stay far enough from shore to provide safety from the rising waters, a result of yesterday's rains. One indication of possible flooding upstream is the presence of debris or drift, which we encountered more of today. With flood warnings for all the area rivers, we will watch the water levels closely the next few days.

Our perfect camping place is an island again. Luckily, this island is much quieter than yesterday's. The only noises heard (besides the wind) have been raccoons fighting (a common occurrence within the coon population) and a turkey gobbling as it flew onto our island at dusk. (Yes, turkeys do fly.) With the turkey's entrance, we enjoyed a conversation between the squabbling raccoons and the new arrival. The raccoons growled, grunted, and screamed as if they were killing each other. In response, the turkey gobbled, translated to humanese (I know that isn't a word, but it works) means "shut up!" Surprisingly, the raccoons stopped their quarrel, becoming silent for a moment before returning to their domestic disturbance. The raccoons and turkeys repeated the scenario several times until the raccoons finally gave up or one raccoon won (lost).

The wind! Because of the wind, John put up our UST tarp (the same one he used this morning) in front of the tent as a windbreak. Unfortunately, as soon as John put a stake in the soft sand, the wind put enough pressure on the tarp to pull the stake loose. John put on his "MacGyver hat" and gathered some large sticks. He used one of the sticks to dig a trench. He then put another stick through the loop of the tarp line, burying the "anchor" in the trench. His MacGyver expertise worked great!

I stepped back and watched John work. I don't get the chance at home to experience John's resourcefulness. At home, he doesn't need to be resourceful; he has all the tools he needs. If something breaks, there is a tool made for the task of repairing it. If a hole needs dug, John walks to our cute, yellow garden shed and retrieves a shovel. (A few years ago, I convinced John we NEEDED the cute, yellow garden shed. We hired an Amish crew to transform a scary, dark, old granary into a sunny, yellow building with a porch and windows, complete with window boxes.) I noticed how he placed the orange tarp at the exact angle needed to protect our tent from the wind. He attached the tarp to the limbs above the tent and the bottom in the sand using his MacGyver method. The tarp successfully sheltered the grey tent from the wind.

Tarp secured, we found a downed tree behind the tent and sat on it to dodge the wind—unsuccessfully. We enjoyed (as much as you can, hunched behind a tent and tarp) a spaghetti dinner with garlic croutons and Parmesan cheese with mud pie for dessert. After devouring our food, we performed our getting-ready-for-bed tasks: brush teeth, wash face, remove contacts, go pee, and, of course, move the kayaks. Wait, the last task isn't usual. Yes, John moved *Work* and *Pray* to higher ground because in the couple of hours since we had landed, the water had risen. Even though the sun remained above the horizon, we retreated to the tent to escape the cold and wind.

The wind!

04-21-2015

Who Put Orange Juice on the Beer Shelf (guest writer John)

Weather conditions:

High: 59

Low: 38

Skies: clear early becoming cloudy later in the day

Wind: W 14 - 32 mph with gusts 40-50 mph

Today's mileage: 10 miles

Total mileage: 223 miles

Where we traveled: Fulton Islands at the mouth of Flint Creek to Attica, Indiana

It was the best of times, it was the…. Oh, wait. That line has already been used before.

Gobble, gobble. Apparently, the same turkey that was annoyed by the fighting raccoons last night was still on our island, and he was an early riser. The commotion started just before first light and continued pretty much non-stop for the next two hours. Oh, well, it sounded cool echoing through the woods, and we needed to get up anyway.

The first job was to check on the kayaks, water level, and flood warnings. It was a good thing we had pulled the boats to higher ground late in the evening, or I would have needed to wade out to get them. Regardless, they are always tied off…just in case. Kayaks, ok. Check.

The river is definitely higher again with a lot more floating logs and debris from the flooding upstream, but manageable. River, ok. Check.

Then the wind started. Like the flick of a switch, it went from dead calm to very windy. The warnings were for 40-50 mph again today.

It was just too windy and cold to comfortably set up the stove and make a warm breakfast. So today, it was a cold breakfast of homemade granola full of dehydrated fruits and nuts bathed in Nido, reconstituted powdered milk. LaNae could sell this cereal mix as it's absolutely delicious. Filling cold breakfast eaten. Check.

By the time we tore down the tent, the wind had reached gale strength. Pretty interesting folding a bunch of ultra-light poly in a gale, but we've gotten good at it. Tent packed. Check.

Next, we packed *Work* and *Pray* and pushed-off into the swollen river full of everything from large trees to blue plastic barrels. All is well.

We came across six more eagles today and two nests, but this occurred on a long, straight, west-southwest stretch of the river, which was directly into the teeth of the wind. There was very little opportunity to stop paddling and mess with a camera to capture those images. Attention to detail is warranted in those conditions.

The waves were amazingly big at times today for a river of this size. We had gone from simple white caps to two-foot rollers that often crashed across our bows and cockpit skirts. To not have skirts on today would have surely meant swamped boats. Well prepared for the rough waters. Check.

There were no clouds today. No, I don't mean I had to search to find a cloud. I mean there were NO clouds. The sky was a brilliant azure for as far as the eyes could see.

So what clouds don't cause the potential for rain? When I was a kid, I remember looking at the different types of clouds as displayed and described in our ivory white set of Encyclopedia Britannica. (You know, the source of all knowledge prior to the internet.). Each type of cloud was described by how it contributed to precipitation in some way. I remember thinking to myself, "So when I'm lying outdoors with my dogs and looking up at cool clouds on a beautiful 'sunny' day with no rain, what type of clouds are those? They aren't producing rain?" Of course, I now understand that the mere presence of clouds doesn't mean that it would rain. Regardless, there had been no risk of rain today.

I soon decided it would be a good time to try to capture some action shots with the iPhone. I would have done this with my GoPro camera, but I didn't have a GoPro camera. The GoPro was only a level 4 on our priority list, a "want," and so it didn't make the budget cut. So, placing the Overboard waterproof case lanyard around my neck, I started the video recording and propped the unit between my chin and life jacket, hoping to provide a first person view of the action. After about 90 seconds of video, I looked and discovered that the result was a video of the beautiful blue sky and, well, just the beautiful blue sky. Oh, once in a while, you would see my gloved hand and paddle shaft streak by the lens, but other than that, just the beautiful blue sky. Action video attempt. Failed.

LaNae and I talked about pretty much everything as we made our way down the river. These are great times. We never have trouble finding topics to discuss, but are also very comfortable just hanging out in silence. We can talk or not talk for hours.

We finally turned more southernly and found a bit of respite from the wind, waves, and spray on the outside bend of the river. It was about then that we saw the tall steeple of the Catholic church in Attica. Today was a short, as planned, ten-mile paddle since the rising river was forecasted to crest today. For this reason, we thought it best to make it a short day and end up in civilization in order to keep an eye on the water conditions. If the river broke its banks, we wouldn't want to be on it tomorrow; and I wanted to be sure that we were safe if we needed to hang out for a couple days until the levels dropped.

As we approached Attica, I went on ahead of LaNae to confirm a good place to pull out, which I found to be a cement boat ramp. Once I was up on shore, I walked back upstream to greet my favorite girl and tell her where she should pull out. Just then, LaNae let out an adorable squeal as we experienced our first Asian carp. These accidental transplants had been introduced into our American waterways via the bilges of international shipping. Unlike our native carp, these guys spend a lot of time feeding near the surface and are really jumpy. No, I literally mean "jumpy." An approaching boat, paddle stroke, or other distraction freaks them out and often causes them to launch themselves through the air. It was this unexpected leap across LaNae's bow that gave rise to her shriek. I chuckled. She wasn't amused. Fortunately, for me, they jumped two or three more times before she reached the ramp. I chuckled. She wasn't amused. OK, I must confess that I had experienced the carp earlier as I approached the boat ramp. Yeah, I squealed like a schoolgirl. And I hadn't really run back up stream to tell LaNae where to land but instead simply wanted to watch her experience the carp and have a good laugh. LaNae's squeals were much cuter than mine.

The Attica riverfront is really nice and a change from the usually non-exploited riverfronts we have experienced at most towns so far. There is a well-kept boat ramp along a mown strip next to a driveway where people had pulled up to look at the river while they ate their lunches. The ramp is shaded by old stand cottonwood trees. Immediately behind the trees below the ramp is a large well-maintained area with rows of neatly planted saplings and a landscaped sign that reads, ""Ouabache Park Wildlife Sanctuary."

Once out of our boats, we dumped all our empty plastic food bags into a trashcan and went in search of a rest room. There were some cars parked down by the river, so we thought it best not to expose the occupants to us exposing ourselves via a public urination. A restroom would be appreciated by all.

We came across what appeared to be a newly constructed restroom facility and pavilion located just off the river. But, as we have found at previous stops, it was apparently too early in the season for the restrooms to be open. We walked on towards town.

A McDonald's close enough to the river, from which to see our parked kayaks, made a good place to do some on-line work and use a working bathroom. While LaNae used a working bathroom, I, on the other hand, used the non-working bathroom marked "restroom closed" because the good ole' boys hanging out at McDonald's told me bluntly, "Heck, everybody else is using it, you might as well too." So I did. Bladders emptied. Check.

I chose this time to send a quick email and make a phone call to the city offices. We wanted to be sure that it was ok not only to pitch a tent in their riverfront park for the night, but also to do so behind the trees in the Ouabache Wildlife Sanctuary in order to get out of this brutal wind. "Sure," they told us, as long as we were careful around the newly planted saplings. Secured an approved place to camp. Check.

While we were working, I remembered the discomfort in my left butt cheek and back of thigh that I had been experiencing the last few days. The pressure from sitting was causing a sharp pain in my butt and down what I believed to be my sciatic nerve. At times, it made it really difficult to find a comfortable position in my kayak. I had experienced this on a much worse level when kayaking in Lake Huron off Drummond Island, Michigan, last summer. Since then I had removed the adjustable seat back that came standard and replaced it with a much less intrusive back band as suggested by fellow kayaker and friend Barry Hollowpeter and his gal Robin. The switch to the back band had helped significantly. However, it seems that long hours in the seat were still causing some discomfort. Hmmm..., what to do.

I decided a piece of foam might help so I told LaNae my plans and set off in search of some cheap relief. The first stop was the local hardware store. Air conditioner window seal. I don't think so. Next stop, the local CVS pharmacy. Perfect. A 5" by 10" piece of memory foam. I don't remember what its intended use was, but it looked like it would do the trick.

By then the perfectly clear skies had become polluted with thick cumulous clouds that moved the day from sunny to partly cloudy. Blocking out the sun made the air feel even colder as we walked towards our boats to set up camp.

As we approached the waterfront park, we came across a historic marker with the title "Attica & Covington Canal Skirmish," which describes a dispute between the two towns that took place back in 1846. As we would learn later, the differences between the two towns didn't end then.

We could not have imagined the unbelievable amount of hospitality we would experience in Attica. I had just finished securing my newly procured foam pad to my seat bottom with Gorilla Tape when a truck pulled up, stopped, and a guy jumped out. It was the mayor of Attica, Bob Shepherd. His son had hiked the Appalachian Trail, and the mayor has a real interest in the river, adventure, and exploration. Once he learned we were here, he came to welcome us and learn more about our trip. No sooner had the mayor introduced himself than a car pulled up and another gentleman joined us. "Oh, by the way," the mayor said, "this is Doug, a reporter for the local papers. I took the liberty of letting him know you were here. He would like to interview you. I've also made arrangements for you to have dinner at Robie's restaurant and bar tonight." Dignitaries met, interviews given. Check.

The mayor left briefly and returned with Robie, proprietor of Robie's restaurant and bar, the local theatre, Pizza King, and the furniture store. Robie offered us a night in his rustic cabin on Big Pine Creek. Gracious offer, but too much work to tear down and move *Work* and *Pray* back upstream. Regardless, we hiked over to Robie's bar where we were given a great dinner on the town. Then Robie himself came by our table and asked if he could show us his property and cabins. We hopped in Robie's truck after dinner and made the short drive to what looked more like a state park than a private property. A 120' drop from the top of his highest hill down to clear and bubbling Big Pine Creek. (This is Indiana?) His cabins (yes there are two) are amazing. Hand built log houses constructed by him and a friend using old barn timbers. They looked 200 years old—absolutely fabulous.

Well, I hear our nightly serenade—the train—so it's time to crash and get some rest for the push into Covington tomorrow. Good night.

04-22-2015

Just Eat the Meat

Weather conditions:

High: 50

Low: 32

Skies: Overcast, light rain

Winds: W 13 mph with gusts 36

Today's mileage: 26 miles

Total mileage: 249 miles

Where we traveled: Attica, Indiana, to Perrysville, Indiana

Hmm… Shoo Goo. Who came up with a name like that? It sounds like something I would scrape off my shoe after walking in a cow pasture. Yesterday, when John told me he needed to hit the local Do-It-Best Hardware Store to buy Shoo Goo, I thought he was making up the name. John is famous for creating words. I believe he could create a new language—Johnlish. After I gave him the is-that-really-a-word look, he promised me it really did exist. Since this was a new invention to me, I was dying for him to produce the evidence.

He explained, "I need to buy it to fix my boot where I snagged the neoprene on the end of a sharp tree root the other day. I'm tired of my socks getting wet every time I step into the water. And then it takes forever for them to dry." John's socks are always hanging around drying.

Returning from the store, he proved the goo's existence, applied it to the damaged area, and placed the boot in a secure place to dry overnight.

First thing this morning, he inspected his repair job and deemed it good. We have officially added Shoo Goo to our gear list.

In addition to purchasing the Shoo Goo at the hardware store for boot repair, he purchased a product from CVS he hoped would 'repair' the pain he has been experiencing in his back. The last couple of days in the kayak have been uncomfortable for John, as he has battled some sciatic nerve pain. He doesn't normally ask to stop and rest but has declared "time out" several times over the last couple of days in order to try different positions and stretch, without much relief. Lucky for John, the pain subsides as soon as he climbs out of his kayak.

He unpacked his purchase from the plastic CVS bag. I giggled when I saw what he held in his hand. "You bought a pillow? Is there room for that?"

"It's NOT a pillow. It's a block of memory foam." Was he trying to convince himself or me?

"Hmm… Keep telling yourself that. It looks like a pillow to me."

John ignored me as he secured his pillow—I mean memory foam—into the perfect place in his kayak with Gorilla Tape. This is another invention new to me. I guess it is even better than duct tape –who knew? I hope this adjustment provides some relief to John as he paddles. Has John discovered a new use for a pillow—I mean memory foam?

After eating breakfast, tearing down camp, packing *Work* and *Pray*, taking advantage of the restroom at McDonald's, removing the wheels and then re-packing the back hatches, we launched our kayaks for an 18-mile paddle to Covington where our Week #4 package awaited us at the post office.

Keep us upright and safe.

Although the temperature rose into the mid 50's, the wind and clouds made today feel like one of the coldest days we've experienced on the water. Luckily, the swollen rivers pushed us along; we paddled to Covington in only three hours. If you do the math, we traveled about six mph. I could get used to this pace.

Once we pulled ashore, we attached the wheels to *Work* and *Pray*, towed them to a safe place on the bank, and prepared for our trek into town. Before leaving the boat ramp area, we scoped out the camping potential. The DNR operates and owns the area at the boat ramp. Although no restroom or water was available, some flat, grassy areas survived in the midst of the mud—an acceptable place to camp. As John has done previously when arriving in other towns, he planned to find the proper official to ask permission to spend the night.

Goals: find a restroom and use it, locate the post office, retrieve our package, and gain permission to camp at the boat ramp. We trudged uphill for what seemed like miles. (I think I should mention here that everything is uphill from the river.) Remember, we had paddled 18 miles—we were tired. At the top of the hill, we spotted a convenience store. Yeah! Restroom, here I come. While I emptied my bladder, John met an insurance man, Dave, from Lafayette, Indiana. Dave had recently finished listening to *The Adventures of Huckleberry Finn* (Twain's classic set on the Mississippi River) on audio books. He expressed his enthusiasm by echoing our mantra "you're doing it!" He's right—we ARE doing it!

After taking care of nature, we headed to the post office to retrieve our nourishment for the next week. Super nice and helpful Beth at USPS gave us our Week #4 package. From the post office lobby, John called the city department to gain permission to pitch a tent in their somewhat rough, isolated riverside "park." Soon after explaining our situation to the proper official, John set our box down on the floor and started pacing. "We are no trace campers. You won't even be able to tell we were here…. Okay, have a nice day." I had a feeling things didn't go well.

John confirmed my suspicions. "Sorry, babe. We need to move on." This was the first time we received a "no" response when we have asked permission. Do we continue to ask permission or practice asking forgiveness?

"I'm so tired. I hate the thought of crawling into my kayak and going back on the river. It's so windy and cold." Tears threatened to escape my eyes.

"Can you make it another eight miles? Jerry Hay's map shows a potential spot around the highway 32 bridge." *Sleeping under a bridge. Are we officially homeless?* I nodded my head. I couldn't think of any other option. John put his arm around my shoulders and tried comforting me. "And in another one and a half miles, we will reach the half-way mark of the Wabash."

"Okay." Reaching the halfway mark in one and a half miles TODAY didn't comfort me. I would have been happy to stay in Covington tonight and reach that milestone TOMORROW.

We shuffled back to the boat ramp. Earlier in the day when we arrived in Covington, we thought we would be setting up our tent by now, not preparing to climb back into our kayaks. On the road back to *Work* and *Pray*, we met a man working in his yard. He stopped working and peered at us with curiosity. He knew we weren't from these parts because Covington's a small town and we were dressed, well, uniquely in river attire—wet suits and boots. In addition, John was a carrying a box on his shoulder like a massive boom box as we lumbered towards the river. The man asked the usual question, "Where y'all goin'?"

"We're kayaking from the headwaters of the Wabash to the Gulf of Mexico. We just picked up our next week's worth of food at the post office and are headed back to our kayaks," John replied as he adjusted the package on his shoulder.

"Really! I have a golf cart in the barn. Can I give you a ride?" John later told me he resisted the urge to say, "to the Gulf of Mexico?"

At this point, we could see *Work* and *Pray* from his yard, you know, like 40 yards away. But we decided before this trip began if someone wanted to help us, we would say "yes." What we really hoped for was an invitation to pitch our tent in his backyard. But he didn't offer.

"Yes, thank you."

Retrieving the golf cart from his barn took longer than walking the rest of the distance to our kayaks would have taken. However, we didn't want to squelch his giving heart—a complete contradiction to the poor image set by the town officials who told us to "move along." Typical "thank yous" and "good lucks" exchanged, we watched our Covington bright spot drive up the path, returning to his yard work. We then reloaded *Work* and *Pray* with our provisions and launched, eager to arrive finally at our home for the night.

A little farther downstream, we saw a sight you don't see every day —an abandoned old bus sitting on the bank by the river. Wait a minute, that's not true. I did spot one yesterday—on stilts. Maybe I will notice one every day. These two bus sightings caused all kinds of questions to bounce around in my head. *Why were the buses there? How long had they been there? How did they get there? Does anyone use them for anything?* John and I have previously discussed buying an old bus and converting it into an RV and touring the country. (Another excursion perhaps?) I have also read about buses permanently parked and converted to homes. I don't think the buses we have observed the last couple of days fall into either of those categories. Sights on the river.

Paddling to our resting place for the evening, we passed a man-made field of tall prairie grass. The grass blocked the view of the bank. However, we soon knew what inhabited the area—birds—lots of them. I could hear hundreds (thousands?) of birds. John and I struggled to hear each other talk over the hullabaloo of their tweets, squawks, calls, and songs. This made me think (surprise)… Birds used to live in nature without any help from humans. Now, since we have intruded on their living space, we build special habitats for them. Not only large habitats, but also smaller ones— various bird houses and feeders we hang in our yards, hoping to catch close-ups of our feathered friends. Have we, out of guilt, "created" nature?

"I hope we're almost there. I'm really tired," I complained.

"I'll look at the map." Coasting, John studied the map in the plastic sheath secured in front of his cockpit. I know I have stated this before; the maps from Jerry Hay's book have been indispensable. Before we left home,

John printed off the individual pages so they would be easier to manage in the kayak. Current map on one side and next map on the other side makes transitioning as easy as flipping over the map sheath. They provide landmarks, potential camping spots, towns, restocking areas, etc. Using the map enables us to have an idea of where we are, where we are going, and what we'll find there. "The bridge should be just ahead."

"Good," I expressed with relief. Then it came into view—the bridge. I paddled faster in anticipation of exiting *Pray* for the day, eating, and relaxing.

Unfortunately, once we reached the bridge, our day continued. We still needed to decide where and if we could land our kayaks and pitch our tent. We floated under the bridge. From the river I noticed some chairs on the bank—private property. *We couldn't stay in Covington, so I doubt staying here would be acceptable.* We pulled up to the bank. John climbed out of *Work* to investigate while I waited in *Pray.* I was feeling discouraged again. *How much farther could I paddle? To where?* This was the first time in 19 days I have fretted about where we would spend the night. I felt homeless and helpless.

"This is definitely private land," John reported when he returned. I cried. "Oh, please don't cry. I think if we paddle back under the bridge, we can scale up the bank to the edge of a farmer's field."

I trusted John. Turning *Pray* around, I paddled back upstream to a small creek that branched off the main river. The challenge was to paddle into the mouth of the creek while fighting the current pushing us away from our targeted area. I was tired. Having used what felt like the last bit of my energy, I made my way into the creek, landed, and soon placed my feet on terra firma for the rest of the evening.

By the time we stopped, we noted nine eagle sightings and two nests. Jerry Hay notes the next thirty miles have the largest concentration of eagles on the Wabash.

After a meal of chili and cornbread (perfect for this cold evening) and strawberry shortcake (perfect for any evening), we have retreated to our tent to escape the wind and cold. Now, as I write here in our portable canvas shelter, I hear fish (probably Asian Carp) landing in the small creek. Hearing the splash, I can almost picture the fish catapulting out of the stream and plopping back in the water, causing a splash. I wonder if these are the same fish that jumped at me as I entered the creek earlier, triggering a squeal much like the one I uttered yesterday when approaching Attica. Wow! After my pounding heart returned to a normal beat, I contemplated the unfortunate possibility of the fish jumping into *Pray* with me. My cockpit is not big enough for a 20-pound fish and me! Perhaps my cockpit skirt will become part of my daily attire.

Enough fish talk, I am going to snuggle in my sleeping bag to escape the cold!

By the way, John's feet and socks are dry. Shoo Goo! Who knew?

04-23-2015

...And Then I Mowed My Yard

Weather today
High: 57
Low: 36
Skies: clear skies
Winds: WNW 5-17 mph, gusts to 26 mph

Today's mileage: 25 miles
Total mileage: 274 miles
Where we traveled: Perrysville, Indiana, to Montezuma, Indiana

"Yay, no snow!" What? No, my thirty-year-old daughter Tiffany, who hates snow, hasn't hijacked my journal. Anyone who knows me realizes how much I LOVE snow. However, this morning's joyous "no snow" statement came after reading reports of snow falling back home. For once, I was thankful it fell there and not here. If I were at home, though, I would have been cheering.

I really do love snow, any time. Actually, one winter when it kept snowing and snowing and snowing, one of my friends sent me a text—"Quit praying for snow!" I am already looking forward to next winter when I am sitting in my dining room, coffee cup in hand, gazing through my bay window, watching snow dancing across the fields. I can almost hear the wood burner blowing as the fire's glow radiates through the stove's window. Oh, and the smells that accompany winter. Nothing beats a whiff of burning wood and the aroma of freshly brewed coffee. I LOVE winter and snow!

However, kayaking in the snow doesn't sound appealing. Or does it? Let me rethink that statement. The more I consider the scene, kayaking in the snow could be a beautiful experience. Imagine the setting…. The white, fluffy snowflakes float from above, disappearing as soon as they hit the water. On the bank, green grass pokes its head through the thin white blanket. A snowflake lands on my nose, leaving a cold wet spot. The quietness of nature allows the snow to be "heard" as it floats and settles. I think I have changed my mind— kayaking in the snow would be a beautiful and peaceful experience.

Although no snowflakes floated from the sky here, this morning started out cold. I awoke shivering and continued quivering all through breakfast. I lusted for a little warmth from my wood burner at home.

After eating breakfast casserole and packing up *Work* and *Pray*, John instructed, "Grab your toiletries bag."

"Why?" I asked, cold and a little annoyed at the suggestion.

"We are going to climb the hill. I'll grab the dromedary."

"Where are you going to find water at the top of the hill? I didn't see anything there."

"I saw a water tower from the river yesterday. And Jerry Hay's map shows a town called Perrysville at the top of the hill. Maybe there will be a place to clean up and get water."

His plan sounded reasonable until I studied the steep and rocky hill he suggested we climb. I still didn't see any town. Before I could become too worked up, John added, "Yesterday, when I was scoping out a place to camp, I noticed a path I think leads to the town."

Gathering everything we needed for a trip to society, we clambered to the path. Unfortunately, a path to the path didn't exist. While shimmying along a narrow ledge, clinging onto trees, and clutching our toiletries, we guarded our steps from the roots waiting to grab our feet and bring us crashing to the ground. Having safely made our way to the path, we climbed the hill. The map was right. At the top of the hill stood the town of Perrysville, Indiana. (Population 456—saaaaa-lute!)

Leaving the path, we entered a residential part of town with small houses and small yards. Strolling on the sidewalk in the direction of what appeared to be downtown, I noticed the tulips, daisies, and other spring flowers punctuating our excursion into town. Observing the buds made me think about my garden at home. *What will it look like this year?* I think I enjoy spring flowers more than those of summer or fall because they represent a new beginning after everything has lain asleep during the winter. In my flower garden, I sometimes forget where I planted certain flowers and am surprised when they peek their heads through the ground. I smile when Mother Nature blesses me with these surprise floral gifts.

We continued moseying until we reached the intersection of Jackson and Main. Apparently, we were on Main Street. To the left on Jackson stood remnants of a once bustling town center. Traces of a painted 1776 flag have survived the elements of time on the side of one brick building. The circle of stars frames the numbers 76. *Did someone paint the mural in celebration of the 1976 bicentennial 39 years ago? Was the downtown thriving then? Did a parade pass down Jackson Street in honor of the birth of our country?* Like so many towns in this area, it thrived while the Erie Canal prospered; but with the canal's abandonment in 1865, the town now mimics a ghost town.

A lone white pick-up truck sat parked on the street in front of the only store that gave the impression of thriving. The other storefronts resemble an old western movie set. I'm sure at one time the streets and sidewalks were bustling and the stores ready for business, Now the streets and sidewalks are empty except for an occasional weed growing in the cracks. The paint on the storefronts is peeling, the windows and wood in need of repair. When did a customer last enter the doors? Are there still people who can share stories about life behind the empty walls of the once thriving businesses?

Another existing business almost every town has no matter its size stood in the opposite direction on Jackson—a convenience store. There we filled our dromedaries and freshened up. Unfortunately, John forgot to unload the trash. Even without emptying the trash, we accomplished two of the three "must dos" in civilization—fill water and use the restroom. The trash will have to ride along a little farther.

Refreshed and water containers filled, we started back to *Work* and *Pray*. On the way, John stopped on Jackson Street and stared at the water tower. John sometimes is random. I asked, "What are you doing?"

He explained the reason for dawdling. "Yesterday as we were paddling towards Perrysville, I noticed the water tower didn't have the town's name painted on the riverside. I wanted to see if Perryville was painted on the highway side. It is."

We are finding that when signs are considered, the river view isn't taken into account. Approaching a bridge from the river view, I always wonder what road I am passing under in order to pinpoint my location. The bridges are the only permanent landmarks giving us clues as to where we are. Without markers revealing the road's name, knowing our exact location is sometimes a guessing game. Even bridges we have passed over all our lives and have recognized from the road look different from the river. Conversely, bridges crossed on the road usually have a sign with the name of the body of water it spans. Ironically, you don't need the marker on the road to aid you in knowing where you are since there are other identifiers indicating your location. Signs where you don't need them—no signs where you do. Ironic.

Returning to *Work* and *Pray* required shimmying, clinging, clutching, and guarding again. I didn't realize going to a restroom to freshen up could be so dangerous. Safely back at the campsite, we launched our kayaks for a 25-mile paddle to Montezuma, Indiana.

Keep us upright and safe.

With temperatures in the upper 50s and a slight wind to our backs, the weather and water provided perfect conditions for a day of paddling. Today, we were excited to count nine more eagles and eight nests. Of all the eagle's nests we've sighted so far, only one was not in a Sycamore tree. We are assuming eagles build their nests in sycamore trees because these trees are tall and have deep "V's" at the intersections of the large main branches. In addition to the eagles, we observed a Great Horned Owl glide overhead. Cool!

Here's a random fact John discovered during his investigation of the dangers many people warned us about before our trip.... More people are killed by cattle every year in the U.S. than by snakes. I mention this because we encountered some cows by the river today. Luckily, the black four-legged bovines stood at the water's edge, watching us pass without incident. During a trip on the river, I expect to catch a glimpse of a snake or two (notice, I plan to catch only a glimpse, not a full-blown encounter) but the cows' emergence along the river surprised me. Based on statistics, we are lucky we survived!

After the close encounter with the cows, we passed our first power plant of the trip and then approached an unusual structure. From a distance, it seemed to float in space. Paddling closer, I thought we had entered a time capsule and were transported 100 years into the future, à la *Mad Max*. The openings of the boxy, bay-like windows jutting out on each side of this oddly shaped framework were blackened as if by fire. From the river, the dimensions of the construction's main portion were difficult to distinguish, perhaps ten foot by ten foot. A six-foot tall pillar of the same width and breadth supported the structure high off the ground. From one end, building height walls enclosed two sides of an extended deck, leaving the remainder open. The deck sat atop four poles, one on each corner. We hypothesized the use of this futuristic-looking object. Perhaps it once served as a lookout tower of some sort. *But what did it overlook?* Although it resembled a futuristic construction, there were indicators of abandonment. *How can something look old and futuristic at the same time?* Still discussing the details of the first, we come across another in the same state of disrepair, possessing a similar blackened appearance. Now we were even more confused. *How could both structures have identical fire damage?* A mystery we may never solve.

We reached Montezuma around 3:30 p.m. Of course, as soon as I stepped out of *Pray*, I needed to pee. Imagine my excitement when I reached the top of the boat ramp and detected a restroom. With a spring in my step, I pranced to the structure. Approaching it and spotting the red construction tape, my step lost its spring. I hoped the exterior was the portion under construction, perhaps an addition to the building. I knew deep down, however, when I pulled on the handle, the door wouldn't budge. I turned the corner of the building, checked for the correct women's sign and tugged on the door. It didn't budge. This is the third town with unopened restrooms close to the boat ramp. The devastation of a closed pee station is like being lost in the desert for days, glimpsing a puddle of water in the distance; and as you draw near, it disappears. I shuffled with a heavy heart back to the boat ramp. Coming to civilization is not always a reprieve. *Now what?* I cried. My last resort was to find and squat behind a large tree while John kept watch. (Remember, I have a one-piece, zipper-less wetsuit and, as a result, expose too much to an unsuspecting world.) The wilderness is much more convenient for such needs!

We sauntered into town to investigate Montezuma's businesses, hoping specifically for a laundromat. We stopped at the library and talked with Crystal (Cris) about the amenities of the town. Montezuma offered little, not even a laundromat. *Where have all the laundromats gone?* Montezuma— another nearly abandoned canal town.

Although the town is no longer thriving, the residents show pride in their heritage. Where the canal once passed, a sign stands, reminding all who travel through the significance of this place in history. The Erie Canal, the longest canal built in North America, which ran from Toledo, Ohio, to Evansville, Indiana, was abandoned about 1865. Montezuma was its main port in Parke County, Indiana. I wonder how many years Montezuma thrived after the canal became history.

We returned to *Work* and *Pray*. Approaching the boat ramp, we passed a sign with the picture of a mule pulling a boat, providing more information about the grassy area in front of us.

Established August 24, 1961
Welcome to Reeder Park
Site of the
Wabash-Erie Canal
Montezuma, Indiana
Western Gateway to the Parke County Covered Bridge Festival

A tree-less, well-kept campground with electrical hookups and water occupied the area between the sign and the river. Close to the unopened restroom stood a pavilion with several picnic tables and playground equipment. During the Covered Bridge Festival in October, I am sure visitors, attracted to the area by the festival, fill this location. I wonder, during the rest of year, how many visitors the Wabash-Erie Canal's history attracts? How about river travelers?

Although inviting with its proximity to water, availability of electricity, and provision of picnic tables, the campground area didn't have an open restroom or any trees for shade. Therefore, we chose to stay closer to our river under some trees. After we pitched the tent, we ate tuna parmesan chowder and vanilla pudding with trail cake. Yum! Then to bed, plan for tomorrow, and enjoy some warmth.

The temperature is dropping as I write—tonight's low 31. Isn't it the end of April, and aren't we traveling South? Oh yeah, we are still in Indiana, where the seasons sometimes are confused. At least we don't have any snow. Brrrrr…

04-24-2015

Why Is There a Goat Standing on the Bridge

Weather conditions
High: 63
Low: 31
Skies: cloudy
Wind: SSE 5 mph

Today's mileage: 10 miles
Total: 284 miles
Where we traveled: Montezuma, Indiana, to Clinton, Indiana

I am sitting in the laundromat! What an exciting way to spend a Friday afternoon. No, I am serious—I am EXTREMELY excited to be sitting in a laundromat. When you possess only three sets of clothes, a laundromat is a great place to hang out no matter what day of the week it is. Now, if only we could find a shower!

At 31 degrees with a light frost, this morning was the coldest yet—even colder than the morning at Huntington Reservoir when we had heavy frost. As I shivered, a dinner entrée for breakfast sounded warming. I pulled ham and beans with cornbread from our dinner bag. Doesn't everyone eat ham and beans for breakfast on cold mornings?

The ham and beans had started simmering just as a car pulled up and two DNR officers climbed out of the vehicle. I'm glad they didn't arrive last night because I would have been concerned their purpose for stopping was to ask us to move on. (Our you-can't-stay-here Covington encounter has caused some paranoia.) The officers explained they were making their rounds and came over to check on us. They asked the same are-you-being-safe questions the other DNR officer had asked us at Markle, Indiana. I wonder if, when DNR officers receive their formal training, they are required to pass Kayak Questioning 101. Satisfied with our answers, they returned to their truck and drove off.

I watched them leave and then turned around. *Oh, no!* Smoke poured from the pot of ham and beans. I had completely forgotten about dinner, I mean breakfast. Directions for this dehydrated recipe are simple: add water, rest for five minutes, boil for one minute, and stand for 10 minutes. I failed the boil-for-one-minute step. Upon further inspection, I decided breakfast wasn't a total loss, only scorched. What a relief. Perspective lesson: If I had thought I prepared the meal perfectly and found it scorched, I would have been disappointed. However, since I thought I had burned the ham and beans, I was happy with scorched. Scorched or not, the hot meal warmed my bones. Unfortunately, John found the blackened pan hard to clean. (I cook. John cleans. What a deal!)

After John scrubbed and scrubbed the pan as clean as he could get it, we launched for a short ten-mile paddle to Clinton, Indiana.

Keep us upright and safe.

Even with a frigid beginning, the temperature today rose to a comfortable 63 degrees. Occasionally, we encountered a wind gust; however, after the last couple of days, today's "wind" felt more like a breeze. More perspective! (At what point does a breeze become a wind?)

Today we counted five eagles and two nests. I will never tire watching these birds propel themselves through the air with a tranquil flap of their wings.

After our short ten-mile paddle, we arrived in Clinton at 1:00 p.m. without incident. John exited *Work* first. He was in the process of helping me from *Pray*—maneuvering on the slimy, sticky, gooey mud-covered ramp was difficult and dangerous—when we heard stones crunch under the tires of a vehicle. We ignored the sound until we heard a truck door open. We glanced up. A gentleman dressed in dirty overalls, purple t-shirt, and ball cap climbed out of a gray truck pulling a long-bed trailer, transporting a red lawn tractor. I assumed he had come to the riverside park to mow the grass. But when he limped towards the boat ramp, I realized he intended to talk to us. (We do tend to draw attention.) I wondered what events had led him to arrive at the boat ramp at the moment we pulled off the river. John and I have labeled these "chance" meetings as "just happened to be" moments.

Forgetting he was in the middle of helping me out of *Pray*, John greeted our "just happened to be" visitor. I sat in my kayak, listening to the dialogue between my traveling partner and our new acquaintance—soon to be friend and hero.

Our visitor introduced himself, "Hi. I'm Jeff Gosnell. I was driving across the bridge and noticed you approaching the boat ramp. I could tell with the stuff strapped on the top of your kayaks that you aren't the typical day kayaker. Where ya' headed?'

"We started at the headwaters of the Wabash and are headed to the Gulf."

"Wow!" He asked the usual questions.

Then John focused the conversation on Jeff. "Where are you headed with the mower?"

"I mow lawns. I was traveling between jobs and saw you as I was crossing the bridge. I actually almost continued after crossing. Then I thought maybe you might need some help, so I turned around."

"What do you do when you aren't transporting your mower all over the country?'

"I study the history of this area and collect coins." He put his hand into his pocket, pulling out a rare old coin. John remembered I existed and carried the coin over to me. From John's hand, I respectfully took it, knowing I would never hold a coin as valuable as this again. Leaving me sitting in *Pray*, he returned the coin to Jeff. Jeff gave us a short history lesson of the area. Jeff is also active in the Clinton Boat Club and previously served as a member of the Wabash River Heritage Corridor Commission. He was the person to meet: He knows everyone! "Just happened to be"? I think not.

"What can I do for you?" Now was Jeff's chance to become our hero.

"Where is the closest restroom, and is there somewhere we can take a shower and do laundry?" John replied.

"Dairy Queen is at the top of the hill over there. You can use their restroom." I made a mental note of where "at the top of the hill over there" was.

He continued, "And there is a laundromat…" He provided the directions, but I didn't pay attention. I had all the information I needed for the moment—the location of the restroom. I hoped John was listening to the laundromat directions.

"But as far as a shower…" Then I started paying attention again. "I don't know of any."

After providing answers to the important questions in our mind, Jeff continued, "I am going to contact the *Clintonian Newspaper* and the mayor. They need to know you are here." One thing we've learned is river enthusiasts like to use our trip to leverage local leaders with more reason for continuing the riverfront development. "Just happened to be"? I think not!

Almost as an afterthought, he added, "Oh, I have some people you have to meet. They are avid hikers and outdoor people. I will call them."

I didn't think anything of his last comment. I didn't have any reason to believe he would follow through. I assume others won't usually do what they say they will do. This is a protection technique. The lower my expectations, the easier they are to meet—success for everyone involved. The higher my expectations, the harder they are to meet—hopes dashed, causing hurt and disappointment. Here's another matter of perspective. No matter what the expectations are, the same non-follow-through result often occurs. With lower expectations, no problem. With higher expectations, disappointment.

Before leaving, Jeff made sure we had everything we needed, saying he would make the proper contacts with a promise to return. (I doubted he would return.)

John FINALLY helped me out of my kayak. We put the wheels on *Work* and *Pray* and pulled them to the top of the short boat ramp. Some towns encourage the use of the river with parks, picnic tables, pavilions, water, trashcans, and parking. Clinton falls into the category of these river-friendly towns. The only necessary detail to me at that point, though, was the restroom and it wasn't in eyeshot. I chose to verify Jeff's restroom-in-Dairy-Queen information before exploring the large park area for a camping spot with John. I found Dairy Queen and the restroom as Jeff had described. What a relief. (Literally!)

On my trek back to the kayaks, I kept my eyes open for potential camping spots. *Here's the perfect place! It is flat and close to the restroom.* I thought if I could find an ideal spot in close proximity to the restroom, my stay in civilization would be more convenient. Upon my return I shared my findings with John. He didn't agree with me, saying my perfect spot would encounter too much traffic. Our goal is to be out-of-sight-out-of-mind, decreasing the odds of someone asking us to leave. (Covington, Indiana. Need I say more?) Leaving *Work* and *Pray* in the parking lot, we began searching on foot. At one end of the riverfront, we found a path leading to an area by the train track bridge. At the mouth of the path lay a level spot with a tree. This was an option, but the path could see a lot of traffic. We kept exploring. We climbed to the top of the hill where a flat, grassy area greeted us. A pavilion with tables and a trashcan stood at one end. Near the street a blue-handled water faucet called to us. John lifted the handle. Nothing—not even a drip. *Why would the pump work? What were we thinking?* We made note of another potential restroom option across the street—Clinton F.O.E. Away from potential activity with trees lined on one side of the park, we found it—home!

Before we set up our tent, John announced he had to use the restroom. He chose the Dairy Queen option thinking the F.O.E might not be open. I wondered why he didn't use a tree as he usually does but didn't ask questions. After he left, I sat on *Pray*, pondering what our next couple of days will look like. We are planning to stay in Clinton for two days because thunderstorms are in the weather forecast for tomorrow. By default we chose tomorrow as our next day of rest (our "Sunday). *What will the next couple of days bring?* My agenda: laundry, shower, relaxation, journaling, etc. I think Dairy Queen has Wi-Fi. We may HAVE to spend some time there. And while we are there, we will HAVE to buy something. Have I mentioned how much I like ice cream?

From my landed kayak, I gazed at the river beyond the hill. Signs of spring covered the hill—trees budding, and a single redbud tree coloring the landscape with a splash of lavender. Gazing at my spring view from land, I thought about my spring view from the river—trees budding, the ground greening, the swallows fluttering and swooping under the bridges, and birds resting on nests. Spring views.

As I peered at the water, the view from my landed kayak differed from the view I witnessed on the river barely an hour before. From land, I detected more of the train track—the portion meandering across the land in addition to the portion floating over the river. From the river, I observed only the underside of the tracks. As I inventoried the area surrounding me and *Pray*, an approaching train blasted its horn. Before our trip, I equated a train's sound with waiting at a railroad crossing, feeling annoyed. Today, I equate a train's sound with traveling down the river, feeling at peace. More perspective.

After a few minutes of contemplation, I watched for John, wondering what was taking him so long. *Did he get lost?* He soon approached from the direction of Dairy Queen carrying something. As he grew closer, I realized John had two purposes for his trip—restroom usage and ice cream cone purchase. Have I mentioned I LOVE ice cream! (I think John should go to the restroom more often.)

John bringing me an ice cream cone AND eating one of his own is part of a transformation. Soon after John and I were married, I enthusiastically suggested traveling to White Cottage, a local ice cream shop, for a sweet treat. With a less than eager response, he informed me he didn't care for the scrumptious frozen creamy delight. Seriously?! We should have had this conversation earlier because his lack of fondness for ice cream may have been a deal breaker. Over the years he has learned to feign interest. However, he still orders boring options—vanilla, chocolate, or strawberry—no matter how many and varied the menu options are.

Stray ice cream drips licked from our fingers, we assembled our home. Even after several weeks of setting up our tent almost every night, when I unzip the zipper and crawl into the tent to prepare our home for the night, I sigh. Our tent is one of my favorite places in the world: Obviously, I don't need a lot of space or possessions to feel relaxed and complete. I hope these priorities remain when I return to a house much larger than my tent, where the possessions in my closet wouldn't fit into our two separate boats. This seems to be a common theme on this trip—how can I simplify my life on land?

Our next goal—wash our clothes. Collecting and bagging our two outfits in preparation of walking to the laundromat took but a moment. As we trekked in the direction Jeff had described, a car parked. Two gentlemen approached us. Jeff Gosnell had called two members of the boat club. *Boy, he made those calls fast. Maybe I should raise my expectations of Jeff Gosnell.*

The gentlemen introduced themselves as Mike Kelley and Mike Harper. (Yay, I had to remember only one name—Mike.) They stopped by to introduce themselves and see if we needed anything. After talking with them, John mentioned he needed a pencil. (John wanted to use a pencil to mark on the maps.) Mike "One" said, "I'll be back." He strolled to his car, opened the trunk, gathered some items, and returned to us carrying a pencil, roll of toilet paper, and a lighter. (Doesn't everyone have a pencil, roll of toilet paper, and a lighter in their trunk?) After giving us all the "necessities," he offered us a ride to the laundromat.

And this story brings me here... excited about spending my Friday afternoon in the laundromat. Once our clothes are laundered, we will return to the tent and make supper. Tonight I will avoid distractions while I re-hydrate our meal so we won't have scorched food again. Tomorrow is a day of rest. Yay!

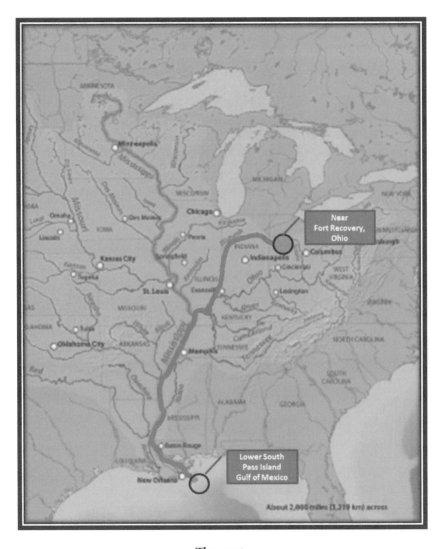

The route

Our river—the Wabash

A lot, and not so much. We had everything we needed,
and needed everything we had.

One week at a time. Food parcels prepared for caching along the route.

04-01-2015 The source of the Wabash River

04-01-2015 The Wabash River begins as a backyard creek.

04-04-2015 Lining *Pray* around a strainer

04-05-2015 River view of the New Corydon bridge

04-07-2015 You camp where you can. (tough weather—Bluffton, Indiana)

04-09-2015 Clothes drying in the tent

04-09-2015 Our Goal Zero solar panel charging our battery pack

04-09-2015 Wind, cold, and rain were the norm during
the early days of the trip.

04-10-2015 Wheeleez portage wheels—a lifesaver

04-11-2015 Hanging Rock, National Natural Landmark

04-12-2015 Mike Beauchamp, our new like-minded friend

04-15-2015 Views you can't get from land.
Welcome to Logansport, Indiana.

04-18-2015 Our Wabash River is getting bigger.

04-20-2015 Refilling our dromedaries (thirty liters worth)

04-22-2015 A cold dinner table for two

04-22-2015 John always had easy access to his charts.

04-26-2015 Power plant seems out of place in nature.

04-26-2015 Rare picture of the two of us

04-27-2015 Laundry day

04-30-2015 Mud-mire-quicksand launch

05-01-2015 Picking up food cache #5 from
St. Francisville, Illinois, post office

05-02-2015 A floating lunch break

05-06-2015 A little shade with our dinner

05-06-2015 Who knew? Sandy beaches on the Wabash
in southern Indiana.

05-07-2015 Just the two of us

05-07-2015 The much larger Ohio River

05-08-2015 Dredging the Ohio River

05-09-2015 E-Town (floating) Restaurant Elizabethtown, Illinois

05-13-2015 Locking through Smithland Lock

05-13-2015 Tow and its barges stage to enter Lock 52

05-17-2015 Olmstead Locks and Dam under construction

05-19-2015 Welcome to the Mississippi River

04-25-2015

Three Guitars and One Amp

Weather conditions:

High: 53

Low: 45

Skies: rain

Winds: E 10 mph

Today's mileage: 0 miles (day of rest—rain)

Total: 284 miles

Where we stayed: Clinton, Indiana

Visitor. Beer. Wine. Rain. Sleep. "Knock, knock." Breakfast. Shower. Relocate. Dinner. Catfish. Philosophy. Friends. Our life the past 24 hours.

The recap actually begins yesterday afternoon in the laundromat. As we packed our clean clothes into our laundry bag, Jeff Gosnell, Clinton's "welcoming committee," surprised us when he "just happened to" walk in. (He had mentioned, when we met him earlier in the day, he would try to come by. My expectations of Jeff Gosnell rose a little more.) He had driven by our weekend home, noticed our absence, and thought he might find us taking advantage of the local laundromat. We graciously accepted his offer to provide us a ride "home."

Back at the tent, while we put our clothes away—threw them on our sleeping bags—Jeff gathered a chair, a six-pack of beer, and a red and white striped gift bag from his trunk and carried them to our campsite. A visitor!

I like entertaining. Actually, a spiritual gift test revealed one of my gifts is hospitality. The result of that same test indicated John has the gifts of leadership, fiscal stewardship, and discernment, which in John's case translates to being bossy, cheap, and judgmental. Interestingly accurate!

Jeff placed his beer on the ground (I couldn't offer him a table.), opened his chair (I'm glad he realized this was a BYOC—Bring Your Own Chair—location), and offered us the gift bag. Not giving John the chance to accept the package, I snatched the bag with red tissue paper from Jeff's hand. *I love gifts, but then again, who doesn't?* My hand dropped unexpectedly from the gift's weight. *You know the action that happens when something is heavier than anticipated.* I unpacked the articles one at a time. I was touched Jeff took the time to gather the gift items, package them, and give them to us. The first thing I removed was a grey t-shirt with the logo "TJ Haase" on it. *That certainly isn't what made the gift bag so heavy.* I expressed my appreciation, "Thank you so much. Since we don't have extra cash to buy souvenirs, this will be a great memento of Clinton. What is TJ Haase?"

"TJ Haase is a local winery," Jeff explained.

"I like wineries and wine!"

Then I pulled the next gift from the bag. "John gets a t-shirt too." I was glad I didn't have to share my t-shirt AND my pillow.

The next item was my favorite. "A bottle of wine!" I enjoy wine, red or white, dry or sweet; I am an equal opportunity wine drinker. Even though I only treat myself to an occasional glass, John makes fun of me in the presence of others by putting his hand to his mouth indicating I drink heavily. Of course, he made the she-drinks-too-much signal as soon as I pulled the bottle from the gift bag. John and Jeff chuckled. I rolled my eyes. Saving it for a special occasion—perhaps the end of the trip—we didn't drink any tonight. We discussed how the bottle would fare for three months in our kayaks. In addition, since there wasn't enough room for my pillow, which is soft and smooshes down, I doubt there is enough room for a bottle of wine. We solved our bottle-of-wine dilemma by deciding to ask John's brother

Delno to take it home when he visits us at Terre Haute in a couple of days. I hope he won't charge any babysitting costs.

I dug to the bottom of the bag—there was more. "Bags of dehydrated soup. We'll enjoy eating something different."

"Thank you so much, Jeff. How thoughtful," John added.

Gift giving completed, Jeff settled into his folding chair—with a back; we sat on our tiny stools—without backs. While I prepared chili and rice pudding for dinner, he interviewed us for an article in *The Daily Clintonian*. When we had finished telling our story, we asked him questions. Jeff is quite a remarkable man in his own right. In addition to being an expert on the local history, he has led an interesting life, possessing a lot of depth and knowledge on topics such as literature, history, and cars. Regretfully, sprinkles with a threat of rain caused us to cut the night short. I hope we connect with him again before we leave.

Good-byes exchanged, we quickly prepared for a rainy evening and perhaps following day of rest in the tent. I sighed as I slipped into my sleeping bag, zipped it up, placed my head on my pillow, and listened to the raindrops plop on the rainfly. (Have I mentioned how much I love our rainy nights and days in the tent?!) No matter how hard the rain has fallen, our transportable home has kept us cozy and dry.

This morning, we awoke around 7:00 well rested—even me. Since the temperature last night was warmer than previous nights, I spent the hours of darkness sleeping instead of shivering. The rain's pitter-patter on the tent and the laziness that accompanies being warm and toasty in our sleeping bags was the perfect beginning to a relaxing day. About twenty minutes into a what-do-you-want-to-do-for-breakfast conversation, someone greeted us with a "knock, knock." Being the only ones in the area, we knew the greeting was meant for us. Another visitor! We have had more of a social life on this trip than at home.

The voice on the other side of the thin wall of nylon introduced himself, "I'm Mark Davis. Jeff Gosnell called me. I would like to take you to breakfast." *He must be the adventurous person Jeff wanted us to meet. Jeff Gosnell is a man of his word!*

We answered, "Yes," since that's what we say on this trip. Throwing on our going-into-town clothes, we emerged from our tent to a dreary day.

Mark, a physically fit man in his fifties dressed in casual sporty clothes and billed cap, shook our hands. Within fifteen minutes of hearing "knock, knock," we climbed into the silver F150's crew cab. Sitting in the back of this stranger's truck, I thought about how trusting we have become even though our parents instructed us as children not to talk to or get in the car with strangers. In the last 25 days, John and I have not heeded our parents' warnings, having continued talking to and accepting rides from unfamiliar people without questioning the safety of our actions. Mark appeared harmless. The thought that we were in danger never even crossed my mind. On the other hand, if Mark had pulled up in his truck in our hometown asking us to breakfast, I would not have opened the vehicle door and jumped in without reservation. *Why are we not taking the same precautions while we are on our trip?* I didn't have an answer but assumed we would meet more strangers who would offer us rides in the next three months and we would say "yes" without hesitation. Trust? Faith? Stupidity?

Still contemplating the fact that we readily accepted a ride and breakfast invitation from a stranger, I heard Mark invite us to shower and stay at his and Kathi's home for the night. Now, I started considering this scenario from a different perspective—the Davises' point of view. Not only were we accepting an invitation from strangers, but these strangers were also planning to allow a couple they recently met into their home. They didn't know us. I'm sure Mark had discussed with his wife the possibility of offering us a shower and bed before he even met us. Inviting a stranger you have only just met into your home is one thing, even if you don't know him or her, but entertaining the thought of hosting someone you haven't even met is another. At least you can make some judgment, accurate or not, about someone you have seen. If you haven't even set eyes on them, you can't make conclusions based on their appearance. Maybe the Davises deemed us safe based on what we are doing. Does our trip give the impression we are less threatening? Thoughts…

John replied to the invitation with hesitancy, "I don't know. We can't leave the kayaks for that long."

Mark had a solution, "I have a trailer we can put everything in."

"I'll have to think about it," John wasn't convinced. Although we agreed to say "yes" on this trip, John was hesitant to accept an invitation that included moving *Work* and *Pray* because of potential damage to them during transportation.

The conversation flowed easily on the drive to Benjamin's Restaurant. *Did we really meet this man only a few minutes ago?* Mark parked in Benjamin's parking lot; we sprinted inside, trying to avoid the pouring rain. The outside door opened to a small vestibule. Opening the interior door revealed a small locally owned restaurant with yellow painted walls and wood wainscoting below a chair rail. The hostess asked if we would prefer a table or booth. We chose the booth option.

Soon after we sat down, a casually dressed tall man stepped through the door. He glanced around the room, spotted Mark, and approached our table. He partially unzipped his navy zippered sweatshirt as he sat down. Mark introduced him as his hiking buddy, Mike Fisher. (The third man named Mike we have met in Clinton.) Mark, Mike, and their wives, Kathi and Amy, share our outdoor and adventurous passions. After three hours (yes, three hours) of sharing stories and bucket lists, we climbed back into Mark's truck. On our way back to the tent, Mark revisited his invitation. John still wasn't sure. I finally voiced my opinion, "John, can I say something?"

"Sure, babe. What is it?"

"We've met a lot of people, but we have mainly talked with men. I really would like to talk with a woman."

"Done. Okay, Mark. We will take you up on the shower. I still haven't decided about spending the night."

Mark drove us back to the tent to gather our shower essentials before traveling on to his white country home. Showing us the guest restroom, Mark explained Kathi was at an exhibition but would return in a couple of hours. Showers complete (I even put on a little makeup), we sat at the Davises' round table chatting with Mark while our electronics charged on the floor behind us. From the table I surveyed their comfortable, inviting home. A bar separated the dining area from the large kitchen. In the cozy family room beyond the sit-at island, I could imagine myself curled up on their comfy couch reading a book on rainy days such as this. As John and Mark talked about their careers, through the window behind Mark I watched the falling rain. Although I love our rain days in the tent, spending a rain day sitting on a chair with a back, leaning on a table while conversing with someone like-minded refreshed my soul.

Discussion continued for another couple of hours until Kathi bounced through the door, greeting us with a contagious smile. I immediately felt at ease with this fifty-something, sandy-haired, petite woman. There are two types of people in this world—those you could tell anything and those you wouldn't even tell what you ate for dinner. The comfort you feel doesn't depend on how long you have known them; it is a result of a connection between the two of you. Kathi fell into the first category. I felt I could even tell her how much I weighed—hmm, maybe not. (John doesn't even know that.) Making sure Mark had offered us all the hospitality usuals—drink, healthy snacks, etc.—Kathi joined us at the table and in the conversation. I hadn't realized how much I have missed girl talk. Most of the people we have met have been males since men are more commonly interested in the river and spend more time there than women. And since venturing far from the shores isn't safe because we don't want to leave our kayaks and possessions, by default our interactions have been with men more than women.

Although the Davises have not undertaken an extensive kayak trip, they have embarked on a couple of long distance backpacking trips with their family. We discussed the similarities between these two types of adventures and the type of people who tackle them. Each trip requires an extensive amount of planning, minimal extras, lightweight and compact options, modesty check, and a willingness to leave behind conveniences. (We even talked about poop issues.) The people who are attracted to these ventures desire to live outside the box and be free of societal constraints. A simpler, liberating, and eye-opening lifestyle is their reward for their efforts—at least for a brief moment in time.

Through conversation, we discovered entertaining strangers isn't uncommon for the Davises. They have rented rooms to visitors and vendors for the local annual Covered Bridge Festival in October on and off for several years. Actually, they have a girl living with them right now who is working at the local crisis pregnancy center and needed a short-term place to stay. Conveniently for us, she went home this weekend.

The hands on the clock spun as we shared our lives with new friends. Although I wanted to continue our conversation, we needed to make some decisions. Mark and Kathi invited us to dinner with their friends. *Should we accept? Where should we sleep for the night?* I was in favor of saying yes to each. John needed a little more convincing. Dinner was an easy sell, but packing up our all our belongings and kayaks and loading everything into a trailer still didn't appeal to him, even after spending time with and getting to know Mark and Kathi.

John voiced his concerns, "It's raining. Everything that is dry will get wet."

"Since my trailer is enclosed, we can just lift the tent and place it in the trailer as is. Your gear will dry out overnight. Then in the morning, you can pack dry stuff into your kayaks." Mark's solution sounded reasonable to me.

"I'm afraid the kayaks will get damaged. If they do, our trip could be over."

"I understand. I have a lot of straps—everything will be secure and enclosed."

More conversation finally convinced John to consent. Yahoo!

John and Mark attached the trailer to Mark's truck and drove the nine miles to Clinton and our possessions. Kathi and I stayed at the table, continuing to talk.

Minutes later (well, it seemed like minutes), the truck and trailer passed the window. However, something didn't look right—long straps held the back of the partially opened trailer closed. The tip of *Work* stuck out the side resembling the nose of a yellow dolphin. Mark's trailer is 15 feet long—*Work* is 17 feet. Do the math. Loading the kayaks, Mark and John noticed the dilemma. However, with some creativity and maneuvering (and lots of straps and bungie cords), they were able to transport both *Work* and *Pray*. Where there's a will, there's a way.

Mark pulled the trailer into the barn; we gathered our toiletry and clothing dry bags and carried them to the guest room. I anticipated sleeping in a bed with a regular-sized pillow.

We spent the rest of the afternoon talking until Mark and Kathi's friends Bob and Janie Pound arrived. Bob, with a full head of gray hair, beard, and mustache, and Janie, who was much shorter than everyone else in the room, are a little older than the Davises are. Kathi and Janie immediately started talking as close friends do. It's amazing what you can learn about others by eavesdropping—I mean listening.

We all clambered into the Davises' SUV and traveled to Marshall, Indiana, to meet Mike and Amy Fisher at Under the Arch for dinner. Under the Arch is named appropriately because it is located "under" the Arch of Marshall, which was constructed in 1921 as a landmark to improve the downtown area's appearance.

Entering the restaurant, we found Mike and his wife sitting at a large round table covered with a black and white checkered plastic tablecloth. I almost didn't recognize Mike without his baseball cap and sweatshirt. Blonde-haired Amy, about the same age as Kathi, shared a bright smile after introductions. I scooted around the table, sitting next to Amy for more girl talk. Amy asked many questions about our trip. Up until today, most questions about our trip have come from men directed at John. After a few questions, I realized I was answering different types of questions than John does and enjoyed the variety. No one has asked John how he goes pee in the wilderness or if he's been warm enough. Actually, sharing gave me a renewed passion for the trip. I realized this is OUR trip—not only JOHN'S trip.

In the midst of the personal interview, I ordered and consumed the best catfish I have ever tasted. A road trip (traveling by road will require less time than by river) to visit this place again may be in the future. What a gratifying time making new friends!

We ate too much before bidding farewell to Mike and Amy and driving back to the Davises' home. Janie and Bob left us around 9:00—past my bedtime. Although our alarm would sound early tomorrow morning and I heard a full-sized pillow calling my name, I found saying goodnight difficult since this would mean the conversation with our new friends would end. I think the others felt the same way because we philosophized until after midnight. Even though my feet dragged as I climbed the stairs to the guest bedroom, I felt refreshed and rejuvenated. I was ready to push forward knowing Mark and Kathi supported us. Although they had barely met us, they didn't criticize or question what we were doing. At home, many friends, and even our family, didn't back us. Many regarded us like "OK. I don't understand why you are doing this, but good luck. And come home safely."

I needed today and tonight. Mark "knock, knocked" less than 24 hours ago, but we connected with him and Kathi as if they were life-long friends. Tomorrow, we leave Clinton and new friends. My eyes are brimming with tears.

04-26-2015

I'm Gonna Go, but I May Not Like It

Weather today
High: 59
Low: 37
Skies: clear
Winds: NNE 10-18 mph, gusts to 23 mph

Today's mileage: 19 miles
Total: 303 miles
Where we traveled: Clinton, Indiana, to Wabashiki Fish and Wildlife Area—near Terra Haute, Indiana

Ahh! Pillow! I slept great last night with a real, fluffy, non-compact pillow under my head—one that would occupy half of one of our holds. I'm sure John's list didn't include this pillow since it's larger than his backpack guitar! (John also had a pillow of his own so I didn't have to share!)

Dressed, we gathered our "luggage" and trudged out to the barn to pack *Work* and *Pray*. Remember, yesterday John and Mark picked up our tent, contents and all, and placed it in Mark's trailer. So, before rolling up the tent, we needed to remove everything out of it. Because of Mark's brilliant idea to wait to tear the tent down in his barn today, everything was dry. Although convenient, tearing down camp and loading the kayaks on a cement floor felt like cheating. Even though we have put away everything we own day after day for the past three weeks, the sleeping bags, wool blanket, and sleep pads seemed unfamiliar in this foreign environment. *Were these really our possessions? Where do they belong in Work or Pray?* I asked John several times where to store various items. Veering from our routine created uneasiness between John and me. I don't think Mark was aware of the friction, but I heard the frustration in John's voice. I was relieved when the barn floor was clear and we strolled hand-in-hand back to the house to enjoy egg sandwiches.

The egg sandwiches tasted better than a dehydrated meal. Actually, egg sandwiches are one of John's favorite breakfasts at home, a close second to bacon and eggs (two eggs sunny-side-up, four pieces of bacon, and two pieces of unhealthy white toast—one with only butter, and one with butter and jam...routine). I ate my sandwich slowly, reveling in the last few minutes of conversation with our new friends. I knew that once I ate my last bite we would climb into the truck, transporting us back to the river. We would then settle in our kayaks and return to the wilderness.

Even though we have gone from wilderness to society and society to wilderness several times, I am still surprised when, dragging my feet, I am faced with a change in my environment—no matter which way I am moving. I adapt to each new way of living within minutes and want to stay there, forgetting the advantages or disadvantages of the other. I forget the switch occurs quickly and painlessly. I wonder if the final transition months from now from wilderness to society will be as quick and painless.

Almost before I had swallowed my last bite, John blurted, "OK. Let's go."

He is always anxious to go. Whether on our way somewhere or on our way home—he's always in a hurry. This morning I know he used every bit of patience he had to permit Kathi the opportunity to make us a sandwich and then eat it in the kitchen instead of on the road. If he had had his way, we would have eaten a granola bar in our kayaks floating down the river. We are both changing, adapting, growing.

When we arrived at the boat ramp, a couple of men we had met on Friday, JD and his friend John, were waiting to see us off. *How did they know we were going to launch this morning? Small town?* These guys had lost a homemade houseboat when the ice broke up last winter and hinted, "Keep an eye out for it." They described their missing boat so we would recognize it if we came across it. *Did they really need to provide the details? How many random homemade houseboats can there be adrift on the river?*

John and Mark pulled the kayaks from the trailer and down to the water. We put on our life jackets, spray skirts, hats, and paddling gloves before picking up our paddles, prepared for the day. Before we climbed into *Work* and *Pray*, Kathi offered, "Can I take a picture of you two?"

"Sure." The picture she shot is one of my favorite pictures of the trip so far. We have hundreds of pictures, but few of both John and me. Most are of me since John normally has the iPhone.

Even at home, pictures of the two of us are rare because we have neglected to record our life together with photos. I don't realize how few pictures we have of us until I look at another couple's framed portraits when I am visiting their house. I make the excuse that I don't want to take the time to schedule a photographer, go to the photo session, pick out a portrait from the (*what is the word for the collection of all the pictures the photographer snaps?*), buy the perfect frame, and find somewhere to display the print. I am afraid someday I may regret my busyness.

Speaking of pictures. Scrolling through the pictures from dinner last night, I was shocked to see my gray roots glowing. Since I rarely gaze in the mirror, I hadn't detected the skunk stripe. I regularly have my hair colored every three weeks; my last hair appointment was almost five weeks ago. I brought bandanas to help cover up my signs of aging and plan to add one to my daily hair attire. *Vanity!*

Ready to shove off, to those whom we had said hello with a handshake yesterday we said good-bye with a hug today. New friends... like minds... a few tears....

Keep us upright and safe.

In addition to seven eagles plus two nests, we spied a beige car resting perpendicular to the river. *Was it beige or just rusty and caked in mud?* While the trunk lay in the river, several inches of mud covered half the hood, leaving the other half and the main body as the only visible portions. Perhaps the nearby trees' entangled roots, bushes, and weeds that partially covered the hood kept the mud-sunken vehicle from sliding farther into the water. I'm assuming someone placed the vehicle there on purpose. Just as the two buses above Perrysville, Indiana, didn't simply appear. Why does our society deem the river an appropriate garbage dump? Humans.

We approached a large modern-looking white building with a smoke stack. It reminded me of the other power plants we have identified, but I still asked John for verification (since he had the map).

John reviewed the map, "Yep. It's a power plant."

Then I started philosophizing, "Doesn't that big building seem out of place out here in the middle of nowhere?"

"The map shows a road all along the river here," John reported. Throughout history civilizations have settled along the river using it for transportation purposes and availability of food—fish and wildlife that drink at the river. Has our modern society forgotten the importance of the rivers?

"I have a hard time realizing society is so close to the river since I can't see it. I wonder if society realizes the river is so close to them."

"Probably not. Until it floods."

We paddled fifteen miles towards Terre Haute, Indiana. The air crisp, the sun shining, the sky blue, and the wind at our backs! We couldn't have asked for more picture-perfect conditions. Life flowed along smoothly until we reached an area between two railroad bridges above Terre Haute. There the water conditions changed, creating some unstable paddling. I'm not sure what lay beneath the water causing the strong currents and whirlpools. The water usually has "stripes" where the current flows down the river. This area had "circles." Everywhere. The "circles" caused *Pray* to jerk, moving almost sideways down the river. A couple of times I thought I might flip. Encountering waters like this on the Wabash scared me. I can't imagine what kind of currents and whirlpools we will face on the mighty Mississippi. I am a little (well, maybe a lot) nervous.

Jerry Hay's book indicates Terre Haute should have a boat ramp. Even when his book shows a boat ramp in a town, we are not sure exactly where it is, so we start searching for it as soon as we discover clues of civilization. Since Terra Haute is river-friendly with Fairbanks Park located on the banks of the Wabash, when we noticed people, picnic tables, and a pavilion, we began scanning the bank for the ramp. Passing more and more of the park, we began wondering if the ramp still existed. Then we spotted a boat dock (not a ramp—a dock). I hoped the "Port of Terre Haute" dock wasn't what Jerry considered a boat ramp. Although I have become proficient at climbing in and out of *Pray* on land, doing the same on a boat dock requires different maneuvers I haven't mastered or practiced. I didn't want to embarrass myself in front of the crowd enjoying the day at the park nor did I want to get wet if I dumped. (Remember, dumping is my biggest fear whether en route down the river or along the shore.) Paddling past the dock, we hoped we wouldn't have to make a return trip upstream. Then we saw the cement ramp as far away from the activity of the park as it could be. I guess the location does make sense. If I were backing a boat into the water, I wouldn't want to worry about a small boy darting behind me as he chased a ball he had missed in a game of pitch and catch with his sister. Safety in the distance. Someone was thinking.

Soon after landing another "just happened to be" (a common thing anymore) meeting occurred at the boat ramp. Having secured *Work* and *Pray* on the bank out of the way from the boat ramp, we were setting out to find the restroom when a couple approached us. At first glance they appeared to be an ordinary couple taking advantage of the beautiful spring Sunday. Wearing a lavender hooded jacket, the tall thin woman tucked a strand of long straight brown hair behind her ear. Her husband, graying and balding, carried a newspaper under his black jacket clad arm. Of course, they asked the usual question, "What are you doing?"

"We are kayaking from the headwaters of the Wabash to the Gulf of Mexico," John explained.

Turning to his wife, the guy hinted, "Sounds like a story."

We didn't think much of his statement until she explained, "I am with the *Terre Haute Tribune Star*. I'm not on duty but will make a few phone calls to get someone down here." Seriously! She and her husband "just happened to be" walking at this end of the park away from all the activities at the moment we landed. *Coincidence?* I think not.

After the couple left, we found the restroom, returned to *Work* and *Pray*, and gathered our lunches. We were heading towards the other end of the park to find a place to eat when the couple returned (they kept showing up as we were leaving), explaining, "I have a photographer and another reporter on their way, but I was afraid you would leave before they got here. I want to record a quick video clip."

As the lady was ready to push record on her iPhone, an energetic, twenty-something girl with an ID swaying on a lanyard around her neck and a camera case hanging on her shoulder approached us. The photographer shot many pictures from interesting angles while the other woman interviewed us via a video clip. *I would love to have some of the pictures.* This was our first video clip interview. The video portion of this interview made me more nervous than verbal interviews because I was concerned about my appearance (no make-up), and I don't like the sound of my voice. *Vanity!* The amount of publicity—nine interviews and ten newspapers—we have encountered without calling a single newspaper surprises me. I pray this publicity will enhance the awareness of our chosen charity, The Fortress.

Interview complete, John admitted, "I'm starved! I need to eat. I saw a group of college students playing cricket. Let's go watch them." Gathering our lunches a second time, we hiked to the other end of the park, seated ourselves on the hill in the sun, and watched the game as confused spectators.

The most intriguing part of watching cricket is trying to figure out the rules. *Does anyone really understand this game?* My theory is they make up the rules as they go. Maybe the reason the match lasts so long (days) is the rules don't specify when the game ends. As a result, the game finishes when both teams tire of playing and agree to quit. Just a thought. (I know that's not true, and I'm just ignorant.)

Eating our peanut butter wraps, we watched for the arrival of John's oldest brother and sister-in-law, Del and Becky, and their dog, Cocoa, who journeyed three and a half hours from Fort Wayne, Indiana, to visit us. They were the reason we chose to spend the afternoon in Terre Haute, Indiana. Supporting us from the beginning, they attended the launching at Ft. Recovery, Ohio, twenty-two days ago; brought us ham sandwiches, coffee, and lemon meringue pie at Markle, Indiana; and plan to pick us up at the end of our trip. While they have been encouraging, some family members and friends have barely acknowledged we are taking a trip.

I thought about what has influenced the perceived lack of support for us on our voyage. Some contemplations…

- *Is the response due to how closely they are related to us?* I don't think so. My mom is supportive, but my dad isn't.
- *Does it depend on how much they have to lose if we don't return?* Maybe a little. Kasie, John's only child, told him as he hugged her good-bye in her foyer, "Don't make me an orphan."
- *Are they not interested in a trip like this?* I don't understand this one because I am extremely interested in trips like this. I need to be careful, though, not to impose my interests on others.

- *Even if there is interest, are they too busy with their own lives to pay attention?* Probably. I didn't follow my cousin's trip on the Appalachian Trail (AT) closely, even though I was secretly jealous. I simply didn't take the time.

Soon after we finished eating, Del's red car pulled into the parking lot. Collecting our lunch trash, we left the on-going cricket match. (Apparently, the players hadn't decided the game was over yet.) After Del parked, we performed our good-to-see-you hugs and sat on a bench facing our river.

I don't think I will ever tire of gazing at the river, whether from the water or land. Why do I feel such a connection with this meandering body of water? Maybe because I have felt such peace and simplicity living in my wilderness home next to the river over the past few weeks. As a result of leaving the banks and entering a new world, I have become one with nature, day and night. We float through the animals' habitat by day and sleep in their environment at night. The sounds are perfect and natural—no man-made sounds (except for the train). Our schedule is no schedule. (Although, we have a routine.) What a great way to live—outside in the wilderness, away from the inside world of society.

Del and Becky didn't bring us any pie today but did provide a donation for The Fortress, pencils (now we have an abundance), two fuel canisters for our stove, and two freeze-dried ice cream bars in honor of our dehydrated diet. *Are we dehydratarians?*

To make the afternoon even better, Del left briefly and returned with Starbucks coffee and warm, soft, chocolate chip cookies. Yes, warm! The melty chocolate chips threatened to drip on our clothes with each bite. I even had to wipe a little chocolate from the corner of my mouth. Simple pleasures.

Sitting shoulder to shoulder on the bench, we drank the bold coffee, ate the gooey cookies, and shared one of the non-frozen ice cream bars. I contemplated the mystery of how closely the freeze-dried ice cream bar resembled the fresh un-freeze-dried variety. Even the ice cream's cold sensation was present, without the ice cream's drippings trickling down my fingers. Were it not for the Styrofoam texture, I doubt if I could tell the difference in a blindfolded taste test. Notice we shared ONE of the ice cream bars. If you do the math, one ice cream bar remains. My opinion is the remaining "frozen" treat should be mine since we have established John's lack of ice cream fondness.

Soon after we enjoyed our treats, the on-duty reporter from the *Tribune Star* arrived to do an official interview. Two interviews in one day!

Our second interview of the day complete, we enjoyed the beautiful park a while longer before Del and Becky climbed into their car (with our bottle of wine from Jeff Gosnell) to travel back to their home in Ft. Wayne, Indiana. We climbed into *Work* and *Pray* to travel to tonight's home in the wilderness. Already 5:00, I was eager to find a place to camp. John suggested concentrating on the RBD (Right Bank Descending) because someone warned him not to go ashore near the prison on the LBD (Left Bank Descending), and he was unsure of its exact location. We found a spot three miles downstream in the Wabashiki Fish and Wildlife Area. The bank appeared easy to pull up to and get out on—fairly flat. Notice, I said "appeared" easy. Unfortunately, the mud-muck-mire goo on this bank was the worst we have encountered yet. With each step the quicksand-like goo caused our feet to sink to within an inch of the top of our boots. The anxiety that our boots would not follow when we pulled our feet from the "mud glue" replaced the initial worry of water flowing into our boots. No boots lost, we landed and set up our "home."

During the three weeks we have been on the river, we have fallen into a comfortable routine when stopping for the day. First chore is setting up the tent. Then, I carry the wool blanket to the tent and begin readying our home for the night. John unpacks the kayaks and brings the bedding: sleep pads, sleeping bags, second wool blanket, and, of course, my pillow. I'm not sure what John does while I set up the bed, but I know he's busy. Bed made, I climb out of the tent to gather other belongings needed for the night from *Work* and *Pray*: Clothing dry bags (mine is green, John's is yellow), toiletry dry bags (mine is green, John's is blue), iPad (mine is green, John's is blue), charts, bear spray, Sherpa, radio, and our Petzel headlamps (mine is aqua, John's is red). The red poop bag attached to the rain fly strap provides easy access to it in the middle of the night and marks the guy-line. All our gear is organized and has a purpose. We have everything we need and need everything we have.

This afternoon, when I went to retrieve our Petzel headlamps from our deck bags, they were missing. I assumed John had already carried them to the tent and didn't think any more about them.

Everything set for the evening, we began dinner. That's when John discovered what he perceived as our first serious error of the trip. John reached into his lifejacket's left pocket to retrieve our multi-tool to open our bags of dehydrated food for supper. The pocket was empty. "Babe, do you know where the multi-tool is?" This multi-tool isn't just any multi-tool. I gave him the Swiss army gizmo as a gift for Christmas soon after we were married.

"No, I haven't seen it since Friday night at supper. Where all have you looked?"

Typically, when I ask John this question, he says, "I haven't," indicating he expects me to know where the missing object is, saving him time. However, this time, he answered in a somber tone, "I've looked everywhere."

We both hunted in every logical (and illogical) place, trying to retrace our steps. No luck. Plan B— use the small back-up knife in my deck bag to complete dinner preparations.

Later as we prepared for bed, I remembered I hadn't put our headlamps in the tent. I asked John, "Hey, did you get our headlamps?"

"No. Don't tell me those are missing too."

The atmosphere became strained. Anger replaced concern. "We never should have moved our gear from the river when we visited Mark and

Kathi. I didn't follow the normal routine. I didn't put things where they belong. I knew better. I am so pissed at myself. I know better."

I texted the Davises, asking them to check in their trailer and barn. They didn't find them in either place and offered to bring us a couple of theirs.

When I told John about the conversation, his cross response surprised me. "I wish you hadn't done that. I will be so mad if they bring us theirs." Apparently, our "saying yes" motto on this trip doesn't apply to "saying yes" when you really need help.

After another frustrating search, he gave up for the night.

We sat in silence the rest of the evening. I didn't want to upset John, and he didn't want to say something he would regret. Sometimes silence isn't merely golden, it is necessary.

I hope the lost is found soon—I miss my fun-loving John!

As usual, before retiring for the night (before dark), John posted a marker (stick) at the water's edge to keep an eye on water level changes. After setting up the tent, unloading all needed gear (except for the "missing" headlamps and multi-tool), and eating a dinner of black-eyed pea soup and rice pudding, we welcomed sleep.

What "just happened to be" event will we experience tomorrow? (Hopefully, the missing will "just happen to be" found.)

04-27-2015

There Was a Squirrel,
a Rare Squirrel

Weather conditions:

High: 60

Low: 37

Skies: clear AM turning partly cloudy in the afternoon

Wind: N 10-20 mph

Today's mileage: 22 miles

Total: 325 miles

Where we traveled: Wabashiki Fish and Wildlife Area—near Terra Haute, Indiana, to Darwin Ferry Crossing (Indiana)

Chatter, chatter, chatter. The noise teeth make when they clank together uncontrollably while the body is trying to stay warm. Unlike yesterday morning, I did not wake up in a warm bed with a fluffy pillow under my head. Instead, I was shivering and my jaw was moving involuntarily when the alarm sounded. However, the weather forecast indicates a warming trend later this week. Unfortunately, tonight is going to be another chilly one, in the 30's. I know it is still April, but I think the air should be warmer than this. I was not mentally prepared for such a long cold stretch.

• • •

Life with the Abnets is returning to normal (normal for us on the river, anyway) because what was once lost is now found. This morning when we woke up, John, still angry with himself for misplacing the multi-tool and headlamps, conducted another search. He started systematically in his rear hatch. He moved the mesh laundry bag, thinking it empty, out of his way and noticed an unexpected weight. Rummaging in the mesh bag revealed the wayward things safe and sound. (Laundry bag, really?!) He doesn't remember placing the items in the bag but must have thought at the time they would be safe there; he let the Davises know he found them. My fun-loving John has returned.

This morning for breakfast, we combined a couple of one-serving meals, couscous with apples, and oatmeal with blueberries and home-made granola. The meal planning and preparations over the past year were worth the effort because now mealtime is relaxed—pull out a bag, cut it open, add some water, heat the contents, and eat the rehydrated food. How much simpler could meal prep be? The pull-out-the-bag step, and the anticipation of what we are going to eat, is almost like the anticipation that comes with Christmas. I reach my hand into our food stores, sometimes with my eyes closed, and pull out a meal. I can't wait to open my eyes and see what I've grabbed. At home, the most stressful part of fixing a meal is deciding what to make. Therefore, the pull-out-a-bag step removes the stressful what-shall-I-make-for-dinner decision. However, unlike Christmas, the bags didn't magically appear like the presents under the tree. I remember the stress of dehydrating and vacuum sealing over 700 meals and snacks during the last year. One day in early March, feeling sorry for myself as I worked on our meals for the trip day after day after day after day, I had a revelation. Standing in the kitchen tired with an achy back, I thought to myself—*For four months, all I will have to do is boil water. I won't have to plan meals, make a grocery list, or buy groceries. Hmm… I think I can handle that.* My attitude changed after that eye-opening moment.

Breakfast complete and cleaned up, we packed up and carried our dry bags to *Work* and *Pray*. Climbing down the hill, I was surprised by the water level—it had risen about ten inches as we slept, causing the river to move approximately four to five feet up the slope of the bank. *Work* and *Pray* still rested on land, but a few more inches and they would have been floating—more proof of the necessity of tying the kayaks off every night. Thankfully, with the rising of the river, water covered the "quicksand" from yesterday. Confused, however, I asked John, "I don't understand how the river could rise that much after the dry and beautiful day yesterday?"

"Remember, Saturday was an entire day of rain. The water from the fields has to go somewhere," he explained.

Saturday seemed like a year ago; I had forgotten the rain. Until this trip, I didn't realize how long rain from upstream takes to affect the conditions downstream. Research has told me a raindrop takes 90 days to travel down the Mississippi. I wonder how long that same raindrop would take to travel the entire Wabash.

Keep us upright and safe.

The weather conditions today, similar to yesterday's, provided a great day to paddle 22 miles. On today's journey, we spotted eight more eagles and two nests. No matter how many we identify, I am still in awe each time we encounter one.

We entered the boundary waters of Indiana and Illinois. Indiana is now to our left and Illinois to our right. John and I can now navigate on the same river while in separate states. John had an idea, "After lunch I want to take a picture of you across the river. Or should I say in another state?"

"Sure." I didn't think any more about his comment and continued paddling.

On shorter days, we have eaten lunch in our kayaks instead of fighting the Wabash River banks. However, considering the distance of today's paddle, we made a conscious effort to stop for lunch, complete with another muck-mire-quicksand bank exit. Reminding us of the reason we ordinarily eat in *Work* and *Pray*!

As we approached our lunchroom for the day, several jumping Asian Carp greeted us. John reached the bank and climbed out to wait for me. He possessed the camera, providing him the opportunity to videotape my reaction to the flying fish as I paddled into the shallows. I'm sure I responded as anyone would who encounters this species of fish—I squealed like a schoolgirl. John enjoyed capturing this moment on video so he could share it with the rest of the world on Instagram! I'm glad I could provide him (and the rest of the world) such enjoyment.

After his videotaping amusement, John took care of some business on the phone during lunch. He called Fluid Fun, the outfitter from which we purchased our kayaks and some of our other gear, to discuss his broken cockpit skirt zipper. Fluid Fun contacted the manufacturer, arranging for them to send a replacement skirt along with a return label to our Week #6 package pick up at the St. Francesville, Illinois, post office. Amazing what you can do along the river with technology and a supportive outfitter like Fluid Fun.

Underway after lunch, John instructed, "Stay here close to this bank." (Meaning—paddle in Indiana.)

I followed his instructions and continued paddling where I was, wondering why he had given me directions to stay in Indiana.

Then almost immediately, he added, "I'm going to paddle over there," and proceeded to the other side of the river (Illinois).

I thought he had changed his mind about where he wanted us to paddle, so I followed him.

Arriving in Illinois, he gazed across the river, expecting to catch a glimpse of me in Indiana. Imagine his surprise when he heard me paddling behind him. He barked with some annoyance in his voice, "What are you doin' over here!? I asked you to stay over there."

"I know, but when you started paddling over here. I thought you had changed your mind," feeling a little defensive.

"I wanted to take your picture while we were in separate states. I told you that before lunch."

"Oh! Why didn't you say so? I didn't realize you wanted to do that NOW." I laughed at my misunderstanding.

John wasn't laughing as he paddled back to Indiana instructing me to STAY in Illinois so he could snap a picture of me in another state. I guess I need to do as he says not as he does.

This stretch of the river, calm and uneventful, caused my mind to wander as I became lost in my thoughts. You know, senseless stuff, like which weighs more, a head of lettuce or cabbage. About that time, a woman's voice startled me. Not just any voice, mind you, but what struck me as a middle-aged British woman's voice. "Hellooo." A cockney tone with rising inflection interrupted my thoughts. "I'm Paddling Enda." At first, based on the content and references to what I assumed was a live audience, I thought I was listening to a radio DIY show.

My head swung around in the direction of the "show," finding nothing but trees, water, horizon, and, of course, John. Yep, John. Therein lay the source of the British greeting.

"What a lovely audience we have with us. I'm just all a twitter that you joined us for today's show," sounding a bit like Robin Williams' Mrs. Doubtfire.

The show (i.e. John) went on and on, discussing the topic of compasses. "Edna" was attempting to describe the importance of a compass for navigating in the wilderness, but a confused young lady in the audience thought the subject was about a drawing compass. Wow! You had to be there. John (or should I say Edna) continued trying to explain the differences to the young lady. Becoming more and more frustrated, he (she?...I'm so confused) huffed, "Hen…Henry (apparently Edna's producer), please help that young woman understand. She's disrupting the show."

Thank goodness for *Paddling Edna* to break up the slow day. I wonder if she will show up again.

Although Jerry Hay's river map may show something exists, without "road signs," identification is difficult. Thus was the case today. This morning before venturing onto the river, John referred to the guidebook to select a possible campsite and had determined Darwin Ferry Crossing a potential camping spot tonight. Having traveled close to twenty miles, we began hunting for hints indicating the existence of a ferry crossing.

"What's that on the right? A sinking ferry boat next to the broken down boat dock?" Paddling closer, I made out a road leading from the boat dock to a few buildings at the top of the hill. Hmm…. Using my detective skills, I examined the other side of the river for more clues. In order for a ferry to be effective, access is required on each side of the river. I searched for another boat dock or ramp and a road. Seeing what I thought might be questionable evidence, I asked, "Is that a boat ramp on the left? It looks like a bunch of mud. And if this is a ferry crossing, shouldn't there be a road leading to the river?"

Darwin Ferry Crossing, like many of the towns on the river, was once a thriving area; however, now the town and ferry crossing appear somewhat abandoned. I wouldn't want to attempt floating across the river on the sinking ferry.

"I think we should stay," John announced. I assumed he planned to pull up on the right bank since it appeared more accessible with a boat dock, road, and limited civilization.

Surprised when he started paddling towards the left bank, I asked, "Aren't we staying in Illinois?" —hopeful I could change his mind. I didn't want to risk losing my boots in the mud.

"Nope. You know staying in civilization isn't always as convenient as you assume. I think Indiana is the better option."

"Okay." I pouted a little; although, deep down I knew he was right.

We steered to the left. As I assumed, we encountered a lot of mud, causing John's boot to sink and sink and sink. Soon mud covered his boot to the top, and water spilled into it. Yuck! Wet boots and socks! *This was his idea, right?*

At the top of the hill from the muddy boat ramp, we had to choose between camping to the left or the right. John scoped both sides while I walked in every direction trying to gain cell coverage. Interesting, although we had cell coverage a few minutes before in the MIDDLE of the river, no matter how I held my mouth or which direction I pointed the phone (you know the drill), "NO Service" appeared in the top left corner of my phone.

At first I was frustrated. *What will we do without the Internet to post our daily journal entry, check the weather, check e-mail, post on Instagram, check Facebook, and who knows what else?* Then I was relieved. The upside—without technology to eat up our time, we had hours to take advantage of other activities, like reading and playing guitar. How ironic that technology, designed to save us time and connect us with the world, causes exactly the opposite. Often so busy using technology, we don't take the time to relax with non-technological activities. Additionally, while connected with the rest of the world, we are disconnected from the people we are with. How often have you sat in a room of people who do not talk to each other while they are conversing with one (or more) people hundreds of miles away? While they know where "Suzie" is vacationing, what she had to eat for dinner last night at some famous restaurant, with whom she ate, and maybe her waiter's name; do they know what is going on in the lives of those in the same room? Technology—a blessing and a curse—makes a great servant but a poor master.

Returning from his camping spot search, John deemed the left choice the best. Camping spots along the river are not the manicured mowed spots found in a commercial campground. This spot came with last fall's dead straw-like grass interspersed in this year's two-month growth of sharp grass. The "lawn" crunched with each step. I won't complain, though, because the ground was flat.

As on most sunny days, we took advantage of the rays by charging the Sherpa. A fully charged Sherpa is comforting. We also pinned some clothes to the clothesline stretched between the sterns of *Work* and *Pray*. Our clothes weren't the only items needing drying—John's socks and boots also sunned themselves.

Remember the Gorilla tape (even better than duct tape) John purchased a few days ago in Attica (along with a "pillow")? We have officially added Gorilla tape to our gear list. A couple of days ago, I detected the material of one of our Grand Trunk stools pulling loose from the stitching. With each "sit" more material came unfastened, causing the stool to become unsafe. John used the tape to secure the seat to the poles in an effort to hold us over until he can contact Grand Trunk and secure a replacement. They have been supportive of our journey; I am sure they will rectify the problem. Until then, we sit gingerly.

In addition to fixing the campstool, John fixed my finger. Not with Gorilla tape but with Neosporin and a Band-Aid. I don't know how the injury occurred. I glanced down at my right index finger and noticed blood oozing from a u-shaped cut on my first knuckle. I wound a Kleenex around my finger to soak up the blood. For a small cut, it bled forever. (Well, maybe not forever.) Once it quit bleeding, I removed the yellow medical dry bag from the top of *Work*. I pulled out the Benadryl, Tylenol, Ibuprofen, Excedrin, scissors, gauze, tape, Tums, sewing kit, ice pack, magnifying glass with tweezer, sting relief pad, nasal sponges, foil emergency blanket, gloves, and moleskin before I finally found the Neosporin and Band aids. (Why is everything you want at the bottom?) I carried what I needed to John, asking him to fix my boo-boo for me. I will need to watch the cut since keeping it clean in this environment will be difficult but imperative. (Side note. To protect me from contaminated water and blood during the trip, the doctor recommended receiving a series of Hepatitis A & B vaccinations. Which I did. John had received his when his workplace offered them a few years ago.)

We ate corn bark chowder with ham, and rice pudding with bananas for dinner tonight (bags opened with the found multi-tool). I shared the last freeze-dried ice cream sandwich with John even though John "pretends" not to like ice cream. Proof that I really am a nice person. I would have had no problem eating it all by myself.

Tonight, no technology interrupted our connection with each other. Little things—reading, playing guitar, dancing, and eating freeze-dried ice cream sandwiches—make us happy!

04-28-2015

You Look the Way You Look, You Smell the Way You Smell

Weather conditions
High: 64
Low: 38
Skies: clear
Wind: NNE 6-10 mph—gusts to 16

Today's mileage: 18 miles
Total: 343 miles
Where we traveled: Darwin Ferry Crossing (Indiana) to Hutsonville, Illinois

My view this morning as I crawled out of the tent reminded me of the song "Winter Wonderland." The grass, kayaks, and deck bags sparkled with a white, cold substance—not snow, but frost. No wonder I shivered again last night. (When will I stop opening my journal entries with a recap of my shivering the night before? I'm running out of creative ways to describe my "uncomfortableness.") I am looking forward to the promised warming trend.

Just as we did a couple of days ago on the beach, we awoke to the sounds of a turkey. (They are early risers.) Since this wasn't the first time to hear morning gobbles, we didn't think much about its call until we exited the tent, noticing a truck by the boat ramp. John, spotting the truck, motioned for me to be quiet. Assuming someone arrived to hunt turkeys while we slept, he didn't want to disturb his or her hunting. I wonder, as the hunter approached his or her hunting spot, if he or she was as surprised to see a tent and kayaks as we were to see a truck. Fortunately, for the turkey, (but not the hunter) no shots were heard.

As I have said before, part of our morning rituals includes checking the weather. I'm not sure why we think being aware of the weather forecast is important, but I am sure the need to possess some sense of control is the ultimate motivation. Although we can't control the weather, we can control how prepared we are. Rain suits, heavy coats, gloves, etc. Without cell or Internet service this morning, we eliminated the check-the-weather step in our routine and, as a result, our control of being prepared. Prepared or not, the weather is going to be what it is going to be. How did people plan 100 years ago? If it was cold, they put on a coat; if it was hot, they took off their coat; if it rained, they sought shelter; if it snowed, they put on boots. Easy! Sometimes, planning actually creates more stress. How many times have I become upset when un-forecasted rain begins falling since I didn't grab a raincoat on my way out the door? If I didn't have expectations, what I viewed as inaccurate planning couldn't disappoint me. Today, we lived as they did 100 years ago and went with the flow. (Pun intended.)

Pulling *Pray* to the boat ramp this morning, I again thought about how different my river view is from my road view. Since no rain has fallen since Saturday, I was still surprised the river had risen again while we slept. Not only would I have not noticed from the road how much the river had risen, but I also don't think I would have looked. I love my expanded river view and focus.

Keep us upright and safe.

John always helps me launch *Pray* first. Then I hang out on the river, waiting for him to catch up. Sometimes he takes a while to join me, so I use the time to think. (Go figure.) This morning while hanging out, I pondered the inactive ferry location at Darwin. What was life like in the area when the ferry connected Indiana and Illinois? Were the communities agriculture-based, river-based, or small-town-based? What was the population? I tried imagining the type of vehicles waiting on the ferry to cross the river and land at the boat dock. Were they trucks, cars, or tractors? Did families, businessmen, or farmers occupy the vehicles? What style of music filled the air from the radios? Unfortunately, not many clues existed to aid in answering these questions. On the Illinois side of the crossing, the dilapidated ferry sits at the bottom of the ramp, giving the impression it will sink if someone steps on it. Why is it still there? My gaze followed the road to the top of the hill where a couple of buildings stand. From my vantage point on the river, I had a difficult time distinguishing if they are viable businesses, and if so, what type of establishments are they. If I approached this same area from the road, would I find more clues to solve the mystery?

The Indiana side of the river provided even fewer clues. The only remnant of a ferry landing is a muddy ramp. A stone road connects the ramp to the top of the hill where the road continues to the right, leading to somewhere. To the left lie the woods and the grassy area where we camped last night. There are no buildings or signs of buildings. Did commerce once thrive here? If not, why the ferry? What is the process for shutting down a ferry crossing? When did the ferry perform its last run between states? How many people came to use the ferry finding it was no longer running? Farmers certainly used the ferry to transport equipment from one side of the river to the other, from one field to another. Since the nearest bridges are 22 miles north or 17 miles south, changing their route would have had significant consequences. Changes causing changes. I had so many questions with few answers, all in the couple of minutes while I waited on John to join me for the day. Before the trip, I expected to see wilderness and perhaps an infrequent town along the river. I did not expect to catch a glimpse of the past. I did not expect to witness what used to be.

• • •

Today, we spotted three more power plants, bringing the total to five for the trip. The power plant's black smoke stacks towering as artificial trunks of concrete trees above the natural tree-lined bank felt intrusive in the midst of the wilderness along the river. However, in our modern society, we need industry and industry needs power. Power plants along the river use water to produce steam as part of the electricity production process, an example of how closely society and wilderness coexist. When a man flips on a light switch ten miles from the river, he isn't aware of what is happening at the source of his electricity in the wilderness. He doesn't appreciate the squirrels playing in the trees, the deer walking down the path to take a drink of water, or the eagle soaring above its nest in the sycamore tree. From his view on land, he is disconnected from nature even though the power plant exists in the world of the animals. He enters a light-filled room not realizing society and wilderness exist together by the river a few miles away. From the river, I experienced the source of his electricity and coexistence of society and wilderness—where the two separate domains meet.

In addition to power plants, we encountered two more abandoned buses, bringing the total to four for the trip—one in a tree, two on the ground, and one resting half in the water. Sights not observed from the road. Hmmmmm... More questions...

The eagle sightings are decreasing. We witnessed only three today. This makes me sad.

Some of the banks are not as steep as they were at the beginning of our trip, making stopping for lunch more convenient, which we did today. Don't get me wrong, not every bank is accessible, just more of them are. Today's lunch-break bank was the easiest place we have exited from *Work* and *Pray* in a long time—if not the entire trip—easy slope and no muck-mire-quicksand. After landing in style, we ventured into the woods and located a fallen tree, providing a comfortable place to sit and a lunch table. Sitting on the tree in our peaceful lunchroom, I inspected my surroundings in all directions taking in the signs of spring. The beginnings of the green may-flower leaves and tree seedlings covered the recently brown, bare winter ground. The dark brown lines of the tree trunks created a contrast against the green of the ground. The budding trees provided shade where the winter sun had shone through. What perfection and peace exists in nature. Even when the tree we sat on at lunch originally fell, nothing went wrong. The falling was all part of the cycle of life. Nothing goes wrong in nature. Even if the tree had fallen on me, it might have been unfortunate for yours truly, but it would not have been a problem of nature. Nothing goes wrong in nature. The fallen tree serves a perfect purpose in the perpetuation of Mother Nature, as it decays and breaks down into dirt, returning nutrients to the ground. Nothing goes wrong in nature.

Enjoying my river view, I savored a new addition to our usual wraps and fruit roll-up lunch. Our Week #5 package contained caramelized walnuts, walnuts covered with a mixture of brown sugar, oil, and soy sauce. This is one treat I plan to make and consume at home—yum!

Another episode of *Paddling Edna* helped ease the monotony of traveling on the smooth water of the Wabash. Today's episode again included some "studio audience" confusion as to exactly who was being paddled and who was doing the paddling. "Hello! I'm Paddling Edna. On today's show we...yes, young man, do you have a question? What's that? When will I be paddling Edna? I am Paddling Edna. You'd like to watch? I'm sorry, but I don't ..., OH! No, no, no, young man, it's an adjective. I am called Paddling Edna. I'm not about to paddle some young lass named Edna. Oh, dear. Please control yourself." Edna still maintains that the *paddling* portion of Paddling Edna is an adjective, not a verb. I laugh simply thinking about Edna's naivety.

We traveled a total of eighteen miles today to Hutsonville, Illinois. The river's slow current and the boat ramp's mud-free cement provided a stress-free landing (next to the floating, dead carp). Kraemer Memorial

Park, located at the top of the hill (everything is uphill from the river), is well kept and includes a fire ring, picnic table, and bench facing the river. An engraved stone memorial reveals the existence of a ferry connecting Hutsonville to Indiana in 1939. Unlike Darwin's Landing, there isn't any evidence of the crossing, not even a sinking ferry sitting by a dilapidated boat dock or a muddy boat ramp with a stone road leading to who knows where. The memorial is all that remains of the ferry. Again, many of the same questions I asked myself this morning popped into my head this afternoon. The use of the Wabash River has changed as society has transformed. Sites eliminated and added—ferry landings to power plants. The water's purpose has changed—transportation to energy.

As usual when entering society, upon landing in Hutsonville, we were eager to find three essentials—water, trash receptacle, and restroom. Today, we added cell service to our list. Two out of four were available close to the boat ramp. Unfortunately (fortunately?), this is the second day in a row my phone shows "NO service" in the upper left hand corner, which equates to no accessible Wi-Fi, with little hope of having any tomorrow.

Having taken advantage of the picnic table for dinner, we are now sitting on the bench facing the river with the sun setting behind us, watching the fishermen run their nets and launch their boats. Without the internet, we will enjoy another evening of reading and maybe dancing. No technology equals peace and relaxation.

Since we haven't connected with the rest of the world for a couple of days, will anyone start to worry about us?

04-29-2015

Being by Myself Is So Much Better with You

Weather conditions
High: 70
Low: 42
Skies: clear
Wind: N 6-21mph, gusts 26mph

Today's mileage: 20 miles
Total: 363 miles
Where we traveled: Hutsonville, Illinois, to sandy bank between Hutsonville, Illinois, and Vincennes, Indiana

I wish I could tell you last night was everything I hoped it would be—a relaxing evening spent reading, dancing, and "wasting" time with John. Unfortunately, it turned into a technology jam session accompanied by the eating of junk food. Here's what happened…

After sitting on the bench watching the fishermen check their nets, talking to each other, and playing guitar, we strolled to the convenience store's restroom one last time to perform our nightly prepare-for-bed ritual of brushing teeth, washing faces, and peeing. We had planned to go to bed early and read uninterrupted by technology. Stepping out of the convenience store, having completed our tasks, John pondered, "I can't believe they don't have Wi-Fi here. Sit at the picnic table and wait while I ask."

Sitting at the picnic table, I watched several people go in and out of the store. A family pulled up in their mini-van and climbed out. Noticing the two older boys wearing baseball uniforms, I assumed they had finished their ballgame and stopped at the store to pick up some snacks. I watched for them to exit the store so I could determine if I was correct. I was spot on. They came out with large 32 oz. drinks and big bags of chips. Even though we don't routinely drink mega drinks or eat chips, I was jealous. As I was making my judgment calls regarding mid-America eating habits, I realized John had been gone longer than I expected. Soon the door opened. Smiling as if he had bought me a new diamond ring, John strutted to the table and placed two bags of chips in front of me—Cheetos and Doritos. Score! (Don't judge me!!)

John announced his accomplishments, "They DO have Wi-Fi, and I thought we'd need some nourishment as we catch up on our journaling and Instagram postings. I'll go get the iPads."

I struggled between clapping and crying. I knew I needed to keep caught up on my Internet chores. On the other hand, I was looking forward to relaxing, reading, and doing nothing productive. At least I enjoyed some unhealthy chips as a reward for my diligence. (Of course, we finished both bags of chips, not wanting to stow any leftovers in our kayaks. Remember, John didn't think there was room for my pillow….)

John returned with our technology gadgets. We proceeded to go our separate ways, performing separate tasks on separate devices, requiring little or no interaction with each other—except for the occasional bumping of hands as we reached into the same chip bag. By the time we finished our chores, the sky was dark, and we were tired with no time left for reading. At least we were productive….

This morning was another frigid start to the day. I'm tired of waking up COLD! I want to feel my toes, and sleep all night without my shivering body waking me. I can do this! I know the time will come when I will lust for a little of this coolness.

Remember, soon after our arrival in Clinton on Friday, John "went to the restroom" returning with two Dairy Queen ice cream cones? Well, this morning he pulled another going-to-the-restroom trick. I was in the middle of making breakfast, when John announced, "I'm so sorry. Babe, but I really have to poop." Making breakfast is my task, so John going to the restroom wasn't a big deal.

I had finished reconstituting Cheese Blitz casserole when I heard John approach from behind. (By the way, John didn't care for Cheese Blitz casserole at home but loved it this morning. I wonder how many other trip-favorite dehydrated meals will not taste as yummy when we return home and aren't as hungry. Does hunger make your taste buds less finicky?) Even though I heard John's feet squash the grass, I didn't see him approach; so when he placed a carry-out sack and a cup on the table beside me, my heart melted with appreciation.

Standing tall with his chest puffed out and wearing a heart-warming smile, he announced, "Warm, homemade, cinnamon rolls and coffee." Even though I like Cheese Blitz casserole, my mouth watered at the thought of the ooey, gooey, doughy, cinnamon treat. The square Styrofoam container squeaked as I pulled it from its white paper bag. Opening the to-go box, I caught sight of the white frosting dripping over the sides of the warm, yeast treat. The roll smooshed down as I used the enclosed white, plastic fork to cut the first bite. What is even better than eating a warm, homemade cinnamon roll on a chilly morning? Chasing it down with an aromatic sip of black, dark roast, hot coffee.

The rest of the morning was uneventful as we ate two breakfasts (we ate the Cheese Blitz casserole too), packed up, and launched from the mud-free boat ramp.

Keep us upright and safe.

As we paddled down the Wabash minding our business, out of nowhere a turkey flew across the river, barely missing us. I ducked to avoid encountering it up close. This was not the white, farm-raised, Thanksgiving variety. It was the deep brown, wild, almost our national bird variety. Regardless, they are big birds!

This near miss flying-bird incident reminds me of another time we scarcely escaped a collision with a large bird. A few years ago, we were on our way home from an end-of-the-road trip to Northern Manitoba and Saskatchewan. If you study a map, you will realize there are few towns in interior Canada. At the beginning of the trip, we had stopped at one of the few restaurant-gas station-shower-motel-combination businesses at an intersection for dinner. On our return trip home, we planned to eat again at this one-building-holds-all. However, on our way home, tired in addition to hungry, we decided to take advantage of the motel portion of the "retreat." Unfortunately, others were tired as well—there was no room in the inn—forcing us to continue and pull an all-nighter.

John typically does the driving. He likes driving; I like riding—a good combination. As the sky grew darker and the hour later, John's eyes stayed closed for long blinks one too many times to be considered safe, so he asked me to drive. John sat with his head resting on a pillow against the passenger window sleeping (perhaps drooling). Minding my own business traveling down the road, I witnessed a moose cross the road in front of us. Since I am from Indiana, encountering a moose cross the road caused me to shout, "A moose!" John reacted by sitting up, grabbing his glasses, and scanning the area in panic. I don't know if he panicked more because of the moose or my sudden outburst. By the time he gathered his senses, we had passed the moose area; but unfortunately, no moose remained.

"Sorry. Go back to sleep," I apologized. John removed his glasses, settling back into his sleeping position, soon making sleepy noises.

I continued driving while humming to the radio. (And maybe "dancing" a little. You know. The noggin nodding, shoulder shuffling, toe tapping, hand hammering sort-of-thing.) Then, I noticed something white sitting in the opposite lane but couldn't quite make out its identity. I drove closer. I slowed down. I squinted. Suddenly, the white object spread its wings, taking off as we passed. I stared directly into the eyes of a PELICAN. I ducked. He banked up just missing my driver window. I exclaimed, as calmly as I could, "A pelican!"

John jumped up, grabbed his glasses, and insisted, "Let me drive. I can't sleep with all this commotion. What are you driving through, a zoo?"

Can you imagine explaining the being-hit-by-a-pelican incident to the insurance company?

Me: "A pelican hit my truck."
Insurance adjuster: "So you hit a pelican."
Me: "No. A pelican HIT my truck."
Silence…

Back to the Wabash. In addition to the turkey, we spotted three eagles, which, thankfully, kept their distance as they soared (ignoring us) gracefully above the trees.

With the widening of the river, we aren't experiencing any minor rapids, causing many of our days to drag on monotonously (except when turkeys try taking us out). Today was one of those days. The smooth, mirror-like river created a duplicate bank and cloud-dotted sky in the water, providing us with an uneventful paddling day. So we passed our time by discussing things we miss.

Convenience: full service bathroom—warm water and privacy
Comfort: sofa—chair with a back
Activity: time with our YSB (Youth Service Bureau) girls—miss them

These are little parts of our life we took for granted until they were no longer readily available. I wonder if, with time, our lives and our normal will change so much that what we are missing now will soon become something in our past. Will we, our lives, and our normal change that much over the next couple of months? Is this a good or bad change? Are all changes good or bad? Or simply changes? On the other hand, I don't want to miss new experiences because I feel obligated to the old. Hmmm…. Thoughts and questions with no answers right now. The questions may be answered as time passes without our realizing they have been resolved or remembering what the questions were. I need to quit thinking.

For supper we ate unstuffed peppers and pineapple upside down cake. Again, delicious! (At least we think so today.)

We are spending tonight on a sandy bank in the middle of no-where and are without cell phone service again; therefore, no Internet connection. Tonight, since there is NO chance to stroll to the convenience store and ask about Wi-Fi, buy and eat a bag of Cheetos and Doritos, give an interview, or have dinner with a mayor, we WILL read and perhaps play the guitar. (If we can stay awake.) I guess it's only John and me. I love my life on the river!

That's all I have for today. Here's Johnny…

So, she wants me to write. Well, we spent the first few miles of today's trip trying to identify "Trapper John's" cabin. Apparently, he's a bit of a local celeb for his appearance on a Discovery Channel show called *River Men*. Maybe we too would be on TV if we had a necklace made from a dried raccoon penis. (You can't make this stuff up.) Well, we didn't see a cabin that fit the image we had, so on down the river we went.

There appear to be fewer ducks, geese, and turtles than we had been encountering earlier. (Or is it just because we are now usually farther from the river's edge than we had been when the river was smaller?)

One of the most interesting things we saw today was a huge colony of mud swallow nests and the hoard of swallows that occupied them. We were going under an old pivot-style railroad bridge (interesting on its own) when we noticed the nests around all of the edges of the concrete pilings. There were hundreds, if not thousands, of nests. As we approached, we were suddenly surrounded by all the beautiful, dark blue, iridescent swallows as they darted overhead and around our kayaks. Pretty cool.

According to Jerry Hay's Wabash River book, this is "one of the three remaining swing bridges on the Wabash." A large gear affixed to the top of the center span enabled that middle section of the bridge to rotate, allowing large steamboats to pass through when they used to travel the Wabash as far upriver as Logansport. Very unique remnant of a time that is no more.

Well, after our planned 21 miles (yes, we were pretty pooped), we began looking for a place to camp and the three required landing criteria… An eddy, an accessible bank, no immediate downstream hazards. Safely ashore on the RBD (RBD = right bank descending), we determined there was a good spot to pitch a tent just above the slope of the bank. We also had plenty of southwest sky to allow us to get a good charge from the solar panel, trees behind to block the winds, and a "beachfront" view of the river. We even found a small clear stream, which was not on the charts, full of minnows just down from camp. As an added bonus, the bank was covered in coyote tracks. Coyotes kinda' freak out LaNae. Home for the night.

One of the questions a reporter had asked us in days past was, "What is there about the river that others don't know?" We simply replied with the answer "more." There is simply so much more going on at the water level than what is seen from a brief passing over a bridge. It seems we usually only notice a river when it encroaches into our world, such as during a flood. I would suggest, however, that everyone should spend some time on the river, even if for only a few miles. Then maybe they would notice the river and its peculiarities. Most who assume the river is simply a single current flowing between two banks would soon learn, that aside from the main current (which is always changing and relocating), there are many other currents. Even in the middle of a 300-yard wide river, there are numerous rogue currents, whirlpools, and the rare but always threatening hazard such as a submerged tree. Despite what we may think when we pass over, the river is never lazy, and its world is never boring.

04-30-2015

You Can See the Elephant from Here

Weather conditions:

High: 64

Low: 39

Skies: sprinkles in the morning, partly cloudy in the afternoon

Wind: N 12-28 mph, gusts 33 mph

Today's mileage: 22 miles

Total: 385 miles

Where we traveled: Sandy bank between Hutsonville, Illinois, and Vincennes, Indiana, to

Kimmel Park, Vincennes, Indiana

Nature never sleeps. Animals often interrupt the stillness of night. We humans thought WE invented second and third shift—wrong. Last night after we retired to our tent for the night, wakeful-wildlife noises surprised us. First, a turkey gobbled in the distance. Then a large bird's wings (probably turkey) flapped barely above our tent, owls hooted in the trees, and fish plopped in the water. Thankfully, even though footprints proved their existence in the area, coyotes didn't yelp in the vicinity! Since we were without cell coverage last night and unable to check the weather forecast before going to bed, middle-of-the-night rain noises surprised us. Oddly enough, even with the rain, the river levels decreased by morning—I don't understand how this works!

Leaving the dryness of our tent this morning, we encountered drizzling skies, causing everything outside to drip. As a result, we were "forced" to eat a cold breakfast of homemade granola. It tasted delicious! At home, I had packed a small bag of powdered milk (Nido) in with the granola— enough to pour over the cereal and enough to drink. To my surprise, the powdered milk (Nido) is good enough to drink. I don't know if the Nido brand is so much better than others are or if the quality of powdered milk in general has changed, but it is better than the powdered milk I remember drinking as a kid.

The falling river level uncovered a mud-mire-quicksand combination, which we fought during our launch. Luckily, no lost boots. Unfortunately, once John climbed into *Work*, he flew too close to the sun when he tried rinsing every bit of the mud-mire-quicksand off his boots, filling the right one with water. More wet socks to dry.

Keep us upright and safe.

Floating down the river while waiting for John to launch and join me, I met our first eagle of the day perched in a dead tree on the bank. He stared at me. Our eyes met. He watched me float by. He must be comfortable in his feathers (or old and blind) because, without leaving his station, he also let John pass. Today we counted six eagles.

Once the sky quit leaking and the sun made its appearance, today turned into another beautiful paddling day—we are becoming spoiled.

Coming near to a left-hand bend in the river, we witnessed the effects of erosion and the benefits of erosion prevention side-by-side. A peninsula covered with trees and brush survived in the center of the bend. On each side of the peninsula, the banks were steep with few trees. Approaching, we noticed large cement pieces covering the lower portion of the peninsula bank. I doubt if someone chose to prevent erosion (creating a peninsula) in the small area by placing cement along the bank while allowing the rest of the bend to erode unprotected from the Wabash River as it carries away small pieces of land. However, from this unplanned experiment, I reached three conclusions. One—don't build too closely to the river; the building may end up floating to the Gulf. Two—erosion prevention can protect buildings erected next to the river. Three—the river is constantly changing.

The changing river reminds me of a quote by Heraclitus "No man ever steps in the same river twice, for it is not the same river and he is not the same man." Changes—in the river and me. Although the changes in the river are visible, the changes in me are not as readily determined. They are slight and internal, not easily recognized by those around me. I have to concentrate and take time to distinguish the slight shift. Just as the banks erode, unprotected parts of my soul can wash away. However, most view bank erosion as negative, but I view my soul washing, because of my time on the river, as positive. My views of the river have given me a new perspective of nature and society. I know I will not be the same woman in four months because these changes in me are evident even after a few weeks on this changing river. I welcome the changes occurring within me and anticipate who I will be in August.

Thinking about the new me, I reflected on what our lives will look like when we return home. Mine in particular. Life is too short to exist doing the expected—why not the unexpected? What is the unexpected? Who decides what is the unexpected? Is everyone's unexpected the same? What will this trip teach me? Hmm… I have three more months to ponder and pray. One more thought. Is *not doing* the expected the same as *doing* the unexpected? John and I go out of our way NOT to do the expected.

One example of our desire to go against the grain happened on February 14, 2004. John and I were in Gordon Food Service (GFS) gathering mints, mixed nuts, paper plates, and other bits and pieces necessary for our April 3 wedding reception. Standing in the checkout lane. I felt stressed. I considered John. He was staring in the distance at nothing. *Was he thinking what I was thinking?* I blurted, "Why are we doing this? I don't want to make a guest list. I don't want to pick out music, I don't want to.... I just want to get married."

John's furrowed brow relaxed. He smiled.

I concluded, "Because everyone EXPECTS us to. That's the wrong reason."

We studied each other. Without a word, we turned the cart around and started returning its contents back to the shelves. John later admitted to putting the mints in the wrong place—just because.

Empty cart returned to the cart station, we strutted to the parking lot, called our pastor from the car, and asked him about his availability the next Saturday. His calendar was clear. We were married on February 21, 2004, in the children's chapel of our church under inflatable fish. We didn't do what was expected, so was it unexpected?

Arriving at Kimmell Park boat ramp in Vincennes, Indiana, about 2:30 p.m., we were greeted by a group from Ball State University taking six large (12 -15 pounds each) invasive Asian Carp from their boat.

"How did you catch them? With a net?" John inquired.

"We caught them via electric shock all within five minutes. It took us longer to launch our boat than to bag these guys. We're doing a study on the different diets of the carp upstream and downstream," they replied. Sounded interesting. We left them to their work.

Having pulled *Work* and *Pray* from the water and deposited our trash in the proper receptacle (remember the three missions we hope to accomplish when entering society—trash, restroom, and water), we began our quest for the restroom. Spying a restroom (and perhaps shower) on the hill by the campground, I smiled. A restroom and shower—a dream come true. Easy access all night. Maybe wash some laundry. However, someone nearby overheard my enthusiasm and burst my bubble by informing us the restroom building was closed. This is the fifth CLOSED restroom located by a boat launch we have encountered. Disappointment! Surveying the area for another option, we detected what appeared to be an abandoned, white block building.

"Let's see if there is a restroom we can use there," John suggested.

The building didn't appear promising. But what did we have to lose? We turned in the opposite direction of the campground, which seemed counterintuitive. Approaching, we first noted a sign defining the building's purpose—"Boat Club." On the other side of the window, a blue sign provided insight into the boat club membership. It read…

WANTED
GOOD WOMAN
Must be able to cook.
Clean, Sew, Dig Worms
Clean Fish
MUST HAVE A
FISHING BOAT!
Please Send Picture of Boat

Peering in the open door on the other side of the sign, we saw exactly what we expected to see—several older gentlemen sitting at tables in the middle of a dark, smoke-filled room—the stereotypical regular meeting of the "good 'ole boys." You know, the meeting where they discuss everything and nothing daily while drinking beer and smoking their weekly cigarette allowance.

John talked with the seven "boys" briefly, then, gesturing towards me asked, "Do you have a restroom she could use?"

One man, moving his chew to the inside of his cheek, pointed to the back of the room and explained, "Yeh—just make sure there's toilet paper." (I was not optimistic about the cleanliness.)

Uncomfortably stepping into the room of men, I felt like I was the first female they had beheld in several days. I sensed every eye following me as I made my way to the back of room. The bathroom was as I envisioned—dirty. I checked for and found the hoped for toilet paper, put the seat down, unfastened and pulled down my wetsuit, feeling more uncomfortable at my state of undress than I would have felt behind a tree next to the boat ramp. Mission two accomplished, I made my way to the sink. Using soap pumped from an orange container of GOJO hand cleaner, I washed my hands. Definitely a man's restroom!

After thanking the men for my use of the facilities (John had already used a tree soon after we landed), we strolled back to the boat ramp, attached our wheels to *Work* and *Pray*, and hiked the quarter mile uphill (everything is uphill from the river) to the campground. Drawing near the campground, we first spotted poles with several electrical outlets strategically placed at every campsite. We hoped that, unlike the restrooms, they were available for use. Then we caught sight of a water spigot at each site—water at each site too. No way! Since the campground was empty, except for one camper, we wondered what the odds were each site would have water AND electricity. First, we tried the spigot—water rushed from the opening. Mission three—water—accomplished. We plugged the phone in the outlet and heard the welcome *ping*, indicating the phone was charging. Even with convenient access to water and electricity, I was still concerned about my restroom options (or lack thereof). The Boat Club was too far away, and the meeting of the minds would soon adjourn for the day.

Oh, well, we were hungry and decided to worry about the restroom later.

While we were enjoying chili soup and chocolate pudding cake (thanks, Cyndy Evers, for making sure each weekly supply package makes its way to our each destination), one of The Boat Club members pulled up. Through his rolled-down truck window, he asked if we needed anything. (Someone is watching out for us.)

"Do you know how we could get the restrooms unlocked?" John asked.

Pointing to the camper, the man replied, "The manager, Ray, lives in the camper over there. He should be home from work this evening."

Later, when Ray arrived home, John walked to the camper, introduced himself, and inquired about the restrooms.

"You're welcome to use the restroom all evening and tomorrow morning. You can even take a shower, but the water will be cold." Ray gave John the key and instructed, "Put the key under the ash tray tomorrow before you leave."

John returned to the campsite waving the key in the air. Life is good!

Even though we were the only ones in the campground, we didn't want to become complacent with our possessions by leaving them unattended, so we took turns taking our first shower since Clinton—five days ago. I jumped in and out of the frigid water several times as I washed my body and hair. I even managed to shave my legs, or should I say goose bumps. The cold, speedy shower felt heavenly. Well, maybe not the experience itself, but the clean feel and smell afterwards were worth a little discomfort.

Shivering all the way back to our campsite from my cold shower, I observed John texting.

"Who ya' talkn' to?" I asked.

"Kerri Lehmann," He answered. Our neighbors, Kerri Lehmann and her family, are taking care of our dogs while we are gone.

John showed me the text dialogue.

Kerri: "The water spigot at back of house is not working. Started to work this AM when I came down to feed and water, then quit running water as I was filling. Came back to check tonight and still no water."

John: "Hmmm, ok, thanks for letting us know. There is a spigot (pump handle) just inside the "2nd" south side barn door (2nd from east). Hopefully, you can draw water from there. I'll have Travis check in the house."

Kerri: "We tried the one in the barn too, but no luck."

John: "Ok. Let me do some checking and I'll get back with you."

John then texted my son Travis, explaining the water situation and that the fuse above the pump in our basement was likely blown. John asked Travis to replace it when he goes out to check on the house tomorrow. We could not have taken this trip without our support system at home. Lehmanns—dogs. Travis—house. Evers—food parcels.

Once clean, John lugged our laundry to the restroom and attempted washing it (four shirts, four pair of underwear, four pair of socks, and two pair of pants) in the dirty, rusty sink. Unfortunately, some of our shirts accumulated dirt and scale from the sink and now have new dirty spots. At least they smell better. At home, we would have placed our newly "clean" clothes back in the laundry basket of "dirty" clothes, waiting to be washed in the next full load. Definitions are changing—it's all a matter of perspective. John tied the clothesline between our kayaks and hung our clothes to dry. They won't dry before we leave in the morning so we will hang them out every time we stop for the next few days. This is our new normal.

Even with pleasant daytime temperatures, as soon as the sun starts retreating, the temperature drops. A cold shower didn't help at all. We were cold. Without a campfire to warm our bodies, we climbed into the tent and snuggled in our sleeping bags, trying to capture some body heat.

We had just burrowed into our sleeping bags with a "this feels wonderful" sigh when a vehicle pulled into the campsite next to us. Then another. And another. And another. Soon a loud crowd had gathered, listening to country music, oblivious to the tent 10 feet away—with people trying to sleep. Apparently, this campground is a hangout for the college students.

I'm ready to go back to the wilderness and the "quiet" of nature. Again, definitions are changing—it's all a matter of perspective.

Side note: Jerry Hay notes that at this location in the river, the Wabash has grown to where it is the largest non-navigable (not possessing channels adequate for commercial traffic) river in the United States.

05-01-2015

Your Skin Is Soft…Like Lard

Weather conditions:

High: 55

Low: 39

Skies: clear

Wind: NNW 2-13 mph, gusts to 21 mph

Today's mileage: 12 miles

Total mileage: 397 miles

Where we traveled: Vincennes, Indiana, to St. Francisville, Illinois

Today is May 1—one month since the beginning of our adventure! I cannot believe how fast this trip is flying —August will be here before I know it. As I write, I am sitting by our third campfire of the journey. This one is compliments of Leroy Wease (another "just happened to be" moment). Shall I start at the beginning of the day?

The beginning of the day actually began late last night with our noisy neighbors' arrival in the campground. The intruders shared their country music with us until the early morning hours. As a result, John woke up with a country twang and "hankerings" and couldn't quit singing the chorus to "Take This Job and Shove It." In addition to the country music, the students treated us to the glow of their campfire. At one point, the fire became more than a glow, causing concern on my part that the tent would burst into flames at any time. Lucky for us, their plan didn't include staying the entire night. Almost as if someone announced the party's end, car doors creaked and slammed, engines roared, and gravel crunched under tires. I haven't a clue what time they left, but it wasn't soon enough for me.

Unfortunately, the fire's glow didn't contribute to my warmth. I shivered all night, executing the try-to-keep-my-toes-warm moves. With each shudder of my body, I wondered when warm weather would arrive. After all, it's May.

After the chill of the night, the lack of frost or ice on *Work and Pray* surprised me when I crawled out of our "bedroom" this morning.

I made breakfast while John readied our kayaks to launch. Having told him our quinoa breakfast was ready, I assumed he would sit down next to me within minutes, if not seconds. However, I soon realized the error of my assumption. I waited and waited. *Where is he?* I couldn't imagine what was taking him so long. Having only a 12-mile paddle to St. Francisville, Illinois, we were taking our time preparing to launch this morning; but I was becoming a little impatient—I didn't want to eat a cold breakfast. *He's not being considerate of my time. What distracted him this time?* (John tends to become easily distracted, especially if he passes through our study at home and spots his guitar sitting on the stand. He can't drift through the room without picking it up, sitting in our rocker, and playing a song, or two, or three. Sometimes, forgetting what his original plans were.)

My frustration intensified. The weight of his steps pressing into the moist spring grass signaling his approach didn't even help lower my annoyance level. *It's about time.* I was ready to ask him bitingly what took him so long when he reached his arm around me, placing a steaming cup of coffee on the table.

"Awe." I smiled, feeling guilty about my impatience. He had taken the time to light the stove, warm the water, and make instant coffee in order to surprise me. One of John's gifts is surprising me with treats. On this trip, he has surprised me by continuing to surprise me, even when it is inconvenient. What a great guy! I think I'll keep him.

We leisurely ate breakfast (coffee included), packed up, used the restroom one last time, and placed the restroom key under the ashtray outside of Ray's camper. Pulling *Work* and *Pray* to the dock, we passed the area previously occupied by the college students. Even if we hadn't heard them last night, we still would have known they had been there because of the amount of trash left behind. A couple of guys wearing maintenance uniforms and gloves were placing beer cans, pizza boxes, and other litter into a trashcan.

"Do you know if there were college students here last night?" one of them asked.

"There certainly were."

"We keep asking the police to patrol this area. They won't listen to us." How frustrating to clean up, knowing you will perform the same task again in the near future (reminds me of housework).

Soon after reaching the boat ramp, John realized he forgot to fill his dromedary. Back to the campsite about a quarter of a mile away. While I stayed at the dock with *Work* and *Pray*, a couple pulled up and asked the usual questions… "Where are you from?" "Where are you going?" After my answers and the usual once-overs, the woman shared a little of Vincennes's history. The bridge we had passed under yesterday on our way into town was the Red Skelton Bridge, in honor of the famous comedian who grew up here in Vincennes. *I wonder what Red Skelton was like as an eighth grade student.* (Later, after she left, I realized our kids probably don't know anything about Red Skelton. A few years ago, when asked, they didn't know who Laurel and Hardy were. *What kind of parent doesn't introduce their children to Laurel and Hardy?*) She also informed me the next bridge we would pass under was the George Rogers Clark Bridge, also known as the Lincoln Memorial Bridge. Huh?

This area is historical. Yesterday, the man from The Boat Club shared the history of the beautiful stonework pavilions and landscaping located throughout Kimmel Park. German prisoners of war during WW II built them. I am sure the prisoners didn't have any idea or even care how much their effort would be appreciated many years later. What are we as a nation building today that will provide enjoyment to those living seventy years from now? Do we have any idea or even care?

Side note—I have poison ivy and haven't a clue where I was exposed to the plant and its oils. I am a little concerned about contracting it more frequently since we will be traipsing through many wooded areas during the next three months. (I can officially write three months now—not four!) I haven't always been allergic to poison ivy. About 10 years ago when John and I were clearing the land in our woods for a cabin, I carried armload after armload of logs without a thought, knowing I had never dealt with a reaction to the plant before. A couple of days later, I was miserable as the seeping, itching rash kept me awake. I covered myself with the unsightly, pink Calamine Lotion. (The doctor later told me to take Benadryl. I now take Benadryl with the appearance of the first blister.) During my time of misery, you would think since John loves me so much he would bend over backwards to take care of me. But no—he doesn't have any sympathy for me at all. He has had poison ivy more times than he can count during his fifty-three years on this earth. He harrumphs and ignores me any time I say that I think I have poison ivy. If I continue breaking out, this could be a long trip for both of us.

Once John returned with the full dromedary, we launched *Work* and *Pray* on our way to collect our Week # 5 package at St. Francesville, Illinois.

Keep us upright and safe!

Passing The Boat Club in *Pray* revealed a difference between today's river view and yesterday's land view of the building. It now appeared to be a quaint building with a fireplace; benches and rocking chairs faced the river on the full-length porch. If I hadn't met the "good 'ole boys" yesterday, I would have assumed the building housed a quilting club, whose members were white-haired grandmas drinking coffee while discussing the church bizarre. Different views—different perspectives.

In addition to the single eagle sighting today, we encountered a partially submerged pick-up truck. The only portion above water of the vertically stuck vehicle was its teal blue bed. Was the driver in the truck when it landed in the river? I hope not! Or was it originally resting on the bank when erosion caused its terra firma platform to give way, causing it to land in the water? What is keeping the truck from floating down the river?

Speaking of erosion, or should I say erosion prevention, downstream from the dead truck we watched the up-down motion of a pump jack as it worked a live oil well. Pump jacks erected close to the banks of rivers cause a potential problem if erosion is not contained. Stone and rock lined the bank in this area, creating a solid foundation for the pump to function without fear of the same fate as the truck. Accidental polluting of the river is avoidable.

Today, we floated under our second pivot bridge of the trip, the Cannonball Bridge. (The first being close to Riverton on April 29.) The Cannonball Bridge was originally a train track connecting Indiana and Illinois by rail. Upon closing the track to train traffic, a gentleman purchased the bridge, converting it to a toll bridge. Minimal changes were made during the installation of the running plank, making the bridge accessible to cars. Years later, ownership of the bridge changed to St. Francesville, Illinois, and finally to the State of Illinois. The toll bridge is still open to traffic, costing one dollar to cross. Gazing up, I considered the wooden "tracks" on which the vehicles must drive with precision. One erroneous move right or left and the wheel would drop off the side of the tire-width plank. Floating under had to be less stressful than driving on it would be. I tried snapping a picture of the planks but failed, as all I ended up with was an unplanned, unflattering selfie.

• • •

Leroy Wease, the Leroy I mentioned at the beginning of this entry, greeted us as we arrived at the Port of St. Francisville, Illinois (established 1812), when he "just happened to be" driving down to the river the moment we pulled up to the boat ramp. Leroy—sporting smiling eyes, a well-kept beard and mustache, and baseball hat—was probably older than he appeared. He explained he works out of town each week; so, ordinarily, he wouldn't be in town on a Friday morning. However, he was enjoying some time off this weekend, spending part of it (like most people in small towns along the river) driving down to the river, scanning it, and then returning to town. That's how he "just happened to be" driving his red truck down to the river at the exact moment we landed.

He asked the typical, "What'cha you doin'?"

Answering with the typical "Paddling from the headwaters of the Wabash to the Gulf of Mexico," we told him we stopped in town to pick up our next food parcel at the post office.

"Can I give ya a ride?" he asked, without hesitation.

"Yes," John replied, since that is what we say on this trip.

On our way to the post office, we observed the oldest Catholic Church in Illinois. Sounds interesting and beautiful, right? The only problem was half of the church lay in a heap on the ground with only the back wall, bell tower, front pillared porch, and steps still standing. We stopped for a moment, taking in the sight and some pictures of the demolition. The excavator's mechanical yellow arm reached towards the building, effortlessly taking bites out of the walls, working its way from the rear of the building towards the bell tower, pillars, and steps. Soon all that would remain of this historic church would be a pile of bricks, plaster, and dust. A crowd stood on the sidewalk watching. I'm sure many had tears in their eyes as they remembered running through the halls before their mother sternly reminded them, "Don't run in church." Maybe, their memories were of standing on the steps on their wedding day or shedding tears during the baptism of their children. Unfortunately, in the United States, we are quick to tear down old buildings regardless of their history or value to the community. Many times the excuse is "The cost to rebuild is less than the cost of upkeep on the current building." Can you put a cost on preserving history?

Leroy waited for us while we picked up our Week # 5 package and replacement cockpit skirt at the post office from Peggy. Unlike some post office workers who treat us as an interruption in their usual day, Peggy showed interest in our trip, treating us like a new friend.

John's skirt's (Seals spray skirt for the kayak—need to keep this in context) zipper malfunctioned a few days ago. One call to Fluid Fun, where we bought our kayaks and many needed accessories, over a lunch break earlier this week was all John needed to do (technology—gotta love it). Fluid Fun contacted the manufacturer, arranging for a new skirt to be drop-shipped to St. Francesville, Illinois. New skirt opened, John placed his defective skirt into the enclosed self-addressed envelope and mailed the skirt back to Seals.

Post-officing (I know this isn't a word—it's sort of like banking) complete, Leroy gave us a tour of the small town. (Population 800—saaaaalute!) We passed one restaurant—only open for lunch; a closed school—bought by the city for one dollar; one bar—only serves Totino's pizza and the coldest beer in town (the only beer in town, so by default it has to be the coldest); one ball diamond— overgrown and rarely used; and a Catholic church—soon to be history instead of historical.

At the end of our tour, we parked along the street near the demolition site, watching the church's bell tower fall to the ground in a cloud of dust. How long had the builders taken to erect the bell tower 99 years ago, considering the short time required for the mechanical jaws to push it down? As the dust settled, the cross on the church's steeple, a symbol to many over the years, stood alone. *I wonder how the bell faired.* Such a sad sight, and I don't even have any ties to the church.

After we took a few videos and pictures of the destruction, Leroy delivered us back to *Work* and *Pray*. We pulled them up from the boat ramp to the other side of one of the nicest, river-friendly parks we've encountered so far. The park had OPEN restrooms, a pavilion, water, trashcan, and electricity! What motivates a small nondescript town such as St. Francisville to have such a nice river park? Or should I say, why don't larger towns exploit the river by creating a usable area?

The number of people who drive down to admire the river and drive back to town surprises me. The driving down part isn't what bewilders me; it's the not staying. I know I have stated this before but I still think if I lived in a river town, I would need to drive to the river, as these locals do, but I wouldn't drive down, glance, and leave; I would exit my vehicle and sit awhile, watching the river. I can't merely glimpse at the river; I need to study the constant changes. I wonder if the draw to the river for me is its proximity to nature and the feeling of peace and relaxation it creates. Whatever the reason, I know even after traveling on the river several hours each day, when we pull to shore at the end of the day, I don't want to venture far from the banks. I never grow tired of surveying the river—it is becoming my home and a part of who I am.

Before setting up camp, we hung our clothesline between *Work* and *Pray* to dry our day old, still wet laundry. By the end of the evening, all laundry items smelled better and were dry, even if the rust and dirt from the Vincennes's restroom sink endured.

As we were taking the tent out of *Work's* back hatch, a blue truck drove down to the water, turned towards our campsite, and parked. Parking was an unusual activity by the river so we assumed we were the focus of their stop. An elderly man dressed in a blue and tan coat, jean shirt (complete with paper and pen stuffed in the pocket), and dirty jeans climbed out of the driver's side of the truck; the passenger stayed seated.

"I'm Lomar Gute," the gentleman greeted us. Pointing to the truck, he introduced the other occupant. "This is my wife Dorothy. She didn't want to get out." He asked the usual "what are you doing" questions and then relayed an interesting story. "Yeah, we're on our way home. We delivered a 'coon outside o' town. We've been havin' problems with 'coon, so I set a live trap. Well, I caught this 'coon. He's a good one. You know what I mean. There are good 'coon and bad 'coon. You can tell by their personality. So, since this was a good one we decided to haul him north o' town and set him free. I'm sure he'll beat us home. Oh well." *I'd like to meet this good 'coon.*

Not sure how to respond to the raccoon story, John stated, "We're taking pictures of the people we meet on our trip. Can we take one of you and your wife?"

Lomar turned to the truck, motioning for his wife to join him, "They want to take our picture. Come out here."

Dorothy reluctantly opened the truck door, slid out, adjusted the bobby pin in her hair, and joined her husband. I assumed their trip to relocate the raccoon had been a spontaneous one since she was still wearing her gardening gloves. I could picture the scene...

Dorothy, cleaning the fall and winter debris from her flowerbed, jumped when Lomar came around the corner of the garage carrying a live trap, a raccoon cowering in the corner of it.

"Dorothy, into the truck. We're taking this critter north o' town."

Dorothy knew the drill. Thinking she would soon return to complete her gardening, she clambered into the truck without saying a word or removing her gloves. Raccoon relocated, Lomar made his usual trek down by the river but, noticing us, took a detour.

Dorothy, wanting to return to her gardening, grumbled, "What do ya think you're doin'?"

"I'm gonna find out what those people are up to."

Here's where Lomar and Dorothy entered our lives.

John snapped their picture. Then as quickly as the Gutes arrived, they left. John and I glanced at each other. *What just happened?*

While John arranged the tent, I made lasagna, complete with parmesan and garlic croutons (one of our favorite dehydrated meals), for lunch. Starved and now having an excess of dinners after picking up our food package from the post office, we ate dinner for lunch. While I cleaned up after lunch, John made a phone call at the other end of the park—the only place where he could receive a signal, a weak one at that— to Travis to check on the status of the no water situation. Travis explained the breaker to the pump was tripped. He reset it, and now life is good. Technology—gotta love it!

While John fixed the world, Leroy brought us some wood for a fire.

This brings me to the point at which today's journal entry began—sitting by our third campfire of the trip. What a treat to sit by the fire journaling while John plays his guitar. Once I deem this daily journal entry complete, I will pull up my book on my Kindle. Yes, I am using technology to read. There wasn't enough room for my pillow; do you really think there would enough room for a book?

Here's to May! What adventures will this next month hold? Whom will we meet? What unique river views will we experience? Where will we camp? Can't wait for each new day to begin!

05-02-2015

I Don't Allow the Truth to Tie Me Down

Weather conditions:
High: 77
Low: 62
Skies: clear
Wind: SSW 2-13 mph, gusts to 17 mph

Today's mileage: 15miles
Total mileage: 412 miles
Where we traveled: St. Francisville, Illinois, to Mt. Carmel, Illinois

Today began and ended with socialization, with a few miles of paddling in between, meeting more people in one day than we have so far on the entire trip. Here's how our day progressed…

Our first encounter with others began soon after we finished eating breakfast casserole, one of our favorite meals, when TWO sets of visitors came by. First, our neighbors dropped in from their nearby campsite. They arrived yesterday in their new camper to visit relatives in this area, which they do often. What a great place to camp frequently —by the river!

Second, Virginia Berry from *The Francisville Times* performed our tenth interview. Sixty-something Virginia, casually dressed in her slacks and sandals, arrived with a lime green notebook in hand and a camera around her neck. Not long after leaving us, she drove back. As she parked, I glanced around to see if she had forgotten something. *Why else would she return so quickly? Maybe she had thought of another question. She didn't need to take our picture; she already had.* She climbed out of her car. Handing us a package of vanilla crème-filled pastries and two bananas, she explained that when she was conducting the interview, she wanted to give us something. On her way home, she remembered the yummy treats she had purchased this morning, so she drove home, gathered them from her kitchen counter, and returned.

"Thank you. How kind. We may have these for breakfast tomorrow."

Keep us upright and safe.

We identified two eagles today. Cool. I set eyes on my first snake in the water. Not so cool. John noticed one a few days ago. (Maybe weeks—I don't remember.) As long as the snake is in the water and I am in *Pray*, life will be good for all.

I'm not fond of snakes—or mice either. I had a conversation with God once after stumbling upon a snake in my yard. "Why do we need snakes?" I asked.

"To eat mice," God answered.

"Why do we need mice?"

"To feed snakes."

"Then why can't we get rid of both?" God apparently didn't agree with my logic since snakes AND mice still exist.

Now that the banks are more accessible, we land and eat lunch on shore more often. However, trying to find a place for our lunch break on land to-day, we found the banks too muddy again. So we chose a floating lunch, planning a snack break later at Mt. Carmel, Illinois (15-mile mark for the day), before continuing to Patoka Island farther downstream to camp for the night. Whether spending our lunch break on the banks or floating in the river, I feel blessed to eat surrounded by the sights and sounds of nature.

During a floating lunch, my body sways with the water's movement while I survey the bank. From this vantage point, I hear birds talking to each other. I gaze up at the trees and flowers decorating the bank, catching an occasional glimpse of a squirrel or bird. Since I haven't entered the squirrel's world by crossing the line between land and water, if I sit silently, I can watch him scurry around doing what he does to survive in the wilderness. No human provides him crumbs from a sandwich or seeds from a bird feeder. Nature cares for him. And he does just fine.

If we are fortunate to stretch our legs and eat lunch on land, I sit on a fallen tree or my kayak, gazing at the river I was recently one with. The water ripples slightly as it continues flowing downstream without me. Even though my body welcomes the change in position (and opportunity to pee), I long to return to the water, joining its journey. My life in the wilderness!

Prior to today, we have come across a few weird currents, but today they were more prominent. We now recognize the warning sound—a splash. Hearing the warning splash, we examine the area for the source in the water so we can avoid it if possible. If there isn't room to miss the disturbance or it materializes before we have a chance to maneuver around it, *Work* and *Pray* dance sporadically to a melody only the water hears. As with the rapids, I consider these unpredictable currents scary. And if John is honest, I'm sure he does too.

Passing through the area where the Grand Rapids Dam used to operate (just above Mt. Carmel, Illinois), we encountered some of these weird currents. All that remains of the dam is a wall on the left bank and some rocks on the opposite bank. The Army Corps of Engineers built and maintained the dam from the 1897 to 1931 to improve navigation on the Wabash. In addition to improved navigation, the dam created pools of water, enhancing the fishing in the area. In 1922, Frederick Hinde Zimmerman built the luxurious Grand Rapids Hotel on his family land to take advantage of the tourist activity created by the fishing. Suspiciously, the hotel burnt to the ground in 1929, soon after the United States Senate Committee on Commerce announced it was removing the funding for the dam. I'm glad the obstacle no longer remains. However, I would love to travel back in time to stay at the hotel and cast a line into the river.

Late in the afternoon—break time—we arrived at Mt. Carmel, Illinois, where the White River joins the Wabash. Although we have experienced confluences of other rivers with the Wabash, its size increased dramatically with the addition of the White. Almost directly across the river from the confluence sits a boat dock and Twin Rivers Restaurant. Deciding since we hadn't made landfall since setting out this morning and I had to pee, we would rest our paddles in this historic area.

Not surprisingly, we encountered another "just happened to be" moment when we landed at Mt. Carmel. Jim "just happened to be" driving by the boat dock in his golf cart as we climbed out of *Work* and *Pray*. Jim, sporting a pair of glasses hanging from the front of his white t-shirt, pushed his baseball cap back as he asked the usual questions. After providing the essential information, John added, "We stopped here, hoping to use the restroom at the restaurant."

Jim offered to drive us up the hill to the restaurant (everything is up hill from the river). We accepted, "Yes." (Since that's what we say on this trip.) He moved his hand-whittled cane from the passenger seat as I climbed in. My trip with Jim was uneventful. John, on the other hand, set out for the restroom and, of course, came back with a place to camp AND dinner arrangements. While in the restaurant, he met Brooklyn Adams, who "just happened to be" working.

John introduced himself to Brooklyn, asking her the meaning of her tattoo, which he recognized as a Japanese character form known as "Kanji." As usual with John, his listening skills suffered—he immediately forgot her answer. However, this did provide an opportunity for more conversation, "My wife and I are kayaking through on our way to the Gulf."

The usual disbelief, questions, and answers followed. Then John, assuming I was too tired to continue paddling to Patoka Island, asked, "Could we pitch our tent behind the restaurant?"

"Your stuff won't be safe here, but you can camp a little downstream at my family's camp," Brooklyn volunteered.

John agreed, and she provided clear directions (or so we thought).

Having had arranged our overnight accommodations, John exited the restaurant onto the deck. Jim yelled up at John, "Hey, that's the owner." Jeff Wyatt, the Twin Rivers owner, "just happened to be" standing outside the restaurant when John stepped out of the building.

After a brief conversation about our trip, Jeff expressed interest in discussing the headwaters of the Wabash. John told Jeff, "We are camping at Brooklyn's and are planning to come back to your restaurant for dinner."

"You better come back for dinner—on me."

Jim returned John to the boat dock and me. Although wondering what was taking John so long, I wasn't surprised when he relayed the events that had transpired. "Just happened to be" moments don't shock me anymore. I almost expect them.

Launching *Work* and *Pray*, we proceeded to Brooklyn's. Our journey to our camping spot was not without challenges.

Challenge number one: find Brooklyn's camping spot. She had given John directions, "Downstream, on the right bank, about a quarter of a mile, red building, stairs..." Again, directions on the river differ from directions on the road.

We paddled what seemed like the correct distance. *How do you determine a quarter of a mile on the river?* John described the situation, "We are looking for a red building with stairs. I see a red building, but I'm not sure if those are stairs. Let's go a little farther."

A little farther produced some stairs but not a red building. John made a judgment call, "Let's turn around." Turning around meant paddling upstream. This didn't thrill me because it was late in the day and my body ached with fatigue. However, since the alternative was traveling farther downstream to the island, paddling upstream appeared to be the best option.

Reaching the red building we had passed previously, John yelled for Brooklyn, hoping she would materialize out of nowhere. And she did. A twenty-something girl with shoulder length hair and glasses appeared and beamed down at us. I assumed this girl dressed in jeans and a white t-shirt with PINK in gold sparkly letters on it was Brooklyn.

I was right.

Relieved to see her, John asked, "Hi, Brooklyn. Is this the right spot?"

"Yep." She smiled, revealing straight white teeth and dimples.

Challenge number two: Dock *Work* and *Pray* next to a pontoon raft floating in front of the mud-covered unusable stairs, tie the kayaks to the remnants of the unsafe stair railings, and then climb up the steep, muddy bank. This was the first time we had docked *Work* and *Pray*, i.e. tied them off, allowing them to float.

I placed myself between the raft and the bank on one side of the stairs while John paddled around the raft to the other side. I held onto the raft, watching John steady *Work* against the bank by placing one end of his paddle on the back of his kayak and the other on the bank, creating a type of outrigger. Then he pulled himself into a seated position on the back of *Work*. So far, so good.

Next step, John needed to place his foot on the steep, slippery bank while trying to keep *Work* from floating away or tipping and himself from falling. Watching his comical flailing, I wavered between laughing and crying because I knew my turn was next. If he had a problem, I would probably face the same dilemma. One foot out—he started sliding. If only he had another paddle he could use to steady himself and keep from slipping. Finally, he steadied himself. Carefully, lifting the other foot out, he swiftly moved his paddle from the horizontal position across his kayak to a vertical position in the mud. He stood up. So far, so good.

Next step, John needed to make his way from *Work* to *Pray* on the other side of the slippery, sharp-edged, metal stairs while trying not to slide down the bank into the water. The railings presented the biggest obstacle. He could climb over, crawl under, or scale to the top around the steps and down the other side to me. Nervously, I watched him go up and around the steps. *What if he fell? What if he tore his neoprene on a stick or the top of the jagged stairs?* He reached me safely and helped me perform similar steps to climb out of my kayak that he had only a moment ago used to emerge from his. Fortunately, I had the advantage of using him to steady myself while my paddle still lay horizontally on the back of *Pray*.

John handed me a stick. "Now, use this for balance and climb to the top of the hill."

"Sure, No problem," I choked. I stabbed the stick into the mud, placing one foot sideways beside it before placing the other foot next to the first with a little sliding in between. Stab, place, slide, place, stab, place, slide, place... until I reached the top of the hill.

Challenge number three: Decide which items we needed from our limited amount of possessions. Then, transfer them from *Work* and *Pray* to the top of the bank without dropping anything in the water or mud, damaging equipment, or tearing clothing. This is a great spot for a family camp and fishing base; but with many metal and sharp edges, the environment is not safe for lightweight camp gear and neoprene. John, trying to stay upright while not losing a boot with every step, threw each article up the hill, hoping I would catch each one. (Playing pitch and catch with our dry bags reminded me of our first night on the river when John threw our gear up to me from *Work* and *Pray* on the steep broken-pieces-of-cement bank.) I wasn't always accurate in my catches. Every time I missed an article, I prayed it would land on the top of the hill and not roll back down through the mud into the water. Success! Last challenge met!

I studied the family campground; to my left stood the landmark red building; to my right, four feeble, spindly poles held up a scrap tin roof of the pavilion. An unusual mix of chairs, some for outdoor and some for indoor use, were positioned around the pavilion's perimeter. The mud-caked chairs and floor provided evidence of recent flooding. A couple of ashtrays lay on the table ready for the next gathering. In the corner, a large, blue, plastic barrel served as a trashcan.

Brooklyn confirmed my assumption, "We are still cleaning up from a flood a couple of weeks ago. We get a flood every year in the spring." She pointed to an area I had overlooked. "This is where my dad cleans fish for our big fish fry on the Fourth. He feeds 200 to 400 people, depending on if we have a band or not. Many stay and camp out here, y'all should come." Even though we had recently met Brooklyn, the invitation didn't feel out of place. I found myself wishing we could accept this year, but we will still be living on the river at that time. Maybe another year.

The fish-cleaning station included a white poly table with a piece of green hose for rinsing. I envisioned the area filled with people. Kids playing tag as they ran too closely to the fish-carcass-littered area, sternly reminded to play by the swing set slightly beyond the pavilion. I could almost smell the unique stench associated with fish cleaning no matter what kind of fish it is.

Brooklyn interrupted my thoughts. "The red hooch is my uncle's. The smaller brown one over there is my dad's."

I had never heard a building called a *hooch* before, but the term fit the two rugged metal buildings with steel roofs. Brooklyn stepped around the corner of her uncle's building. "You can stay in my dad's, even though it's missing a door. He can put that up for you."

Although Brooklyn had offered us a building to stay in, I like sleeping in our tent. It is home. John must have read my mind, "Your dad doesn't need to. We can stay in our tent."

"If you're sure..." Brooklyn paused, waiting for us to change our minds. "You can put your tent anywhere."

"Thanks."

"Hey, I need to get back to work. I'll be back later tonight."

Exchanging good-byes, we returned to our pile of chosen must haves.

Due to the nature of the area and recent flooding, we watched for hidden fishhooks, lures, and other sharp objects during our search for a site to pitch our tent. We found a danger-free spot between the pavilion and the swing set.

Our home for the night in order, we changed for dinner. Changing for dinner doesn't require much time when your lone outfit option is your only set of "clean" clothes. And since I have sworn off wearing make-up (at least for the trip), I save even more time. As we were changing, we heard men's voices on the other side of the tent. I felt a little uncomfortable knowing all that separated me from the men was a thin piece of tent material.

Emerging from the tent, we discovered the source of the voices—six men sitting under the pavilion, most of whom were an Adams or a friend of an Adams, including Jeff, our dinner date. After introductions and brief conversation, Jeff offered to drive us to his restaurant. We accepted the ride and climbed into Jeff's vehicle.

I gripped the door handle as Jeff swerved or slowed down for the many potholes in the dirt road leading from Brooklyn's camp to the restaurant. We parked in the stone parking lot and strolled to the building. Earlier in the day when I approached the building, my mind was focused on finding a restroom so I didn't pay much attention to my surroundings. A portion of the tan building, known as Twin Rivers Family Restaurant, rests on stilts. *I wonder how often the floodwaters rise higher than the stilts, causing the restaurant to close.* Entering the door, I remembered the cash register to the left and kitchen door behind it; to the right the one- person restroom I had used earlier; straight ahead the first of three dining rooms.

A friendly waitress escorted us to a table in the center of the third dining area. Many un-curtained windows filled the gray-paneled walls, providing a clear river view. (I never grow tired of staring at the river.) Unlike many restaurants, Twin Rivers Family Restaurant had different sized tables instead of booths. A tube of paper towel rested on each table instead of rolled silverware.

Deciding what to order, I asked Jeff for a recommendation. He bragged about their famous catfish, so that's what I chose to eat. After the waitress wrote down our requests, Jeff began his inquiry. Jeff, with a salt and pepper mustache and goatee, didn't portray the image of a restaurant owner in his jeans and a green t-shirt. Pushing his glasses to the top of his graying hair, he inquired, "Where does the Wabash really begin? Some maps show Ohio and others Indiana. Since y'all have been there, I'll finally get the correct answer."

John provided the accurate information, "It starts in a field behind a turkey farm outside of Ft. Recovery, Ohio. We had to hike the first 18 miles before the river becomes navigable. It remains narrow until after the dam at Huntington."

Curiosity satisfied, Jeff provided us with a brief history of Mt. Carmel— the mussel boom, the Jumbo Adams story, the historic black pearl, and also some of his own colorful history. What an interesting man! He should write a book.

Returning to the Adams' camp spot, we relaxed in Brooklyn's uncle's red hooch. The building, in disarray during the flood clean up, housed two large tables—one an oval wood-veneer pedestal table with one leaf, the other wood with tile inlays. Mismatched chairs—kitchen, desk chairs with rollers—bordered the tables. In the middle of the first table rested three ashtrays, reading glasses, a deck of cards, a 20-ounce plastic convenience store soda cup, papers, and mosquito repellent.

John and I sat at the wood-veneer table with Brooklyn, now wearing a three-quarter length black and gray t-shirt with "Brooklyn" in white cursive letters across the front. Billy, her father, sat next to her. Her three-year-old nephew, Kadon, with a smile that melts your heart and eyes that make you suspicious of what he is contemplating, grabbed at his grandfather's arm to gain his attention. Meanwhile, Billy's brother-in-law, Dale, sat quietly smoking cigarette after cigarette. His weathered face and partially baldhead were tan despite the fact that May has barely begun.

Fifty-something Helen, Billy's sister and Dale's wife, sat at the other table, legs crossed easily under her; her brown fur-lined moccasins rested on the mud-caked floor beneath her. Long brown hair, parted in the middle, outlined the sharp features of her nose and chin. Rarely without a smoke in her hand, she wore a dainty necklace around her neck, a contrast to her jeans and t-shirt.

Listening to the southern drawl of our hosts, I took inventory of everything crammed into the small one-room building. One corner housed a fish-cleaning station, including a large open chest-style deep freeze located next to it, waiting to be filled with the catch of the summer. Next to the freezer, sat a wood stove with a pink "pig" teakettle—the pour spout was its snout. Along the wall opposite the wood burner and deep freeze, a coffee pot rested on a cabinet. Shelves all around housed other kitchen-type essentials, including paper plates, cups, and utensils. A large flat screen TV blared background noise and produced flashes of light from the wall above the tile inlayed table.

Sitting there, I imagined several of the Adams family and friends gathered around the table playing cards while the fire crackles in the background. The room is warm, filled with cigarette smoke. Occasionally, a commercial on the TV distracts someone from the game, causing the others to prompt, "*%*#$, Frank, it's your turn." Oh, the laughter, memories, and stories these walls must hold.

Billy, Helen, and Dale told some great stories of their family and many people they've met along the river, including a 70-year-old man who had traveled through on the river in an inflatable kayak. He deflates it, puts it in his backpack, proceeding on land with his kayak on his back. Interesting and convenient. He has kayaked in many places in his unique, transportable kayak, including the Amazon.

In addition to the stories, Billy warned us to check for snakes in our cockpits in the morning. Hmmmm... And I repeat... As long as the snake is in the water and I am in *Pray*, life will be good for all. A snake in my kayak is not a desirable scenario. Most of the reported potential hitchhiker threats come in the form of common water snakes, but apparently, a copperhead makes an unwanted appearance now and then. (Remember, more people are killed by cattle each year in the U.S. than by snakes. I am counting on this statistic to hold true.)

We said goodbye to our new friends, who traveled to their houses, leaving us to ours—our tent. On his way out the door, Dale turned around and placed some money in my hand. "It isn't much, but I want to give this to the charity." My eyes brimmed with tears at his generosity. Unexpected blessings.

We were brushing our teeth when a truck pulled up. *Who could this be? Did someone forget something?* However, we didn't recognize either the couple or dog that climbed out of their vehicle. I think they were as surprised to find someone camping in this spot as we were to see someone pull up.

In order to avoid accusations of trespassing, John quickly introduced us, "Hi. We are John and LaNae. We're kayaking from the headwaters of the Wabash to the Gulf. Brooke invited us to camp here for the evening."

"I'm Mike's (another Adams brother and owner of the red hooch) daughter, Jenna. This is my boyfriend, Brent. We're planning to build a fire and sit by the river. You're welcome to join us." Sitting in the pavilion and talking, we watched their dog play with a ball before leaving them to the fire.

Good night. I can't believe how much socialization can happen in one day while traveling on the river. Didn't we leave our new friends of St. Francisville a year ago—not only this morning?

PS. One of our river angels in Clinton, Kathi Davis, gave me a tube of lavender essential oil when we stayed at her house a few days ago. I rubbed some on my poison ivy—miracle cure—no more itching. Works better than the pink stuff and doesn't make me look like a freak! Another addition to our gear list. Lavender oil, who knew?

05-03-2015

The Toilet Is Clean—You Can Defecate at Will

Weather conditions:
High: 79
Low: 61
Skies: clear
Wind: S 6-17mph, gusts to 25 mph

Today's mileage: 18 miles
Total mileage: 430 miles
Where we traveled: Mt. Carmel, Illinois, to a sandy/shell beach

This morning was not one of our typical mornings. First difference: At Billy's recommendation, John checked our cockpits thoroughly for snakes. I hoped this would be the first and last time. Unfortunately, John informed me that "de-snaking" will become a morning ritual. Glad he's the one performing the task and not me. Second difference: Transferring our possessions from the top of the hill down to where *Work* and *Pray* floated in the water, we faced some of the same challenges we did yesterday— keeping all items out of the mud and river as I threw them to John while he tried to stay upright without losing a boot. He was better at catching than I was, or maybe I was a better pitcher than he was, since he didn't miss any gear like I did yesterday. Even so, I was glad we didn't have an audience.

Mission accomplished, John stuffed the articles into the appropriate storage places in our kayaks.

Work and *Pray* ready to launch, I set our collapsible blue cooler on the table under the pavilion. (The blue cooler lives in John's kayak behind his seat. It came along to provide a safe place for fragile items such as fruit and other treats. Occasionally, when we haven't found a garbage can for a while, trash finds its way into it.) I unpacked our breakfast—the package of vanilla crème-filled pastries and two bananas we received from Virginia Berry yesterday. (Was it only yesterday morning she handed us these treats as we were leaving St. Francisville?) As I unwrapped the plastic wrap from around the pastry package, my mouth watered. Although my stomach asked for food, I closed my eyes as I savored the crème filling in my mouth. I luxuriated in each bite, not wanting the experience to end. The pure sugar delighted my taste buds. I was pealing the healthy portion of our breakfast when a vehicle we didn't recognize parked beside the pavilion. A man in a t-shirt and faded overalls climbed out, along with his German Shepherd.

The man's smile peeked through his full beard and mustache as he introduced himself, "Hi. I am Richard Johnston." Pointing to his dog, he added, "This is DJ." Richard is an Adams Family friend. The Adams family campground must provide a get-away for many in Mt. Carmel.

After John provided Richard with the details about our trip, and us, the rest of our breakfast called. But not wanting the conversation to end, John invited him to stay, "We were just finishing our breakfast. We don't have much to offer you, but please stay."

Richard declined our breakfast offer but continued sitting in the pavilion around the glass-topped table while John and I finished our bananas. Conversation flowed with Richard as we talked about our trip, his dog, and stories of the area, causing us to long for a return visit to meet more Adams family and friends.

John glanced at his watch, "Oh my. I didn't realize it was this late. We need to get movin.'"

We gathered the pastry container and banana peels and placed them into the blue trashcan, thankful we didn't have to find a place in *Work* and *Pray* to stuff our garbage while we searched for a trash receptacle later. A trashcan—a luxury. Who would have thought?

"We really enjoyed getting to know you, Richard." John extended his hand to our new friend.

Shaking John's hand, Richard inquired, "Do y'all have any way to listen to music?"

"Not really. We have our iPads but need to save our battery power for journaling."

"Wait." Richard moseyed to his vehicle, opened the door, pulled out a battery powered AM/FM radio, and offered it to John.

John took the radio. Examining it in his hand, his brow furrowed. I wondered what he would say. We had decided we would say "yes" on this trip—unless we couldn't find a place to store the gift. Remember, everything has a place, and there is a place for everything. (My pillow even has a place now.) I could tell by John's delayed response, we probably wouldn't be taking the radio with us. "Richard, thank you so much for your thoughtfulness. But I can't accept this. We just don't have room." He placed the radio back in Richard's hand. I thought saying "yes" on the trip was going to be difficult. Saying "no" is definitely as hard, if not harder.

Richard accepted his gift back. "I understand," he whispered as he lowered his hand to his side.

After saying goodbye to Richard, we cautiously sidestepped our way down the hill to our kayaks. The time had come to leave Mt. Carmel, Illinois.

Keep us upright and safe.

I reflected as I floated away from the Adams family camp. (Every time I write "Adams Family," I think of the TV show *Adams Family* from the

60s. But Brooklyn, Billy, Kadon, Dale, and Helen are nothing like Morticia, Gomez, Uncle Fester, Lurch, Cousin It, Wednesday, or Pugsley.) We visited this town for less than 24 hours, but left many new friends behind.

Today, we paddled under our third pivot bridge of the trip, complete with a large swallow colony and their mud nests. If I were traveling on this bridge instead of under it, I'm not sure I would recognize it as a pivot bridge since I wouldn't notice the more robust center pillar. In addition, the bridge would hide the pivot mechanism at the top of that large column. And I know I wouldn't detect the swallow colony housed on the supportive columns and pivot. I love my river view.

Each of the pivot bridges we have encountered is now defunct. Pivot bridges were necessary in the early 19th century to allow passage for the large boats and steamships traveling on the Wabash. In the late 19th century, traffic stopped because erosion, due to farming and runoff, made travel for the ships down the river impossible. The Army Corps of Engineers could have dredged the Wabash to solve the problem but chose not to because railroads were becoming the preferred means of travel along the river. This decrease in commerce on the waterway is one factor contributing to the decline in the river towns' prosperity—creating a ghost town ambiance in many. Oh, I would love to go back in time to experience the hustle and bustle of the river and the towns depending on it.

We stopped for lunch at a boat ramp in the middle of nowhere near Crawleyville, Indiana. When I say it was in the middle of nowhere, I mean it was in the middle of nowhere. We observed no signs of people or the town—only the wooden sign at the boat ramp.

CRAWLEYVILLE
PUBLIC ACCESS SITE
DIV OF FISH AND WILDLIFE
DEPT OF NATURAL RESOURCES

Relaxing on the ramp's cement ledge, I savored my view of the yellow, spring wildflowers blooming in the midst of the sparse green grass. The river splashing on the rocks along the boat ramp hypnotized me, causing my eyes to close for a brief moment. This trip is hard work but relaxing all at the same time. The quiet atmosphere and nature views cancel some of the exhaustion.

Today, we spotted five eagles, sang our "Do Wah Diddy Diddy" song, endured a *Paddling Edna* episode—"Paddle Shaft Options" (you can imagine the miscommunication...), paddled nineteen miles, and are now camping on a sandy, shell beach. Nothing eventful. Oh, wait. The sandy, shell beach is significant—NO mud!

We are seeing more and more beaches such as this. I didn't realize the Wabash River had so many sandy beaches punctuated with beautiful shells. In northern Indiana, I equate the Wabash with mud—not shells.

After John's initial I-have-to-pee moment upon landing on this beach, he searched for the perfect site to pitch our tent. I was still taking care of my FULL bladder (remember, while John needs only to unzip his wet suit to pee, I have to undress) when John called, "I found it." I redressed before joining him in the brush under a tree. His perfect spot *looked* perfect—flat, soft grass, shade, protected from the wind. However, as I inspected our potential home for the night, I swatted at least ten mosquitos. His perfect spot didn't *feel* perfect.

Standing in the midst of the blood-sucking creatures, I recalled a trip we took several years ago to interior Canada. Since it was my first trip to Canada, I wasn't mentally prepared for the multitude of mosquitos we were forced to live with for a week. I assumed that with the colder weather of the North, their number would be fewer than in Indiana. I was wrong. The main event revealing the extent of the multitude-of-mosquito situation occurred when we (I) decided we should hike several miles into the forest to view a waterfall, camp, and then hike several miles back out. Armed with our bug suits and enough deet to protect a small army, we proceeded into the forest for what we thought would be a peaceful journey. I have always viewed wooded areas as quiet retreats. I soon realized this is not always the case. The forest hummed, yes hummed, from the buzz of mosquitos assembled in battalions primed for attack purposes. I could barely hear John talk above the roar. (If you ever want to torture someone, place him or her in a room filled with the recording of a swarm of mosquitos.) Too stubborn to admit this could be a mistake, I bravely (stupidly) kept trudging. John continued ahead, as he usually does, to protect me. With the swarm of mosquitoes surrounding him, he reminded me of Charles Schulz's Pigpen character and his ever-present cloud of dust. Following John I could feel my swinging hands hitting mosquitos mid-flight. Eventually, I couldn't tolerate the buzzing, swarming, or hitting any longer. Admitting my error, I begged John to return to the truck.

I shuddered as I recalled the Canada memory, trying to focus on the situation at hand. Performing a stay-off-me-mosquito dance, I asked, "Can we camp on the beach? The mosquitos weren't as bad there."

"Let's take a look."

I couldn't leave the mosquito-infested area fast enough. Moving away from the bush onto the sandy, shell-covered beach provided relief. We chose a location far away from the mosquitos. However, the beach proved to be an obstacle when John attempted securing the tent with the stakes. He employed the same MacGyver trick he had used a couple of weeks ago when securing the tent in the sand.

- gather sticks
- dig hole
- place stick in loop of tarp line
- place stick laterally across the bottom of the hole
- bury stick

I wonder how many times he will need to use this trick in the future.

Tent secured, John examined our surroundings. The location was remote, the beach sandy (not muddy), and the air relatively warm. Noticing he smelled a little gamey, John took advantage of the circumstances, taking the first river bath of the trip. He first confirmed the absence of observers in the area. He then stripped down before taking a cold, but refreshing and cleansing, soak in the river. The water is still a little too chilly for me. (I prefer skinny-dipping in warmer water!) I still smell gamey.

Dinner of black bean stew and mud pie consumed, we retreated to the tent at 5:30 p.m.; not because we were tired but to escape the mosquitos. I need to text Cyndy tomorrow, asking her to put our bug suits into our Week #6 package.

05-04-2015

That Bungee Has Both Hooks

Weather conditions:

High: 84

Low: 62

Skies: clear

Wind: S 7-17 mph, gusts to 24 mph

Today's mileage: 15 miles

Total mileage: 445 miles

Where we traveled: Sandy/shell beach to New Harmony, Indiana

Swat, squirm, flinch, swat, squirm, flinch, repeat… The stay-off-me-mosquito dance.

On this warm morning, as we crawled out of the tent, the mosquitos prevailed on land, in air, and near water. Can't wait for our bug suits to arrive in a couple of weeks. They will serve as our armor. Despite the need to swat, squirm, and flinch to evade the mosquito squadron, we enjoyed eating couscous for breakfast. The smell of food definitely attracted those mosquitos.

Before packing up our gear, we applied the much-needed mosquito repellent and then sped through completing all needed tasks while listening to the flying flotilla chorus. Even though the repellent defended me against becoming a pincushion, I couldn't launch *Pray* fast enough to escape those buzzing battalions.

Keep us upright and safe.

Today's high of 84 was the warmest temperature we have had to date. What began as a welcome breeze, eventually turned into an annoying, tiring wind as we maneuvered *Work* and *Pray* directly into gusts on long, open stretches. Fortunately, the wind still wasn't as strong as the 50 mph winds we experienced a couple of weeks ago on our trek to the Huntington Reservoir.

Approaching a beach to stop for lunch, I was concerned we would encounter mosquitoes again. *Did we experience the mosquitoes last night and today because of the time of year or because of the location?* I cautiously emerged from *Pray* and wandered onto the beach, conscious of my location in reference to the woods. As long as I stayed close to the water, the biting, flying soldiers didn't visit me as I undressed (remember my wetsuit doesn't possess a zipper—I'm not bitter) to empty my bladder. Note to self: stay on larger beaches.

We spotted four eagles and another pump jack as it worked a live oil well today. We paddled north, south, east, and west on the winding Wabash while encountering sandy beaches and islands.

We also came across a collapsed railroad bridge. The portions still securing the bridge to the bank stood while the middle, the actual track, was gone. *Where did it go? How did it collapse? Was it still in use when it collapsed?* I would love to travel back in time, observing life before certain buildings and bridges became abandoned. Just think, they all were new at one time. Which of our current day bridges and buildings will cause future generations to stop and ponder the reason for collapse or abandonment?

Pondering collapsed bridges and abandoned societies, my mind wandered to the hindrance of peeing in civilization. (Odd, I know.) Why would entering civilization complicate the use of a restroom, you ask? After all, urination has to be more convenient in society. Sitting on a porcelain potty is more desirable than squatting in the bush. Right? Wrong. In the wilderness, I merely find a tree, which are plentiful, and hide behind it. *Come to think of it, from whom do I need to hide—the fish?* In civilization, a tree usually isn't sufficient for hiding behind, assuming a tree can be located. In addition, as we have found in many cases, a restroom is frequently not located near a boat ramp; and if it is, it may be locked. Since the riverbanks are becoming more accessible, we are able to eliminate the I-need-to-pee-right-now syndrome when entering civilization by simply stopping in the wilderness a few miles before landing in society.

Today, since we were planning to stop in New Harmony to spend the next couple of nights, John checked the charts for a possible pre-civilization pee. He found a fishing boat ramp outside the city limits, an ideal place to use nature's restroom.

When we stayed in Wabash, Indiana, we learned of the Wabash River Defenders. A couple of their goals are providing access to the river and placing white "Wabash River Water Trail" signs with a blue map of Indiana in the center. We are now aware of these signs, confirming land access from the river.

Today, approaching the boat ramp area indicated on the map, we began searching for the marker. John thought he noticed the ramp, "I think the ramp is on the left, but I don't see a sign. You hang tight. I'll check it out." John went ahead while I back-paddled, watching his progress. When I was certain he was parking on the ramp, I joined him. Then we saw it—the sign—bent over, almost lying on the ground. *How did the sign get damaged?* A car couldn't have hit it; it wasn't close to a road or driveway. Caked mud on the cement and debris indicated some flooding in the recent past, probably the root cause of the problem, proving nature's power.

Urination mission accomplished—the reason for stopping—we proceeded to New Harmony. Although today's paddle lasted only four-and-a half hours, because of the heat and wind, the muscles in my body ached as if they had moved *Pray* through the water twice that length of time. I was hot and tired.

Pulling *Work* and *Pray* out of the river upon arriving in New Harmony, we met a U.S. Coast Guard boat and its three occupants approaching the boat ramp. We exchanged greetings and the usual what-were-you-doing-on-the-water and where-are-you-going questions. They explained they had been collecting water samples in the area. *What were they checking for? What did they find? Should I be concerned?*

After they left, we hiked to the top of the boat ramp and perused the area for a camping spot, restroom, and shade. (I was in dire need of some shade as the hot sun burnt through my shirt, causing it to cling to my sweat-drenched skin.) The criteria for a camp spot in civilization are different from the wilderness. In the wilderness, the ideal site is flat, root-free, and away from brush. (Think mosquito free.) However, when camping in a populated area, the perfect spot is reasonably close to the boat ramp and a restroom, free from manmade-hazards, and tucked away from nearby activities. Out of sight, out of mind. The area before us was wide open with several roads connecting the incoming road to the boat ramp, parking area, and visitor center about 400 yards across the expansive lawn. A historic pioneer utopian village sat next to the visitor center. At first glance, I didn't identify any potential camping spot. The restroom located in the visitor center and quite a distance from the boat ramp would close at the end of the day. I was discouraged, not to mention tired, hungry, and hot.

With tears in my eyes and feeling sorry for myself, I shuffled to the visitor center to use the restroom and gather information about New Harmony. Before leaving, I had thought about changing from my boots to my shoes but was too disheartened and hot to exert the energy to do so; I simply wanted to be as unhappy and uncomfortable as possible—you could say I was pouting. I clomped the 400 yards to the Atheneum Visitor Center.

Approaching the white door, I made note of the hours—open daily 9:30-5:00. To any normal person that would mean the souvenir shop was open from 9:30-5. My interpretation was the restrooms would be available from 9:30 a.m. to 5:00 p.m. I just wanted to pee. I grabbed the large silver c-shaped handle, entered the foyer, and then opened a second set of doors. The visitor center's interior was predominately white—hospital white—with lots of angles and crisp lines. I wondered if the all-white décor was to perpetuate the flawless community ideal. To my left was an information desk, straight ahead a black brochure rack, appearing out of place against the white backdrop, but easy to find. Several white folding chairs in straight rows faced a TV on the wall where a video of New Harmony's history played.

Entering the modern building, I imagined everyone staring at me. While they were dressed in clean touristy clothes, I was wearing my muddy wetsuit and dirty shirt. While they had probably enjoyed a shower this morning, I was hot, sweaty, and gamey. (Remember, I DIDN'T bathe yesterday.) I had expected the mud on my boots to rub or fall off in the grass on my way to the visitor center; but when I inspected my path from the door to where I stood, I was mortified to catch a glimpse of a dirt trail on the pristine white floor. *Did they think I was homeless?* I don't think I have ever been so embarrassed by my appearance. At home, much to John's consternation, I conduct a critical inventory of my appearance before going into public. *Am I wearing non-lounging, non-work clothes? Are my clothes clean and hole-free? Do I smell fresh? How does my hair look? Is almost every curl in place? Makeup applied?* So, when I assumed my appearance didn't pass the going-into-public test, I was embarrassed. Am I vain? Maybe. Probably. Definitely.

I looked for, located, and proceeded, leaving a trail, to the restroom. The restroom followed the building's theme—all white—walls, stalls, tiled floor, paper towel dispenser, sink, vanity, and soap dispenser. My dirtiness felt even dirtier. I was sure I could fix some of my deficiencies with a little water and a glance in the mirror. But, I was afraid to face the mirror. *When was the last time I gazed at my reflection?* Peering into the looking glass confirmed my suspicions—I was not going-into-public worthy. Many of my curls had escaped my ponytail holder, my face was red from sun-exposure and streaked with dirt, and the armpits of my shirt were wet with perspiration. I don't think make up would have helped. I did my best to make myself more presentable. I washed my face and redid my ponytail. However, I couldn't do anything about my clothes. Somewhat refreshed, I left the restroom and entered society.

I located a young man wearing a nametag wondering aimlessly. He studied me, then the dirt trail, and me again. Trying not to feel offended, I asked, "Is there anywhere close by where we would be allowed to camp?"

He ambled over to the pamphlets and pulled out a map. Handing it to me, he explained, "Harmonie State Park is right outside of town."

A glimmer of hope. "Is it on the river? Do they have a boat ramp?"

"I am not familiar with the park." Flipping the pamphlet over, he pointed, "Here's a phone number."

As I studied the park map, he shuffled behind the counter and brought out another map. "Here's a map of New Harmony."

"Thanks so much for your help."

Leaving the all-white building, I noted four golf carts parked along the sidewalk. I must have been a little preoccupied since I hadn't noticed them a few minutes earlier. A sign in front of the line of carts read:

New Harmony
Golf Car Company
To rent your golf cart
See front desk
Golf cart parking here

Eyeing the golf carts, I wished I could hop into one and drive back to the boat ramp. (John claims the common characteristic of golf carts is the keys are always in them, making them an easy snatch.) I walked.

I reported my findings to John, who was sitting on W*ork*. "I have a map and phone number for the state park, which is downstream. I glanced at the park map. I think there is a boat ramp. However, I don't know how far the campground is from it."

"Can I have a look?" I handed John the map. He examined it. "The best way to find out is to call." He located and dialed the number on the back of the pamphlet. Yes, there is a boat ramp, but the campground is not within walking distance, and we could not camp by the boat ramp. My shoulders slumped as I tried to think of a solution. None came. *What are we going to do? I don't want to climb back into my kayak. I've got sweat running in between my boobs. I'm HOT. I'm TIRED! I just want to stop!!*

John put his arm around me, "I told you I would find a place to stay tonight and I believe I have. Follow me." We strolled hand-in-hand past the wooden June Barrett Public access site and rules sign.

- No camping or fires
- Park clear of boat ramp
- No swimming 100 ft. of launch ramp
- No mooring
- Please, do not litter

We continued down a mowed path opening to a clearing with a shade tree. The water treatment plant's hum provided a pleasant backdrop. Out of the way, shady, and private. Perfect! We rolled *Work* and *Pray* to our home for the next couple of days, set up camp, cleaned up, dressed in our going-into-town clothes, and placed the solar panel in the sun to collect some afternoon rays. Then, using the map I received at the visitor center, we wandered up town.

My first impression of New Harmony was favorable. It is a well-kept small community (Population 915—saaaaa-lute!) with a lot of history and unique stores. During the early part of the 19th century, New Harmony was the site of two attempts to establish Utopian communities, which explains why it gives the impression of perfection. Almost too perfect, giving off a bit of a "Stepford Wives" vibe. I doubt any weeds dare poke their heads through the ground anywhere in this town. I felt uncomfortable in the midst of the perfection. *Why?* Maybe because my flaws glowed in contrast?

Spring flowers adorned the well-kept, Victorian style houses. Many houses had a plaque either on the house or in the yard relaying their history and significance. This town has preserved its history more than other river towns we have visited. I'm sure the other towns have an interesting past—if only someone would take the time to preserve the history and promote it. I think discovering the roots of an area is fascinating because I like imagining how people lived in another time. I am looking forward to exploring New Harmony tomorrow on our day of rest.

We were hungry and hoped to find somewhere to hang out tomorrow, use free Wi-Fi, drink coffee, and relax. With the aid of the map, we found Sara's Harmony Way, a small coffee house downtown. The bright yellow, blue, and pink metal chairs sitting outside against the brick wall beneath the painted words "Wilson Furniture Co" would have been inviting had the temperature not been so hot! I wanted to sit in an air-conditioned building, enjoying hot coffee—sounds contradictory, huh? Upon entering the corner entrance, we avoided knocking over the construction tools and scaffolding, providing clues that Sara's was in the midst of a remodel. Even with the added clutter, the restaurant was welcoming.

I stared at the wall-sized chalkboard menu behind the counter. I didn't care how I looked or smelled. I was in a coffee house. *Which coffee drink shall I order?* I hadn't ordered a specialty coffee drink in over a month. A few entries on the menu caught my eye: Magical Coffee, Shake Rattle & Roll, Milk & Honey, and Why Bother (decaf latte). I chuckled as I read the last option, Why Bother. This reminded me of my thirty-year-old daughter, Tiffany. Every time I offer her decaffeinated coffee, she grimaces, "Why bother?" I decided on one of my favorites, caramel macchiato. John, a creature of habit, selected his usual dirty chai.

Anarae floated through the opening in the chalkboard wall, took our order, and gave us a hospitable welcome to New Harmony. Her blue shirt and colorful skirt matched her artistic and free spirit. We hope to see her and become better acquainted when we return tomorrow.

Sara's was divided into two areas: a coffee-lunch area and a bar-dinner area. Sitting in the coffee area, we enjoyed a latte and late lunch while using their Wi-Fi. Can you believe this is the first meal we have purchased since we left home four weeks ago? Remember, we've been rehydrating meals and enjoying the hospitality of strangers in their homes and at local restaurants.

Eating our bowls of pasta salad and paninis, we spied the words Sara's Harmony Way painted on the window. This continued an ongoing conversation between John and me. Not long after we were first married eleven years ago, the second time around for both of us, we were lamenting the fact we didn't have any children together, discussing what might have been. Our daughter would have been beautiful, well-mannered, adventurous, and fun. We agreed on the name Sara. But then the disagreement began—how to spell her name. I insisted on Sara, without an "h." John thinking it should be spelled Sarah, with an "h," was obviously wrong. Peering at the coffee house window, I was intent on pointing out the spelling on the window—Sara—no "h." I won today.

Internet chores complete, we came back to our home for the next couple of days and raced the mosquitos to our tent. This is the first night since the beginning of our trip we haven't slept in our long underwear or under our wool blanket. Only a couple of nights ago, I still shivered all night despite the fact that I wore my long underwear while snuggled under a wool blanket. With the changing weather, we will send some cold weather clothing home to make room for our bug suits, our armor against the lances of the mosquito hordes!

No worries for the time being. Tomorrow is a no-alarm-Tuesday (N.A.T.)! Day of rest.

05-05-2015

Made with Real Milk

Weather conditions:

High: 85

Low: 61

Skies: clear with scattered clouds in the afternoon

Wind: S 7-14 mph, gusts to 20 mph

Today's mileage: 0 miles—day of rest

Total mileage: 445 miles

Where we stayed: New Harmony, Indiana

Today was a N.A.T. (No Alarm Tuesday)! We slept in until 9:00 a.m. No wait, that was a dream. It really was a N.A.T, but unfortunately, our alarm went off as usual at 6:00 a. m.—not on our phone—our internal alarm. How frustrating! Oh, well. Even though we didn't sleep in, we enjoyed a relaxing morning of reading, journaling, and ordering our summer NRS Hydroskin pants made of ultra-light-weight neoprene. We didn't originally have lightweight "summer" neoprene in our gear collection because we planned to wear shorts or our quick-dry Columbia brand pants. However, once we realized how easy neoprene is to clean and dry, we decided we wanted it year round. They will arrive in our Week #6 package at Cairo, Illinois. Once they arrive we will send our one-piece wet suits back to our food cache coordinator, Cyndy. We love our wet suits because they keep us warm and we aren't concerned about them becoming muddy or wet; but as the daily temperatures increase, we will need the lighter, cooler option. Another advantage of the pants, for me, is the ease of peeing—all I will need to do is pull them down. Can't wait until all I expose is my tush when taking care of business.

As part of our couscous breakfast, we treated ourselves to a cup of coffee. Stress slips away with the fist sip of the thick black aromatic brew. Even though we are coffee snobs, at this point an instant packet of Folgers hits the spot.

Morning chores complete, we dressed in our going-to-town clothes (our cleanest clothes) and hiked uptown to buy some baby wipes (I use these to freshen up every morning and after taking off my smelly wet suit) and other health and beauty needs. Remembering the downtown area's cuteness, I wasn't confident we would find a store selling the items we needed. Proceeding to the major intersection, we glanced left and right, choosing to turn right—towards what appeared to be the majority of businesses. The flawless storefronts matched the colors of the chairs in front of Sara's—yellow, turquoise, and pink. Where else can you find a town with color-coordinated chairs and storefronts?

New Harmony's storefronts differ from those in most of the river towns we have encountered. I remember specifically the "ghost town" of Perrysville, Indiana. Actually, I found distinguishing the open businesses from the closed ones difficult in Perrysville—not the case here in New Harmony. The storefronts here invite me in. Passing the window displays of the antique shops, bookstores, and craft shops, I wanted to enter and browse. However, following a strict budget and not having room for any extravagances (and some necessities, like pillows), going into the stores seemed like a waste of time. *Why browse when you can't buy?* I limited myself to quick glances at the merchandise beckoning me through the windows and then continued on my way.

Glancing in the New Harmony Soap Company window, I spotted a sign for soap making classes. Soap making intrigues me. Over the past few years,

I have made my own cleaning solutions and laundry soap. My next venture may be bar soap making. Maybe on my next visit to New Harmony, I can attend a class. Even though traveling by river took a little over a month, driving by car would take less than five hours. A nice weekend road trip, perhaps?

Still contemplating the soap making classes, I spied a blue sign with gold letters—*Chris' Pharmacy*—exactly what we needed. Entering the brick building's door, I felt I had stepped back to the year 1960, when every town possessed a small downtown pharmacy. The wood floor creaked with each step as I picked up a blue shopping convenience basket with metal handles. The wooden shelves filled with only essentials did not hold many imported trinkets. On the end of aisle 4, a handwritten paper sign instructed "Take an additional 50% off all items on this shelf." I expected to turn the corner, finding my grandma checking out the latest sales while waiting for the pharmacist in the back of the store to fill her prescriptions. Here I am digressing to the past again…

Necessities purchased, we crossed to the other side of the street, beginning our search for the town hall. However, finding the government building wasn't as easy as locating the pharmacy. We returned to the intersection, glanced right, and detected a historical marker. My curiosity and love of history caused me to wonder what was engraved on it. Turning right, we strolled to the sign for closer investigation. It read…

New Harmony
Location of two attempts
At communal living:
Reverend George Rapp. 1814-1825
And the Owenites under
Philanthropist Robert Owen. 1825-1826.
New Harmony remained
An important cultural center
For many years thereafter

I would love to go back to 1820 to experience communal living under Reverend Rapp. Notice, I didn't choose 1814—the start—but instead chose 1820—the middle—because by then they should have worked out some of the kinks in the system; but by 1825 something had gone awry. Reverend Rapp's experiment operated for 11 years (successful or stubborn?) while Owenites maintained that living style for only one year. You would think Robert Owen would have learned from the Reverend Rapp's mistakes and adjusted accordingly. I wonder how they differ from present day communal villages. I think visiting one may be in our future.

Detecting the sign and being curious worked to our advantage because after reading the sign, we peered across the street and found the town hall. The building housing the town's government possessed a similar historic exterior as many of the other businesses. When considering building upkeep, New Harmony appears more concerned with conserving the past than the associated maintenance costs. My view is that much of the United States would rather tear down a building and replace it, stating the cost to repair is more than the cost to rebuild. (Remember St. Francesville, Illinois, and the historic Catholic church? Don't get me started.)

We crossed the street, climbed the steps, and entered. The building's interior, a seventies remodel, didn't follow the historic theme of the exterior. In the midst of the flowered wallpaper, a woman smiled at us from behind a metal desk adorned with family pictures.

Formalities complete, John explained the reason for our visit. "We're kayaking through on our way to the Gulf."

The usual response, "Wow!"

"We would like to camp in the area behind your water treatment plant. We won't build a fire or leave any remnants behind. We want to be sure we won't be in the way of a maintenance man wanting to mow the yard."

I held my breath, waiting for her answer. Ever since the police in Covington, Indiana, told us to move along, I worry every time John asks permission to stay anywhere. Since we are staying here a couple of days, he felt the authorities should know of our presence, thinking they might keep an eye on our possessions when we venture away from the campsite. She finally answered, "I don't see a problem. I think that area is scheduled to be mowed on Friday and y'all will be gone by then," I exhaled.

John, on a roll, asked, "Is there somewhere we can take a shower or find a laundromat?"

She thought for a moment. "No. I'm sorry. We don't have a laundromat, and I can't think of anywhere for you to take a shower."

"Thank you so much." We left, feeling relieved about our camping accommodations but a little discouraged about the lack of opportunity for cleanliness. I'm sure we smelled, and with the heat, I doubted the situation was improving.

John knew a coffee house would lighten my mood. "Let's go see Anarae at Sara's." (Have I mentioned a coffee house relaxes me?)

Entering Sara's, we observed two grayed-haired men, probably in their sixties, sitting at a round table. The illustration on the olive green t-shirt of one man brought a smile to my face—a picture of a partially filled glass in white with the words *half full* written under it. The relaxed mood of the t-shirt contrasted with his coffee partner's business-like appearance of a plaid button-up shirt and khaki pants. Overhearing them as I ordered my coffee, I thought their heavy New York accents sounded out of place in the midst of the "y'alls" heard in the area. John, being his social self, stopped to talk with them after placing our order. He discovered the New Harmony transplants from the New England area often enjoyed their morning coffee at Sara's. We designated this meeting as another "just happened to be" moment because the man in the button-up shirt previously worked as an executive with a barge company on the Mississippi.

In his New York accent, he provided insight into what we can expect later in our journey, alleviating some of my fears about tows and barges. Who would have thought we would learn about the Mississippi while still on the Wabash?

The tows and barges scare me. Probably because I don't have any idea what to expect—nothing to hang my hat on. Gestalt Theory says I match all incoming information with what I know in order to make sense of it. Possessing no previous knowledge, I can't form a true opinion or face it with reality. Ignorance is fear. Being ignorant of the tows, I am fearful. Gaining more knowledge from someone who has experience helped alleviate some of my anxiety. Even if some of my distress is warranted, knowing what is real helps me create a plan to face it and overcome the obstacle. When fear is based on facts, it is kept at a manageable level and doesn't escalate.

Another interesting fact he mentioned is the food quality served on the towboats. He suggested if given a chance to eat on one, we should take advantage of the opportunity. Informed, I no longer dread encountering the tows. A change in outlook all because of knowledge.

While we were enjoying our coffee and performing technological chores, Anarae became one of our newest heroes. I noticed her approaching our table carrying a clear plastic Ziploc bag but didn't think anything of it; but when she handed us the bag containing half-a-dozen, still-warm cookies, my mouth watered. She knew they would be a good complement to our coffee. (Although becoming better at accepting gifts, I am still surprised when someone gives us something. I hope I never lose the sense of surprise and start expecting acts of generosity.) On the outside of the bag, Anarae's handwritten "Safe Journey and Good Fortune" and two hand drawn kayaks lit up my face and lifted my spirits. She then explained, "They are lavender cookies." They sounded healthy—anything made out of herbs has to be healthy, right? They tasted anything but healthy. Each warm bite began crisp, yet as I chewed, the shortbread cookie melted in my mouth. Delicious! I have added lavender to my herb garden plan.

Even better than the delectable cookies was our conversation with Anarae. She showed us her book of drawings and writings, asking us to write a message in it. Just as her skirt and shirt did yesterday, today's "I heart Me" t-shirt and flowy patchwork skirt reflected her personality and outlook on life. She is comfortable in her skin, reveling in her uniqueness. I love this part of the trip—meeting people!

During our conversation, John asked if we could fill our dromedaries somewhere. She pointed, "There is a spout on the side of the building."

Anarae returned to her place behind the counter. I stayed and enjoyed the atmosphere of Sara's while John returned to the campsite to retrieve our dromedaries. As the door closed behind John, I stared at the remaining cookies on the table, begging me to eat them. *If I eat the rest of the cookies and discard the plastic bag, will he forget about them?* A quandary similar to "the last Easter candy dilemma" of a few weeks ago challenged me. *He needs to quit leaving me alone with food.* A good girl, I ate only three. *What would you have done?*

John had scarcely stepped back into the coffee house with the water dromedaries in hand when the Hamiltons (Nate, Liz, Grant, Emma, Eva, and Katie) arrived. Nate and Liz, long-time friends of John's niece Jennifer, who lives in Fort Wayne, Indiana, reside an hour away in Newburgh, Indiana. They heard about our adventure from Jennifer and brought their home-schooled children to meet us as part of a field trip. (I never imagined I would be interesting enough to be included as part of someone's field trip.) After John filled the dromedaries, he loaded them into the Hamiltons' van. Then Liz, the children, and I drove back to our campsite; John and Nate walked.

Arriving back at the campsite, Nate and Liz spread a blanket on the ground and unloaded picnic lunches from the back of the van for their family and us. Our crisp lettuce wraps and fresh veggies were a refreshing treat! I have expanded my definition of treat—anything from lettuce wraps to ice cream. In other words, if I didn't dehydrate it, it's a treat.

While eating, our visitors "interviewed" us. Although I think the intent was for the kids to ask most of the questions, the parents took over when Grant, Emma, Eva, and Katie began wandering away from the "table," ready to move on to the next segment of the field trip—New Harmony State Park.

Lunch complete, we gave them a brief tour of our "home," taking about 30 seconds. Obligatory pictures shot, they left—new friends.

John taking our days of rest seriously, decided to enjoy a nap. Guess what I did—I sat on a stool without a back, journaling. Typical day of rest.

Once John felt well rested, we strolled back to Sara's to update the website and put a final charge on the devices. After working awhile John took a break to investigate the bar and restaurant side of the building. I kept working, but after a few minutes, John didn't return. *What is he doing this time? He didn't leave; I would have seen him exit through the door.* I set off in search of my traveling partner. There he sat in the bar area on a couch, in heaven, playing a guitar he had found leaning against the wall near the seating area. He can't lay eyes on a guitar without touching it.

Remember our favorite reporter from *The Paper of Wabash County* in Wabash, Indiana, Emma Rausch? The one who brought us apples, caramel, and fuel for our stove? During our conversation with her in Logansport, she mentioned her mom lives close to New Harmony; Emma wanted us to meet her. She stated if the timing were right, she would travel to New Harmony to join up with us and introduce us to her mom. Soon after arriving yesterday we contacted her. Unfortunately, she couldn't leave work today but told us her mom wanted to show us around the town and treat us to dinner. During most of the day, we corresponded through text with Emma's mom, Rebecca. Finally able to escape life and meet us for dinner, she sent us a text "Meet you at *The Red Geranium* at 7:30."

All arrangements made, we journeyed by foot to our meeting place. (I'm thankful for small towns.) *The Red Geranium*, part of the *New Harmony Inn and Conference Center*, maintained a historic and perfect exterior similar to the other buildings in New Harmony. Sauntering up the brick path, we encountered immaculately sculpted hedges and a flower garden. From the front of the restaurant, I observed an outdoor dining area in the back. A paneled lobby with a grand piano greeted us as we entered the restaurant.

Waiting on Rebecca to arrive, we examined the pictures and read more history of the quaint town where we are spending our day of rest.

When Rebecca arrived, a pleasant dark-haired hostess, Ronda, escorted us down the hall to the main dining room, seating us by a window overlooking a garden and walking path. We found the food delicious and the conversation with Rebecca a pleasure. What a kind and personable woman!

Our hostess, Ronda, (whom John continued calling Betty for some weird reason) and our waiter, David, provided excellent service. As the evening progressed, they joined in the discussion of our trip. During the conversation, the topic of showers came up (i.e. our lack of one). They offered to open the fitness room at *The New Harmony Inn* so we could bask in a hot shower. Of course, we replied, "YES!" Dinner finished, Rebecca drove us back to our tent to gather our bare essentials (that's all we have) and returned us to the restaurant. David drove us in a golf cart (our second golf cart ride of the trip) to the inn. He led us to the fitness room, showed us where to find the towels, shampoos, and lotions, instructing us to take our time and call him when we finished. Then he locked us in.

The water washed the dirt, sweat, and smell down the drain. I wanted to stand under the flow of water for hours but resisted because I didn't want to interrupt David's evening too long. I hurriedly performed the basics—wash body, shampoo hair, shave underarms and legs. Even though the shower passed quickly, it helped erase some of my embarrassment from yesterday's incident at the visitor's center.

Crisp and clean, we called David to let us out. He unlocked the door and offered us some local tourist event t-shirts. The t-shirts will come in handy when doing laundry—we can wear them while washing ALL three of our other shirts. Approaching the golf cart, we were surprised to see Ronda sitting on the passenger side. I climbed into the back of the cart, enjoying the cool night air blowing through my freshly shampooed hair as our wait staff transported us back to our tent. As we crawled out of the golf cart, they gave us bottles of water and some other goodies. What a privilege meeting all these wonderful, giving people!

Tonight we set our alarm. Tomorrow we return to the river after a day of rest, rejuvenation, and a shower. Now, all we need is a laundromat.

05-06-2015

I've Seen How You People Sleep

Weather conditions:

High: 85

Low: 58

Skies: clear with scattered clouds in the afternoon

Wind: SSE 4-14 mph, gusts to 20 mph

Today's mileage: 22 miles

Total mileage: 467 miles

Where we traveled: New Harmony, Indiana, to a sandy beach

Beep, beep, beep. *What IS that noise? It is still dark! Oh yeah, we set the alarm last night for 5:00 a.m.* Considering the uncomfortable conditions paddling into New Harmony on Monday, we had a planning session, determining what changes we could make to avoid traveling on the river when the sun is beating down on anything not protected by shade. After discussion and much to my chagrin, we decided to set our alarm for 5:00 a.m. I am not a fan of rising early—especially in the dark.

During our discussion we identified making, eating, and cleaning up breakfast as a time eater, causing a delay in our launching. John had a brilliant idea—eat lunch for breakfast and breakfast for lunch. In this ideal world, I prepare lunch before going to bed at night. In the morning we eat our lunch for breakfast. Then when we stop for a mid-day break, we eat our breakfast for lunch. The first part of the plan, lunch for breakfast, worked well today. The treats Ronda and David handed us last night as they delivered us to our tent were perfect lunch-for-breakfast food. I smiled as I beheld the spread displayed on our "kayak table"— a loaf of bread, individual peanut butter containers, strawberry jam packets, and honey pouches—resting on a napkin tablecloth, also provided by Ronda and David. Bread instead of a tortilla. What a treat! Peanut butter and honey sandwiches are a favorite of mine.

I remember eating peanut butter and honey sandwiches as a kid. Yum! I loved peanut butter sandwiches but rarely ate a plain one. A plain peanut butter sandwich is boring unless you dip it in chili soup. I know dipping a peanut butter sandwich into chili soup is not normal. I developed this habit during my elementary school years. If chicken noodle soup and chili appeared on the lunch menu, you knew the sides would be peanut butter sandwiches with the chili and butter sandwiches with the chicken noodle. Before leaving our classroom, we formed two queues—one for chicken noodle and one for chili. I always chose to stand in the chili-with-the-peanut-butter-sandwich line. In order for the lunch ladies to know which line was which, the first person in each group wore a crown with the name of the soup the followers wanted to enjoy. Memories.

At home as a kid, I enjoyed numerous non-boring varieties of peanut butter sandwiches: peanut butter, grape jelly, and brown sugar; peanut butter and mustard pickles; peanut butter and homemade freezer strawberry jam; peanut butter and banana; peanut butter, mayonnaise, and lettuce. Don't judge me until you try them for yourself.

Lunch for breakfast worked. With the changes in our routine, we launched by 8:00 a.m. Score.

Keep us upright and safe.

Today is May 6. We have paddled almost every day since April 4—thirty-four days. The first couple of days of the trip were stressful for me: small rapids, fallen trees, and strainers (remember a fallen, impassable tree is known, sadistically, as a strainer). Since then, except for windy conditions creating waves and the few mysterious rapids at Logansport, the water has been smooth. Sometimes, I refer to this as "Slicin' da Butter"—drawled with as much of a southern accent as someone from the north can muster. (Would you call it a southern-northern accent or a northern-southern accent?) I love these conditions as I glide effortlessly, creating only a minor disturbance in the glass-like appearance of the water as the trees on the bank reflect a second landscape in the liquid mirror. With not much to maneuver around and through, paddling can become monotonous. Left paddle in, right paddle in, left paddle in… Yawn. (John is so proud of a picture he snapped, catching me in the middle of a yawn. *Thanks.*) Keep eyes open. Stay awake. I have drifted off more than once. Time sometimes creeps. Singing our daily "Do Wah Diddy" song helps. (John thought it important to capture our song on video. Evidence that we're not very good.)

"Helloooo!" Well, I am learning these startling outbursts from John indicate the beginning of another *Paddling Edna* episode. I think I should take time here to reflect on Edna's mannerisms. You see, I have learned Edna can be quite naïve. Add to this her propensity to unintentionally make some risqué innuendos or her marginally inappropriate use of words or terms, and you end up with some rather uncomfortable moments. For example, this episode's featured topic was hand operated bilge pumps. Yeah, you can already guess some of the faux pas that can likely result from that topic. As Edna attempted to describe the proper way to handle and use a bilge pump, she received some middle school-ish reactions from her studio audience.

"Excuse me, young man. Why are you giggling? I will thank you to please control yourself so as to not disrupt. Thank you…. So, as I was saying, you firmly grasp with one hand and begin to …Young man, please stop giggling…Henry, Hen…Henry (Remember, Henry is her producer.) ….Why is that young man giggling?"

On and on the dialogue continued. Wow, never a dull moment. I wonder if I can change the station.

Today, our adventure sightings featured five Bald Eagles soaring in the sky, an abandoned school bus teetering on the side of the bank, and a train approaching and crossing a bridge. Read on to learn more about each.

How many eagles have we seen? At the end of the trip, I need to reread this journal and add them up. *Will we see as many on the other rivers?* I certainly hope so. Many times the sighting begins with a black dot in the sky. I usually ask John, "Is it an eagle or a vulture?" John is more of a bird identification expert than I am. However, if John weren't here, a close study of the soaring bird would leave no doubt in my mind. No other bird floats through the sky with such grace and ease as a Bald Eagle. One or two flaps of its wings propel the majestic bird for minutes with no additional effort. The eagle soars with flat wings while the vulture's extended wings arc upwards, almost forming a "U." And of course, when the sun gleams off the white tail or head of a mature bird, I am certain it is an eagle. Sometimes it is even close enough for me to watch it lower its distinct orange talons to catch prey or grasp a branch.

How many buses have we seen? Not sure I want to keep tally of this sight. Lying precariously on the side of the bank, today's bus was held in place by only a small tree. Was it once on land and then the earth eroded, causing the bus to slide closer to the river? Or did it float downstream during a flood, landing on the bank when the height of the river lowered? Will it float farther downstream with the rising and falling of the water, possibly ending up in the Gulf? Although a school bus resting on the riverbank isn't a natural wonder, it is something I would not have experienced from the road. What can our society do to decrease this type of pollution in the rivers? Many continue to view the river as a convenient garbage dump, pushing trash into the river as an easy means of disposal. "Out of sight, out of mind." I think, or at least hope, this practice is becoming less prevalent as the media publicizes the ramifications of such actions. Proof that media can have a positive impact.

Trains and train bridges. We've passed under several train bridges, but today the experience included the train's presence. Approaching the bridge, John gave his usual instructions, communicating where he planned to paddle under the bridge. "Second opening from the left bank." Although not experiencing as many obstacles as we did in the beginning, we are continuing the established routine for the rest of the trip of John's leading and providing direction, especially since the Ohio and Mississippi will certainly create more than a few tense moments.

Noticing a train making its way onto the bridge, we paused, letting *Work* and *Pray* float towards it. John used the iPhone to video the train's trip across the bridge. Drifting under the overhead train was a little intimidating as I watched the bottom of each car pass over me on the open slats in the track. A different view from the river than from the road. This is the first time I have floated under a bridge (second opening from the left bank) while a train cruised overhead—the loud clackety-clack of the train's wheels rolling on the track bounced from the water to the bridge and back again. The reverberations I felt in my chest resembled those I have experienced while traveling at a high speed down the hill on a roller coaster without the accompanying fear of my stomach staying at the top. According to Jerry Hay's book, this is the last train bridge we will paddle under on the Wabash.

In addition to the last train bridge, we also passed under the Wabash River's last automobile bridge —The Wabash Memorial Bridge, connecting Illinois 141 and Indiana 62. The next bridge we encounter will span the Ohio River. I can't believe we will soon complete the Wabash, entering the next of our three rivers, the Ohio. If all goes as planned, tonight we will spend our last night on the Wabash, reaching the Ohio tomorrow. I will miss our friend the Wabash. We drive over it almost daily near our landlocked residence in Berne, Indiana. Our friend connects our land home to our current river home. This is our river, our home.

When John checks the maps every night or morning, he determines if we may encounter any dangers during our paddle, locates potential places for a break, and selects possible camping spots. Today, he had picked out two potential camping spots: a DNR boat ramp and a sandy beach. Reaching the DNR boat ramp after paddling about 15 miles, we stopped for a break, a snack, and a discussion about staying or proceeding another seven miles.

John asked my opinion, "How are you feeling? Do you need to stop?" Although he generally has his preference, he asks for my input before expressing (or not expressing) his ideas.

"I'm doing OK."

"It's not too hot yet, and we've gone only 15 miles. I think we should keep going. The map shows a sandy beach seven miles downstream. That may be a nicer place to camp."

"Let's do it!"

Arriving at the spot indicated on the map, we found the promised large and expansive sandy beach. Glad we didn't stay at the DNR boat ramp, I commented, "This is beautiful. Who knew the Wabash had beautiful beaches?" Another sighting we would not have appreciated from the road.

Although today's paddle was seven miles longer than Monday's to New Harmony, we weren't as exhausted when we stopped for the day. Perhaps the early start, allowing us to avoid paddling on the river in the heat of the day, was the key. I'm sure our endurance is inversely proportional to the temperature. Higher heat—less endurance. And we are still in Indiana! I wonder what adjustments we will need to make to withstand the heat in Louisiana.

A small turtle greeted John as he stepped out of *Work*. Before the turtle could run away, John gently picked him up. While I was still in *Pray*, John carried his prize to me. As he strutted towards me, I caught a glimpse of a seven-year-old John showing the girl next door his treasure. I wanted to squeeze him—John, not the turtle. The green and yellow striped turtle was about the size of John's thumbprint. *How did John see it from his kayak?* Admiring John's new friend, I realized it hadn't pulled its head and legs into the security and protection of its shell. *Wasn't it scared? Were we the only humans it had encountered?* (Rest assured no turtles were harmed during the taking of this beach.)

Scoping out the campsite possibilities, we detected many coyote tracks crisscrossing in the sand near the water's edge. Not a comforting sight to me. I don't mind interacting with a turtle, but the thought of encountering a coyote at close range causes my heart to pound. A few days ago, a coyote trotted along a beach, watching us pass. A safe view from afar.

Staying on a beach has its positives and negatives. Positive—combatting fewer mosquitos. Negative number one—transporting *Work* and *Pray* up the beach far enough from the water to ensure they are secure and close enough to the campsite to allow accessibility. Negative number two—finding shade on a beach to ensure protection from the afternoon sun.

Overcoming negative number one— transporting *Work* and *Pray* up the beach. Having selected the perfect spot to place our tent, we stood motionless, scanning the distance from *Work* and *Pray* to the selected campsite; the distance growing with each scan. I asked, "Are we going to carry all our gear all the way up there? Why can't we camp closer to the kayaks?"

John, being wise, answered my concerns, "The river is unpredictable and can rise considerably overnight. We need to be a good distance from the water to be safe. And no, we aren't going to carry our gear. I want *Work* and *Pray* up there so they're secure and accessible." Jerry Hay warns "water rising only 1 foot can completely submerge a sand bar." And, as we have experienced, it can happen rapidly.

"Then how are we going to get the kayaks up there? They're too heavy for me to carry that far."

"Let's try putting them on their wheels." He is so smart.

We put *Pray* on wheels and tried pulling her through the sand. He is so dumb. The kayak's weight caused the wheels to sink into the soft sand, making pulling it nearly impossible. Even with John tugging and me pushing, progress crept along. John had another idea. "Let's leave this kayak here and try dragging the other one, without wheels. You know, like a sled." He is so smart.

We plodded back to where *Work* waited by the water. John pulled. Surprisingly, this worked better. I couldn't pull or push, so I felt guilty standing there watching John pull, rest, pull, rest...

We, or should I say John, finally moved *Work* and *Pray* to our campsite. Overcoming negative number one—accomplished.

At 4:30 p.m., we sat in the tent to escape the sun and heat. (Only two weeks ago, we climbed into the tent to escape the wind and cold.) With the tent's sides pulled back, a cooling breeze blew through. Peering through the opening, I observed the untouched sand in both directions (thankfully, no coyote tracks on this portion of the beach). I'm beginning to realize the Wabash River's landscape is as diverse as Indiana's weather, from high steep muddy banks in the northern portion to flat sandy beaches in the south. Changes not witnessed from the road.

"Hey, Irene sent us another conversation topic. Can we look at it?"

"Suuuure," John acquiesced.

I pulled up her text on the phone. "Adam and Eve. First ten minutes of conversation after leaving the Garden. Go..."

Most people would sit for a couple of minutes, thinking about their answer, before putting their thoughts into words. Not John. "Go" barely out of my mouth, he began his answer.

"'Hey, try this apple...Yeah. Great idea, Eve. First you talk me into calling that curly tailed thing a peg.' John's words flowed without any pauses.

'I said PIG...PIG! When will you get it right?!'

'Ok PIG. Whatever. The point is you've always gotta have your way. All that great stuff to eat, and what do you give me? Fruit from the ONE tree we're not supposed to eat from. Now we can't stay in that awesome Eden anymore.'"

Apparently, John has some hidden angst I didn't know about.

Answering Irene's question made me think of something I hadn't previously considered. "Can you imagine what Eve thought when she started her first period? I bet she thought she was dying when she started bleeding from down there. She didn't have a mom telling her what to expect. She didn't have to sit through the embarrassing movie in 5th grade, receiving tampon and sanitary napkin samples."

Even though John couldn't relate, he had to add something to the conversation. "I'm sure she blamed Adam."

"Huh?"

"You know. For…"

"Is that all you think about?"

"Only every three seconds."

"Oh, brother. That brings me to another thought. What about when she became pregnant? Her belly started growing. Can you imagine her face when the baby kicked? She probably yelled for Adam to come feel her belly. I wonder what he said."

John couldn't resist. "Hey, this is just like that Alien movie."

"You're impossible." I kissed his cheek. "I love living with you."

Later, emerging from the tent at 6:15 p.m., I smiled at the scene in front of me. Placing *Work* and *Pray* on their wheels to lift them off the ground, John (my personal McGuiver) had angled their noses towards each other, almost touching. This left the kayaks' sterns about eight feet apart, the right distance to stretch a clothesline. Increasing or decreasing the angle of a kayak provided an easy adjustment to make the clothesline tighter or looser. Blue, plastic clothespins held two sets of laundered clothes in place. Laundry day—our clothes are "clean-ish," having been washed in the river (replacing one smell with another). On *Pray's* bow, the kitchen sink (a compact handy collapsible bowl made by Sea to Summit, actually called "the kitchen sink"), which John had used to do the laundry, hung upside down drying. The wetsuits lay on *Work* airing out. Wetsuits have a certain odor after wearing them all day. We refer to this odor lovingly as "wet suit stench." Did the scene give the impression of homelessness? Probably, but I still tenderly called the scene "home."

Overcoming negative number two— finding shade on a beach. John had placed the centers of *Work* and *Pray* the right distance apart to stretch our UST HexTarp, which, up until today, he had used only for protection from rain and wind. Placing the reflective side up, John's goal was to reflect the sun away from our shady area. All I could distinguish of John were his legs. I peeked under the tarp. He was sitting on a stool leaning over, trying to fit his 6'1" frame in a space about four feet tall. He appeared older than seven now but still as cute as could be. I wanted to squeeze him—AGAIN. His shoulder-length hair curled from under his black baseball cap. He was wearing his orange, button-up, going-into-town shirt while his paddling shirts dried on the clothesline. From his red Nalgene bottle, he poured water into the pan of dehydrated chicken Mexican rice, resting next to the MSR camp stove and red fuel canister. The multi-purpose tool John had used to open the vacuum-sealed Food Saver bags, red lighter, and hand sanitizer remained on the foil table. Our green and blue cups with matching sporks rested on the table, waiting for us to use. (Remember the breakfast we planned to eat for lunch? Didn't happen—we were too busy. Now, we are one meal behind. We may have to revisit this plan.) Overcoming negative number two—accomplished.

The time now is 8:20 p.m. The sound of our alarm at 5:00 this morning seems like days ago. Dinner eaten. Laundry dry and put away. *Work* and *Pray* packed and placed close to the tent in case an animal (coyote) decides to investigate our presence. Face washed. Teeth brushed. We're now lying on our sleeping bags enjoying an active dialogue between some owls. The air is finally cooling off. Tomorrow is our last day on the Wabash River. Wow!

05-07-2015

You Look Better Now That You're Dressed

Weather conditions:

High: 85

Low: 64

Skies: clear with scattered clouds in the afternoon

Wind: S 4-16 mph, gusts to 20 mph

Today's mileage: 30 miles

Total: 497 miles

Where we traveled: a sandy beach to Old Shawneetown, Illinois

The *first* shall be *last* and the *last* shall be *first*—today's theme. We have traveled from our *first* day on the Wabash River, a little over a month ago, to our *last* day on our river today. Today, our *last* day on the Wabash became our *first* day on the Ohio. Endings and beginnings.

Today, our *last* day on the Wabash River, began with our alarm sounding at 4:30 a.m. Many have heard me say, "I want to see 4:30 only once a day, and that is in the afternoon." This trip is an exception. Now I say, "I want to be in the heat of the sun at 4:30 only once a day, and that is in the morning." (I know the sun hasn't risen yet at 4:30 in the morning, but it works for this statement.) Considering our uncomfortable afternoon yesterday, hungry and in the sun, we held another planning session. Decision number one: Get up even earlier—4:30 a.m. Ughh! Decision number two: Eat breakfast and lunch in the normal order. Today we ate hash brown, egg, and sausage casserole for breakfast. Yummm! The early alarm enabled us to launch by 7:45 a.m.—a record!

Keep us upright and safe.

Our paddle today included some sightings that have become ordinary on the Wabash—three eagles and another bus on stilts. In addition to the regulars, we encountered something you certainly can't spot from the road—a house on the verge of falling into the river because of erosion. Of course, inspecting the teetering house caused my mind to go into overdrive. Why wouldn't the homeowner protect the house by taking precautions to keep the bank from eroding? How many years passed as the river's edge inched towards the house and finally under it? How long before it is on its way to the Gulf of Mexico? How many other houses have become houseboats? Can you imagine watching the debris float by?

This apparent lack of care for one's property makes me think about our "disposable" society. How many broken or old gadgets are disposed of and replaced instead of keeping and fixing them—for convenience sake? I agree purchasing a replacement at the store or on-line and then disposing of the old object is easier and consumes less time. Fixing something requires the following: determining the problem, deciding what parts are needed, finding where these parts can be purchased, going to the store, locating the parts in the store, standing in line at the check-out, paying for your purchase, going home, and fixing the broken possession. But is the practice of disposing and replacing being a good steward of our money, possessions, and environment? Our landfills are overflowing with what we deem as "disposable" goods. Companies didn't manufacture these items and label them disposable. Our toaster may not even be broken; we are merely interested in the release of the new and improved version with four slots and a setting for frozen bagels. When new is purchased, we change our classification of the old valuable from "needed" to "disposable." It's a sad society when even our homes have become disposable. Allowing a house to fall into the river isn't only poor stewardship of a material possession, it is also poor stewardship of a natural resource—the river.

We stopped on a beach to eat our *last* snack, the usual granola bar, on the Wabash. Said granola bar would have to wait: of course I needed to pee. However, we were on a beach with no trees to duck behind for privacy. Remember, I have a zipper-less wetsuit (no bitterness here). I voiced this quandary to John. "I have to go pee so badly. But where am I going to go?"

"Seriously? Just go anywhere. Who's going to see you?" John mocked, unsympathetic.

I peered up and down the river. Trying to secure my case, I pointed upstream. "There's a house over there."

"There isn't anyone outside, and they'd have to use binoculars to see you. Go anywhere." John chuckled.

I didn't have a choice. I unsnapped my wetsuit, pulled it down, exposing more than anyone would want to behold, and took care of nature. John snickered.

After I put myself back together, trying to forgive John for his lack of sympathy, I agreed to a selfie of the two of us. Ever since taking a crash course in photography a few years ago, John is proud of his "artsy" pictures. Today's selfie was unique—a picture of our shadows on the sand. Holding hands with the sun to our backs while John held his paddle upright, creating a shadow resembling Grant Wood's *American Gothic* painting, John snapped the picture. I hate to admit to John's cleverness, but this is one of my favorite pictures of the trip so far because it represents our togetherness and common goal. I love that man!

Soon after returning to the river, Paddling Edna joined us for one *last* episode while on the Wabash. "Helloooo"…boomed John's poor excuse at a British accent. "I'm Paddling Edna. On today's show we will be discussing hygiene. As you all know... Yes, young man... You there waving your hand. What is it?... Well, hello to you too. Now, as I was saying. Today we will be discussing hygiene. On the river, it is...Young man, what is it?... I said hello already. Now... Henry...Hen.... Henry, please see why that young man keeps interrupting.... What's that? ... His name is Gene?... And he wants to say hello? No, no, no. I'm not saying, 'Hi, Gene.' It is hygiene. Personal cleanliness. Now, as I was saying..." On and on he rambled.

Being on this trip with John is one thing, but adding his alter egos is another. Oh, well, at least she, I mean he, is entertaining.

Not long after the merciful conclusion of *Paddling Edna*, we came to a split in the river. To the right, with less water, spread the original river. Not only was there less water, but it also was closing up and becoming marshy. To the left, with more water, a river reroute. The flooding in 2008 and 2009 caused a river reroute, creating a short cut to the Ohio River, eliminating approximately seven miles. Of course, we chose the shorter route with more water.

As we paddled our *last* mile of the Wabash, its confluence with the Ohio River loomed in the distance. The opening horizon filled me with sadness. While paddling the *last* mile, I contemplated leaving our view for the past 487 miles, the Wabash River view. I was heavyhearted that we were leaving this view because we were saying good-bye to our friend and home for the last five and a half weeks. Where we had a view visible only from the river—the river view. Where we met so many new friends. Where "just happened to be" moments made us smile. Will I feel the same way when we come to the end of the Ohio and eventually the end of our trip? Coming to the end of the Wabash reminded me again of the quote from Lewis Carol's *Alice's Adventures in Wonderland*: "Begin at the beginning and go on till you come to the end: then stop." We began at the beginning of the Wabash River and went on till we came to the end; but then we did not stop—we continued on the Ohio River.

The Wabash River "T's" into the Ohio. As everyone does when turning onto a road at a T-intersection, we looked both ways. To our left, the John

T. Myers Locks & Dam appeared intimidating as it towered like a large grey citadel in the hazy distance. On the Ohio, we will encounter two or three locks. Since the Ohio and Mississippi converge below the Mississippi's last lock and dam, we won't encounter any more once we leave the Ohio. Glancing left, we turned right, entering the next leg of our journey—133 miles of the Ohio River.

Turning onto the Ohio River caused another set of emotions. We were there! The excitement of attaining this goal was similar to what I felt several years ago when we traveled to James Bay via the Moose River. Approaching the mouth of the bay, John continued tasting the water for saltiness in order to determine when it became brackish—where the fresh water of the Moose and the salt water of James Bay meld. John finally put his finger to his lips, smiling with tears in his eyes, and announced, "It's salty." Witnessing John's lifetime goal reached brought tears to my eyes. Today's goal wasn't solely John's vision, though; it was both of ours. After a year of planning, we had reached our *first* goal, the Ohio.

Where the two rivers meet at Ohio River mile 848, three states share the river—Kentucky, Indiana, and Illinois. Leaving the Wabash, we placed our paddles for the *last* time into the waters of Indiana. We will now paddle with Kentucky to our left and Illinois to our right until we reach the Mississippi. *Good-bye, Indiana!*

Waves created by a head wind and the larger body of water intimidated me after the calm, smaller waters of the Wabash River. The choppiness reminded me of the waters we encountered last September in Lake Huron off Drummond Island. During a "trial run" paddle in the great lake, we experienced waves larger than any we had encountered on previous kayaking trips. I remember being concerned, and asking John, "Will the waves on the Ohio or Mississippi be as large as these?" (I didn't ask about the Wabash because I guess I assumed the waves on it would be doable because of the river's size.)

"Probably," he answered. Even though John's response wasn't what I wanted to hear, I continued paddling and didn't die.

Today, the waves scared me, but I embraced them. The "trial run" trip to Drummond Island, intended to prepare us emotionally and logistically for this trip, was a success—we survived the large (huge to me at the time), rolling Lake Huron waves. I had survived those waves; I could survive these.

While concentrating on staying upright, I squinted to determine the identity of the white speck approaching in the distance. Still not able to distinguish what it was and assuming John's eyesight was better than mine, I asked, "What is that?"

"Without binoculars (they didn't make the gear list), I can't be sure." He studied it more intently and replied, "I think it's a boat."

As it grew closer, John updated his opinion, "By its shape and size, I'm sure it's not a fishing boat. I think we're seeing our *first* yacht."

Waiting for the yacht to cruise close enough to read the name, he readied his VHF radio for a radio check. When the boat's name, *Panacea*, came into view, he turned on the radio, pushed the "talk" button, and addressed the captain, "This is kayak *Work* trying to raise the *Panacea* for a radio check."

"Loud and clear," the pilot of the *Panacea* responded.

After John finished playing with the radio, I mean making sure it worked properly, we noticed a beach on the RBD (Right Bank Descending). John suggested, "I think we should pull off there and take a break. I need to change my charts from the Wabash to the Ohio."

We landed *Work* and *Pray* on the sandy beach for our *first* break on our new river.

Removing the Wabash charts from his waterproof pouch, John replaced them with those for the Ohio. Watching him tend to the maps, I realized how much I have trusted and depended on him during this trip. He is the one who examines the charts. He is the one who uses the charts to be aware of the dangers. He is the one who knows where we are. He is the one who determines how far we may travel each day. He is the one who considers the weather, assessing if the conditions are safe for river travel. He is the one who searches for a campsite. He is the one who… Trusting him has provided a sense of peace for me. I have enjoyed not dealing with the stress of making decisions—the worry about making a wrong decision. *Does all this responsibility stress him?* I don't know. If it does, he is doing a great job of hiding it. *Have I taken him for granted?* Probably. I haven't even considered picking up the charts. *Does he know how much I appreciate all he is doing for me? Have I expressed my thanks?* I hope so. Watching him continue to take care of me by simply changing the charts, I fell in love with him all over again.

Charts organized, we discussed camping there on the sandy beach or going another eight miles to Old Shawneetown, Illinois. Taking the short-cut at the end of the Wabash had eliminated seven miles from our paddle, and we had plenty of energy. We also were running on adrenalin as a result of the milestone we had just completed. Onward.

Close to Old Shawneetown, we encountered our *first* tow and barge. John radioed the captain of the tow, *Caleb Dean*, to be polite and confirm our approach. This way both knew the other existed.

Watching the large steel mass come nearer, I worried about my approach. The tow was a BIG boat—bigger than any fishing boat, ski boat, or yacht I had encountered. I knew the size of wake a ski boat puts out and the importance of turning the bow of *Pray* into the wave so she wouldn't capsize. In my mind the aftermath of a vessel the size of the tow and barge had to be larger than that of a smaller boat. As the tow passed, I pivoted *Pray* to face the wave, preparing myself for a moving ridge capable of forcing my kayak on its side. Much to my surprise, as the *Caleb Dean* glided through the water next to me, it didn't create much of a disturbance. *Pray's* bow paused as it perched briefly on the top of the small swell. I beamed, realizing I had survived my *first* tow and barge!

Even though I survived my *first* tow and barge, I would lie if I didn't say I am nervous about tomorrow's paddle. *Will other tows be traveling faster and produce more wave action? How many will we encounter back to back? Will we be aware of a tow and barge approaching from behind? Will they always see us?* The unknown creates fear. I'm sure tomorrow night I write that the tows weren't as bad as I thought they would be.

We arrived at Old Shawneetown's boat ramp around 2:30 p.m. I stayed with *Work* and *Pray*; John investigated our water-filling and camping options. While out and about, he met a woman gardening and inquired, "Is there someplace we can fill our water containers?"

She pointed up the street to the lone building with a sign out front and non-boarded up windows, offering, "The bar will, as soon as they open."

"Thank you."

As John headed towards the potential water-fill station, a car pulled up in front of the bar and a woman hopped out.

"Are you here to open the bar? John inquired. When will it open?"

"Consider it open," she replied.

"Hi, I'm John. We're kayaking through. Is there someplace we can fill up with water?"

"I'm Monica. You can use the outdoor pump."

"Thanks. By the way, we may pitch a tent by the gazebo at the top of the hill for the night." Notice, John didn't request permission—he mentioned our intent. Since our Covington, Indiana, rejection, we hesitate to ask.

Having obtained the go-ahead to fill up with water, John joined me at the boat ramp. He relayed his success," I've located water and a place to stay. The only problem is the long, steep hill we have to pull the kayaks up. We'll have to take several breaks on the way. Are you up to this?"

I stood up. "Do I have a choice?"

Picking up the front of *Pray* and pulling her up the hill, I affirmed, "Let's do this."

We crossed the ramp, turned, and were ready to start up the hill when the woman with whom John had originally inquired about water pulled up next to us. She introduced herself to me as Laura. She and her friend Bentley wanted to make sure we had found access to water. The kindness of people will never cease to amaze me. She stopped what she was doing and made a special trip to check on us. Why? We were an interruption to her day. Would I be as willing to stop picking tomatoes, climb into my car, and drive to check on some strangers? I doubt it. I am too selfish with my time. Hopefully, our interactions with others on this trip will open my eyes and cause a change in my priorities. Picking tomatoes can wait…

Watching them drive away, we took a deep breath before starting our long, hot climb up the steep hill. (Have I mentioned everything's uphill from the river?) When I thought I couldn't go any farther, I focused on the small gazebo resting on the top of the hill, the reward for my effort. I tried to imagine sitting in the gazebo as the cool breeze dried the sweat from my temples. Ahh!!!

Of course, John traveled faster than I did and was soon ahead of me. Realizing I was no longer beside him, he glanced back, noticing my struggle. He sat down *Work*, trekked back to me, and pulled *Pray* to where *Work* was resting. He then transferred *Pray's* rope back to me, picked up the front of *Work,* and started pulling his boat beside me until he was ahead of me again. We repeated the same drill several times until we reached our goal.

At the top of the hill, the road curved to the right and back downhill. I stopped a moment, taking in the view from my high vantage point. To the left I surveyed an unobstructed view of the river. I examined where we came from today and where we would paddle tomorrow. We definitely are not on the Wabash any longer. The Ohio has its own personality. Gone are the calm waters of a smaller river. Even from the banks, the unpredictable swirls of currents were visible. The bridge we will pass under tomorrow is much larger than the bridges on the Wabash. The river from this view scared me! I couldn't imagine paddling on such a big body of water. On the Wabash, no matter where we paddled, we traveled next to each other. On the Ohio, if we paddle on opposite sides of the river, we could be nearly a mile apart. I feel like we are beginning a new trip. The sites are foreign, not the familiar ones of the last month. *Will entering the Mississippi create similar feelings?*

As I scanned the area to the right, Old Shawneetown (Population 193—saaaaa-lute!) lay at the bottom of the hill. Old Shawneetown used to be simply Shawneetown, which flooded frequently. During the historical flood of 1937, the local bank resorted to doing business from a second story window. (Instead of a drive-through, float-through perhaps?) The three-story partial brick, partial block Greek revival style bank is impressive with its story-high steps and still stands as a historical landmark. Because of the severity and frequency of the flooding, the government eventually moved the town three miles from the river. The name Shawneetown moved with the town (known by locals as New Town). The remaining few houses, abandoned businesses, and bar—*Nate's Bar and Grill*—by the river are now known as Old Shawneetown. I know what a pain moving a household of stuff is. I can't imagine the logistics of moving an entire town.

I wonder if the few who stayed in Old Shawneetown regret their decision every time water inundates the town as the river exceeds its limits. I can hear the conversation....

"The water is coming under the door again."

"*#&#*, Frank! I told you we should have moved when the town moved."

"Grab the dog. Let's go."

Those living by the river regard the river the same and yet differently than I do. While we both are aware of its power, I view it as a means of transportation, providing me with scenes of nature only witnessed from the river. They perceive it as a means of devastation as a result of the events in nature.

Back to my land view this afternoon. In front of me stood the promised gazebo on a small grassy patch above *Nate's*. Our home for the night, conveniently located close to water (and a restroom. Score!). While I organized our tent, John filled our dromedaries.

Settled, we strolled down the hill to *Nate's* to use their Wi-Fi and charge our electronics. *Nate's* interior reminded me of many other small town bars with neon beer signs, pub tables, and a pool table. In addition to the expected décor, a red truck door with *Hardware Bar and Grill* painted on it and an orange and white safety life preserver ring hung on the brick wall. In the rear, ropes separated a few slot machines from the rest of the bar. Entering the restrooms in the corner required going up a step. (This seems like a bad idea for a bar.) *Nate's* is a place where everyone knows your name probably because it is the only place to eat in town. Young and old, 13 to 80, sat at the bar talking with dark-haired, 30-something, bartender Monica.

We ordered drinks, found a table next to an outlet, and climbed onto the pub-height chairs. We plugged in one iPad and our phone. (Packing only one iPad charging cord may have been a mistake since we have two iPads.) As our devices charged, I journaled while John posted some pictures on Instagram. In the background, *Gilligan's Island* played on the TV. Interesting choice of programs for a bar.

On our way out, we met a gentleman seated at the bar who was building a catamaran, intending to sail around the world. I thought we were adventurous! I found his story intriguing, but I wish I had paid more attention to everything he told us. I don't remember exactly where he was from; I think some other country. He came to Old Shawneetown to build the boat, but I don't remember why he chose this area. He has spent several years building it, but I don't remember how many. The expected amount of time to complete his trip is … I don't remember. I asked all the right questions; I just don't remember. Oh no, I sound like John, who asks questions but rarely pays attention to the answers.

After relaxing and charging our devices over cold drinks, we returned to the gazebo and fixed Southwest lasagna and chili for dinner with chocolate pudding for dessert. Once we had finished eating, cleaning up, and making a last restroom trip to *Nate's*, we secured everything we weren't using into the kayaks and crawled into our tent for our *first* night on the Ohio River.

What a monumental day of *firsts* and *lasts.* We spent our *last* day on our *first* river, the Wabash. We spent our *first* day on the Ohio while leaving Indiana and entering Kentucky. Bittersweet.

05-08-2015

It's Mr. Weenie Time

Weather conditions:

High: 85

Low: 61

Skies: clear in the morning with rain late afternoon

Wind: SSW 4-22 mph, gusts to 28 mph

Today's mileage: 23 miles

Total: 520 miles

Where we traveled: Old Shawnee Town, Illinois, to Cave-in-Rock, Illinois

Today started even earlier than yesterday—3:30 a.m.—in order to miss some wind, heat, and storms during our 23-mile paddle to Cave-in-Rock, Illinois. My preference of seeing 3:30 only once a day is the same as seeing 4:30—in the afternoon. By the end of the day, however, I was glad we woke up at 3:30 a.m. I hate to admit John was right—again!

One advantage of waking early is the beauty we witness in the sunrise. Today's sunrise of deep purples, oranges, and pinks, reflecting on the river, provided double splendor. The colorful background set a backdrop for a life-size painting of the silhouetted trees on the opposite bank. The sparse clouds accentuated the subdued colors in the sky with a deeper purple hue. There may be more sunrises than sunsets in our future from now until the end of the trip as we rise early, trying to beat the heat in the afternoon and enter a state of sleep before the sun retires for the night.

• • •

Before I start with the recount of today, I need to talk about my eventful night. Even though I was exhausted by the time I crawled into my sleeping bag, my churning gut prevented me from falling asleep. I assumed I would feel better if I made a trek down the hill to Nate's. Although I didn't know if I could reach the restroom without an accident, I finally convinced myself that hiking there was better than other options. So I put on my shoes, clenched my butt cheeks, trudged down the hill, and arrived at the toilet just in time. Healed (or so I thought), I stumbled back to the tent. Having ridded myself of some toxins, I fell asleep—for a while. Suddenly, my agitated belly woke me. Apparently, this wasn't over. Unfortunately, the bathroom was closed by this time. *Now what?* Camped under a security light by a road, I longed for the privacy of the wilderness. Still wanting to avoid a mess, I put on my shoes, clenched my butt cheeks, gathered the red poop bag, and traipsed towards the boat ramp, thinking the amount of traffic on a boat ramp in the middle of the night had to be less than that on the road. I picked out a spot halfway to the river, removed the shovel from the poop bag, slid it from its sheath, and opened it. I pressed it into the ground. The ground laughed at my feeble attempt at digging a hole. By this time, I couldn't think of anything but quieting my stomach. In the words of our granddaughter when she was younger, "I got the diarrhea!" I squatted towards the long grass beside the road and…. Even if I had been able to dig a hole, confidence in my accuracy was low. I traipsed back to the tent, repeating this scenario several times during the night and into this morning.

This brings me to breakfast. After eating granola with milk for breakfast (I struggled to eat all mine) and packing up, we rolled *Work* and *Pray* down the hill to the boat launch. Although not as tiring as going up a hill, rolling our kayaks down a hill presents difficulties of its own. The wheels roll faster than I walk. I tried pulling it beside me but had difficulty controlling the speed. Then, I had the brilliant idea of proceeding in front of it, thinking I could regulate the speed with my body. Although I was lucky I didn't face plant when *Pray* tried to push me, this option proved to be the safest because I could maintain a little more control. Arriving safely at the boat ramp, we launched by 6:30 a.m. Just think, earlier in the trip, we set our alarm for 6:30 because of cold temperatures. Now we leave by 6:30 because of heat. Living directly in the elements dictates our daily activities.

Keep us upright and safe.

In addition to a queasy stomach, I was weak most of the morning. But thankfully, I didn't need to make any emergency pit stops. By lunch I was hungry and welcomed the peanut butter wrap in my lunch bag. When preparing for the trip, I hadn't thought about sickness. Had I, I might have added Imodium AD and Pepto-Bismol to our gear list. Since I can't remember the last time I tasted Pepto-Bismol, and I'm not sure if I have ever purchased Imodium AD, I didn't automatically consider them as essential line items on the Excel spreadsheet of gear.

The river's width is affecting both the way we paddle together and our communication with each other. Previously, the narrow river provided two options for traveling together—close to each other or single file. Conversation flowed easily. With the gift of room, we now navigate farther apart because the currents and larger waves could push us into each other. However, this gift creates a communication obstacle since we are often out of hearing range. We have found ourselves saying "what" more than we like. Sometimes the word *what* creates tension on both sides of the conversation—speaker and listener. The listener, who can't hear, is annoyed because she didn't catch what the speaker relayed. The speaker is annoyed because he has to repeat his statement. Miscommunication is especially frustrating when telling a joke— the punchline is lost upon the second uttering. So we invented a system to help alleviate some tense moments. If the listener says, "what," the speaker determines if the statement is necessary to repeat. If not, he says, "I love you." The listener then goes on with life. This seems to work well.

We have also had some humorous moments as a result of the hearer misunderstanding a statement, responding to what she THOUGHT she heard. Her response usually doesn't make any sense in the original conversation. For example, one time John yelled (I learned later), "There are not many boats, crazy waves, or others out here today."

My response, thinking John uttered something about goats grazing with whales and their mothers, was, "How can a whale possibly graze with goats?"

Deciding previously to have fun with these misunderstandings, instead of saying, "I love you," the original speaker simply goes with the flow (pun intended) and responds to the unexpected reply, thus creating an entirely different dialogue than expected. John's comeback, therefore, was, "Well, they are mammals you know. Don't you know anything?" I'm glad there's no one else out here to hear us.

Our eagle count fell to one today. I'm sure they are still present; but since the river is so wide, and we're rarely near the bank, the probability of our spotting perched or nesting eagles is reduced.

Approaching what bore a resemblance to a tow with barges, we paddled closer to one another in order to discuss our theories. Making sure we gave the large object enough room, I remarked, "I don't see a wake. Is it moving? Why would it be sitting in the middle of the river?"

John examined it. "You're right. Maybe it's broken down."

Approaching, I noticed the red and white barges weren't attached in the front as they usually are. "The barges are on the side of the tow."

"And look at all the equipment on the tow." John concluded, "I bet that's a dredge. I read about these." He continued explaining that the Army Corps of Engineers employ these boats and their accompanying barges to maintain the nine-foot deep sailing channel needed for the larger boats. This trip has been so educational. Where in Berne, Indiana, would I come across a dredge?

Since I don't encounter them, I wouldn't have a reason to investigate the existence of them. I am eager for the exposure to knowledge I don't know exists. You don't realize what you don't know until you know it. (Clever, huh?)

As I predicted yesterday, the barge traffic didn't intimidate me as much as I thought it would. The river's size provides plenty of room to maneuver away from them, so by the time the wake reaches our kayaks, the impact is minimal. Actually, the wake from a powerboat creates more havoc. In addition, John uses our radio to keep in contact with the tows, providing an element of safety. We know their plans, and they know we exist.

Many of the dangers others warned me about have proven to be safer than they described. Was their advice the result of experience or something they heard? Were they afraid because they didn't know? Were they too scared to face the fear and find out if it was as bad as they thought? Ignorance breeds fear. If they would jump off the bank and face the unknown, become familiar with it, many fears would float away. I know there are certain entities we should be afraid of—a healthy fear. But how is the difference distinguished? How do we force ourselves to experience life before making judgment on what is fear-worthy? Many want to stay in their ignorance, using fear as an excuse not to proceed, instead of living adventurously. The result is staying inside, living adventures vicariously through people on television or in books. Many feel safer when they stay away from what they fear. Is staying ignorant and not overcoming the fear really safer? It may be safer, but are they missing something? If I had stayed home because of all the dangers others warned me about, I would have missed so much. Avoiding the fear isn't worth what I would have missed. What do I fear in my life? What am I ignorant about and therefore fearful of? What am I missing because I am still sitting on the bank watching my fears float by? Grace Hopper reminds me, "A ship in port is safe, but that is not what ships were built for."

Continuing on our first full day on the Ohio River, I took inventory of all the differences between this river and the Wabash. The width of the river increased—more than doubled; odd currents intensified—making it more difficult to keep *Work* and *Pray* tracking straight; boat traffic increased—boat traffic was almost non-existent on the Wabash. With the addition of commercial boats, the Ohio River has navigational aids—buoys and mile markers. Green buoys and mile markers on our right as we travel downstream, red ones on our left. To remember this, we use the mariner's saying "red right return." Most outgoing trips head downstream with their loads. Once free of their loads, they "return" upstream at which point all the red markers are indeed on their right. Easy to remember. In addition to the distinguishing colors, each can be identified by shape: red are triangular, called "nun" buoys; Green are square, referred to as "can" buoys.

Another difference—the wind produces larger waves on the larger body of water. Today, the calm wind at the beginning of our paddle increased about five hours into our journey. Okay, here's a math problem. If we paddled six hours and the wind increased five hours into our journey, how long did we have to endure the nagging wind? Correct answer is one hour. Extra credit. If we had set our alarm for 6:00 a.m. and not 3:30 a.m., how long would we have paddled in the wind? Answer—three and a half hours. Again, John was right to force me to see 3:30 twice a day.

Even though we paddle farther from the bank, we are still close enough to appreciate its diversity. Beautiful sandy beaches stretch next to low cliffs with visible rock striations. Some portions of the cliffs have fallen into the river, creating huge boulders. Approaching the town of Cave-in-Rock, Illinois, we observed houses built on the edge of the cliff. This is not an exaggeration, one wrong step off the porch, and... Yard maintenance is minimal, though, if nonexistent. This picturesque view of the cliffs and beaches can be appreciated only from the river. I feel privileged! On the other hand, those living at the top of the cliff also enjoy an equally breathtaking view—the land view of the river. If I lived on the cliff, I would witness the daily and seasonal changes of the river from my porch while relaxing and drinking my morning coffee on my wooden Adirondack chair (feet propped up on a footstool, of course). The downside to living on the cliff—the challenge of accessing the river. So close, yet so far. I did note one home with a ladder reaching part way down the cliff. *Do they extend the ladder when they are ready to use it? Or is the ladder used only when the river is higher?*

A little farther downstream, we discovered the reason for the town's name, Cave-in-Rock, where we plan to spend the next two days. From the river view, a cave peeks out of the rocky bluffs; a sandy beach connects it to the river. Beside the cave, a bridge provides on-land access. I wonder if tourists and visitors have violated the cave with litter and graffiti. Interesting how my thoughts about the area changed as soon as I noted the bridge, providing society's access to this part of nature. I automatically assumed humans ruined that which was naturally beautiful before they touched it. How can others be convinced to appreciate and experience nature without leaving a mark?

Rounding a bend soon after the cave in the rock, we spotted a ferry, the *Loni Jo*, a white towboat with an attached open red barge, transporting a pick-up truck, a car, and a heavy-duty commercial truck from Illinois to Kentucky. Waiting for the ferry to leave the Illinois side of the river, John radioed the *Loni Jo's* operator and received the "OK" to land. Docking next to the ferry provided a new experience with challenges. We had to stay out of the way of the ferry while avoiding the large rope used to secure the boat to the dock. (John later told me he kept a close watch on a snake he caught sight of at our landing point. I think his decision not to alert me of the existence of the creature was probably wise. He knew I would *freak* out.) We also had to land and exit *Work* and *Pray* quickly while avoiding the breaking wake. If caught by a crashing wave, there is a danger water would swamp our kayak. We didn't have to worry about pummeling waves on the smaller Wabash. New experiences, new challenges, new skills. I wonder how many new experiences will eventually become an ordinary part of our trip. How many experiences were new at the beginning of the Wabash but are now such a seamless part of our existence that we forget they were once new? How many times do you have to repeat an activity or experience before it becomes part of your life, no longer new and exciting?

The main reason we chose to stop at Cave-in-Rock was to pick up our Week # 6 package. As soon as *Work* and *Pray* were on dry ground, John checked the post office's hours—8:30 a.m. to 12:30 p.m. Time on John's watch—12:50 p.m. I guess we should have set our alarm for 3:00 a.m. Hmm, maybe not. Tomorrow's hours are 9:00-10:15 a.m. We have a second chance; however, we can't miss that small window of opportunity or we won't be able to move on until Monday.

Realizing we didn't need to hurry to the post office, we placed the wheels on our kayaks and pulled them to the parking lot. Across the street, members of the fire department oversaw inmates spraying mud off the parking lot with the high-pressure hoses from the firetruck. Apparently, this area flooded a couple of weeks ago. I sat with *Work* and *Pray* while John sauntered over to inquire about the town's amenities—camping, restrooms, laundry, shower, water, trash, etc.

Sitting on *Pray*, watching the vehicles wait in line for the ferry to return from across the river, I speculated the reason they were leaving Illinois and traveling to Kentucky. A lone man in a vehicle—returning to his office after a business lunch? A mother with young children—visiting grandma? A 20-something man in a dirty, sweaty t-shirt—on his way to the next landscaping job? As I examined them and judged, they examined me and judged. What were they thinking? What was their assessment of me? Since they observed me sitting on my kayak, I am sure their conclusions were different than if they had met me on the street. At the beginning of the trip, I was concerned about what others thought of my clothes or smell. I was vain. I don't care as much now. I can't remember the last time I considered putting on makeup. This is who I am—this is me. Will I still be content with who I am once we return home? When I live in society again with access to a shower and a washing machine, I will look and smell more like the others I meet. Will I still be content with being me even if it means I am different? Interesting, I am LESS concerned about being different when I AM different. Yet MORE concerned about being different when I am NOT different. Evidently, if I stand out, I want to REALLY stand out—stand out on purpose.

Meanwhile, John approached the man who appeared to be in charge. "My wife and I are kayaking through. I was wondering if there's a place here by the river where we could pitch our tent."

"You mean like…camp?" the man replied.

"Yes," affirmed John.

The man pointed to the sign next to the parking lot. "How about right here behind the sign that says Cave-In-Rock Campground?"

John stared at the sign, "Ummm…Yeah."

The two continued to become acquainted. John learned his name was Perry and he was sort of the town overseer. He explained to John that they hoped folks would use the river for recreation and had recently put a shower and rest room next to the city office up the street. I think Perry, knowing someone had paddled in and would use them, was as excited for us to use the facilities as we were to take advantage of them. A win-win situation!

Returning to me with the information required for our stay, John, my hero, suggested, "I think our kayaks will be safe here. Let's find the restroom before we go to the campground." No complaints from me.

As we lumbered up the hill (have I mentioned lately everything is uphill from the river) in search of the restroom, a man on a four-wheeler passed us and blurted without even slowing down, "If you want good food, go to *Rose's*." Coincidently, David from New Harmony had also suggested eating at *Rose's*. As the dust from the four-wheeler settled, we turned to each other, "*Rose's* it is." How can you not eat at a place after receiving two recommendations?

Entering the main portion of town, we came to the intersection. Two impeccable bicycles, one bright pastel green and the other yellow, stood on opposite corners. A bouquet of plastic flowers rested in the baskets. Art. Moving my attention from the bicycles to the buildings on each side of Main Street, I noted that most of the flower containers in the town held similar plastic flower arrangements. "Rose's Kountry Kitchen" adorned with two roses was painted on the side of a building. A "Welcome Bikers" sign in large letters hung beneath it. There must be some kind of motorcycle festival here although the sign didn't list any dates. Across the street from *Rose's* stood the closed-down Riverfront Opry House, the post office, and a small white church. That was the entire burg. Cave-in-Rock. Another once thriving river town.

Restrooms visited, we trudged back down the hill to the parking lot, retrieved *Work* and *Pray*, and pulled them across the now dirt-free parking lot to the campground. While we were erecting the tent, a local state park DNR officer dressed in his khaki-colored, DNR issued, button-up shirt parked beside our campsite. Twenty-something, sandy-haired Shawn had driven his all-terrain vehicle from the state campground to deliver a package from the Peru, Indiana-based Orion Safety Products. An Orion employee, Duane Stuart, discovering our trip, sent us two complimentary flare signaling kits. Since these items are pyrotechnics, a DNR officer needed to deliver them instead of USPS. (I hope we never have to use this gift!) Raising his mirrored sunglasses, Shawn showed John where to sign on the paper secured to the clipboard. Shawn informed us we could use the showers at the state campground an eighth of a mile down the road. Wow, TWO shower options. Now, if we could find a laundromat, life would be perfect!

Our signal kits delivered and signed for, we continued assembling our tent. Placing the pole in the corner loop, I glanced at the tree next to me. I inched closer to see if what I saw was what I thought I saw. Embedded in the trunk was a pair of electrical outlets with a cord running down the side of the tree to a conduit pipe stuck in the ground. The tree had grown around them, causing the outlets to become part of the tree. *Is this considered "green electricity"?* Excited for access to electricity so conveniently located outside the tent door, I retrieved my iPad and charging cord. I plugged it in—silence. No "I am charging" ding. Being teased by possible electricity created a feeling similar to finding a locked restroom. Excitement dashed.

Luckily, the tent was secure when the wind picked up and the skies grew dark. Protected from possible rain in our Frogg Togg lightweight rain suits (John's is gray, mine is blue), we gathered our iPads, phone, and chargers in preparation to travel to *Rose's Kountry Kitchen*. The plan was to charge our battery-powered pieces of equipment (since the electric trees didn't work) and check out Wi-Fi options. We also anticipated taking advantage of the access to dessert and coffee too. (We had to buy something, right?) Trudging up the steep gravel path directly behind our campsite, we passed by the post office on our way to the downtown area—how convenient. Across the street from the post office stood a white building adorned with three red benches and a fern growing in a yellow pot—*Rose's*.

Noticing our entrance, the owner, Rose, and her daughter, Renee, chorused, "Welcome."

Forty-something Renee's purple tie died t-shirt, "holey" jeans, and matching purple baseball cap fit her spunky personality. Flashing us a bright smile, she asked, "What can I get y'all?" Pointing to a whiteboard behind the counter, she added, "Here are the specials."

"Do ya have any desserts?" John asked.

Directing us to the display case full of scrumptious-looking desserts, Renee beamed, "We make all these here."

My mouth watered. Since I couldn't have one of each, I blurted, "I think I'll take the peach cobbler."

"Do you want it warm? With ice cream?"

"You just made her day when you mentioned ice cream," John informed Renee.

"Yes, please," I confirmed.

John pointed at the third shelf, "I'll take the blueberry cheesecake. Oh, and can we get two black coffees?"

"Seat yourselves. I'll bring everything to you."

Scoping out the available seating along the walls, I scanned under the tables for handy electrical outlets. Finding the perfect spot by the front window, we sat down and unpacked. Waiting on our desserts and coffee, I studied this highly recommended diner. Décor and sayings filled every available space on the paneled walls. The tables and chairs were a hodge-podge—some wood grain, others metal. The padded metal chairs were either all black, all red, or red and black. Black electrical tape covered holes in the cushions created by years of use. Even though no one has updated *Rose's* in a couple of decades, I prefer this comfortable outdated atmosphere over that of a modern five-star restaurant—I didn't have to worry if I used the correct fork. And I was confident the food would be comparable to my grandma's.

Renee delivered our dessert and coffee. The melting ice cream on the non-dehydrated dessert on the porcelain plate formed a white puddle in the middle of the warm peach cobbler. Grasping the handle of the fragile coffee cup, I raised it to my lips. The bold fragrance of the non-instant coffee wafted to my nose. I almost forgot the collapsible green handle-less tumbler and instant coffee packets packed in the front hatch of *Pray*. I'm not complaining about what we are eating or drinking on our trip or our table service. I'm surprised at what I now consider a luxury. Two months ago, I would have ordered my dessert and coffee without much thought. I would have eaten my first, second, and third bite using a non-collapsible fork or spoon without paying attention to the characteristics of the plate. I would have picked up my coffee cup by the handle not thinking another option existed. I wonder how long after I return home from our trip before I slide back into the rut of non-observance or lack of appreciation for the little pleasures in life.

As we savored our peach cobbler with ice cream and blueberry cheese-cake, the dark skies began leaking. The falling rain cemented the wisdom of our earlier decision to set our alarm for 3:30 a.m. If we hadn't, we would have been on the river or setting up our tent in the rain. I guess John had the right idea even if he forced me to see 3:30 twice today. I'm glad he over-looks what HE considers are my quirks.

Dessert enjoyed, I decided to use *Rose's* Wi-Fi. I turned on my iPad, selected settings, Wi-Fi, and waited for a network to appear. None. Not even a locked *Rose's* network.

John caught Rene's attention, called her over, and asked, "Do you have Wi-Fi here?"

"Sorry. We barely have cell coverage in town. I have to stand at the intersection down the street to get a signal."

I checked my phone. Sure enough, "No Service" glared at me in the upper left hand corner. I was disappointed—I had planned to accomplish some chores on-line over the next two days. Again, the dependence on technology caused stress. Twenty years ago, maybe even five or ten, I wouldn't have even considered *Rose's* having Wi-Fi; so I wouldn't have known to be disappointed. Once you experience a convenience, its absence creates discontent. All of a sudden I can't live without something I lived without fine before, because it didn't exist then. In the past, I didn't know I should miss it. How many new stresses have the inventions of technology and conveniences created? I thought about the stress and disconnect I experience the moment I realize I forgot my cell phone at home. I think *What if someone needs to call me?* Twenty years ago, I would have left the house without considering the need for the phone. If someone called while I was gone, he or she would leave a message on my answering machine. And before the invention of the answering machine, he or she would continue calling back until I answered. Conveniences invented to reduce stress sometimes create stress. Ironic. Fewer conveniences equal less stress.

The rain finally subsided, so we clambered down the stone driveway to our tent. Even though we had eaten dessert, we were still hungry. I pulled quick beef stew from our dinner bag, added water, heated it, and we devoured it for dinner. While we sat on a bench with a back and ate dinner, a nearby church played hymns over the loudspeaker. Listening to the songs, tears came to my eyes as I reminisced about the hymns sung in my childhood church. Listening, I recalled a poster I had read on the wall at *Rose's* advertising a revival in town. I have missed going to church, so I asked John if we could go.

After dinner, John ventured uptown to check out the possibility of attending the revival. He not only returned with a ride to church, but he also arranged to have the electric tree turned on. I have found on this trip that when John leaves to go to the restroom or find something out, he often returns with something wonderful like ice cream, cinnamon rolls, or other random surprises. He is my hero!

At the arranged time, a red crew cab truck pulled up. I peered in the window at the man in his forties with a graying beard and mustache sitting in the driver's seat. John introduced me to Perry—the fire chief and previous mayor, with whom he had talked soon after our arrival. His dirty, gray t-shirt revealed his involvement in the parking lot cleaning earlier in the day. He, along with his sandy-haired, approximately ten-year-old son, had come to drive us to the local Baptist church.

John opened the rear door of the truck, and we climbed in. Arriving at the church and watching the greeters at the door, I felt underdressed. I have going-to-town clothes but not going-to-church clothes. Not to mention the fact that we smelled as if we hadn't showered in days. (Well, we actually hadn't.) However, the well-dressed churchgoers overlooked our attire and smell as they gave us a warm welcome.

The sanctuary was almost identical to the one at the small country church I attended as a child. Two doors bookended the center stage. I'm not sure where the doors in this church led to; but in my childhood church, the stage-left door opened to a hall leading to the restrooms and steps to the basement. The other door provided access to the pastor's office. In front of the left door in both churches stood the piano, mirrored on the opposite side by the organ. A center aisle separated two sets of pews. The rack on the back of the pew in front of me held two hymnals, a Bible, and a paper fan attached to a wooden handle. I removed the paper fan and began cooling my face. It resembled the fans

I used in summers past, minus the Yager Funeral Home advertisement printed on the back.

After taking in the surroundings of the sanctuary, I studied the people. I wondered how many were related to each other. How many were sitting in "their" pews? I gazed at the third pew on the left from the front and could almost picture my grandparents and great grandparents sitting on personal cushions in "their" pew, holding hymnals with "their" names written on the first page inside the front cover. The small congregation of my church consisted mainly of my aunts, uncles, and cousins. I looked forward to going to church; it was like a family reunion every Sunday.

Tonight, in front of us sat a family with three tow-headed children—two boys and a girl. The freckled little girl, dressed in a red sleeveless dress, turned around to catch a better view at the strangers sitting behind her. Was she scrutinizing who was sitting in her aunt's pew? Turning around, she put her hands over her nose. Oh, now I understand. She was searching for the origin of the foul odor. Only a child would be brave enough to express discomfort so openly. Adults would feel too awkward to turn around, let alone cover their nose—even if they desperately wanted to. With age, do we become wiser or less honest? The innocence and honesty of childhood.

Oh, the visual memories. I leaned back, allowing the tears to flow as I reflected on the impact that small country church had in forming who I am today. My spiritual foundation, my desire for family bonding, my aspiration to be a missionary, my… I don't think I'm aware of a fraction of the ways my childhood church affected me then and still does today.

Every Sunday morning, Sunday night, and Wednesday night, I sat with my parents in "our" pew one row in front of where we sat tonight, where the little girl in the red dress sat. Mom had an arsenal in her purse to help my two siblings and me defend against the boredom of sitting quietly on a hard, wooden, church pew for at least an hour—black and white magnetic Scottie dogs, silly putty, pencil and paper, and pennies. I placed the pennies under the paper, then using the pencil to rub over the top, created a two-dimensional image. I also used the pencil and paper to write stories. I still have a small tablet of stories I wrote when I was around eight, and I've been writing ever since. My favorite piece of entertainment, though, was one I carried—a small purse with a drawstring my mom made by cutting off the bottom of a dish detergent bottle and then crocheting around the edge. This little purse was unique because pulling down the sides converted it to a doll baby basinet, revealing a small doll complete with a pillow and flowered blanket. She even wore a small hand-crocheted pink hat and diaper. I never played with these toys at home; Mom saved them for church, keeping them extra special.

Singing the familiar old hymns comforted me. In our church at home, we usually sing modern praise songs and sometimes re-lyriced secular ones, following the words projected on a screen. Holding a hymnal and singing the old standards was a perfect addition to the evening. The message was Biblical and Southern Baptist. At the end of the message, John and I each received a visualization of the story in the form of a small scarlet ribbon, which now adorns the bow loops on each of *Work* and *Pray*.

At the completion of the service, many greeted us, asking about our journey. (They knew by our clothes and river stench we weren't ordinary people.) We even signed an autograph for a long white-haired, older gentleman. Encouraging him to follow us on our website, he told us, "I don't do computers or Internet." Will he ever know if we live up to the autograph?

Autograph signed, we returned to the tent, retrieved our toiletry bags, and strolled hand in hand to the public shower. The shower felt wonderful and we smell so much better now. If only we could wash our dirty clothes!

Back in the tent refreshed, we are ready for bed. The time is 10:30 p.m. I am exhausted. What a day! Remember the alarm that sounded this morning at 3:30—23 miles ago? A lot has happened in 19 hours—including some diarrhea. Tomorrow, we are staying here because of the forecasted storms, and we need to pick up our food between 9:00 a.m. and 10:15 a.m. Whom will we meet tomorrow in Cave-in-Rock?

05-09-2015

The Pictures Are in English

Weather conditions:

High: 81

Low: 64

Skies: mostly cloudy with scattered showers

Wind: S 5-10 mph—gusts to 21

Today's mileage: 0 miles (day of rest)

Total: 520 miles

Where we are: Cave-in-Rock, Illinois

What is the connection between sitting on a bench outside the restroom in the small town of Cave-in-Rock and the Internet? Read on….

Today we slept in until 6:00 a.m. I remember at the beginning of this trip when 6:00 a.m. used to be the time we set the alarm for, not the time we slept in to. Last night we didn't even set the alarm, making today an N.A.S. (No Alarm Saturday). We didn't need to set an alarm; our only agenda for the day was to pick up our Week # 6 package between 9:00 and 10:15 a.m., and we knew we wouldn't sleep *that* late.

As John does every morning before he leaves the tent, he checked the radar and suggested, "Hey, if we're going to take a shower this morning, we better do it now before the storm blows in." We gathered our shower paraphernalia and "clean" clothes, trudged up the hill (everything is uphill from the river), and relished a warm shower for the second day in a row—a new record!

Smelling fresh, we ate couscous and savored the last of the bread given to us by Rhonda and David at New Harmony.

Breakfast finished, we called (trying not to move from the exact spot where we had cell coverage) my son Travis, who is taking care of our yard and house, to check on a few details. He is doing a great job making sure the house doesn't collapse while we are gone. He has already dealt with no water—the breaker on the well pump kicked off. And too much water—the sump pump needed replaced. He is our hero from Berne, Indiana!

Our local hero, Don, who turned on the electric tree last night, came to collect our $15 camping fee for two nights and bring us a trash can. While he wrote our receipt, we discussed last night's revival meeting, which he also attended. You know you are in a small town when you have a social life within 24 hours of arriving.

As soon as Don left, John checked his watch. "It's 8:55. The post office opens in five minutes. Let's go. I want to be at the door when they open." Since the post office was conveniently located next to the steep gravel path directly behind our tent, we entered the lobby at 8:57 and greeted Kelsey as she unlocked the main door promptly at 9:00.

John introduced us, "Hi. We're John and LaNae Abnet."

The twenty-something girl behind the counter reserved her full smile until she was sure she could trust us. "Hi. I'm Kelsey. How can I help you?" Not a single hair of Kelsey's tight bun on the top of her head was out of place. I had the impression the post office wasn't the main entry on her to-do list for the day since she wasn't wearing the typical post office uniform, but instead sported an olive green sweater jacket over her purple tunic.

Kelsey's smile grew when John added, "We're kayaking from the source of the Wabash River to the Gulf and should have a general delivery package for John Abnet."

"Just a minute." She sauntered to the back and returned with the white box we had purchased at our local post office before our trip and labeled "6" with a black Sharpie.

After explaining our trip and food parcel boxes in more detail, John observed, "Kelsey, you have the greatest job in the world. Yesterday, you worked 'til 12:30. And today you're here only from 9:00 until 10:15. What a great gig!"

Stepping out the door, John added, "Thanks, Kelsey. Enjoy your day."

We trampled back down to our tent and began unpacking the box and placing the food in the correct meal bags. Opening each supply box is like Christmas. Since I packed them a couple of months ago, I don't remember the contents of each box. At the top of today's box lay our bug suits. I had to refrain from jumping up and down screaming, "Our bug suits are here! Our bug suits are here!" Our deet-free protection from those nasty swarming, buzzing, biting creatures had arrived.

Food organized, we traveled to Rose's with the goals of charging our battery-powered necessities, drinking coffee, and reading—that's what we do on our days of rest when no Internet is available. Not long after sitting down, John mumbled, "I have a hankerin' for a cheese toastie."

Did he say "hankerin'"? Okay, that's not a surprise. John started having "hankerin's" at Vincennes, Indiana, when the college students kept us awake most of the night with their blaring country music. *Did he say "cheese toastie"?* His term choice didn't surprise me because "cheese toastie" is what John and I grew up calling what most of the world refers to as a "grilled cheese." But I was concerned about the time of the request—9:45 in the morning. So to clarify, I asked, "What? Did you just say you had a hankerin' for a cheese toastie?"

A little louder this time, he teased, "Yes. Do you have a problem with that?" I had to remind myself we aren't on a normal schedule. (And John isn't normal!) John ordered and savored every bite of the buttery toasted bread with cheese dripping from the edges onto his small white plate, not caring what the time was. Confession—I stole a bite and enjoyed it.

Having relaxed a couple of hours, we started packing up to return to the tent when the rain started falling. More coffee anyone?

The rain ended after about an hour; we packed up a second time. As we exited the eatery, cool air and a gentle breeze blew in our faces. On the river a nice breeze translates to waves; but on land it means great laundry drying. We gathered our laundry, scrambled to the restroom and hand-washed the essentials. Although we washed our clothes in the river a few days ago, they weren't spotless. No matter how many times I rinsed them, the rinse water contained brown river water. Even so, our clothes now look cleaner (notice, I said *look* cleaner) and smell fabulous. (Well, fabulous is relative.) We hung our clothes to dry on our clothesline stretched between our separate boats. A foundation for our clothesline is only one of *Work* and *Pray*'s many functions, having been transformed into backrests, vanity, table, and more.

Laundry chore complete, we ate lunch and relaxed on a park bench at the campground. I read while John played his guitar. I know I have whined about John's guitar making the packing list and not my pillow, but I must admit I'm thankful he took the time to strap it on the back of *Work*. In an attempt to protect it, John had pulled a lawn and leaf trash bag over each end and then cinched the overlapping portions around the guitar's neck using a rubber band. He then stuffed it into the heavy rayon bag it originally came with. Regardless, he had real doubts about it surviving the trip and warned that my Christmas gift to him two years prior would likely need replacing when we return home. As a result of his efforts, we have both received comfort and relaxation as he plays and sings. Sometimes, I join—even if I don't know the words.

At intermission, I remembered Irene had texted me our next conversation topic yesterday. I suggested, "Hey, Irene sent us another topic. What do you think?"

He didn't sound as excited as I, but still agreed, "Sure."

"Your name has been drawn from the lottery to recreate America's political system from top to bottom. What changes would you make regarding political parties, political title, criteria to hold office, responsibilities, and the American voting process?"

Despite the question's depth, John didn't ponder his answer long before he responded, "Term limits in congress. Get rid of the two party system. Get money out of the campaigns," and on and on and on he bloviated. Apparently, Irene had struck a chord.

Next on our agenda—check out the Cave-in-Rock landmark from the bank and view the river from the cave. Cave-in-Rock is more than an interesting natural cavern; it is part of Ohio River's history. During the flatboat days it became home to bands of pirates. They would persuade passing boats to stop and then proceeded to steal their goods and/or kill those on board. I didn't know pirates created problems on the Ohio and Mississippi Rivers.

I felt small as we hiked along the bank next to the boulders and cliffs I had glimpsed in the distance from the river yesterday. I studied the water we had paddled in from a different view—from the bank. Even though the wind caused some waves, the river represented peace and quiet—no people creating distractions and interfering with nature. As we approached the opening, the number of tourists increased. I felt suffocated. The red painted graffiti at the mouth of the cave sickened me. *WHY would someone do this?* The defacement continued into the cavern. I was angry! At that point I stopped to consider how different my reaction would have been if I had entered and found prehistoric drawings covering the walls. In some sense, they are the same. Both are writing on the wall. But why does one anger me while the other enthralls? Perhaps, because of the intent. What is the intent of graffiti? What is the purpose? Cave paintings were a means of communication, of telling a story, of recording history. Once again, modern society disgusted me.

People! The number of people increased when we entered the cave, or maybe I felt that way because of the small space and slippery floor. I placed my feet down deliberately while trying to find a spot clear of intruders so

I could snap a picture of the river through the cave's opening. I thought I had a clear shot and at that moment someone stepped in front of me. The result was a picture of a shoulder. People! Tourists! Hey, wait a minute. The definition of *tourist* is someone sightseeing. I was one of those people, one of those tourists. How quickly I judge and miss that I could be part of the problem. Careful, LaNae.

After viewing the river from a different perspective, we trekked back to camp to relax some more—John napped. (Surprise!?) Love our days off!

While John napped, a different type of towboat motored past. This one was literally towing, not pushing. A small white yacht was towing a white fishing boat. Interestingly, this small towboat put out a larger wake than the huge ones pushing barges.

For dinner, we ate ham and beans with corn bread, and banana nut bread. Replete with adequate nourishment, we strolled to the public restrooms. (Thanks again, Perry! Hey, I just realized Perry was another "just happened to be" moment. Yesterday, when we arrived at the dock, Perry "just happened to be" there with the fire department cleaning the mud off the parking lot and directed us around town.)

Before returning to our tent, we sat in one of the few areas in town with cell service—on a bench outside the restroom. Focused on my task of using this brief moment of Internet service to finish my journal entry and post it on our website, I didn't notice the white car pull up until John exclaimed, "There's Winnie!" I stared at him. *Who's Winnie and how does he know her!? I've been with him every minute since we floated into town.*

She parked by the sidewalk. John introduced me to her, "LaNae, this is Winnie. I met her last night when I was searching for information about the revival." *Oh yeah, I forgot he did leave me for a little bit last night.*

"Nice to meet you," I replied.

Jovial Winnie gave us a little history of the town. I love my wilderness life, but meeting people like Winnie makes coming to society bearable. Whom will we meet in the next town?

• • •

This brings me to the present, sitting on a bench outside the restroom in the small town of Cave-in-Rock, taking advantage of the weak cell signal to finish and post this journal entry on the Internet. We plan to climb into our tent soon because tomorrow is another early day in order to beat the heat of 86 degrees. In addition to the heat, the winds are predicted to increase around 2:00 p.m. I'm scared to ask John what time he is setting the alarm for. Loved our day of rest and hate for it to end!

Good night Cave-in-Rock— population 350—saaaaa-lute!

05-10-2015

It's Not a Nice Enough Day to Be a Crook

Weather conditions:

High: 88

Low: 70

Skies: Light rain in the morning, clear in the afternoon, thunderstorms in the evening

Wind: SSW 5-15 mph, gusts to 28

Today's mileage: 17 miles

Total: 537 miles

Where we traveled: Cave-in Rock, Illinois, to a sandy beach between Elizabethtown, Illinois, and Golconda, Illinois

The alarm blared at 3:45 a.m. Unfortunately, the early rise was not necessary, in my opinion anyway, since we didn't end up launching as early as we had hoped. Having checked the radar and detecting severe weather in the area, John concluded we had time to eat breakfast casserole, pack our belongings, pull *Work* and *Pray* to the river, remove the wheels, and prepare the kayaks to shove-off. But instead of launching, we hiked up the hill to sit on the bench outside the public restroom waiting AN HOUR for the storm to materialize. *We could have slept another hour!* The system tracked north of us. Confident we wouldn't be in danger of thunderstorms, we returned to the ferry landing and started on our way.

Keep us upright and safe.

Around seven miles into our day, large swells on the choppy river caused concern on my part. I wondered how far John planned to travel today because paddling and maneuvering in the wind and waves tired me both physically and mentally. Constantly aware of the next wave's direction, I pointed *Pray's* bow into the mountain of water. Not allowing her to follow the course of least resistance required strength. I was tired. Keeping up with John was difficult. *Isn't he tired? Doesn't he realize he is pulling ahead of me?* I felt like he wasn't aware of my plight. I was frustrated (maybe even angry) with him as well as the circumstances. *How many more times can I dig the paddle into the water and pull myself along?* I had a hunch that even though we got a late start, John still wanted to paddle the same distance he had originally planned. I couldn't (didn't want to) go that far! I was tempted to tell him how I felt but didn't want to be a wimpy traveling partner or liability. And if I did tell him, what could he do? There wasn't any place to pull off. I felt trapped and wanted to pout.

Then I set eyes on a welcoming sight—a tan building with red umbrellas poking above its blue roof—E-town River Restaurant in Elizabethtown, Illinois. An orange life ring hung on the side of the floating building while a plank walkway wrapped around the eatery. John had read about this barge-turned-restaurant establishment in Jerry Hay's Ohio River guidebook, making a mental note to stop here if we could. Stopping would give me a break! Knowing of a potential respite made paddling easier. The wind and waves hadn't changed, but my attitude had. A possible end in sight gave my body and mind an energy boost. Each stroke brought me closer to land and farther from the waves. I secretly hoped we would find a place to stay and not have to enter the river again until tomorrow with calmer seas. I hoped!

We docked and exited our kayaks next to the restaurant, but the parking lot was empty. *Oh, no! It can't be closed. Please don't make me climb back into my kayak!* Thankfully, a girl dressed in a gray E-Town River Restaurant t-shirt "just happened to" drive up.

As she proceeded down the plank towards the door, John called, "Hi!" Having gained the employee's attention, he asked, "What time does the restaurant open?"

"11:00."

"Thanks." John glanced at his watch. "It's only 9:40. I don't know if I want to wait that long. That would defeat the purpose of getting up early."

I didn't know what to say. I stared at the turbulent water, not wanting to return there. I felt like I had when I realized we couldn't stay at Covington, Indiana. The thought of climbing back into *Pray* brought tears to my eyes.

John recognized the disappointment on my face. His words comforted me. "We'll wait for them to open. Experiences are as much a part of the trip as traveling the miles."

This trip is changing us. We are both focused, goal-oriented people who find veering from the perceived agenda unproductive, inconvenient, and difficult. We are list "checker-offers." Before embarking on this trip, we would have viewed an hour and twenty-minute delay as a waste of time. We would have continued on the predetermined mission, believing we were being responsible and productive. While proud of these qualities in our personalities and having completed several to-do lists, I am realizing we may have missed many "floating restaurant" experiences. Which is more rewarding—experiences or list completion? I am beginning to appreciate the value of the experience. Here's to not checking items off the to-do list. Maybe I should rethink having a list all together. *Ouch!* I don't think I can go that far. One step at a time.

Waiting to experience the E-town Floating Restaurant, we strolled around the village. The population of Elizabethtown is about the same as Cave-in-Rock—300. However, the people of E-town have preserved more of their historic buildings, one being the oldest hotel in Illinois. The Historic Rose Hotel, an L-shaped white building with a double full-length porch facing the river, operates as a bed and breakfast and is owned by the State of Illinois. James McFarland built the hotel in 1812 to offer lodging to river travelers. 1812!

What did travel down the Ohio River look like at that time? I can almost see the ladies in their puffy sleeved, high-wasted, flowing dresses stepping off the steamboats onto the wood planks of the dock. This was during a major war. Was traveling on the river dangerous? Did each boat have extra security? How did the security then differ from our security now? They didn't have to wait in line, remove their shoes, pass through a special machine, or limit the ounces of liquid in their bottles. A simpler time. I would love to own a time machine to trek through the years and experience the river before roads moved the population away from it. A time when river towns were vibrant, had a purpose, and were a part of life—not only a place that used to be.

Across the street from the hotel stood River Rose Inn Bed and Breakfast, complete with a pool and Jacuzzi. Both lodging options would have been accessible for us from the dock and would have had a place to store *Work* and *Pray*. The Historic Rose Hotel was built specifically for those traveling down the river. However, in other towns, finding lodging close to the river is an unusual occurrence. Had we been aware of these two possibilities, we may have planned differently. We couldn't possibly stop for the day at 11:00 a.m. even if the wind and waves were killing me. How irresponsible would that be?! I know I just said "this trip is changing us," but we are taking baby steps!

The tour of the town didn't require the entire hour and twenty minutes to complete; so we sat on a rock outside the restaurant, removed our iPhone from its waterproof pouch, and snapped pictures of our surroundings. Slipping the phone into its protective holder, I noted an opening in its corner. The seam had failed. Not so waterproof any longer. Although we have a Lifeproof case on the phone, we store it in a waterproof pouch with a lanyard for an extra protective layer and handy access when paddling. What's convenient about this pouch is we can take pictures through the clear plastic and still use the touch pad. I'm sure John will contact Overboard to inquire about a replacement.

We sat back, relaxed, and watched the other people waiting in the parking lot for the restaurant to open its doors. I love to watch people and imagine their story. Since today is Mother's Day, I wondered if most of the patrons planned to eat at the floating restaurant in honor of their mothers. Lucky for us, the owner opened the doors twenty minutes early, allowing everyone to advance on the yellow plank from land to the small front deck and into the dining area. The small inside dining area could hold about forty people. Outside on the large deck, seating for an additional fifty was located under the red umbrellas I had seen from the river jutting above the blue roof. Even though the restaurant is floating, we couldn't distinguish any movement once inside.

We chose a small corner table by the window, providing a clear view of *Work* and *Pray*. With little room between the tables and chairs, the small building's interior made me feel claustrophobic. Ohio River historical pictures (including a picture of Old Shawneetown during the 1937 flood), "fishy" decorations, and a plaque recording the mileage to various river towns decorated the cheery, yellow walls.

Since the menu stated "We catch it, cut it, and cook it," we both ordered the catfish. Actually, even if they hadn't advertised the preparation process, my order would have been the same because any time catfish is on the menu, I normally order it. I have always liked catfish, but I think the main reason I eat it is because it reminds me of fishing with my younger brother, Jeff. When I was young, my great grandfather had a pond in the woods around the corner from where I lived. My brother and I (I don't remember my sister, Cassie, who is five years younger than I, coming with us) would carry our cane poles equipped with the typical red and white bobbers to the pond. Standing on the bank for hours, we watched for the bobbers to disappear under the water.

I loved the thrill of landing the fish. However, that was where the thrill ended. Although I'm brave enough to remove less ferocious fish, I refused to take the mean catfish off the hook. I made Jeff do it. I didn't have any problem putting the squirmy, slimy worm on the hook; but the fear of being "stung" kept me from completing the entire task of catching the fish. I watched my brother hold the catfish cautiously behind the fins as he removed it from the hook. I didn't know how the catfish caused the pain but knew I wanted to avoid it at all cost. I used to think the whiskers would "sting" me but have since learned I was incorrect. I now know the "sting" results from the venomous dorsal and pectoral fins behind the head on each side and on the top of the fish, puncturing the skin. Other fish don't possess the venomous dorsal and pectoral fins, and are, therefore, "safer" to remove.

Eating catfish caught by someone else may not be as gratifying, but it is certainly less painful (and cleaning isn't required). Ordering the fried catfish today wasn't as simple as saying, "I would like to order the catfish dinner." We faced an additional decision—river or pond. I didn't know where they lived (or died) made a difference. I thought catfish was catfish. Maybe because in Berne, pond is the only option. We decided to order one of each type so we could compare the differences. I chose the river and John the pond. We found the biggest difference was in the presentation; the river variety, thick chunks; the pond, a fillet. I preferred the meatiness of river chunks. And the pond may have tasted a little fishier, but both tasted delicious.

Soon after receiving our meal, the gentleman and his wife seated at the table behind me asked us if the kayaks belonged to us. (Was it our attire or smell that gave us away?) We replied "yes," which was followed by a plethora of questions. Soon everyone in the capacity-filled restaurant was engaged in the conversation. In the midst of the interrogation, a sheriff, gun on his hip, stepped through the door. On his way to the counter for a to-go order, he took a detour and found his way to our table. *Now what had John done?* He asked, "Are the kayaks yours?" (Attire or smell?) He also inquired about the design, the rudders, etc. No jail-time today.

Having satisfied everyone's curiosity, we finished our catfish. We hate being the center of attention. However, I know the attention we received isn't even close to what celebrities endure in public. Many even travel incognito so they can live a normal person's experience. Having our meal disrupted and being the object of an entire room's interest interrupted our normal life. I didn't mind the intrusion once, but I wouldn't want my normal life to consist of interruptions in almost all of my activities. I like my quiet normal. Today's "celebrity status" attention continued as we floated away when I observed a lady standing outside the restaurant taking our picture. If only she knew how ordinary we really are!

Our decision to wait for the restaurant to open turned out to be wiser than we knew at the time because the water calmed down while we were visiting the Illinois village of Elizabethtown. If the previous windy and wavy conditions had still been present, I don't know if I could have paddled the eight miles to the boat ramp where John had hoped to spend the night.

Although no eagles graced our skies today, we saw a herd of approximately 40 cattle hunkered under a lone cluster of trees, taking shelter from the sun. (Scary sight, since more people are killed by cattle in the U.S. each year than snakes!) Spotting bovines on or in the river surprises me. I guess because I generally encounter them from the road—in a pasture. Our trip is helping me think beyond MY normal experiences; I realize that life on the river looks different from life on land but is normal for this environment. It makes sense for a farmer with property on the river to use the never-ending water supply. John, always thinking, called it "Jersey Shores." (And yes, he laughed at his own joke!)

Shortly after passing "Jersey Shores," John suggested we begin searching for the boat ramp on the LBD (left bank descending). Most boat ramps have a couple of similarities—rocks piled on the edge of the water and cement or packed dirt angled from the road into the river. We first noticed the rocks, then the angled cement. We reserved our excitement until closer investigation could reveal possible hazards. Even though the boat ramp had the necessary features, we soon decided we could not use it nor had anyone else used it in years. Trees grew from the buckled cement. Although the ramp's condition was not a showstopper, the steep bank was. Onward…

I'm glad we didn't settle because we found the best camping spot we've had on this trip—a beautiful sandy beach with trees. The decision whether to settle on the first possible campsite or take the chance of not finding one within a reasonable distance—especially after a long, hard paddle or late in the day—is a difficult one. A few days ago when we were discussing the stresses of the trip, John indicated selecting a place to camp is one of the most stressful parts of the trip for him. I'm not surprised I didn't realize this was a burden to him. I usually don't recognize when John is feeling stressed because he rarely shows it outwardly. I'm the opposite—he almost always knows when I am anxious. I'm not sure which is better. If I share my stress, we both are stressed. If he keeps his bottled up, I can't help. Maybe we need to find some kind of balance.

If today's beach is any indication of what is in store for us as we travel farther south, I am excited about the places we have yet to stay!

We were in the middle of assembling the tent when the sky darkened and thunder rolled. John checked the radar. A storm was coming right at us. We quickly finished setting up camp. John examined the radar again. What appeared to be coming right at us was now tracking to the north. The second time today a storm missed us, just as many storms have skirted around us on this trip. Luck, I think not.

Tonight I pulled out a bag of tuna cheese soufflé to rehydrate for dinner. Dessert consisted of mud pie—chocolate pudding with homemade granola. Here's a trick I use when making pudding. At home, I combine half a box of pudding and four tablespoons of dried milk in a baggie. Preparing the pudding on the river is easy: add one cup of water to the bag; shake (Warning! be sure baggie is completely closed); set ten minutes (while eating dinner); voilà—pudding. Add homemade granola and you have a restaurant-worthy treat. (Serves two.)

While we were eating dinner, a guest joined us—a groundhog climbed a tree within ten yards of where we were sitting. I didn't know groundhogs climbed trees; I always spot them running across the field or along a river or ditch bank. He lounged on a limb, peering at the water for over two hours.

In the midst of our peaceful evening watching the lazy groundhog, John blurted, "His name is Ed."

"Huh?"

"The groundhog's name is Ed."

"I'm afraid to ask this, but, how do you know?"

"He told me."

"Reeally…"

"Yeah. The conversation went something like this…" John proceeded to relay the chat between him and our visitor.

"I first introduced myself, 'Hi, my name is John.' He turned and gave me a dismissive glance before returning his attention to the river.

I was determined, so I asked him his name. Continuing to peer at the river, he said flatly, 'Ed.'

On a roll, I quizzed him, 'Are you from these parts?'

'Yep. Lived here most of my life,' Ed yawned.

'Do you have any family?'

Ed turned his back and dismissed me."

I stared at John with disbelief. He watched the river, acting as if everyone has conversations with groundhogs. (I think John paddled in the sun too long today.)

John's conversation with "Ed" reminded me that Irene had sent a discussion question earlier in the day so I shared it with John. "Irene texted another question. Do you want to hear it?"

As before, he hesitated, "Suurrrre." Will he ever answer with an enthusiastic "Absolutely!"?

"Here it is. Rename the following animals: horse, zebra, turtle, elephant, and spider. Let me know their new names." I couldn't even start to guess what John would come up with.

He smiled mischievously. "I have an idea. Let's give Irene the new names and she has to decide which name goes with which animal."

"Sounds fun."

"Here are the names: Gray-bellied stomper, quadtrottletops, weak-kneed silk spinner, piano mule, and pluck chicken."

"You're weird."

"Have you told her about our Adam and Eve conversation?"

"Not yet, but I think I should ask her what she thinks Eve's response to her first period was."

I sent her our answer and her assignment. My phone "dinged" a few minutes later.

John, more interested in the conversation topics than he was ten minutes earlier, inquired, "What did she say?"

I read the text to him, "Eve's response to her first period was probably bossing Adam around and sending him out for cocoa beans… Chocolate in its first form. I will get back to you about the animal names."

We laughed. I love these times with John. If we were home, I can guarantee we would not be discussing animal names or Eve's first period.

Early to bed tonight again and early to rise tomorrow. We are hoping to beat the forecasted nasty weather late in the day. Hopefully, we will be eighteen miles downstream at a campground with showers and a place to do LAUNDRY! Or, if the weather doesn't track north again, we may be blessed with another day of rest on the beach. Both options sound appealing! Good night.

05-11-2015

Can I Accomplish It and Not Be Done

Weather conditions:

High: 75

Low: 54

Skies: Thunderstorms with clearing in evening

Wind: SW 5-15 mph gusts to 20 mph

Today's mileage: 0 miles (rainout)

Total: 537 miles

Where we are: sandy beach between Elizabethtown, Illinois, and Golconda, Illinois

Rainy days and rainy nights…

Zip… Pitter…. Patter…Roar… The sounds we heard last evening as we entered the tent for the night. The wind began to blow. (Literally, I heard no wind one second and then heard severe wind the next—I heard the wind begin to blow.) Wind blew, thunder crashed, and lightning flashed. John examined the radar; the storm wasn't tracking north of us this time. Wind blew, thunder crashed, and lightning flashed during two storms last night. Even though yellow and red indicating severe weather filled the radar screen, we were safe and dry in our tent.

• • •

This morning the alarm sounded at 4:00 a.m., just as the thunder from the second storm faded in the distance. After silencing the alarm, John glanced at the colorful radar and moaned, "Go back to sleep." I didn't argue.

He reset the alarm for 7:00 a.m. When the alarm rang again, John viewed the radar and stated, "We're not going anywhere today." No shower or laundry at the campground downstream. Instead a day of forced relaxation. I didn't complain.

John established a "kitchen" (tarp) with plans to cook and eat our cheese blitz casserole breakfast under it. Casserole dumped out of the bag. Water added to the breakfast. Food boiled in the pan. Thunder cracked in the atmosphere. Wind blasted through the trees. Rain poured all around the "kitchen." Rain whirled under the tarp. At this point, we stood up, gathered our breakfast, and huddled in the middle of the tarp. Huddled under the tarp is where and how we consumed our breakfast. During a brief respite in the rain, we left the breakfast dishes (one pan, one lid, and two spoons) unwashed in the middle of the "table" (foil emergency blanket), and retreated to the warm and dry surroundings of our tent.

Another day of rest—literal rest. What else can you do on a rainy day while camped on a sandy beach? That is exactly what we did most of the morning—sleep. When we were finished napping and the skies were finished leaking and rumbling, we crawled out of our tent to wash the breakfast dishes, eat a rare peanut butter AND JELLY wrap (jelly, courtesy of Rhonda and David from New Harmony. Who would have thought jelly could be such a treat?), and hang our rain suits on the clothesline strung not between two separate boats but two separate trees.

John used this gift of time to work on our schedule for the next couple of weeks, particularly where we will pick up our Week #8 package. (Our Week #7 package will be waiting for us at Cairo, Illinois, around May 19.) We have been averaging about 100 miles per week. John uses this fact, Jerry Hay's maps, and the list he created of post offices close to the river to determine where we will be each week in relationship to our need to resupply with food. Today after finishing his calculations, he sent Cyndy Evers, our current food cache coordinator, the following text...

"Hi Cyndy. Here is the information for the next box (I believe it is #8). Please....
- remove panty liners.
- remove 2 pkgs of tortillas.
- add the package of tampons that we previously had you remove.
- add Avon face wash.
- add Equate sunscreen.

Send to:
300 Carleton Avenue
Caruthersville, MO

We will arrive there approx. Tuesday, May 26.

Thank you!"

With Cyndy's help and a year's worth of careful planning of our food and other needs, we are able to be self-sufficient, not needing anything other than what is in the boxes that we prepared in advance. Many have offered to drive us to the store for supplies and have been surprised when we have graciously declined.

Side note—the addition of tampons. Being perimenopausal made packing period necessities difficult. *Would I have a period each month? How heavy would it be and how long would it last? How would I change my tampon and dispose of it?* I decided to include 20 tampons (enough for an average period lasting five days) in my first box. I then included another 20 tampons in every fourth box (assuming I had a normal period at normal intervals). However, when I hadn't had a period by April 22, I asked Cyndy to remove all tampons to avoid an overabundance. (Even though I use OB tampons, which do not have an applicator, every extra item can create a problem by putting stress on our limited space—recall the now notorious pillow.) Having started my period this week, I need to replenish my supply.

Starting my period brings up another subject I need to address: How to change and dispose of tampons. Again, I use OB tampons because they do not have an applicator, thus eliminating some waste. Since exiting the river to change a tampon at regular intervals is not plausible, during my period I change my tampon every time we stop. When not provided the convenience of a restroom or garbage can (which is almost always), I place the used tampons into a Ziploc bag (recycled food bags) and store them in the red poop bag. Then I try to remember to dispose of the tampon bags each time we locate disposal opportunities (i.e. trashcan). This entire process was a little inconvenient until it became my norm. I'm amazed at how quickly I can adapt to a new normal when the necessity arises.

Remember the failing iPhone pouch from yesterday and miracle Shoe Goo from Attica, Indiana? John used our downtime today as an opportunity to apply the Shoe Goo to the hole in the iPhone sleeve's edge, making it usable until we receive a replacement. After spreading liberal amounts of Shoe Goo on and around the tear, John propped the pouch against a leg of his Grand Trunk stool, ensuring the thick goo would stay where intended while it dried. He then piled some dirt on the bottom of the pouch to keep the wind from moving it. The pouch may not be waterproof any longer, but hopefully the hole won't expand.

While John worked I read an e-book on my iPad. Before we began the trip, I chose to download an e-book instead of bringing an actual hold-in-your-hands, page-filled book. (My pillow wouldn't fit. Need I say more?) However, I am beginning to question my decision. One advantage of an e-book is the space it saves. In addition, the illuminated iPad provides the opportunity to read even in the darkest circumstances. Unfortunately, I didn't consider the fact that the iPad has a battery that requires charging. Charging isn't a problem when the sun shines sufficiently to replenish the Sherpa's charge. However, since we've had several rainy days, the Sherpa's charge is dwindling fast. During cloud cover, the first priority is to charge the iPhone. If there is still sufficient charge in the Sherpa after the phone is at 100% and we will soon be somewhere to recharge the Sherpa, I can plug in my iPad. My iPad's battery is now at 30%. I need to save the remaining charge for journaling. Before the trip, I had set a goal of reading four books during our four-month excursion. *If I can't read, what else will I do?* I'm not very good at just sitting. Hmm… I may search for a book at one of our next stops and try to scrunch it in somewhere. I think there may be some room in my deck bag. Problem solved. Now, what can I do about reading in the tent after dark? I know. I can use my headlamp. I have just decided—when we are in Cairo, I am buying a real hold-in-your-hands, page-filled book.

Yesterday the lack of towboat traffic surprised us. Today the large amount of traffic intrigued us. We even witnessed three tows passing each other at once—one traveling downstream, one traveling upstream, and one (empty) also traveling downstream while passing the other two. (I am glad we experienced the increase in traffic from the shore and not the water.) The open barges transport various types of loads—coal, rock, and sand. In addition, there are the tanker barges, which we assume haul everything from cooking oil to fuel.

Watching the tows move up and down the river, I thought about life on a towboat. What an interesting way to live— journeying up and down the river each day. I contemplated the work schedule involved. Of course, different tow companies have different work policies, but plans commonly include days or weeks on and days or weeks off. This type of work schedule with a large chunk of consecutive days off would allow John and me to live a travel-filled life. I shared my thoughts with John.

"Have you ever thought about working on a tow?"

"What?" He sat there for a minute digesting what I had suggested. Finally joining my thought process, he admitted, "I can honestly say, I have never thought about working on a tow. Where did that come from?"

"Well, I was sitting here watching the tows pass in front of us. The crew lives on the river, and I've always wanted to live by the water. What a great job—being paid to live on the water. I remember hearing they work days or weeks at a time and then are off days or weeks at a time. Just think if we both worked on a tow, we would have time to travel when we're off."

"I see where you are going with this. We could live in an apartment so we wouldn't have a lot of stuff to care for. You could be a cook."

"Since you don't have a job to go home to, the possibilities are limitless. We could do anything or live anywhere. This is exciting."

John laughed as he suggested, "Most people wouldn't agree with you. They would probably consider not having a job to go home to a little irresponsible."

We continued planning our imaginary towboat life. I love planning with John. Especially since our plans are unusual to most people. We really do live an exciting life together. I don't know that we will become towboat employees, but I do know we won't let what others consider irresponsible keep us from moving in any certain direction. I treasure this time talking about what our life will look like when we return home—so many possibilities. I feel like an artist peering at a blank canvas, not having an end result in mind, not knowing where to begin or how to get to the end. So many ideas, but only one blank canvas. How to choose? How to begin?

Following a restful afternoon, we chose BBQ beef stew (made with dehydrated BBQ mashed potatoes) and pineapple upside down cake (using my pudding-making trick explained yesterday) for dinner.

After dinner, we completed some post-rain chores. First, we removed our cockpit skirts from our cockpits. Next, we used two important items on our gear list—bilge pump and sponge—to remove the quart of water gathered behind our seats. (Remember, the skirts have an opening.) Then, since the sun was shining brightly, we placed our life jackets out to dry and connected our Sherpa to its solar panel to charge.

Right now, John is enjoying the last bit of our time relaxing by playing his guitar on the beach. Again, I'm so glad he brought it. I would have given up my pillow to ensure he could bring his guitar. (Shhh…. don't tell him!)

Tomorrow is another early morning—3:30 a.m.—so we can beat some of the wind. I won't mind though because the end of my day promises me a shower and laundry! (small joys)

0 5 - 1 2 - 2 0 1 5

If You Wanna Have a Hog Farm, You Gotta Have a Hog

Weather conditions:

High: 70

Low: 48

Skies: clear

Wind: WNW 5-10 mph, gusts 16 mph

Today's mileage: 18 miles

Total: 555 miles

Where we traveled: Sandy beach to Birdsville Resort and Campground near Smithland, Kentucky

As I write, I am sitting in the shade outside the Birdsville Resort and Campground's laundry room near Smithland, Kentucky. We arrived here about 12:30 p.m.; met the owners, Bob and Linda; assembled our tent; and found (and used) the showers and laundry room. We feel (and smell) like new people.

Will doing laundry still excite me when I arrive home? At home I take lifting the laundry basket lid and throwing a dirty shirt on top of the other unclean shirts, pants, and underwear for granted. When the temporary holding spot reaches capacity, I remove the clothes, sort them into like-colored piles, place sorted piles into individual laundry baskets, carry baskets a short distance to my laundry room, fill the washing machine with water, add laundry soap, and stuff clothes into the washer's tub. In approximately 45 minutes, the clothes are clean and ready to dry. When living on land, I wear my shirts until they appear dirty or smell funky. On the river I wear my shirts, no matter how dirty they seem or how rank they smell, until I find somewhere to launder them. In my convenience-based environment, I dread washing my clothes, referring to the task as a "chore." On the river I yearn to wash, dry, and fold my three shirts, three pair of underwear, two bras, and three pair of pants. Interesting that my perception of the same activity changes depending on my environment.

In addition to doing a load of laundry anytime I choose, what other daily life conveniences do I take for granted? Lights, running water, toilet, chair with a back, air conditioning, heat, stove, clean sheets—just to name a few. Did I previously view these conveniences as necessities? At home if my air-conditioner breaks, I don't even consider NOT calling the repair-man. I NEED my air-conditioner—especially when weather conditions exceed my comfort zone of 75 degrees Fahrenheit and 25 percent humidity. In society not only do I view my conveniences as necessities, but I also use them out of habit. Flicking on a light switch, I simply expect the light will indeed work. It's just assumed. How long after I return home will I regard my conveniences as needs and take them for granted? Maybe the question I should ask myself isn't "how long," but instead "how can" I maintain my current mindset?

Let's go back to the beginning of the day and recap the events that brought me to this happy place outside the campground's laundry room. Today began early again at 3:15 a.m. I assume the earlier the sun rises the earlier the wake-up call. The plus side of these still dark "arisals" (I don't think "arisals" is a word, but it works) is an opportunity to view some awesome sunrises. The down side is missing sunsets. Since the sun doesn't set until 9:00 p.m., witnessing both is difficult—I need my beauty sleep. Even though we do go to bed early, I am still exhausted. Some days I use every bit of energy I have just to survive. (Early wake up calls don't help.)

Many people have asked if we "Huck Finn it" (float) down the river. NO WAY! If we did, who knows what we would hit, or more importantly, what would hit us. While on the river, we paddle non-stop, each stroke of the paddle having a purpose. Why wouldn't I be tired? Many mornings I pray for rain as John studies the radar, hoping he will notice storms approaching and say, "Go back to sleep." Yay! Another day for my muscles to recuperate from the constant paddling.

Unfortunately, this morning was not a "go back to sleep" day. We climbed out of our sleeping bags when the phone alarm sounded, performed our usual prepare-for-the-day chores, and launched at a reasonable time.

Keep us upright and safe.

Today's WNW 12 mph wind resulted in a crosswind at times and a tailwind at others, depending on the river's direction. We have discovered not all wind is created equal—each causes different paddling conditions. The crosswind annoys me as it rocks *Pray* and splashes my arm. The tailwind causes following seas (waves moving in the same direction as our kayaks) and rollers (or rolling waves—a wide wave). The rollers give me a sensation similar to what I imagine it would be like to surf as I ride on the top of the waves. However, an awkward moment occurs while paddling on the crest because instead of experiencing the resistance of water when inserting the paddle into the wave, only air surrounds my paddle. The "weightless" paddle resembles picking up something you think weighs 10 pounds but weighs only two pounds. Your arm becomes "weightless," flying up farther than you expect.

We have been on the Ohio River five days and are adapting to the differences between the Wabash and the Ohio. One difference is the presence of the mile markers and buoys I wrote about a few days ago. Last night while I journaled and John played his guitar, we spotted a glowing light on the opposite bank. After some discussion we decided it probably was a mile marker. Then we hypothesized about the energy source used to power the light all night. We eliminated battery power because that would require someone changing batteries in hundreds of mile markers along the river at predetermined intervals. So we concluded the light must run on solar energy.

Today we paddled close to the area where we thought the light had been blinking. We verified the presence of not only a light attached to the top of the pole but also a square green marker and white sign with numbers associated with the location on the river. The numbers on river mile markers increase or decrease with each mile (similar to road mile markers), depending on the original reference point. The Ohio River mile markers increase from its headwaters in Pittsburgh, Pennsylvania. This particular sign was numbered 905.0, meaning at that point we were 905.0 miles from Pittsburgh. When we reach the Mississippi, we will enter at mile marker 954—954 miles from the end of the Mississippi. The mile markers will decrease until we reach the end of the river at mile 0 (the original reference point of the Mississippi). I used to think the Mississippi ended at New Orleans, but New Orleans is actually at mile marker 100 or 100 miles upstream from the river's end.

On the light's base, we discovered the presence of our hypothesized solar panels collecting and converting the sun's rays to energy for operating the light at night. We were right!

We counted four eagles today. If you had asked me before we left home what wildlife I expected to encounter while living on the river, I would have listed squirrels, deer, raccoons, coyotes, vultures, etc.—not eagles. Even though we have observed more eagles than other types of wildlife, catching a glimpse of an eagle is still a rare occurrence in my mind. Probably because during my childhood, we never spotted eagles. However, sightings are occurring more frequently in my portion of northeast Indiana. I wonder if they will ever become as common as Red-tailed Hawks or Red-winged Blackbirds.

While our eagle count today was the largest since we entered the Ohio, our tow count decreased to just one. Conversely, yesterday's barge traffic was non-stop. John and I discussed the difference, each coming up with our own hypothesis. I thought maybe they adhere to a schedule—loading on certain days and transporting on others. John thought since there was such a large disparity between the amount of traffic between yesterday and today, there had possibly been a hold up at one of the locks. That interruption could cause the tows to be backed-up, which, once removed, produced the releasing of a congested group. Nobody knows.

Each night John studies the weather forecast and Jerry Hay's maps, assessing what lies ahead the next day. From the forecast, he determines our schedule based on storms, heat, and wind. These Mother Nature features affect our start and end times for the day. I didn't realize how much daily planning we would incur on this trip. I thought since the major organization transpired before the trip, once we launched from Fort Recovery, we wouldn't have much of a schedule. I was wrong. Considerations that determine our river-based agenda differ from our land-based one. On land, other people—appointments, church schedules, store hours, etc.—influence our decisions. Here on the river, we base most of our decisions on nature—sunrise, sunset, storms, wind, temperature, etc. Even though we still follow a schedule, a time constraint based on nature doesn't create the same stressful feeling that a human-induced schedule produces. It is still OUR schedule.

From Jerry Hay's maps, John can tell where a camping spot—an island, river town, boat ramp, campground, etc.—might exist. Today based on the maps, he chose Birdsville Resort and Campground near Smithland, Kentucky, as today's stop because...

One: campground on the river
Two: boat ramp
Three: conveniently located right above the Smithland Lock

Although camping at the campground enticed John, its close proximity to the lock was the main reason for his choice, enabling us to pass through the lock at the beginning of our day tomorrow. We don't want to attempt locking through at the end of our day in case the process is lengthy. If we go through later and it takes longer than anticipated, our only option for the night may be a less than desirable place to camp at the completion of a long day.

Speaking of locks. Tomorrow's lock experience will be our first. Entering a lock, floating in the big chute as the water rises or falls, and exiting with the flow excites and scares me. Since I don't personally know anyone who has traveled through a lock in a kayak, I am looking forward to telling my story. On the other hand, since I don't personally know anyone who has gone through a lock in a kayak, I don't know what to expect and am a little fearful. During John's investigations before the trip, he researched locking through in kayaks or canoes; we watched several videos on YouTube to understand the proper protocol. As a result of the research, we each have a rope coiled in a dry bag (mine is green, John's is blue) attached to the top of our kayaks. Our understanding is the lock keeper will lower a rope to us. We will then attach our rope to theirs with a carabineer. The rope will prevent us from drifting in the channel as the gates open and close. John plans to radio the lock keeper early in the morning to receive instructions. I wonder if we will share the lock with tows and barges. The prospect of floating in close proximity to such large vessels intimidates me. Using a lock is an unknown. The unknown creates fear based on ignorance. I'm sure tomorrow I will write about how exciting and unintimidating the experience was—like our first encounters with towboats.

Locating our home for the night was not without obstacles. Since we knew the campground was located just above Smithland Lock, when we caught a glimpse of the cement structure looming in the distance, we started scanning the left bank for the campground. We identified a boat ramp but no campground. Confused, John commented, "The map shows the campground is right on the river. All I see is a boat ramp. Shouldn't I be able to see the campground? Let's pull up."

We landed our kayaks and perused the area. The well-maintained public cement boat ramp and parking lot were all that was there. No campers, no houses, no businesses, no restroom—nothing!

John directed, "You stay here and rest. I'll walk up the road and see if I can find the campground."

I didn't argue. Considering our 3:30 a.m. wake up call and the windy and wavy paddling conditions the past 18 miles, I was tired. I sat on the bow of *Pray* and laid my head on my lap. Not the most comfortable position, but I fell asleep and was soon dreaming (and perhaps drooling). I can't remember my dream specifically, but I know it was a "river life" dream. I love that the setting of my dreams has slowly changed from "land life" to "river life" over the last month and a half. I dream about paddling down the river, sitting at our campsite, or other river and wilderness related events. Once in a while, I will have a "bad" dream—I am lost and can't find John. But overall the dreams are peaceful, representing who I am in this chapter of my life. What a sad day (or night) it will be when upon returning to my life on land, my dreams transform from "river life" to "land life."

I didn't wake up until I heard John declare, "The campground is about a quarter mile downstream from here. Just as I hoped, it's right on the river."

We climbed back into the kayaks. Around the bend, several campers occupied sites near the river. We paddled around a pier; many end sections were missing beyond its security light.

Landing easily on a sandy beach, we crawled out of *Work* and *Pray* and climbed a short distance to a grassy area and the beginning of the campsites. Each site had a stone parking pad, picnic table, water spigot, and fire ring. Since no trees grew close to the beach, we rolled a heavy fire ring down by our kayaks to tie them to. (ALWAYS tie off!)

We strolled to the campground office located under the owners' living quarters. There Bob and Linda welcomed us and provided information about the showers and laundry located around the corner in the same building.

Thinking Linda could shed light on our previous night's discussion, we asked her the reason for the fluctuating tow and barge traffic. I hate to admit it, but it appears John was right (that's always hard for me to say). She explained the traffic is indeed directly related to activity of the locks and dams. If being worked on, the lock is closed and the boat traffic stops, causing the boats to line up and wait for the lock to reopen. The subsequent opening of the lock, allowing boats through again, results in a steady stream of traffic. A closed lock today may equate to a lot of traffic tomorrow if it reopens.

That brings me to now. As I sit in my chair with a back, wearing my yellow winter coat and holding my iPad on my lap, the clothes dryer hums through the open screen door behind me. Last night's storms brought in cooler air, causing us to pull our coats from our holds. A stark juxtaposition to yesterday's warm weather when even the thought of wearing a coat would have been uncomfortable.

I gaze at the small, well-kept campground. Bob and Linda told us they "just happened to" reopen a few days ago after cleaning up from flooding. We are lucky to be staying here.

Wait... A towboat is pushing several barges upstream. They must have opened the lock. I wonder if the river will be busy tonight. I just thought of something. If they hadn't opened the lock today, we wouldn't be locking through tomorrow.

I just realized I almost overlooked two blessings—the open campground and lock. I guess not only do I tend to take conveniences for granted, but I also sometimes overlook some "just happened to be" "openings."

Early to bed, early to rise. A new adventure tomorrow—the lock!

05-13-2015

Now, All We Need to Do Is Make Your Boobs Big (guest writer John)

Weather conditions:

High: 77

Low: 55

Skies: clear

Wind: ENE 6-14 mph, gusts 20 mph

Today's mileage: 23 miles

Total: 579 miles

Where we traveled: Birdsville Resort and Campground near Smithland, Kentucky, to Paducah, Kentucky

* Slept in (4:30 a.m.)
* Paddled through first lock
* Didn't die
* Paddled a long way
* Stopped for the night

Well, that's how I would summarize our day. However, when LaNae said I had to write the journal entry for today, she told me I needed to expound beyond simple bullet points. So here goes.

As mentioned before we did, indeed, sleep in until 4:30 a.m. today. That was probably a good thing since LaNae said she had trouble sleeping after midnight. There was some barge traffic in the early morning hours, and the vibrato hum of the tug twin diesels woke her up periodically.

Tonight's campsite is by far our most industrial to date. We are just below (river speak for "downstream") the I-45 bridge near Paducah, Kentucky, where we are close enough to hear the steady whine of tires rolling over the steel grate roadway. In addition to the automobile traffic, the barges are lined up no more than 15 yards from our shore front as they stage for entering Lock 52, which is about another three miles below where we are camped. When we pulled up on the beach where we intended to camp, we immediately noticed the strong stench of dead and decaying fish. Most are large 10 to 20-pound Asian Carp. I'm assuming their propensity (use big word—check) to jump into the path of moving boats has proven quite hazardous, resulting in the premature demise of these foul smelling drifters. Fortunately, we are uphill from the beach and are able to avoid most of that stink. We also noticed quite a bit of trash up the bank, including an old water heater that washed up not too far behind our tent. According to Bob from Birdsville Campground, water heaters are one of the most common items that "accidentally" land in the river. Also just behind our tent, we noticed the massive head of a dead carp. Hmmm…, we didn't want this thing for a neighbor all evening. So grabbing two sticks I found at the base of the trees and using them like oversized tongs, I was able to grasp that smelly cranium and toss it into the water downstream, hoping it would drift down and away from our home for the night.

Between waking this morning and stopping for the night, quite a few other interesting events happened as well. We had been on the river just a short time, having travelled about three miles, when I radioed ahead to Smithland Lock. I wanted to be sure we were cleared to enter and let lock-master know we were lock virgins so he could step us through the process. The lockmaster told us to proceed to the landside chamber, and he would open the gates for us. Sure enough, as we approached, the two massive gates swung open. LaNae and I paddled into the chamber where the massive concrete walls towered overhead. The lockmaster (Chad) then looked down on us from the wall on our port side and pointed out the slide pins positioned periodically along the chamber walls. He told us to either throw a line over the pins or simply hold on. We chose the latter. As we held on, the ominous sounds of banging metal and rushing water began. However, we only slightly felt the movement of the water as we smoothly dropped the 20 feet necessary to put us in line with the downriver side. Then the downriver gates began to swing open. Chad wished us well, the exit horn sounded, and we paddled on our way. Nobody died.

As we neared Paducah, Kentucky, we encountered the most tug and barge traffic thus far. A lot of fleeting (staging and stacking of barges) was taking place along the right bank descending, even though the charts did not indicate fleeting in this area. I'm sure that can be explained by the fact that the Jerry Hay Riverlorian charts (priceless asset) are nearly five years old. Regardless, to alert them of our presence, we made radio contact with potential threats, including the tows *Terry C., Edwin Kennedy, Tom Busser,* and *Tom Frazier.* Once we communicated our intent and desire to stay out of their way, they graciously directed us to the best route. They then allowed us to squeeze between the shoreline and the barges, which sat less than ten yards off the bank. Cool.

Now it's time for dinner (black bean stew with garlic croutons and apple pie) and a good sleep here on "Dead Fish Shore" (as we have christened it) as we prepare for Lock 52 in the morning.

In closing, I'd like to mention a little about birds and the omens they seem to represent. Today we saw five graceful and glorious Bald Eagles. The fifth even rose from his perch on a dead tree to fly ahead of us and over the entrance to the lock chamber, seemingly guiding and blessing our approach. Conversely, as we settle in for the night, a hoard of noisy Black Vultures is settling into the tree overlooking our tent. Hmmm.

05-14-2015

Here's Your Coffee

Weather conditions:

High: 75

Low: 61

Skies: mostly cloudy with light drizzle in the afternoon

Wind: ESE 2-9 mph

Today's mileage: 16 miles

Total: 594 miles

Where we traveled: Paducah, Kentucky, to Joppa, Illinois

Twigs cracked above the campsite, sounding like they could snap at any moment, causing whatever creature looming above to join us in the tent. Last night I lay snuggled in my sleeping bag, listening to the ruckus, thinking it would stop soon. The suspense became overwhelming, so I nudged John, interrupting his sleep breathing, "John?... Are you awake?"

John mumbled sleepily, "I am now."

"Do you hear that?"

He pretended to listen, or maybe he was falling back asleep. "What?... That cracking?... It's probably the vultures landing for the night."

I lay quietly a little longer listening to the ominous sound of each winged beast landing, twigs breaking, branches crackling, and wings flapping. Again, I couldn't keep silent any longer—this was the first time I had tried to sleep below a vulture apartment. I nudged John again, interrupting his sleep breathing. *How could he sleep through all the commotion?* "John?... Are you awake?"

A little agitated, he mumbled again, "I am now."

"Will the branches break? How many are there? Will they be there all night?"

"They won't hurt us. I'm sure this is where they sleep every night." John answered sternly, "Go to sleep."

John rolled over. Hmm… I listened to a hundred or more large birds land and flutter around until the tree above us became silent. I rolled over.

We slept in again this morning until 4:30 a.m. Remember when I complained about setting the alarm for 4:30? Now I consider it sleeping in. It's all a matter of perspective.

We ate dinner for breakfast—Mexican rice meal. (Not sure why we had dinner for breakfast, but we did.) Enjoying our Mexican rice dinner-breakfast (should that be deakfast or brinner?), I counted the hundreds of vultures wake up and take flight for the day. One, two, three,…eleven, twelve, thirteen. Seriously, only 13. The other hundred must have taken to the air before we climbed out of the tent. As they flew away, I realized this is the perfect place for them to hang out. With all the dead fish on the banks, it's a vulture's smorgasbord!

Vultures gone and breakfast complete, I began my typical roll up the bedding chore. As I folded the bottom wool blanket, I noticed a wet spot. *This can't be good!* I checked out the floor. *There is a damp spot.* I ran my hand along the nylon bottom. *What's that poking through? I know I did a thorough scouting of the area for twigs, roots, and man-made hazards last night.* Folding up the tent with John, I kept my eyes peeled for a stick or small weed. Nothing. While John stuffed the tent bag into *Work's* back hatch, I combed the area systematically. *I think this is the spot.* On my hands and knees, I moved the sand around. *What's that?* My hand touched something small, hard, and metallic. *A man-made hazard! A fish hook!!! That wasn't visible last night.* Apparently, our weight had pushed the hook through the sand, the footprint, and then the tent. Thank goodness, we had the wool blanket padding to protect us from the sharp object. Without the footprint as a moisture barrier, we will need to put an extra layer (frog tog pants, perhaps) down between the tent floor and the wool blanket. *This is the trip.*

Our first goal today was to lock through our second lock of the trip. John radioed the Locks and Dam 52 operator last night. Locks and Dam 52 is one of two wicket dams (the other being Locks and Dam 53) still in use on the Ohio River. A wicket dam consists of 300 or more little wooden dams hinged to a foundation on the bottom of the river. These wickets are about four feet wide and up to 20 feet long. In response to the water level of the river, the lock and dam crew raise and lower the wickets from a maneuver boat along the upstream side of the dam by connecting a bar to the back of each wicket. A changing-of-the-wicket position causes a lock closure and backs up traffic. Currently the dam of Lock 52 is up, meaning we will need to lock through. Dam 53 is down, meaning we will not need to lock through and can paddle as if it didn't exist. Once construction is complete, a new dam, Olmsted Locks and Dam, will replace these outdated systems, decreasing lock-through times.

John began his conversation with the lock operator last night by identifying ourselves. The operator asked John to describe our vessels and then told him, "We don't lock through small boats any more. You'll need to portage around."

John responded by politely telling the operator about us, our previous lock experience, and the loaded weight of *Work* and *Pray*. Portaging around, he explained, was not, in his opinion, the best option. Regardless, the operator kept his position and stressed we would need to portage due to safety concerns.

John signed off and turned the radio switch to "off." He sighed through his clenched teeth—he was NOT happy. Our loaded kayaks weigh between 150 and 170 pounds apiece, and everything we own (two spoons, two cups, three sets of clothes, one pillow…) is stuffed into those yellow plastic tubes. If anything happens to *Work* or *Pray*, our trip could possibly be over. *Why wouldn't we be a little overprotective of them?*

This morning John radioed the lock again, but this time he raised a different operator. He began the conversation the same way he did last night. The new operator told John to skirt past the queued up tows and barges, radio when we approached the gates, and prepare to enter the seaside chamber. He'd move us to the front of the line.

John turned off the radio. His eyes brightened as he declared, "Let's pack up."

Yay! We didn't need to worry about damage to *Work* and *Pray*. I was both excited and scared to go through another lock. Yesterday I was scared before we faced our first lock, not knowing what to expect. The unknown creates fear. Excitement replaced my fears as the operator locked us through by ourselves, telling us exactly what to do. Once I overcame my fear, I was like a kid experiencing a carnival ride for the first time, asking when I could go again. Today I wondered if this lock would be like the last one. *Would we lock through with a towboat? Would we hold onto the pins or throw our ropes to the lock operator as we had seen in the YouTube video?* Again, not knowing created some fear.

We quickly packed up and launched.

Keep us upright and safe.

Several towboats and barges had waited all night and were still waiting this morning in front of our beach for their turn to pass through the lock. Paddling past them, I felt a little guilty (just a little) butting in line and entering the lock out of turn.

When we arrived, John radioed the lock again, reaching yet another person. "This is the kayak *Work*. We are approaching the gates and are prepared to enter the seaside chamber on your signal."

"Kayaks?" this different operator replied. "You can't lock through. Head to shore in the small opening to the right of the lock and someone will meet you there with a tow motor to transport the boats to the other end."

John turned off the radio. He stared straight ahead for a couple minutes before mumbling, "I don't like this. This is stupid, unsafe, and a good way to damage the kayaks. I'm NOT happy." However, what could we do? We were at their mercy. We either play by their rules or go home.

We pulled off into the "waiting area," which was nothing more than a small lagoon between the high concrete walls and the shore. The banks were steep, covered in mud in one area and large rocks and concrete in another. If we had been presented this area on the river as a potential stopping spot, we would have definitely moved on. We dismissed the idea of exiting *Work* and *Pray* on the muddy banks, leaving the rocky section the only option. Drift and numerous large, dead fish limited the access to this open area. Oh, the smell!

John parked and exited *Work*. He gingerly climbed the rugged, steep hill of loose rock up to the top in search of someone to assist us in our portage. While he investigated the area, I hung out with the dead fish. Oh, the smell!

John returned with David. David was dressed in his work gear—a large reflective (glow-in-the-dark) life jacket, tan leather work gloves, and white hardhat. With the cloud cover, his sunglasses rested on his hard hat. *How does he keep them from falling off when he bends over?* He and John carried fully loaded 170-pound *Work* up the stone hill and placed it on the narrow concrete ledge bordering the side of the lock. Not a safe maneuver. The kayak's weight, the precarious footing, and the possible long fall into the water on the ledge's seaward side caused a strain on John's back and put our possessions at significant risk.

John then slid down the rocks to assist my parking and exiting. I was nervous. The rocks were uneven and the bank steep. Placing my paddle over *Pray's* stern perpendicular to the rocks, I grabbed the shaft of my paddle close to each blade. I placed my weight evenly on the paddle and started lifting myself out of the seat. The paddle slipped. I peered up at John, "I can't do this."

He moved my paddle to a more stable rock and locked it down under his foot. He encouraged, "Try again."

This time, the paddle stayed in place. I pulled myself up and sat on the back of my seat. The next step concerned me. I needed to place my foot on a stable place on land so I could stand up. *I hate this. I feel so uncoordinated. How am I going to stand up on the rocking concrete? And there are people watching. I will be so embarrassed if I fall or tip my kayak. They're having us not lock through because this is safer? I think not.* I placed my foot on what appeared to be the most stable piece of cement I could find—it wobbled. I tried the one next to it—it moved only a little. I decided to use this cement piece as my exit point. I squatted, gaining my bearings before standing up. John offered his hand, which I accepted. Now we were both trying to keep our balance. If one fell, we both fell. With one quick pull, I stood up. Securing my balance and using my paddle to stable myself, I climbed to the top of the rock mountain. (Deep sigh.)

John and David carried *Pray* to the narrow landing and placed it beside *Work*. Again, a difficult and unsafe process.

I held both paddles as today's operator, Susanna, wearing a red life jacket and sunglasses approached us. I was surprised she didn't have on a hardhat or reflective vest like David did. *Shouldn't wearing all the safety gear be a requirement for everyone working in this area?* Susanna was the operator who had instructed us to paddle our kayaks to the "holding area" for transport.

John voiced his concerns, again reiterating his preference to lock through. Susanna, however, emphasized it was their policy and the tow motor could transport our kayaks safely to the other end.

John's taut voice and guarded answers told me he wasn't convinced.

As John finished his conversation with Susanna, another John, dressed like David—complete with sunglasses on his helmet—arrived with a side-by-side all-terrain vehicle to haul the kayaks to the orange Case tow motor (forklift) waiting at the end of the narrow landing. My John helped put *Work* on the carrier portion at the back of the side-by-side. My heart skipped a beat watching him lose his balance and almost fall into the lock chamber. He muttered a few choice words under his breath. He was clearly pissed.

The stress of the entire portaging process kept increasing. I thought about the anxious feelings I had an hour before regarding the unknown elements of this lock. All previous concerns paled in comparison to the actuality I was experiencing, the possibility of an injury to John. This is proof that worrying about events that haven't happened yet is a waste of time because what we fear many times doesn't come to fruition. Concern yourself with (worry about) the present.

After David and my John had placed *Work* on the side-by-side, my John asked (suggested), "Aren't you going to strap this on?"

Lock-worker John replied, "No. We're just going to the end of the dock."

John's face clouded! He didn't say anything.

I talked with Susanna while watching my John and David shuffle beside the kayak, holding it on as it bounced on the side-by-side down the pier to the tow motor. Once they arrived, they again lifted *Work,* placing it onto the tow motor's forks.

David and the two Johns then returned for *Pray.* However, prior to picking it up, John put on his life jacket for safety while carrying it along the edge of the narrow lock wall. *Whew!* The men transported my kayak to the tow motor and placed it in front of *Work.* Lock-worker John tilted the tow motor's prongs and began the long journey over the rough ground to the other end of the lock. I watched the tow motor precariously transport everything we owned unstrapped up the cement path without my John or David providing support. My hands sweated. *What will we do if one of the kayaks falls off? What if they damage something? Will we go home?*

John and I rode in the side-by-side across the lock to the area where we were going to launch our kayaks. This area, with a dirt boat ramp, was much nicer than the "waiting area" where we landed. Standing next to the launch area, I watched the tow motor bounce down the stone hill, causing *Work* and *Pray* to rock on the forks. Concerned a wheel would fall into a hole causing the kayaks to fall to the ground, I said many prayers waiting for lock-worker John to deliver all our worldly goods to us.

Thankfully, the rest of the story is boring since all arrived safely at the bottom of the hill.

Work and *Pray* safely lowered to the ground and unloaded, we watched a white tug with horizontal red and black stripes push several barges into the channel. The *Mountain State* from the port of Lakin, West Virginia, entered and waited as Susanna drove across a small walkway on a yellow Cushman scooter. She parked next to a pair of long steel levers protruding up from the top of the dock wall. She pulled them. The gates behind the boat clanked as they slowly closed, banging when the gate's two individual parts slammed together. We glanced across the small walkway. Susanna was still pushing the red handled levers! Apparently, she needed to hold the levers in place the entire time the boat was in the chamber. I'm sure Susanna will appreciate only pushing a button when the new Olmsted Locks and Dam are completed.

We didn't stay to watch the entire locking activity; filling the lock with water is a lengthy process. Leaving Susanna to her work, we were on our way to accomplish our next goal—visit Fort Massac, Illinois' first state park, which features a replica of the fort Lewis and Clark visited on their famous westward expedition.

Sliding into the water and taking my first stroke with my paddle, the stress of the last hour slipped away. The calming sense of the water washed John's "pissed off-ness" into the river as it carried the trial downstream. We and our gear were safe; we were where we belonged—on the river.

Along our way to the state park, we passed the still-in-construction Olmsted Locks and Dam. I wondered if the lock operator would have allowed us to lock through if the more advanced lock system were complete.

Did Susanna force us to portage around the current lock because of its inefficiency or the uneasiness of the crew?

Our visit to Fort Massac was quick and disappointing. We found the fort in disrepair and a bit of a letdown. So we ate our lunch, disposed of our trash, used the restroom, performed the obligatory walking tour and photo session, filled our dromedaries, and left. We spent about an hour visiting this historical location.

Our non-educational trip to the fort complete, we proceeded to accomplish our next goal, paddle nine more miles and find a place to camp. We checked that box when we found, landed, and established camp on another beautiful beach.

For dinner, we pulled barbecue beef stew with cornbread croutons, and banana nut bread from our dinner bag. Picking up the banana nut bread, I smiled as I read the handwritten note from our friend Dee on the outside of the vacuum-sealed plastic bag. "Jesus Loves You." In March Dee spent an afternoon helping me pack, vacuum seal, and label some of our meals. At that time I noticed she spent extra time on the labeling process but didn't think much about it. She has no idea how much her act of kindness means to us in the middle of nowhere, away from the people we know and love.

Our day compete, I am now sitting on the beach watching the towboat traffic as John plays his guitar. In between songs, John and I are discussing the correlation between river traffic and highway traffic. We decided—the tows and barges are the semi-trucks; the coast guard is the state police; the Army Corp. of Engineers (mappers, dredgers, lock operators, etc.) are the highway department; the locks are bridges; the sailing line is the interstate; outside the buoys is the berm; the banks are the rest stops; and the boat ramp is the exit ramp. I love my river life! It's a rough life sitting here without a care in the world. I think a stroll on the beach is in our future.

• • •

After a romantic stroll, the hour is now 8:00 p.m., and I have returned to sit on the beach, admiring a rare sunset viewing for us. As the sun peeks around the edge of the trees at the end of the beach, the sky has changed from gold tones to subtle hues of pink and blue. Sparse clouds add their own version of coloring to the end of the day higher in the sky with deeper pink and blue tones. Sunrises and sunsets—God's beautiful bookends to the day.

Good night, sun. Tomorrow we have a short day—four miles to Grand Chain Campground.

05-15-2015

It Was a Barry Bonds Trip

Weather conditions:

High: 84

Low: 66

Skies: clear in the morning, thunderstorms in the afternoon and evening

Wind: S 15-22 mph, gusts to 38 mph

Today's mileage: 8 miles

Total: 602 miles

Where we traveled: Joppa, Illinois, to four miles downstream from Grand Chain, Illinois

Toilet paper. The subject of the day. Curious? Read on…

Today was another day of firsts.

- We reached 600 miles—woohoo.
- The first day storms chased us off the river.
- A towboat captain flashed his lights at us, came out of his wheelhouse, and waved.

Let's start at the beginning of the day, which began at 4:30 a.m. We ate a cold granola and milk breakfast and pushed off by 7:00 a.m.

Keep us upright and safe.

Our goal was to reach Grand Chain Campground and Resort before the storms hit later in the morning. The forecast included storms for the rest of today and most of tomorrow, some of which could be severe. In the event the worst-case scenario came to fruition, the resort would provide a safe place for us to camp and possibly a building for protection. We also hoped to hang out in the lodge, using their WIFI tomorrow during a forced day of rest. In addition, it was imperative that we buy some toilet paper.

Speaking of toilet paper. While packing our weekly supply boxes, I tried to include everything we would need for one week at a time, no more and no less. I didn't want to NEED to locate a store to purchase supplies. In each box I packed a one-week supply of food, daily vitamins (in individual packs for John and me), Q-tips, flossers, and a roll of toilet paper. In addition, I also created an inventory box for our cache team back home. In this box I packed items I knew we would need to resupply throughout the trip—toothpaste, sunscreen, deodorant, shampoo, face wash, ChapStick, etc. Knowing how often each item would need replenished was difficult, so when one of these supplies runs low, I contact Cyndy and ask her to place it in our next supply box. If I had been smart, I would have recorded how much of each item we used over the last few months before the trip. Unfortunately, I didn't have that much forethought. Regardless, everything has worked perfectly. Until now. Our toilet paper is running low.

I remember specifically trying to decide how much toilet paper to place into each box. For some reason (I have no idea why), I thought maybe John would have some insight into how much toilet paper we would need. As I was creating a list of box contents, I picked his brain, "How much toilet paper do you think I should put into each box?"

He offered, "I haven't a clue. Maybe one in every other box."

I didn't think that sounded like enough, so I doubled the frequency and placed a roll into each weekly box.

Early in the trip, we developed what we have coined as "paddle poop." Paddle poop has the consistency of peanut butter and smears everywhere with each wipe, causing the use of an unusually large amount of toilet paper with each poop episode and often a quick below-the-waist bath in the river to complete the process. And we have been "regular" the entire trip. I have realized, therefore, that a roll a week is not enough. When unpacking each weekly supply box, I am becoming more excited about the arrival of another roll of toilet paper than of the food.

Today, only a few squares of toilet paper clung to our last cardboard tube. So in addition to the need for water, we needed more toilet paper.

Today's glassy "slicin' da butta'" water was not typical for the Ohio River, especially considering the storms in the forecast. Paddling in these water conditions was easy and our spirits were high as we navigated the four miles to our destination. To pass the time, John suggested recording our daily singing of "Doo Wah Diddy Diddy" again. That lasted about 11 seconds before John screwed up. Abort.

Having aborted our claim to fame, he decided another "The Paddling Edna Show" episode was in order. Today's installment focused on spray skirts. Obviously, Edna's intent was to speak on a spray skirt's use and purpose, but a "young man" in the audience was confused as to why he would want to put on a skirt. Edna's naivety then got her into trouble again and, well, I guess you had to be there. (Be glad you weren't!)

At the end of our four-mile journey, the desired lodge overlooking the river came into view. We excitedly landed *Work* and *Pray*. Confusion soon replaced our excitement. At first glance from the beach, the A-framed building with a wrap-around porch appeared to be a scenic haven. Upon further inspection we noticed signs of un-use and lack of upkeep. First, dried mud covered the boat ramp. Second, the area was overgrown with weeds and not landscaped in the way expected of a resort. Third, the cabins, with permanent items like grills, coolers, trash, and strollers sitting outside, didn't appear to be over-night accommodations. We also noted the lack of people strolling to the river, children laughing and playing, and vehicles driving (or even parked). In other words, no tourist activity.

A couple of days ago, John had called Grand Chain inquiring about camping by the river; the woman on the phone told him we could pitch a tent on the beach. Of course, we could—nobody was there to stop us. *To whom did he talk? The area doesn't show any signs of life.* Deciding not to jump to conclusions, we considered the abandoned-looking area more closely. Maybe the owners simply hadn't performed their spring cleanup yet.

Trudging up the hill (everything is uphill from the river) to the lodge, we didn't run into or hear another human; the parking lot was empty and the lodge windows dark. We glanced across the road, finding the campground portion of the Grand Chain Campground and Resort—several RVs and a building we assumed was a restroom and shower house. Crossing the street we confirmed the structure's identity. Since using the restroom inside the lodge was obviously not an option in the near future, we decided to take advantage of the campground's facilities.

The new-looking building had two doors on each side. A sign labeled MEN hung on the doors on one side and a similar sign labeled WOMEN on the other. I've camped at several campgrounds—two doors marked the same usually means one is a shower and the other a restroom. I opened the first door marked WOMEN—definitely a restroom with a toilet and sink but no toilet paper. *Oh no!* Out of curiosity I peered into the other women's door, expecting to find a shower. Another restroom—also no toilet paper. *Where is the shower?*

Yesterday during John's phone call to the lodge, he had inquired about showering. The "lodge employee" told him we could use the showers at the campground. Now I was confused—two restrooms and no shower. I thought about the shower dilemma for maybe a second. What I really needed was a restroom with toilet paper. *There had to be a spare roll of toilet paper somewhere.* I studied the area more intently. Then I spotted the shelf on the opposite wall—a great place to store toilet paper. NONE. But I did discover a showerhead on the wall to the left of the shelf. The shower house was efficient and similar to many RV bathrooms—one room does it all.

My opinion is a shower/toilet combo in a public restroom is a bad idea for a couple reasons. One—the floor would be extremely slick after a shower, a danger to restroom users to come. Two—taking a shower requires more time (usually) than using the restroom. If women were taking showers in both rooms, the next woman trying the locked doors would have a long wait. Having detected a drain in the floor and the shower on the wall, I examined the shelf more closely. Instead of toilet paper occupying the space, a variety of shampoos, conditioners, and body washes rested on the shelf. I concluded that the campground must have several permanent spots, campsites rented for the season rather than by the night. Those renting seasonal spots must leave their toiletries in the shower room for convenience.

Even though I had solved the shower mystery, I still hadn't solved my need to use a restroom with toilet paper. So I stepped around the building searching for John and found him waiting on me. His restroom DID have toilet paper and plenty of it—three rolls. I had no other option except to use the men's restroom—on purpose. (I have used the men's restroom in Wal-Mart by accident—but that's another story.)

Still curious about the lodge situation, we strolled across the empty parking lot. The two-toned building with brick pillars adorning the entrance didn't resemble a building old enough to be abandoned. We tried each of the double doors; neither budged. Hmmm.... The hours posted on the door: 10 a.m. – 8 p.m. Time on John's watch—9:00. So there was a chance. Peeking in the window of the door, we spied a quaint table with two chairs in the hall. I imagined us playing two-handed euchre there tomorrow sheltered from the storm. Next to the table was a small store with sparsely stocked shelves. I imagined us standing by the checkout counter purchasing toilet paper.

Meandering around the building hunting for more clues, we came across a lot of weeds and two water faucets. We needed water. Even though we still didn't have any answers about the lodge situation, John traipsed the quarter mile to retrieve the three dromedaries from our kayaks.

While John accomplished his mission, I wandered around to the back of the lodge and onto the deck facing the river—what a great view. Upside down tables and chairs crammed into a corner made me start to believe we had arrived in the off-season. Through several windows I recognized elements of a restaurant. Many bottles filled the shelves of the bar, but the tables were in disarray without any restaurant-type table articles (napkins, menu, salt and pepper shakers, candies, etc…) on them. I peered in a couple other windows and identified hotel-style rooms. Each room was equipped with a perfectly made bed, TV, desk, and chest of drawers. On my way back to the front of the building, I tried the two water faucets—nothing! *Why didn't we try them earlier?* John had hiked to the kayaks for nothing.

As I rounded the corner of the lodge, a middle-aged woman "just happened to" arrive and approach the door with confidence. It was a little before 10:00 a.m., so I assumed she was there to open the lodge.

"Do you work here?" I inquired.

"No," she answered, "My daughter is renting the restaurant for a graduation party tomorrow. I'm meeting her here to set things up. Hi, I'm Nita."

Shaking her hand, I introduced myself, "Hi, I'm LaNae. Is the lodge open for the season yet?"

"The small store is sometimes open. However, the selection is limited. A few lodge rooms are available to rent when someone is here to check you in. But that's all. The restaurant isn't open. The lodge has seen several owners, each not having much luck because the area isn't very populated. The new owner has started a vineyard hoping to make Grand Chain a destination place. But it may be a while for that to take off."

I explained our trip to Nita and that we had stopped to beat the storms, hoping to enjoy the lodge and perhaps buy some toilet paper. We were in luck; she previously managed the lodge and had a key. She unlocked the outside door, but unfortunately, her key didn't work in the store's lock—no purchasing of toilet paper. I remembered the dry faucets on the side of the building and asked if there was a water source nearby. She led me to the kitchen.

About the same time John returned, Nita's daughter and friend, Julie and Misty, arrived. After introductions, they asked the usual questions about our trip, proceeding to warn us about the Ohio River currents. We have received various warnings—some because of fear of the unknown, others due to previous experiences. An undercurrent sucking down a loved-one had inspired their warnings. During the course of our conversation, we mentioned our NEED for toilet paper. Nita offered to go home and bring some back. We said yes. (That's what we say on this trip.) While Nita was gone, John and I filled the dromedaries and spoke with Julie and Misty.

After Nita returned, we thanked everyone for their kindness and carried the dromedaries and toilet paper back to *Work* and *Pray*. With no clouds in the sky, believing dangerous storms could affect our travel was difficult. Considering Grand Chain wasn't what we had envisioned, John referred to the radar to determine when the storms might arrive. The first batch of storms had just missed us, and we had time before the next surge. We discussed staying or leaving. Our batteries and Sherpa were low; so we decided to return to the lodge, use the outside outlets to charge them, and then make a decision about the rest of the day. Surprisingly, our phone showed four bars in the upper left hand corner—the best coverage in several days; so in the shade of the awning, I sat on a bench outside the front double doors and took advantage of the Internet access to pay bills.

Before the trip I paid as many bills ahead as possible—mortgage, insurance, taxes, etc. However, I didn't know the amount due for others, like electric and cell phone, so I had to wait for each company to post the total. Paying those statements is what I accomplished today.

Electronics charged and bills paid, we re-evaluated staying or paddling a few more miles. John checked the radar, determining the storms wouldn't hit for several hours. If we stayed, we could camp down by the water or rent a spot in the campground at the top of the hill, giving us access to showers and restrooms. However, the four miles we had already paddled didn't sound like enough for the day, so we decided to move on. Gathering our electronics, we trekked the quarter mile back to the kayaks. (Today's math question: How many miles did we walk today?)

Keep us upright and safe.

When we returned to the water, an occasional cloud floated in the blue sky. Soon occasional passing clouds became complete cloud cover. The sky grew ominous, the clouds darker and heavier. The wind picked up. Thunder rumbled in the distance. John inspected the radar again. A storm was building out of nowhere. John combed the banks. To the right, John spied a place where we could get off the river and safely ride out the storm. *Paddle hard.* The wind roared. *Paddle.* The thunder marched closer. *Paddle.* Flashes of forked lightening appeared. *Paddle.* The current fought us. *Paddle.* Exhausted, we finally landed *Work* and *Pray* on a desolate strip of wooded shoreline.

John yelled over the wind, "Hurry! We better set up the tent for shelter before the storm hits. It's going to be a nasty one."

By now we have a system. John gathers the tent dry bag from his back hatch. We assemble the tent together. I climb into the tent. John gathers the bedding and throws it in to me. I make the bed while John secures the stakes. Next, he usually puts up the clothesline and any leftover undried laundry. This afternoon he skipped the clothesline step, climbing into the tent just as the first raindrop plip-plopped on the rainfly.

Even though the rain was short-lived, this was the first time since we left Ft. Recovery, Ohio, on April 1, a storm has chased us off the river. The entire episode both scared and exhilarated me.

We were hungry, and since the radar indicated we were in the line of more yellow and red cells, we used the short window of opportunity to fill our stomachs. We ate an early dinner at 3:00 p.m. of black bean stroganoff and banana pudding.

Dishes (two pans, one lid, and two spoons) washed, we stood by the river watching the barges. We waved at a captain; he flashed his lights; we waved again; he came out and waved; John retrieved our VHF radio from the tent (he puts it on his side of the tent every night) and spoke with the captain briefly. The fact that the captain noticed us and then took the time to communicate surprised us. I wonder how he retold the interaction to his crew. Maybe it happened something like this…

Captain: I saw something unusual today as I was approaching the locks.
Crewmember: What?
Captain: A couple kayaks on the bank.
Crewmember: What're they doin' out here?
Captain: I spoke to the guy. They're kayaking to the Gulf.
Crewmember: No way. On the Mississippi? They're nuts!
Captain: That's what I told 'em.

Soon after the conversation with the captain, another incoming storm forced us back into the tent—this time for the night. With storms in the forecast tomorrow, we will probably have another forced day of rest. At least we have toilet paper. Thank you, Nita!

It is now 5:00 in the afternoon; we are sitting in the tent. I am journaling; John is napping. The thunder and lightning have raged with fury while the wind has thrashed the treetops for over an hour. Mud is forming in glossy pools outside the tent. Prior to John falling asleep, we entertained ourselves (and others on Instagram) with a selfie capturing our little area of the world. John captioned the Instagram post, "Wasting valuable battery life taking a 'selfie' while pinned down by roaring winds and thunderstorms." I can't think of any place I would rather be than worrying about toilet paper with my best friend!

0 5 - 1 6 - 2 0 1 5

Who'd Have Guessed I'd Grow up to Be like Me

Weather conditions:

High: 72

Low: 70

Skies: rain most of day with a thunderstorm later

Wind: SSE 4-9 mph

Today's mileage: 0 miles (weather day)

Total: 602 miles

Where we are: Downstream from Grand Chain, Illinois

Rain, rain, go away!

12:27 p.m.

Lounging uncomfortably in the tent. Rolled up sleeping bags, blankets, and sleep pads sit by the doors as we wait for the rain to pass through. Our tent is barely wide enough for our separate sleeping bags to rest side by side, so the 16-inch pile of sleeping gear leaves us little room to stretch out. Not to mention the hard ground that remains after removing all padding. This could be a long and uncomfortable wait. *Why did we roll everything up?*

Earlier this morning as I lay here wishing the rain would stop and listening to my stomach grumble as a result of not being fed since yesterday afternoon at 3:00 p.m., I contemplated the changes we are witnessing. Trains providing background noise while we slept have been replaced by towboat engine roars interrupting our sleep (similar to the sound of a helicopter landing). Bare trees have changed to leaf-covered shade providers. Steep, muddy banks are now sandy beaches. Mud and mire have shifted to sand, stones, and shells. Downed tree obstacles in the river have switched to locks and dams. Every change requires a replacement. If there isn't a replacement involved, it isn't a change; it's a disappearance. Hmmmm... That's pretty good, if I do say so myself.

The rain fell most the night until about 11:00 a.m. When the thunder's roar softened and the rain's plip plop slowed, John checked the radar, determining the storms were moving out of the area. Hoping a return to the river was in our near future, we rolled up our bedding, the bedding that is now infringing upon our space. Even though the sky was still dripping, we emerged from our tent to make dinner (taco mac and cheese) for breakfast under the tarp. Planning to put in a few miles today, I followed my after breakfast routine of making our lunches for later. I was in the midst of doing this when the sprinkles became heavy, fast-falling raindrops. We made a dash to the tent, leaving everything, including our lunch, under the tarp.

Now, staring at the hard tent floor devoid of our cushy sleeping bags and pillow (well, MY pillow), we are discussing how long we should sit here uncomfortably waiting for the skies to quit leaking so we can load *Work* and *Pray.* I voted for five minutes.

7:39 p.m.

We are still here! Rain poured from the time we made a dash to the tent earlier today until 4:00 p.m.; which is too late to load *Work* and *Pray,* paddle a few miles, and then set up camp again down the river.

Realizing we were stuck here another day, we started to regret our decision to leave Grand Chain Resort. Even though it wasn't what we thought it would be, at least we could have hiked up to the building in our rain suits and spent part of the day relaxing on chairs with backs, taking advantage of their WIFI, charging our devices, and using THEIR toilet paper.

John then inserted his wisdom into our conversation, "Remember our decision to reflect and not regret. Regretting isn't going to change this situation. We are here, not there. However, let's reflect on our decision and use that for future dilemmas. We knew it was going to rain. Yesterday, we made a decision based on the present—the sun was shining—instead of on what we knew was coming—the forecast indicated rain. Reflect don't regret."

We spent the rest of the afternoon napping, reading, playing euchre (I won), and pretending to be Robinson Crusoe.

Let me explain. JOHN pretended HE was Robinson Crusoe. He thought collecting rainwater off the tarp by funneling it into our water bottles sounded like a good idea. Unfortunately, the debris on the tarp flowed with the water into our bottles. Discussing various options to "filter" the gravel and sticks from the water, I remembered something I had read. I'm not sure where I read the idea to use a coffee filter for filtering water, but we both thought it sounded reasonable, so we put coffee filters on our "grocery list." (This revelation of perceived wisdom caused John to make his oft claim of "Mind power.") We will buy some when picking up our Week # 7 package at the post office in Cairo, Illinois.

This is the part of our adventure that emphasizes our dependency on and oneness with nature. Although planning to buy something while in society (coffee filters), making the process more efficient, we are using what we own (tarp) and what nature provides (rain) to meet our basic needs. The settlers' lives were difficult and dangerous, but they must have felt satisfaction every time they overcame an obstacle by using what they had together with what nature provided. They didn't have the advantage of the nearest Lowes, collecting all the items needed to build a cabin. They looked into their covered wagon, gathered their axe or saw (what they had), and proceeded cutting down trees (what nature provided). They thought for themselves. With modern conveniences, when facing something we haven't done before, we Google it or play a YouTube video to gather the information we need to accomplish our goal. How often do we think, plan, and execute on our own without any outside instructions? No wonder we feel the need to search for other ways to achieve a sense of accomplishment. And just think of the money we would save if we used what we have in our "wagon."

Let's do a little recap here… We emerged from our tent at 11:00 a.m. and scurried back into it at 12:00 p.m., foolishly leaving our lunch under the tarp. We sat in our tent while our lunch taunted us until the rain released us from the tent at 4:00 p.m. Starved, after spending the afternoon in the tent without access to our food, we ate our lunch, hardly breathing between bites. Even though we've eaten peanut butter wraps for lunch almost every day for the past six weeks, these were the best wraps ever.

Hunger satisfied, we hung our wet paddling clothes from yesterday on some low branches, charged our Sherpa with the solar panel (the sun was shining), and syphoned water from our cockpits with our bilge pump. Oh, and I can't fail to mention John herded dead fish (don't ask). Followed by dinner—beef and bean burritos with Spanish rice and salsa. We resisted dessert because we had recently eaten lunch. Will power.

After dinner we washed the dishes, returned the propane stove to its small pouch, folded the foil table, stowed the kitchen bits and pieces in *Pray's* front hatch, and talked on the phone with my youngest son, Trent, during his commute home. Now to bed. I know 7:30 p.m. sounds early, but John set the alarm for 3:30 a.m. Although the weather forecast is a little sketchy, we hope to paddle tomorrow. If not, we will enjoy another day of forced relaxation, and maybe I'll beat John in another game of euchre.

05-17-2015

Was That the Same Goat? (guest writer John)

Weather conditions:

High: 72

Low: 68

Skies: scattered showers and thunderstorms, clearing later in the day

Wind: S 9-17 mph, gusts to 23 mph

Today's mileage: 6 miles

Total: 608 miles

Where we traveled: Below Grand Chain, Illinois, to Mound City, Illinois

Hi. John here again. LaNae said I have to write the daily journal periodically, which I've learned means "as determined by LaNae."

Today is what we call a "C" day. We've determined that each of our days fall into one of the following three categories:

- "A" days—mileage on the river, efficient, etc. In other words, a day that most would consider productive towards reaching our ultimate goal.

- "B" days—scheduled day off, "Sabbath," to rest and reflect. We try to do this once a week.

- "C" days—"Weather day"…forced into the tent due to inclement weather.

It seems to be taking forever to get to Cairo, Illinois. We have a lot to accomplish in Cairo, and we are anxious to pass this elusive milestone. First, there is the significance of its location. While Cairo is still over two miles from the joining of the Ohio and Mississippi, it is, nonetheless, the generally accepted location of the confluence. Secondly, Cairo is the home of our next gear and food cache. This time we not only pick up food for the next week that our friends Mike and Cyndy have sent us, but we also have our warm weather neoprene "wet pants" and a replacement Overboard phone case that ROC Gear sent to us. We will also be gathering up space-consuming cold weather gear and sending it back home, since the coldest temperatures seem to be over and the days are getting warmer.

Well, much like how that last paragraph dragged on, so goes our attempt to reach Cairo, as this is our third day pinned down by heavy rains and storms.

Our sleep ended at 3:30 a.m. with the hope that morning would bring a reprieve from the bad weather. However, we woke to storms and a radar that indicated another day in the tent was likely.

So, here is the key; enjoy and make good use of each type of day. On a trip like this, one must assume each type of day will happen. Actually, on an adventure such as this the terms "good" and "bad" are somewhat subjective. It is ALL just part of the trip.

So, we killed the alarm, snuggled back into our sleeping bags and got some more rest. Once well rested we woke for the day to a rare lull in the rains. Wanting to take advantage of this brief opportunity, I climbed out of the tent, splashed barefooted across the wet ground to LaNae's kayak, and grabbed the lunch bag. Once I got back to the tent, I went through the typical drill: kneel on the tent floor, taking care not to drag in mud and water; raise feet while they remain sticking out the tent door; reach forward and grab the "tent towel"; lean back while maintaining balance; clean and dry feet. Acceptable, I climbed in, zipped the door shut, and fixed us a late breakfast of wraps and nuts. (Oooh, eating in the tent. This is normally taboo since it introduces scent into the tent that can attract animals. Considering they might not be careful with the zipper when they try to enter, there's a risk they may damage our tent. But in this case, the situation warranted it.) Finally around 1:30 p.m., the rains stopped; the dark and thunderous skies were replaced by low gray clouds and flashes of sun. Aha! We can knock off some miles towards Cairo.

I quickly fired up the stove while LaNae started to break camp. As is our norm, once breakfast (lunch for breakfast and breakfast for lunch) was on the fire, she took over the cooking duties while I started packing the boats. By the way, as I'm writing this—tomorrow—LaNae is playing solitaire and making noises like a seal. No, I don't get it either. Maybe tomorrow's entry, which we'll write tomorrow, since I'm writing about today—tonight (yeah, confusing) will have an explanation.

By 3:30 we were on the water and squeezing past (no, I literally mean squeezing past) the tow *Hamilton* and her barges, which she had pushed within 10 feet of our beach as she waited for some southbound traffic to pass. She was empty so had a draft ("draught" for my British friends) of only about two feet. This meant she could push right in close to shore. (It's a good thing she wasn't there earlier since today was bath day!) Once I let the Hamilton know our intentions, we were underway.

We were soon navigating past Lock 53 in which the wicket dam was open, meaning no need to lock through. About a mile farther downstream we encountered the new Olmsted dam and lock construction project. This monster narrowed the sailing line and forced us into it, so I contacted Olmsted to see if they had any instructions and asked about the barges closing on us from upstream. The tow *Bridget Colley* jumped on the radio, identified herself, and indicated she was the tow coming up behind us and that she was making about 9 mph. Since she was definitely moving faster than we were, we let her know we would simply hold our position and jump in behind her once she made the turn. All was well.

As we passed Olmsted, the river opened up again; and an approaching southerly turn allowed the south winds to have their way. We were soon pushing through two-foot plus rollers that crashed clear up over our deck bags. I communicated (I thought) my plans to LaNae and pushed on, singing (poorly) and enjoying the bouncy but strenuous ride. After a mile or two, I looked back at LaNae, immediately noticed the unpleasant look on her face, and tried, above the noise, to ask her to come closer to my boat. I heard a loud "hbjhffdfgyuivq!" in response and assumed (wrongly) that she had simply said "ok" and would soon be merrily paddling alongside me. So, I paddled on another mile while singing (poorly) as the spray smashed me in the face and then again looked back to see LaNae some distance off my port stern with that same unpleasant look I had seen earlier. I yelled out, "Hey, where ya going?" She responded in an animated way with what again sounded like "hbjhffdfgyuivq!" This time I figured I should wait for her and discuss the situation. Hmmm, it turns out she totally misunderstood where I said we were headed (oops) and really does NOT like wind and big waves (oops). Once I had a good laugh (oops), I clarified my destination intent, and we pushed on. We made landfall at about 5:30 p.m. after completing about six miles.

Cairo and the Mississippi tomorrow?!??

05-18-2015

Can You Italicize a Period

Weather conditions:

High: 81

Low: 56

Skies: scattered rain and thunderstorm, some thunderstorms could be heavy

Wind: S 15-20 mph, gusts to 26 mph

Today's mileage: 0 miles (rain out)

Total: 608 miles

Where we are: Mound City, Illinois

Whoosh, drip, rumble, flash, drip, flash, whoosh, rumble. Sights and sounds of the last three days. In that time we have paddled only six miles in our attempt to reach Cairo, spending the rest of the time checking the radar and wondering if we will be able to move farther downstream any time soon. I understand the anticipation Huck Finn and Jim felt in Mark Twain's *The Adventures of Huck Finn* as they paddled upstream on the Mississippi with Cairo and the Ohio River as their goal. I hope that the fog they experienced, causing them to miss Cairo, won't join the elements of nature impeding our progress to the same destination.

Today started at 3:30 a.m. John studied the radar, determining the storms would miss us. Up as usual—sleepily. John proceeded to pump the water out of *Work* and *Pray* and was in the process of hanging some clothing on the line when I noticed lightning. I squeaked, "Jooohnnnn…."

"It's going to miss us," confident in his recent reading of the radar.

Another flash lit up the sky, followed by a boom and a whoosh. The wind and rain sounds increased in frequency and intensity as the storm progressed our way.

John grabbed his still-wet shirt, wet suit, socks, and boots (John had a little incident falling, I mean climbing, out of his kayak yesterday. Don't ask.) off the line, rushed to the tent, and zipped its zipper as the raindrops bounced off the rainfly. John complained, "The radar didn't show this. It's not supposed to be raining."

Returning to the tent called for a nap. Taking a nap sounds a bit odd at 4:15 in the morning. Maybe we should say we went back to bed.

At about 8:00 a.m., John consulted the radar and informed me we should try leaving again. The scene in the tent was much like the one a couple of days ago—our rolled bedding was lined up by the door, waiting to be packed in the kayaks. Our couscous breakfast was in one of our two pans covered with our one lid, completing the "rest 10 minutes after adding boiling water" step. Lunches—made and packed. John glanced downstream, recognizing the wall of rain heading towards us. We grabbed the breakfast, secured as much as we could, gathered the still-wet clothing from the line, and ran to the tent. Zip…. at the very moment the rain wall reached us. John complained again, "Where did this come from? The radar didn't show this. It's not supposed to be raining."

Breaking unwritten rule number seven yet again, we ate breakfast in the tent. By this time it was 9:30 a.m. John stated, "We're staying here today."

We had intended to travel to Cairo, Illinois, today, where three packages (new lightweight neoprene pants, a replacement Grand Trunk stool, and our Week # 7 package) await us. In addition to a trip to the post office, we needed to search for a store selling books and coffee filters. The rest of the plan was to paddle a few more miles downstream and camp. We must leave here no later than 10:00 a.m. to accomplish all this.

During a lull in the rain, we crawled out of the tent. Lumbering down the sandy hill to *Work* and *Pray* to retrieve some snacks from our hatches, we were shocked. Eight-inch ravines leading to the water had replaced the flat sand we had strolled on earlier this morning. Our tied-off kayaks rested safely a foot away from the erosion. While ambling to the kayaks was now a little treacherous, our situation could have been much worse. If *Work* and *Pray* had been resting a few feet to the right and not tied off, they probably would have been traveling to the Gulf without us. I am so thankful that even when our kayaks are not even close to the river, John still secures them. Erosion was something I had not foreseen as a danger.

Turning to climb up the hill (everything is uphill from the river), I contemplated the trees surrounding our tent; the upper three feet of their root system was exposed—erosion. Surely, a slight breeze could uproot them as easily as a snowplow relocates a mailbox. And this is where we chose to place our tent? Maybe not the best choice.

After the rain finally stopped, we spent the rest of this afternoon waiting for John's paddling gear to dry, removing water from *Work* and *Pray*, shaving (John), and journaling (me). No napping this afternoon. We did that at 4:15 this morning.

Having spent a lot of time in the tent the last three days, we are running out of things to talk about, so I suggested another conversation topic from Irene. John was hesitant but willing.

"Okay. Here is the first one."

John, unsure of his decision to participate hesitated, "First one... You mean there is more than one. I don't know about this."

"It'll be fine. They're easy."

John squinted, "I don't trust you."

I opened her text. "America's obsession with fragrance. Is there really a need for fragrance or just a hang up with the way we smell? From soaps, deodorants, lotions, razor handles (yes...I said razor handles), dust cloths, dish soaps...etc."

As usual, John was off and running. "Well, of course, we need to develop and use fragrances. Stink without pleasant fragrance is like black without white, up without down, wet without dry, ..." (I shouldn't have asked)

"Now, that wasn't so bad, was it? Here is the next one. 'Money. The hotel parking lot where we are staying is filled with high dollar cars. Ferraris, Rolls-Royce, McLarens, etc. If you are born into money, how does it affect your life? The same for being born into a family without money.'"

He had a little more to say on this topic. (He must be more interested in money than fragrance.) "If you're born with money then you can't grasp the lack of it. Everything becomes a 'necessity.' How can I possibly exist without my needed Armani? Without my needed Bentley?

Without my needed trove of homes and women? I have money; therefore, I 'need' in order to be justified. If I'm born with money, then it's simply who I am. I assume it's exhausting, but then again we're all rich when compared to someone somewhere. It's complex."

"Are you up for another one? It's either answer another one or play another game of euchre."

Not wanting to lose another game of euchre, he agreed.

"Elmer's glue. It's a funny kind of thing. Who came up with inventing glue and what did the first experiments look like?"

His face lit up. I knew I was in for a long drawn out fabrication of truth. "Glue was invented in 1726 by Elmer Eustice Stuckey. This is where we get the term 'stuck' that we often associate with glue. Glue does not actually cause adhesion in the sense that we think. Instead, it causes a lack of un- hesion. What most people don't realize is that everything has a natural un-hesion associated with it. You know, the ability NOT to stick. What Elmer did is invent a way to remove the un-hesion characteristics by applying a special sauce…what we now know of as 'glue.' I thought every-one knew that."

John pretends he doesn't like discussing the conversation topics, which actually aren't conversations (defined as two or more people sharing thoughts), they are more of a monologue—he bloviates while I listen. But I know he appreciates them since they are a part of our days of forced re-laxation. Forced relaxation in a beautiful and interesting place. Life's rough.

I love sharing this lifestyle with John. How can we recreate this way of life when we return home? How can we perform the basic survival tasks while spending time outdoors in nature? How can we continue exploring new sights instead of spending all our time imprisoned by our familiar sur-roundings? How can we create a peaceful lifestyle in our typical American culture? I don't have answers to these questions, but I still have two and a half months to come up with a plan. I knew this trip would change me but didn't know how. I knew I would have questions but didn't know what they would be. I don't think I realized how deeply I would think and reflect, even over simple activities such as traveling under a deserted bridge. My eyes are opening and so is my mind. These days of rest provide an opportunity for John and me to reflect together on what we are seeing and experiencing.

The rest of the day was uneventful. The breeze dried John's clothes this afternoon. We also enjoyed a late afternoon lunch and then butternut squash soup, rice, and pudding for dinner. Finishing the last bites of pud-ding, we encountered the same experience as this morning, a wall of rain coming towards us. Scramble to the tent…. Zip….Plop…

05-19-2015

Let's Go Find the Naked People

Weather conditions:

High: 73

Low: 52

Skies: clear skies

Wind: S 7-13 mph, gusts to 18 mph

Today's mileage: 20 miles

Total: 628 miles

Where we traveled: from Mound City, Illinois to…

What a day! We traveled 20 miles, but I feel like we are 100 miles from the beach where we awoke this morning. Today's Milestones…

- FINALLY reached Cairo.
- Left the Ohio River.
- Entered the Mississippi River!!!!!!!!!!!!!!
- Left Illinois.
- Entered Missouri.

Today began much like yesterday—alarm blared at 3:30 a.m. However, unlike yesterday, after checking the radar, we knew we would at last arrive in Cairo! We were thrilled to FINALLY pick up our Week # 7 package and continue on to the Mississippi River, the last (and most dangerous) leg of our journey on the Ohio River.

Even though I was looking forward to today's events, I was scared. Probably more scared than I have been since we left Fort Recovery, Ohio, on April 4. Thinking about all the unknowns, I fought back tears. My first area of concern was the Port of Cairo (pronounced kahr-oh, like Karo syrup, by the locals). I know I said we were eager to reach Cairo—we were. However, I didn't mention what else we would experience in Cairo. A lot of fleeting—groups of barges "parked" near ports. This is accompanied by numerous harbor towboats zipping in and out of harbors as they bring barges in for loading and unloading. When passing one tow at a time, we usually know where they are going and what they are doing. However, in a fleeting area, the tows move from one area to another; entering and leaving the river, sometimes appearing mysteriously from behind parked tows and barges. Up until now we hadn't dealt with a large fleeting area. The unknown creates fear. I had examined pictures—there was a lot going on. And from the pictures, Cairo's boat ramp was tucked behind parked tows and barges. *Will we miss it and then have to turn around and fight the current while paddling upstream? If we want to eat another week and wear our lightweight wetsuit pants, we HAVE to stop at Cairo. We don't have a choice.* Many had warned us to be careful when passing through the Port of Cairo. This was one warning that wasn't merely hearsay; I had pictures and facts. I WAS frightened!

I was also concerned about another milestone we would be accomplishing—leaving the Ohio River. I was familiar with the Ohio. Even with its dead fish and trashy banks, it had become home, just as the Wabash was at the beginning. I knew its currents, the size and movements of the tows, and the breadth of the river. The Mississippi is known for its odd currents and whirlpools; much larger tows will be pushing more sizeable loads; and the river—I have crossed the Mississippi on bridges—is huge!

Moving from the Wabash to the Ohio was as easy as turning right. Passing from the Ohio to the Mississippi may not be as effortless. Many have warned us about the dangerous currents where the Ohio and the

Mississippi meet. *Will they be large enough to flip my kayak? If I flip will I remember how to perform the self-rescue we had practiced in John's brother's pond before our trip?* River Gator (John Ruskey), the expert of the Lower Mississippi, has designated many miles as "wild miles." *Where will we stay? Will we have access to drinking water? What kinds of animals inhabit that area?* We had been warned, but I didn't know—didn't have anything to hang my hat on. The unknown creates fear. (Remember the Gestalt Theory from New Harmony on May 5?)

We launched by 6:00 a.m.

Keep us upright and safe.

We experienced following seas today, much like those we faced May 12 on our way to Birdsville Resort and Campground. Even though they push us, they are difficult to paddle in. Following seas are like any other waves. However, unlike approaching waves I have paddled in, I can't see the swells of those behind me. Therefore, I can't adjust my strokes to correspond with the waves. Many times, as I lower my paddle into the water, taking a stroke, I am surprised to find my paddle doesn't penetrate the water—I simply paddle the air. Not very effective.

In the midst of the following seas, John entertained me, not with a Paddling Edna Episode, but with his one-man rendition (British accent included) of the classic fairy tale "Little Red Riding Hood." (The British accent seems to be a recurring theme with John.) Surprisingly (but maybe not since John was the author), the characters didn't live happily ever after. *Where does he come up with this stuff?* I wish I had a tape recorder—his rendition was priceless! A day in my life with John Abnet.

Shortly before arriving in Cairo, we spotted a pelican. I used to think pelicans existed only in the south until my close encounter in Canada. (In case you missed my description of the "Pelican in Canada" story, reread 04-29-2015 journal entry.) In addition to the pelican, we also counted five eagles today. I can't remember the last time an eagle graced us with its presence. *Are they saying good-bye from the Ohio River?* What a treat!

After we had paddled about five miles, Cairo came into view slightly beyond the railroad bridge. My fears soon became my reality. This wasn't a picture. This wasn't someone else's version of what was here. This wasn't merely a warning. There were tows and barges everywhere! *How in the world will we find the boat ramp? How will the tow captains know we are here—we are so much smaller? Will we have enough time to move out of their way?* I tried not to cry. I stayed close to John, listening carefully to his every word and making sure I completely understood his instructions. I didn't care if he had to repeat every statement in response to a "what." This was too important. I had to trust John's judgment and decisions. No asking "why." A quick reaction in my paddling was necessary. John used his VHF radio several times to inquire about a tow captain's intentions and to alert those in the area of our presence.

From Google Earth and the charts, John knew the approximate location of the boat ramp on the RBD. We combed the bank and observed an area void of barges. There it stood—the Cairo sea wall. This was the first sea wall of any substance we have noted on the trip. I noticed a significant portion of the wall near the boat ramp was painted yellow. Waiting for John to land and emerge from *Work*. I surveyed my surroundings. While back paddling, I caught sight of a weathered sign on the yellow portion of the wall. The upper right hand corner was falling away from the wall. Barely legible, the top two lines of the five-lined sign read "No Tows, barges, or towheads." Thus, the reason this area was clear of fleeting—it's a no parking zone. The other three lines looked like someone had used watercolor paint to write with and then dripped several drops of water on the canvas. I wonder what they used to say and if anyone even remembers or cares.

The rest of the riverfront was in disrepair and barren of landscaping, only rocks and weeds bordered the cement road. I wondered if the absence of character was because of frequent flooding or lack of care. Was the rest of Cairo an extension of the riverfront, or did the sea wall separate two different ways of life? I assumed it was an extension of the riverfront because others had warned us to be careful in Cairo, indicating it can be a rough place. Since many of the other warnings have turned out to be inaccurate, we tried not to harbor any pre-conceived notions.

We stepped out of *Work* and *Pray* in Cairo, Illinois, around 9:30 a.m.

Before heading to the post office, John unfolded the Sherpa and secured it on top of *Pray* to collect rays from the sun that we have seen for only brief moments since we left Grand Chain four days ago. With the missing sun, we have used our electronics sparingly. Which means—no reading!

Usually when John goes to the post office, I stay with *Work* and *Pray* without any reservations. However, because of the warnings about Cairo's state of affairs, John was a little more cautious today. He gave me the radio and instructions on how to use it. Except for carrying it from *Work* to the tent or vice versa, I hadn't held the radio until he placed it in my hand. (John keeps the radio in the tent at night for two reasons. One: to receive weather updates in case we don't have cell coverage. Two: to call for help in case of an emergency.) He set the radio on emergency channel 16 and showed me how to use it to contact a local tow or the coast guard if I had any problems. I was hesitant before he handed me the radio, but now I was nervous. Well, maybe more than nervous, I was scared. John doesn't typically pay much attention to warnings. In fact, he usually poo poos them. So for him to take action because of a warning revealed he was concerned. He's my calming force, bringing warnings down to a manageable level. I didn't know how to process this change.

I sat nervously on *Pray*, the radio clenched in my hands as I watched John hike up the road and disappear through the opening in the sea wall. Sweating, I wished I had a book to read to take my mind off the situation. I hoped John would still allow me to venture into town later and buy a hold-in-your-hands-page-filled book. No charging required. One I could read at any time.

Since I didn't have a hold-in-your-hands-page-filled book to read, I didn't know what to do. The wall blocked the view of the town, so I couldn't people watch. I didn't have any idea what was going on in Cairo. Likewise, because of the wall, the people in Cairo didn't know what was going on in the Ohio River. I wondered how many inhabitants of the town view the river each day. Do they know what the tows and barges do in a day's time? Do they live behind the wall without even thinking about the river—until it floods? Is that what they associate the river with—flooding? There is so much more, if they would simply pass through the gates and look. They would glimpse another world: a world of commerce, a world of travel, a world of nature, a world of…

I turned towards the river and watched the tows pushing barges. *Where are they going? How many people are on each tow? When was the last time the crew spent any time at home? How long do they spend on the boat at a time?* I thought back to the conversation about life on a tow John and I had a little over a week ago while sitting on a sandy beach between Elizabethtown, Illinois, and Golconda, Illinois. I still think I would like to work on one for a time. I would be PAID to live on the river. I love living on the river. I'm sure life on a towboat isn't as glamorous day after day after day as I envision it is during the few minutes it takes for it to pass me by. But I would like to know what that lifestyle is like. I still haven't dismissed the possibility because when we return home, the world is open to us. Something to think about.

After I daydreamed for around half an hour about living on a towboat, John reappeared through the opening in the wall, carrying three boxes (pants, stool, and supplies). Christmas! He brought our goodies back to *Work* and *Pray*. First goal accomplished. Next goals: locate water, a trash receptacle, and a restroom (normal three goals when entering society). He again vanished through the wall to seek those essentials; I unpacked our Week # 7 package. Yay, more toilet paper! Box emptied, I repacked it with the winter clothes I had decided to send back home. I smiled as I removed my long johns, winter hat, gloves, and coat liner from my yellow dry sack (my cold winter clothes bag), and placed them into the box. I enthusiastically did so for two reasons. One: this would free up some space in our hatches, making packing much easier— particularly when we pick up our weekly package. Two: sending back our winter clothing means the weather is turning warmer and I won't begin my journal entries with "I was so cold last night" or "My teeth are still chattering" any more.

I also unpacked our new Grand Trunk stool. The old one is going home. John will enjoy sitting on a stool not held together by Gorilla tape, wondering if, with one wrong move, he will fall to the ground.

When John returned forty-five minutes later with dromedaries full of fresh water, he filled me in on the city and his encounters. On his first trip in to get our mail package, he apparently encountered a gentleman who must have thought happy hour began at 9:00 a.m. John described the guy's sad appearance as he approached, asking, "Have you seen Larry?" Obviously, John had neither seen nor knew the "Larry" of whom he spoke. Regardless, he followed John and asked a few more times before John finally convinced him that he couldn't help with locating "Larry."

On John's second trip back through the sea wall opening to get water, he met some folks working on what appeared to have been a park at one time. They were planting flowers and fixing up an old bleacher in what they described as an effort to host an annual blues concert.

John proceeded to describe the city's architecture. A lot of ornate brick and wrought iron structures that were in serious disrepair. Additionally, there were empty or partially empty lots where remnants of what was remained. It appeared to John that Cairo had once been a beautiful and vibrant city. No more.

After John filled me in on the happenings in Cairo, he directed me to a city maintenance building to use the restroom and change from my Farmer Jane wet suit into my lightweight capri neoprene pants. I followed his instructions and found the building, restroom, and the kind gentlemen who had graciously allowed us access. I separated the two strong Velcro strips at the top of my left shoulder strap one last time, pealed the suit from my sweaty body, and tossed it over the restroom stall. OOOOH, the wet suit stench. I wonder if my new wetsuit capris will develop this rank, unique odor. I slid on my new pants without needing to contort my body into the various positions I did when putting on my one-piece, zipperless wetsuit. And now I can pee without taking off my clothes! I feel like a new woman.

Having changed into my capris, I returned to the kayaks and John. While I was gone, John placed his winter clothes and wet suit into the going-home box. I zestfully laid my wet suit on top and closed it, ready to be sealed at the post office. *Good riddance!* We are sending the box to our house and won't be opening it until we return to our land home. Since our two heavily used wet suits won't air out for two or more months, I can't imagine the smell that will waft out upon opening the box. We may need to put on masks and unpack it outside.

We then held a conference deciding who would trek back into town to purchase a book (no charging required), coffee filters (for filtering rainwater), and more lighters (for lighting the stove). I volunteered because I didn't trust John to buy a book for me.

This is how I picture John's book-buying adventure would unfold. John enters the store, scanning the immediate area for books. After two seconds he thinks, "I can't find it." Since he knows I crave a book, he decides not to give up right away (as he normally does when he can't find something) and asks an employee where the books are located. When the employee directs him to a display in the back of the store, he proceeds to the metal rack. Upon discovering the paperbacks, he removes the one closest to him at shoulder level. He doesn't even read the title, let alone turn the book over to read the plot description on the back. The fear of reading a western novel about gunfights and saloon brawls influenced my quick offer to battle the heat and venture to Dollar General.

I strolled on a brick street in deserted downtown Cairo. A few cars were parked at the curb, but I am not sure why they were there because all the buildings were obviously abandoned with boarded up windows and doors. I stepped under an iron arch with the words "Historic Downtown Cairo" embedded in it, remnants of a once booming town. *"Historic" Cairo. Hmm... Is that the Cairo Huck and Jim would have encountered had they not floated past in the fog?* The present day "historic" Cairo was an eerie place to pass through, even during the day. I wouldn't feel safe traveling that same street at night. I turned at the end of the street, wondering if the next portion of Cairo was as desolate. It was. This street housed more boarded up buildings. I turned again. This time I witnessed some signs of life and Dollar General about a block away.

I entered the store. I had never purchased a book at Dollar General, so I had no idea where they were located. I wasn't even sure they stocked any. My first guess was by the magazines. No luck. Even though the store wasn't big, I didn't want to take a lot of time searching for them, so I asked the checkout girl.

"Do you have any books?"

"What kind?"

"Any kind." She gawked at me confused, so I clarified, "The kind you read."

"Oh, yeah. They are at the back of the store at the end of aisle 3."

I found my way to the end of aisle 3. There a metal revolving stand held twenty or so books, many duplicates. Each book had a sticker on it indicating the genre—romance, mystery, western, etc. No best sellers here. But these books didn't require charging, so I wasn't going to be picky. I chose one labeled "mystery" with the picture of a boat on the cover, located the rest of the items on my list, and checked out.

I passed the same vacant buildings on my way back through the downtown section. Approaching the sea wall, I detected a sign to the left of the opening. "Welcome to Historical Cairo 'Gateway to the South.'" Interesting. The sign wasn't faded or weathered. *How long ago did Cairo's citizens, or, more likely, the chamber of commerce determine the town was the gateway to the south? And why?* This entire visit has me shaking my head. As with many river towns, I would love to go back in time and witness Cairo before the train bypassed the city and the need for steamboats became a thing of the past. The population of the town in 1920 was 15,203; in 2010 it was 2,831. Wow! An 81percent decrease. No wonder there are so many empty buildings.

When I returned to John, we finished packing and sealing the going-home box. Then John left to mail the unneeded items (26 pounds worth). I watched John move through the seawall. With the VHF radio resting in my lap, I held my new hold-in-your-hands-page-filled book. No charging required. I didn't even miss John.

Upon his return, I expected John's hands to be empty, but instead, he carried a white paper sack and Styrofoam cup. I was sure he held a scrumptious surprise—a white sack had to contain food. My stomach growled as John motioned for me to join him in the shade of the wall. I bounded up the hill (everything is uphill from the river). Christmas again. My mouth watered in anticipation of the contents of the white sack. He pulled out two sandwiches wrapped in sandwich paper—catfish and pork barbecue. The Styrofoam cup held ice water. Ice water doesn't ordinarily excite me, especially if I am eating fish, but with the rising temperatures over the last couple of days, all we have had to drink is lukewarm water. The ice water quenched my thirst. I had to resist drinking all the water at once and be sure I saved some for John. John ate half the catfish sandwich while I ate half the pork barbecue sandwich. Then we traded. (I wish I could have eaten the entire catfish sandwich. It was my favorite.)

Sack lunch consumed, John carried out our last errand—disposing our garbage. I sat on *Pray*, reading my hold-in-your-hands-page-filled book. No charging required. I love to read! I didn't even miss John.

Garbage disposed, we departed Cairo at 2:00 p.m. and were on our way to the Mississippi River a couple miles downstream. The weird-current warnings made me nervous. I knew the Mississippi entered the Ohio from the RBD, so I kept glancing to the right while watching for unusual patterns in the water. I glanced—nothing. I glanced—again nothing. In addition to the weird-current warnings, I had read the waters at the confluence differ in color—Mississippi brown, Ohio blue— and the two flow side by side for several miles before combining. I examined the water but didn't distinguish any color variances. (Side note: Tradition has it that if you make a wish as you toss a coin in the river at the confluence, your wish will come true. I didn't have a coin.) I started wondering if we had missed our next milestone—exiting the Ohio and entering the Mississippi—so I glanced back over my right shoulder, discovering a bridge spanning a river smaller than the Ohio. I blurted, "I think we're in the Mississippi."

"Why do you say that?" John asked.

"There's a bridge crossing a river to the right back there."

He turned his body, "I think you're right."

A little confused, I questioned, "Where are the strange currents?" Another warning turning out to be less than I had expected. When will I learn?

Entering the Mississippi wasn't as obvious as entering the Ohio from the Wabash. Entering the Ohio, we arrived at a T-river and turned right. No turning onto the Mississippi—the two rivers just kind of, uh, merge. Distinguishing the moment we officially entered the Mississippi was almost impossible. No "Welcome to the Mississippi River" sign. Some say the Mississippi should have been named the Ohio because where the two rivers meet, the Ohio is larger in volume and wider, causing the Mississippi to triple in volume with the addition of the Ohio River. No matter what the name is, we are traveling on a larger body of water than what we launched onto this morning.

Almost as soon as we realized we were on the Mississippi, we spied a giant white cross on the bluff at Wickliffe, Kentucky. *Is this a welcome sign? Or a bad omen?*

Our intention was to enter the big river and immediately find a camping place. Since we were paddling on the Kentucky side of the river and didn't want to paddle the mile to the Missouri bank, we scanned the Kentucky shores for our home for the night. Wispy clouds floated across the sky as we adjusted to the larger body of water, hunting for a campsite. I'm not sure how far we traveled before we located it—our first camping spot on the Mississippi. Ahead of us Island 1 loomed on the left, offering us a beautiful sandy beach. John proclaimed, "Home."

I zealously paddled with my eye on the prize. However, approaching our home for the night, we encountered some crazy currents and even a drop in river level. I had expected these kinds of conditions at the confluence but not necessarily this far from where the rivers melded. My hands were sweating. *If I can reach the island, I can relax.* I periodically admired the island while maneuvering the whirlpools.

Then I heard gurgling. Studying John, I gulped, "What's that noise?" Early in the trip, we learned that noise indicates something weird, maybe dangerous, going on with the water—not a good thing. Detecting the gurgling, we sought its origin. There it was—a thin white line crossing the river between the beaconing sandy beach and us. Bubbling water. *What is causing the water to bounce with an occasional spray?* Then we noticed the rocks. An entire line of rocks protruding half mile into the river from the shore, blocking our access to the island. We were headed straight towards the rock wall.

John yelled as he turned his kayak parallel to and slightly upstream of the rocks, "Angle upstream and paddle hard. We need to get around this."

I followed John. I paddled hard, watching the strong Mississippi current push us closer to what I knew must be our death. *Paddle. Upstream. Paddle. Upstream.* We were losing our battle as we grew closer to the obstacle but not within reach of safety.

Realizing we couldn't reach the end of the wall, John turned his kayak perpendicular to the line of rocks and called, "Follow me."

I turned my kayak. *Paddle. Follow John. Paddle.* John neared the wall. *Paddle. Follow John. Paddle.* I tried not to cry. I was petrified. *What if something happens to John?*

John reached the wall. The front of his kayak tipped over the wall. *How large is the drop? What's at the bottom? I don't like this! If this is what the Mississippi is like, I don't think I can do this. I want this to be over.*

It seemed like slow motion as John's cockpit followed the front of his kayak over wall. Next his rear hatch. Then, *Noooo!!!!* John dropped beyond the line of rocks.

To be continued...

About the Author

LaNae Abnet has cycled the Appalachian Mountains, kayaked in the Arctic, train hopped through the interior Canadian wilderness, and paddled the big waters of Lake Huron. She is also the first woman to kayak the 1600-mile source-to-sea journey from the source of the Wabash River to the Gulf of Mexico. She and her husband, John, share four children and live in a 750-square-foot home on thirty-two wilderness acres outside of Geneva, Indiana.

LiVEout...
...doors
...loud
...rageous
...dreams

"Inspiring, encouraging,
motivating,
human/ wilderness interaction"

www.separateboats.com

@separateboats